ORIGINALISM'S PROMISE

The foundation of the American legal system is its longstanding written Constitution. However, a contentious debate now exists between originalists, who employ the Constitution's original meaning, and nonoriginalists, who argue for a living constitution interpretation. The first natural law justification for an originalist interpretation of the American Constitution, *Originalism's Promise* presents an innovative foundation for originalism and a novel description of its character. *Originalism's Promise* provides a deep, rich, and practical explanation of originalism, including the most detailed originalist theory of precedent in the literature. Of interest to judges, scholars, and lawyers, *Originalism's Promise* will help all Americans better understand their own Constitution and shows why their reverence for it, its Framers, and its legal system is supported by sound reasons. *Originalism's Promise* is a powerful contribution to the most important theory in constitutional interpretation.

LEE J. STRANG is John W. Stoepler Professor of Law & Values at the University of Toledo College of Law. In 2015 Professor Strang was a visiting scholar at the Georgetown Center for the Constitution, and in 2016 he was appointed to the Ohio Advisory Committee of the U.S. Commission on Civil Rights. In 2017 the University of Toledo awarded Professor Strang its Outstanding Faculty Research and Scholarship Award. During the 2018–19 academic year, Professor Strang was a visiting fellow at the James Madison Program at Princeton University.

Originalism's Promise

A NATURAL LAW ACCOUNT OF THE AMERICAN CONSTITUTION

LEE J. STRANG

University of Toledo

CAMBRIDGE
UNIVERSITY PRESS

University Printing House, Cambridge CB2 8BS, United Kingdom

One Liberty Plaza, 20th Floor, New York, NY 10006, USA

477 Williamstown Road, Port Melbourne, VIC 3207, Australia

314-321, 3rd Floor, Plot 3, Splendor Forum, Jasola District Centre, New Delhi - 110025, India

79 Anson Road, #06-04/06, Singapore 079906

Cambridge University Press is part of the University of Cambridge.

It furthers the University's mission by disseminating knowledge in the pursuit of education, learning and research at the highest international levels of excellence.

www.cambridge.org
Information on this title: www.cambridge.org/9781108475631
DOI: 10.1017/9781108688093

First published 2019

A catalogue record for this publication is available from the British Library

Library of Congress Cataloging in Publication data
NAMES: Strang, Lee J., author.
TITLE: Originalism's promise : a natural law account of the American Constitution / Lee J. Strang, University of Toledo.
DESCRIPTION: Cambridge, United Kingdom ; New York, NY, USA : Cambridge University Press, 2019. | Includes bibliographical references and index.
IDENTIFIERS: LCCN 2019000042 | ISBN 9781108475631 (hardback : alk. paper) | ISBN 9781108468732 (pbk. : alk. paper)
SUBJECTS: LCSH: Constitutional law–United States.
CLASSIFICATION: LCC KF4552 .S768 2019 | DDC 342.73/001–dc23
LC record available at https://lccn.loc.gov/2019000042

ISBN 978-1-108-47563-1 Hardback
ISBN 978-1-108-46873-2 Paperback

[R]ationis ordinatio ad bonum commune, ab eo qui curam communitatis habet, promulgata.[1]

[1] I-II St. Thomae Aquinatis, Summae Theologiae q. 90, a. 4 (Leonis Romae ed. 1892) (law is "an ordinance of reason for the common good, made by him who has care of the community, and promulgated.").

Contents

Acknowledgments   *page* xi
List of Abbreviations   xiii

Introduction   1

PART I A DESCRIPTION OF ORIGINALISM   7

1 **A Brief History of Originalism in American Constitutional
   Interpretation**   9
   1.1 Introduction   9
   1.2 The Long Arc of the Republic's History   12
        1.2.1 English Background   12
        1.2.2 Framing and Ratification Period   13
        1.2.3 Early Republic and Pre–New Deal American
               Constitutional Practice   14
   1.3 Originalism's Eclipse during and after the New Deal   17
   1.4 Originalism's Reincarnation and Evolution   23
        1.4.1 Modern Originalism's First Generation   23
        1.4.2 Nonoriginalist Criticisms Engaged   25
        1.4.3 The Main Outlines of Originalism's Second-Generation
               Conceptual Changes   26
   1.5 Pluralism within Originalism and Originalism's Focal Case   40
   1.6 Conclusion   42

2 **The Constitutional Communication Model of Originalism**   43
   2.1 Introduction   43
   2.2 The Constitutional Communication Model of Originalism   44
        2.2.1 Introduction   44

2.2.2 Preliminary Note Distinguishing Face-to-Face Communication   47
2.2.3 The Focal Case of Constitutional Interpretation:
      The Constitution as Communication   48
2.2.4 The Conditions for Constitutional Communication Support
      the Constitutional Communication Model of Originalism   50
2.2.5 The Process of Creation of the U.S. Constitution Supports
      the Constitutional Communication Model of Originalism   56
2.2.6 Why Original Meaning, Original Intent, and Original
      Methods Were Perceived as Distinct   61
2.2.7 Conclusion   63
2.3 The Deference Conception of Constitutional Construction   63
    2.3.1 Introduction   63
    2.3.2 The *Prima Facie* Plausibility of Constitutional Construction   64
    2.3.3 A Modest Role for Constitutional Construction   66
    2.3.4 Constitutional Construction Is a Subsidiary Mechanism of
          Constitutional Communication   90
    2.3.5 Conclusion   91
2.4 An Originalist Theory of Precedent: Originalist and Nonoriginalist
    Precedent Serving the Common Good   91
    2.4.1 Introduction   91
    2.4.2 Distinguishing Originalist from Nonoriginalist Precedent:
          The Originalism in Good Faith Standard   92
    2.4.3 The Interpretative and Constructive Modes of Originalist
          Precedent   97
    2.4.4 Originalism Preserves Some Nonoriginalist Precedent for the
          Sake of the Common Good   103
    2.4.5 Precedent Is a Key Means by which the Constitution's
          Original Meaning Is Effectively Communicated   141
    2.4.6 Conclusion   141
2.5 The Deference Conception of Construction and the Originalist
    Theory of Precedent Are Both Manifestations of Judicial Legal
    Deference to Other Interpreters   141
2.6 Virtue's Home in Originalism: Originalism Is Fortified by Judges
    Who Possess Judicial Virtue   142
    2.6.1 Introduction   142
    2.6.2 An Introduction to Virtue Ethics   143
    2.6.3 The Key Judicial Virtues   144
    2.6.4 Incorporating Virtue Ethics into Originalism Makes It More
          Descriptively Accurate and Normatively Attractive   148
    2.6.5 Conclusion   157
2.7 Conclusion   157

PART II ORIGINALISM IS THE BEST EXPLANATION OF OUR
EXISTING CONSTITUTIONAL PRACTICE AND THE MOST NORMATIVELY
ATTRACTIVE THEORY OF CONSTITUTIONAL INTERPRETATION   159

3   Originalism Best Explains Our Existing Constitutional Practice   161
    3.1 Introduction: Why It Is Important for Originalism to Fit In   161
    3.2 Summary of Claims That Originalism Does Not Fit Our
        Constitutional Practice   164
    3.3 Our Written Constitution Fits Originalism   166
        3.3.1 Introduction   166
        3.3.2 The Constitution's Text Identifies Originalism as the
              Correct Mode of Interpretation   167
        3.3.3 The Constitution's Provenance Identifies Originalism as
              the Correct Mode of Interpretation   169
        3.3.4 The Amendment Process Identifies Originalism as the
              Correct Mode of Interpretation   173
        3.3.5 Conclusion   176
    3.4 Supreme Court Practice Fits Originalism   176
        3.4.1 Introduction   176
        3.4.2 The Supreme Court's Reasoning and Arguments   176
        3.4.3 Originalism Accounts for the Practice of Constitutional
              Doctrine   180
        3.4.4 Originalist Precedent: Putting the Constitution into Effect   183
        3.4.5 Constitutional Construction: Fitting and Justifying Elected
              Branch Constructions   195
        3.4.6 Originalism's Embrace of Some Nonoriginalist Precedent
              Helps It Fit Our Constitutional Practice   197
    3.5 Originalism Accommodates Societal and Constitutional Change   205
        3.5.1 Introduction   205
        3.5.2 Ongoing, Transformational Change   206
        3.5.3 The Purported Problem Posed to Originalism   208
        3.5.4 Originalism Sufficiently Accommodates Societal and
              Constitutional Change   209
    3.6 Conclusion   220

4   Originalism Best Advances Americans' Human Flourishing:
    The Law-as-Coordination Account of Originalism   221
    4.1 Introduction   221
    4.2 Originalists Must Provide a Normative Account for Originalism   222
        4.2.1 Introduction   222
        4.2.2 A Normative Account Is Needed to the Extent That
              Originalism Is a "Reform Project"   223

4.2.3 Originalists Must Respond to Critics' Frequent Claim That
       Originalism Is Substantively Unjust   223
4.2.4 The Constitution Makes Normative Claims upon Its Subjects   226
4.2.5 Conclusion   226
4.3 Law-as-Coordination Is a "Thin" Account   227
4.4 The Law-as-Coordination Account of Positive Law   228
  4.4.1 Introduction   228
  4.4.2 Human Flourishing, Natural Law, and Virtue Ethics   229
  4.4.3 Social Beings Pursuing the Common Good and Human
       Flourishing through Legal Authority and Law   239
  4.4.4 The Law-as-Coordination Account of Positive Law: Positive
       Law's Essential Role Pursuing the Common Good and
       Human Flourishing   265
  4.4.5 Conclusion   278
4.5 The Law-as-Coordination Account of Originalism   278
  4.5.1 Introduction   278
  4.5.2 The Constitution's Original Meaning Resolves Fundamental
       Coordination Problems to Secure the Common Good
       and Human Flourishing   279
  4.5.3 The Law-as-Coordination Account of Originalism Applies
       to the Whole Constitution   290
  4.5.4 The Law-as-Coordination Account of Originalism Precludes
       Resort to the Reasons Employed by the Framers and Ratifiers
       to Reject the Constitution's Original Meaning   291
  4.5.5 The Law-as-Coordination Account of Originalism Makes
       Sense of the Framing and Ratification in a Manner
       Nonoriginalism Cannot   292
  4.5.6 Judges (and Other Government Officials) Have Sound
       Reasons to Follow the Constitution's Original Meaning   295
  4.5.7 The Law-as-Coordination Account's Limits   307
4.6 Summary   309

Conclusion   310

Index   311

Acknowledgments

The impetus for this book first arose over eighteen years ago during my initial constitutional law courses when, to my surprise, the courses focused almost exclusively on Supreme Court opinions that themselves frequently paid little, and often paid no, attention to our written Constitution. My initial thoughts on constitutional interpretation were formed in conversation with Professor Ken Kress, both in and outside of class. Professor Richard Parker generously supervised my initial scholarly expedition into originalism. Since then and for over eighteen years, in articles, conferences, and debates, I tested various claims about originalism. This book is a product of those discussions.

My special thanks to Professor Randy Barnett and the Georgetown Center for the Constitution for the time at the Center to write the initial draft of this book, and to Professor Barnett and Professor Larry Solum for so generously commenting on my arguments. Thank you as well to Professor Robert P. George and the James Madison Program in American Ideals and Institutions at Princeton University, where I performed the final revisions and received valuable feedback on the manuscript, and to Bill Araiza, Eric Berger, Gonzalo Candia, Eric Claeys, Richard Dougherty, Joaquin Garcia-Huidobro, Scott Gerber, Josh Hochschild, Santiago Legarre, Jason Mazzone, Frank Ravitch, Eric Segal, Steve Smith, Alex Tsesis, Francisco Urbina, David Upham, and Christopher Wolfe, who offered thoughtful comments. I have substantially altered many parts of the manuscript as a result of their input, and it is better for it. The University of Toledo provided crucial research leave and other support that made it possible for me to research and write the manuscript. Carl Bachmayer, Jorge M. Farinacci-Fernos, Akhil Rajasekar, and Mike Stahl provided valuable research assistance.

Earlier versions of this book, as well as parts of it, were presented at many conferences and workshops including the ACS Constitutional Law Scholars Forum, the University of Akron School of Law workshop series, the Central States Law Schools Association annual conference, the Cleveland-Marshall College of Law, the Federalist Society Faculty Conference, the James Madison Program at Princeton University, the Loyola-Chicago Constitutional Law Colloquium, the Midwest Political Science Association annual conference, the Ohio Legal Scholarship Workshop, Pontifical Catholic University of Chile Law School, the University of the Andes (Chile), the University of Dallas political science faculty, the University of Toledo College of Law workshop series, the Valparaiso University Law School workshop series, and numerous debates on constitutional interpretation, where I received valuable feedback and constructive criticism.

Portions of this book appeared in *The Clash of Rival and Incompatible Philosophical Traditions within Constitutional Interpretation: Originalism Grounded in the Central Western Philosophical Tradition*, 28 HARV. J. L. & PUB. POL'Y. 909 (2005), *An Originalist Theory of Precedent: Originalism, Nonoriginalist Precedent, and the Common Good*, 36 N.M. L. REV. 419 (2006), *Originalism and the "Challenge of Change": Abduced-Principle Originalism and Other Mechanisms by which Originalism Sufficiently Accommodates Changed Social Conditions*, 60 HASTINGS L. J. 927 (2009), *An Originalist Theory of Precedent: The Privileged Place of Originalist Precedent*, 2010 BYU L. REV. 1729 (BYU Law Digital Commons © 2010), *Originalism and the Aristotelian Tradition: Virtue's Home in Originalism*, 80 FORDHAM L. REV. 1997 (2012), *Originalism's Subject Matter: Why the Declaration of Independence Is Not Part of the Constitution*, 89 S.C. L. REV. 637 (2016), and *An Evaluation of the Historical Evidence for Constitutional Construction from the First Congress' Debate over the Constitutionality of the First Bank of the United States*, 14 ST. THOMAS L. REV 193 (2018).

Saint Thomas Aquinas is a scholar's role model. He dedicated his life to learning and loving the Truth, and articulating that Truth in an accessible form. He shows that one's commitment to the truth is consistent with and entailed by one's commitment to the Truth.

Finally, special thanks to Elizabeth, who provided the love, understanding, and support that makes possible our wonderful family life which, in turn, created the space for me to write this book.

Abbreviations

AQUINAS   JOHN FINNIS, AQUINAS: MORAL, POLITICAL, AND LEGAL THEORY (1998)

NE   ARISTOTLE, THE NICOMACHEAN ETHICS (D.P. Chase trans., 1947)

NLNR   JOHN FINNIS, NATURAL LAW AND NATURAL RIGHTS (1980)

ST   ST. THOMAS AQUINAS, SUMMA THEOLOGICA (Fathers of the English Dominican Province trans., Benziger Bros. ed., 1947)

Introduction

We the People of the United States, in Order to ... promote the general Welfare ... do ordain and establish this Constitution for the United States of America.

Constitution of the United States[1]

The Constitution of the United States is Americans' most important civic document. It is a source of national identity, substituting for the religious, linguistic, cultural, or ethnic bonds that hold together many other countries. It is the pinnacle of our legal system, and from its perch it decides many of the most important issues of today, not to mention those in the past.[2] The Constitution is our nation's legal and – to only a slightly lesser degree – cultural "trump card" on these important issues. And yet, Americans disagree about its meaning and how to arrive at its meaning.

I argue in the following pages that the correct way to interpret the U.S. Constitution is originalism. Originalism is the theory of constitutional interpretation that identifies the Constitution's original meaning as its authoritative meaning. This meaning is the text's public meaning when that text was ratified. Judges especially, but all federal and state officers – and all of us, as American citizens – should utilize originalism to interpret our Constitution.

I tie originalism's promise to my conception of originalism, which is structured and justified by law's purpose: to secure the United States' national common good

---

[1] U.S. CONST. pmbl.

[2] The Constitution directly decides the substance of many important issues. For instance, it protects Americans' political speech from significant governmental regulation. U.S. CONST. amend. I; *Arizona Free Enter. Club's Freedom Club PAC* v. *Bennett*, 564 U.S. 721, 734 (2011). It also indirectly decides many other important issues by identifying the authoritative decision-maker for such issues. For example, the Constitution identifies states as the primary decision-makers for whether and how to provide education. U.S. CONST. amend. X; *United States* v. *Lopez*, 514 U.S. 549, 564 (1995).

1

and to enable individual Americans to achieve their own human flourishing. Hence, my conception of originalism is Aristotelian and aretaic. Aretaic is from the Greek word for excellence or virtue – *arete* – which is the idea that humans live best when we live full, happy, flourishing lives. Law in general, and our Constitution in particular, are key mechanisms to help make that possible for Americans, on both society-wide and individual levels.

Originalism's promise is to make sense of our constitutional practice while, at the same time, painting it in its best light. Originalism promises that the Framing, Ratification, and subsequent following of the Constitution was a rational process, one that then and today gives Americans sound reasons to follow. Originalism promises that the important and widespread facets of our existing constitutional practice, like precedent, are healthy and good and should continue to flourish. It also promises that utilizing originalism will identify and support the background conditions through which Americans today – both as a community and as individuals – can best pursue the common good and human flourishing, respectively.

The first part of this book, *A Description of Originalism*, begins in Chapter 1 by briefly describing originalism's history. Though originalism has been with us since the Republic's beginning, it was eclipsed in the early twentieth century. Originalism revived in its modern form beginning in the 1970s and has become increasingly sophisticated since the late 1990s.

Chapter 2 details my conception of originalism: the Constitutional Communication Model. This model of originalism views the Constitution as a reasoned act of intentional lawmaking, the purpose of which was to change the law and re-coordinate Americans to secure the common good. I seek to reconcile the major forms of originalism through conceiving of the Constitution's original meaning as the primary mechanism of communication between and among the Framers, Ratifiers, government officers, and all Americans. The Framers and Ratifiers reasonably responded to existing coordination problems and placed solutions to them in the Constitution in the form of legal directives to Americans. The Constitution's original meaning contains the Constitution's reasons that Americans should employ in their practical deliberations as exclusionary reasons, and which coordinate Americans to secure the common good. Chapter 2 also identifies a modest role for constitutional construction – the Deference Conception of Construction – and it describes robust roles for precedent and the judicial virtues. This conception of originalism draws on the Aristotelian philosophical tradition's resources, especially its conceptions of law, legal authority, and virtue.

The second part of this book, beginning with Chapter 3, contains my positive arguments for originalism. My case for originalism has two components. First, I show that originalism is better able to account for the important and the widespread facets of our constitutional practice than other theories of interpretation. This argument runs contrary to a common and potentially powerful argument against originalism: that it cannot fit our constitutional practice, and that adopting originalism would lead to massive and harmful disruption to our legal and social order. For example, Professor Richard Fallon spoke for many critics when he pointed to a number of facets of our constitutional practice that, he claimed, showed that originalism is inconsistent with current constitutional practice:[3]

> If the Constitution's status as ultimate law depends on practices of acceptance, then the claim that the written Constitution is the only valid source of constitutional norms loses all pretense of self-evident validity. As originalists candidly admit, originalist principles cannot explain or justify much of contemporary constitutional law. Important lines of precedent diverge from original understandings. Judges frequently take other considerations into account. Moreover, the public generally accepts the courts' non-originalist pronouncements as legitimate—not merely as final, but as properly rendered. In urging that existing judicial practices should be altered, originalists are not pure positivists, who insist that the "rule of recognition" prevailing in the United States reflects originalist principles. Rather, originalists, like all other participants in constitutional theoretical debates, carry a burden of normative justification. They must attempt to establish that the constitutional regime would be a better one— as measured by relevant criteria—if constitutional practice were exclusively text-based and if originalist precepts were consistently followed.[4]

My argument that originalism best fits the Constitution and our constitutional practice proceeds in two parts in Chapter 3. First, I rebut claims, like those made by Professor Fallon, and show that originalism does, in fact, substantially fit our constitutional practice, and does so better than competing theories. Originalism best fits both the important and the widespread facets of our constitutional practice. For example, I describe how originalism better fits the most important facet of our practice: our written Constitution's text. Second, I acknowledge that some facets of our practice are in tension with originalism, and that those contrary practices should be limited or rejected, as mistakes. In some situations, this is a cause for regret, because of the unsettlement doing so may cause but, in many situations, it will be a cause for celebration because our actual Constitution is saved from the mistakes falsely attributed to it.

Second, in Chapter 4, I lay out the law-as-coordination account of originalism. I argue that originalism is the most normatively attractive theory of constitutional interpretation because it is the one most likely to secure the common good of American society and individual Americans' human flourishing. This argument proceeds in four parts. First, I explain that the end of human beings is flourishing – what the Greeks called *eudaimonia*, often translated as happiness. Human flourishing occurs when we pursue the basic human goods, such as life, friendship, and knowledge, and do so excellently – virtuously.

---

[3] Richard H. Fallon, Jr., *How to Choose a Constitutional Theory*, 87 CAL. L. REV. 535, 545–48 (1999).
[4] *Id.* at 548.

Second, I show that individual human beings can only achieve human flourishing in community with others – in a society that effectively pursues the common
good through legal authority. No person is an island, and every person, at all stages
of life, needs fellow human beings to effectively pursue happiness. Only a society
can provide the organization necessary to produce the goods (broadly conceived to
include material, emotional, and spiritual goods) and provide the conditions (*e.g.*,
peace, structures for the expression of individual personality, and structures for social
cooperation) conducive to individual human flourishing.

Third, I describe how every society of more-than-modest complexity must and
does utilize legal authority to coordinate its members. Every society faces a unique
combination of circumstances, and within each set of circumstances there are
typically a variety of mutually exclusive and yet reasonable means of ordering a
society's pursuit of the common good. For this reason, human societies designate
authoritative persons and institutions, and give to them the task of authoritatively
determining how that society will pursue the common good for its members,
through law. These legal authorities characteristically coordinate members of their
societies through (1) authoritative, (2) prudential, (3) coordinating decisions, (4)
embodied in positive law.

Fourth, I apply this law-as-coordination account to the United States Constitution
and show how the Constitution contains American society's foundational authoritative, prudential, coordinating decisions. Americans, at the time of the Founding as
well as today, point to the state ratification conventions as having the authority to
adopt the Constitution for our society. The Constitution's decisions on how to order
American society are prudential: they are all-things-considered judgments made by
the Framers and Ratifiers. The Constitution's authoritative, prudential decisions
coordinated – and continue to coordinate – Americans' lives toward the common
good and individual human flourishing. The Constitution did so by using its
original meaning to communicate the Constitution's reasons to Americans who
would, in turn, employ those reasons in their practical deliberations and thereby
coordinate their activities. Americans in 1789, and Americans today, access the
Constitution's decisions – and thereby effectively secure the common good and
pursue their individual goods – by utilizing originalism. This gives judges and other
interpreters sound reasons to follow the original meaning.

My two-pronged argument for originalism in Part II first takes an "internal"
perspective. It argues that our constitutional practice itself commits us to originalism. Then, my argument takes an "external" perspective and maintains that our
practice's commitment to originalism is worthwhile because it advances the
common good of the United States and facilitates individual Americans' human
flourishing.

These two claims naturally complement each other because the jurisprudential
foundation for both of my claims is the Aristotelian philosophical tradition. This
tradition provides both the description of law and legal systems, and the justification

for law and legal authority, that I employ to analyze the United States Constitution. This legal theory is relatively uncommon in the American legal academy, so I introduce readers to its key concepts as my argument proceeds.

Many assume that a natural law account of the American Constitution must result in the judicial power to invalidate federal and state law through the use of unenumerated natural law or rights.[5] As John Hart Ely famously (and critically) described this general perspective, "[t]he invitation to judges seems clear: seek constitutional values in—that is, overrule political officials on the basis of—the writings of good contemporary moral philosophers."[6] My argument in Chapter 4 shows that, at least in the context of the United States, that assumption is misplaced. Instead, the Aristotelian philosophical tradition's account of our Constitution requires federal judges to utilize originalism.

---

[5] For a recent counter-example see Jeffrey A. Pojanowski & Kevin C. Walsh, *Enduring Originalism*, 105 Geo. L.J. 97 (2016).

[6] John Hart Ely, Democracy and Distrust: A Theory of Judicial Review 58 (1980).

PART I

A Description of Originalism

1

A Brief History of Originalism in American Constitutional Interpretation

[T]he legitimate meaning of the Instrument must be derived from the text itself; or if a key is to be sought elsewhere, it must not be in the opinions or intentions of the Body which planned & proposed the Constitution, but in the sense attached to it by the people in their respective State Conventions, where it recd. all the Authority which it possesses.

James Madison[1]

1.1 INTRODUCTION

The history of American constitutional interpretation has largely been an originalist one. At the Founding, the Framers and Ratifiers employed originalism when debating, drafting, and authorizing the Constitution. They did so against a background of originalist conventions of legal interpretation. Throughout the nineteenth century and – though subject to greater criticism and exceptions – up to the New Deal, originalism continued to be the dominant method of constitutional interpretation.

Beginning during the Progressive Era, nonoriginalist methodologies made their appearance, and as time went on they made their weight felt. My claims thus far are contested in the literature, though, with few exceptions, the next part of the story is not: nonoriginalism captured the Supreme Court and American legal culture during the New Deal and continued to hold unchallenged sway into the 1970s. Then, slowly at first, and gaining steam in the 1980s, originalism made a resurgence. Today, originalism is a powerful contender for allegiance in American legal practice, in the legal academy, and among Americans more generally.

---

[1] *Letter from James Madison to Thomas Ritchie* (Sept. 15, 1821), *in* 9 THE WRITINGS OF JAMES MADISON 72 (Gaillard Hunt ed., 1900–1910).

Today, originalism is a family of theories of constitutional interpretation;[2] it is not monolithic. Originalists have grounded originalism in different normative theories,[3] they have identified different sources of constitutional meaning,[4] they take varying approaches to nonoriginalist precedent,[5] and originalists have articulated different approaches when the Constitution's original meaning is underdetermined.[6] This chapter argues that, although originalism as a sophisticated theory of interpretation

[2] Lawrence B. Solum, *What Is Originalism? The Evolution of Contemporary Originalist Theory*, *in* THE CHALLENGE OF ORIGINALISM, THEORIES OF CONSTITUTIONAL INTERPRETATION 12 (Grant Huscroft & Bradley W. Miller eds., 2013).

[3] *See e.g.*, RANDY E. BARNETT, RESTORING THE LOST CONSTITUTION: THE PRESUMPTION OF LIBERTY 109 (2004) (arguing that originalism best protects natural rights); KEITH E. WHITTINGTON, CONSTITUTIONAL INTERPRETATION 110–59 (1999) (grounding originalism in popular sovereignty); JOHN O. MCGINNIS & MICHAEL B. RAPPAPORT, ORIGINALISM AND THE GOOD CONSTITUTION (2013) (arguing that originalism is justified because it protects the good consequences that arise from the Constitution's supermajority requirements). Some originalists have argued that no normative theory is necessary to support originalism, beyond whatever normative justification supports the constitutional system generally, because originalism is the best explanation of our constitutional system. William Baude, *Is Originalism Our Law?*, 115 COLUM. L. REV. 2349 (2015); Stephen E. Sachs, *Originalism as a Theory of Legal Change*, 38 HARV. J. L. & PUB. POL'Y 817 (2015). Professor Chris Green has argued that official oath-taking provides the needed normative hook for originalism. Christopher R. Green, *"This Constitution": Constitutional Indexicals as a Basis for Textualist Semi-Originalism*, 84 NOTRE DAME L. REV. 1607, 1643–48 (2009).

[4] Originalists are or have been divided into original meaning, original intent, original methods, and original understanding camps. Currently, the most widespread are original meaning originalists who include Jack Balkin, Randy Barnett, Gary Lawson, Lawrence Solum, Michael Stokes Paulsen, Keith Whittington. Original intent appears to be making something of a comeback. The most prominent original intent originalists are Richard Kay, Larry Alexander, and Saikrishna Prakash. The most prominent original understanding originalist is Robert Natelson. Original methods originalism was articulated by Professors McGinnis and Rappaport. MCGINNIS & RAPPAPORT, *supra* note 3. Most recently, Professor Baude and Sachs have proposed original law originalism. Baude, *supra* note 3, at 2349; Sachs, *supra* note 3, at 817.

[5] *Compare* Gary Lawson, *The Constitutional Case against Precedent*, 17 HARV. J. L. & PUB. POL'Y 23 (1994) (articulating the first powerful argument against nonoriginalist precedent); Randy E. Barnett, *Trumping Precedent with Original Meaning: Not as Radical as It Sounds*, 22 CONST. COMMENT. 257, 259 (2005) ("Accepting that judicial precedent can trump original meaning puts judges above the Constitution . . ."); Steven G. Calabresi, *Text vs. Precedent in Constitutional Law*, 31 HARV. J. L. & PUB. POL'Y 947, 947 (2008) (arguing that the Constitution "is controlling in most constitutional cases"); Michael Stokes Paulsen, *The Intrinsically Corrupting Influence of Precedent*, 22 CONST. COMMENT. 289, 289 (2005) (stating that "stare decisis . . . is completely irreconcilable with originalism"); *with* Lee J. Strang, *An Originalist Theory of Precedent: Originalism, Nonoriginalist Precedent, and the Common Good*, 36 N.M. L. REV. 419 (2006) (arguing that Article III requires preservation of some nonoriginalist precedent); Kurt T. Lash, *Originalism, Popular Sovereignty, and Reverse Stare Decisis*, 93 VA. L. REV. 1437 (2007) (arguing that popular sovereignty-based originalism preserves some nonoriginalist precedent); Lawrence B. Solum, *The Supreme Court in Bondage: Constitutional Stare Decisis, Legal Formalism, and the Future of Unenumerated Rights*, 9 U. PA. J. CONST. L. 155, 184–201 (2006) (arguing for a "neoformalist" conception of constitutional precedent based primarily on its good consequences, such as respect for Rule of Law values).

[6] I describe the various approaches in Section 2.3.

is of relatively recent origin, current originalist theory is a revival and a restoration of the original manner in which Americans interpreted their Constitution. It also suggests that alternatives to originalism are twentieth-century developments reflecting changes extrinsic to the Constitution and not facets intrinsic to the Constitution.

The practice of constitutional interpretation at the Founding was originalist, as that label is now understood.[7] To be sure, it was not the sophisticated, more-fully explicated originalism of today; it was largely inchoate, but both our legal practice's express goal of interpretation and the identified tools of interpretation were originalist. The goal of interpretation was to ascertain the lawmaker's fixed communicated meaning, and the interpretive tools were conventional means to achieve that goal. Importantly, neither the goal nor the tools of interpretation targeted contemporary meaning or normative considerations. Originalism's core is that the Constitution's meaning was fixed at the time of ratification and that the Constitution's fixed meaning contributes to constitutional meaning.[8] The early Republic's interpretive practice, as I show, hewed to originalism's core commitments.

This chapter's narrative of originalism's history dovetails with my Constitutional Communication Model of originalism, described in Section 2.2. The Constitutional Communication Model argues that constitutional interpretation's goal is to facilitate communication among and between the Framers, Ratifiers, government officers, and all Americans (past, present, and future). If, as I describe in this chapter, the conventional interpretive practice at the time of the Framing and Ratification was originalist, then my Constitutional Communication Model of originalism fits the process of constitutional creation and adoption and facilitates Americans' ability today to access the Constitution's communications.

This chapter's description of the early originalist conventions also supports my law-as-coordination normative justification for originalism in Chapter 4. I argue

---

[7] What follows is not a detailed review of the evidence supporting this claim. Instead, this is a summary of the evidence with references to the rich secondary literature that both identifies evidence and incorporates that evidence into more robust arguments. Much of my description is taken from CHRISTOPHER WOLFE, THE RISE OF MODERN JUDICIAL REVIEW: FROM CONSTITUTIONAL INTERPRETATION TO JUDGE-MADE LAW (1986); JOHNATHAN O'NEILL, ORIGINALISM IN AMERICAN LAW AND POLITICS (2005), H. Jefferson Powell, *The Original Understanding of Original Intent*, 98 HARV. L. REV. 885 (1985); and Howard Gillman, *The Collapse of Constitutional Originalism and the Rise of the Notion of the "Living Constitution" in the Course of American State-Building*, 11 STUDIES IN AM. POL. DEV. 191 (1997); *see also* BARNETT, *supra* note 3, at 96–100; PHILIP HAMBURGER, LAW AND JUDICIAL DUTY (2008); Robert G. Natelson, *The Founders' Hermeneutic: The Real Original Understanding of Original Intent*, 68 OHIO ST. L.J. 1239, 1305 (2007); Charles Lofgren, *The Original Understanding of Original Intent?*, 5 CONST. COMMENT. 77 (1988); Robert N. Clinton, *Original Understanding, Legal Realism, and the Interpretation of "This Constitution,"* 72 IOWA L. REV. 1177, 1186 (1987). For a recent counter argument see JONATHAN GIENAPP, THE SECOND CREATION: FIXING THE AMERICAN CONSTITUTION IN THE FOUNDING ERA (2018).

[8] Solum, *What Is Originalism?*, *supra* note 2, at 29–32.

there that the Constitution was the product an intentional act of lawmaking. The Framers' and Ratifiers' purpose was to facilitate societal pursuit of the common good and individual human flourishing. The Constitution was their response to sound reasons for lawmaking, and its authoritative, prudential, coordinating decisions are the product of the lawmaker's response to those reasons. If, as I describe in this chapter, originalism was the early Republic's conventional means of ascertaining legal meaning, then that supports my argument that the original meaning was the mechanism by which our Constitution's authoritative, prudential, coordinating decisions were created, authorized, communicated, and followed by Americans.

Let me be clear before proceeding: I am not arguing that originalism is the best theory of interpretation *because* the Framers and Ratifiers in general, or James Madison (or anyone else from the founding generation) in particular, said it was. That would be a weak argument. Instead, I argue in Chapters 3 and 4 that originalism is the best theory of interpretation because it best fits our existing constitutional practice and best secures the common good and human flourishing. This chapter's description of Founding Era originalism supports these claims.

1.2 THE LONG ARC OF THE REPUBLIC'S HISTORY

1.2.1 *English Background*

The English background dealing with positive law enactments by Parliament developed as Parliament's legislative output expanded and the theory of parliamentary sovereignty arose. The goal of interpretation of positive enactments was to ascertain Parliament's will.[9]

Sir William Blackstone's *Commentaries on the Laws of England*[10] represented, at least to Americans[11] if not in actual fact, the interpretive conventions prevalent in late-eighteenth-century England. As Blackstone described the goal of statutory interpretation: "the fairest and most rational method to interpret the will of the legislator, is by exploring his intentions at the time when the law was made, by signs the most natural and probable."[12] The reason for this interpretive goal, according to Blackstone, was because of parliamentary sovereignty.[13] The goal of interpretation, on Blackstone's account, was to follow the sovereign's communicated will.

Blackstone listed a series of interpretive rules to guide interpreters toward achievement of that goal. The five "signs the most natural and probable" identified by

---

[9] O'NEILL, *supra* note 7, at 13–14.
[10] WILLIAM BLACKSTONE, COMMENTARIES ON THE LAWS OF ENGLAND (1769).
[11] The *Commentaries* were published in four volumes between 1765 and 1769 and were likely the most influential legal authority in eighteenth-century America. Albert W. Alschuler, *Rediscovering Blackstone*, 145 U. PA. L. REV. 1, 5 (1996).
[12] I BLACKSTONE, *supra* note 10, at *59.
[13] *Id.* at *91.

Blackstone were: (1) "words ... in their usual and most known signification"; (2) legal context; (3) the "subject matter" or broader context; (4) "the effects of consequences" of different interpretations; and (5) "the reason and spirit of it; or the cause which moved the legislator to enact it."[14]

Blackstone's prescriptions for interpretation viewed interpretation as communication between the Parliament and interpreters, especially judges. Interpretation's goal, on Blackstone's account, was to uncover Parliament's fixed meaning, and his five rules were the tools to facilitate that goal. The most important tool of interpretation was the statute's text, and judges should resort to the last four rules of interpretation only if Parliament's intent remained unclear after using the first rule of interpretation.[15]

1.2.2 *Framing and Ratification Period*

Americans during the Framing and Ratification period followed in Blackstone's footsteps, though their conception of interpretation must be drawn primarily from their actions because they typically acted unselfconsciously in this regard. At the Philadelphia Convention, the Framers took great care to craft the Constitution's structure, text, grammar, and even punctuation;[16] they did so to communicate as clearly as possible the meaning they wished to convey to the Ratifiers, government officials, and Americans generally.[17] For example, the Framers extensively debated whether the text that became Article I, § 8, cl. 10, should include the words "punishment," "declare," and "felonies," in the grant to Congress of power over admiralty and international law.[18] The Framers took such care because of their commitment to the Blackstonian conception of legal interpretation that identified interpretation as communication and saw the Constitution's text as the primary source of information for later readers. As summarized by Professor Powell, "[t]he Philadelphia framers' primary expectation regarding constitutional interpretation

---

[14] *Id.* at *59–*62.

[15] *Id.* at *60.

[16] For instance, the Framers debated the punctuation for what became the Taxing and Spending Clause, with the possible different implications for the scope of Congress' power under the Clause. MAX FARRAND, THE FRAMING OF THE CONSTITUTION OF THE UNITED STATES 182–83 (1913). *See also, e.g.,* Akhil Reed Amar, *A Neo-Federalist View of Article III: Separating the Two Tiers of Federal Jurisdiction*, 65 B.U.L. REV. 205, 217 n.50 (1985) (utilizing punctuation choice to ascertain meaning).

[17] *See* JAMES MADISON, NOTES OF DEBATES IN THE FEDERAL CONVENTION OF 1787 (June 16, 1787) (1966) ("Mr. Elseworth proposed as a more distinctive form of collecting the mind of the Committee on the subject, 'that the Legislative power of the U. S. should remain in Congs. This was not seconded, though it seemed better calculated for the purpose than the 1st. proposition of Mr. Patterson in place of which Mr. E. wished to substitute it'.").

[18] Powell, *supra* note 7, at 903 n.90.

was that the Constitution, like any other legal document, would be interpreted according to its express language."[19]

This Blackstonian approach was parroted in the later and larger societal debate over Ratification, by both proponents and opponents of ratification. For example, *The Federalist Papers* used Blackstonian rules of interpretation.[20] In *Federalist 83*, Alexander Hamilton expressly invoked "[t]he rules of legal interpretation [which] are rules of common sense, adopted by the court in the construction of the laws."[21] There, he explicitly employed Blackstone's first, third, and fifth rules of interpretation.

Brutus, the most famous Anti-Federalist, contended that application of the well-accepted rules of interpretation showed that the proposed constitution would create a federal leviathan that would subvert the states.[22] For instance, in his explanation of federal judicial power, he expressly relied on the conventional rules of interpretation:

> According to this mode of construction, the courts are to give such meaning to the constitution as comports best with the common, and generally received acceptation of the words in which it is expressed, regarding their ordinary and popular use, rather than their grammatical propriety. Where words are dubious, they will be explained by the context. The end of the clause will be attended to, and the words will be understood, as having a view to it; and the words will not be so understood as to bear no meaning or a very absurd one.[23]

In a series of letters, Brutus utilized these rules of interpretation to review the Constitution's text, structure, background, and purpose to argue that federal judicial power would empower the federal government to swallow the states.[24]

1.2.3 *Early Republic and Pre–New Deal American Constitutional Practice*

Though there was little explicit discussion of interpretive methodology because the legal culture of the time accepted an unselfconscious originalist approach,[25] early American constitutional practice directed constitutional interpretation toward the goal of ascertaining the text's original meaning. For example, James Madison, in his congressional speech opposing the chartering of a national bank – one of the most important constitutional debates in the First Congress – relied on a number of

---

[19] *Id.* at 903.
[20] WOLFE, *supra* note 7, at 20–23; O'NEILL, *supra* note 7, at 15–16.
[21] THE FEDERALIST No. 83 (Alexander Hamilton).
[22] Powell, *supra* note 7, at 905.
[23] THE ESSAYS OF BRUTUS No. XI, *in* 2 THE COMPLETE ANTI-FEDERALIST 419 (Herbert J. Storing ed., 1981).
[24] THE ESSAYS OF BRUTUS Nos. XI–XV, *in* 2 THE COMPLETE ANTI-FEDERALIST, *supra* note 23, at 419–42.
[25] WOLFE, *supra* note 7, at 17.

Blackstone's rules of interpretation.[26] He argued that "[i]n controverted cases, the meaning of the parties to the instrument, if it be collected by reasonable evidence, is a proper guide. Contemporary and concurrent expositions are a reasonable evidence of the meaning of parties."[27] Congressmen on all sides of this debate likewise employed rules of interpretation.[28]

This use of originalism crossed (emerging) party lines. President Thomas Jefferson, for instance, responded to Rhode Island's request for his understanding of the Constitution by stating that "the constitution ... shall be administered by me according to the safe and honest meaning contemplated by the plain understanding of the people of the United States at the time of its adoption ... [T]hese explanations are preserved in the publications of the time."[29]

The Marshall Court similarly used an originalist approach to constitutional interpretation.[30] For example, in *Ogden v. Saunders*, Chief Justice Marshall explained:

> To say that the intention of the instrument must prevail; that this intention must be collected from its words; that its words are to be understood in that sense in which they are generally used by those for whom the instrument was intended; that its provisions are neither to be restricted into insignificance, nor extended to objects not comprehended in them nor contemplated by its framers, is to repeat what has already been said.[31]

Likewise, Joseph Story, in his 1833 *Commentaries on the Constitution*, summarized the governing rules of interpretation: "the first and fundamental rule in the interpretation of all instruments is to construe them according to the sense of the terms, and the intent of the parties."[32] Tying his point to the broader practice of legal interpretation, Story then summarized Blackstone: "Mr. Justice Blackstone has remarked, that the intention of a law is to be gathered from the words, the context, the subject-matter, the effects and consequence, or the reason and spirit of the law."[33]

In sum, both the goal and tools of constitutional interpretation in the early Republic were originalist. Early Americans did not argue that the Constitution's meaning was not fixed. Nor did they claim that extrinsic normative considerations

---

[26] James Madison, *Speech Opposing the Bank*, in 2 ANNALS OF CONGRESS 1944–52 (Feb. 2, 1791).

[27] *Id.* at 1946.

[28] *Id.* at 1955, 1958 (Fisher Ames) (Feb. 3, 1791); 1966 (John Lawrence) (Feb. 4, 1791); 1970, 1979 (Elias Boudinot) (Feb. 4, 1791).

[29] *Letter from Thomas Jefferson to Providence Citizens* (March 27, 1801), *in* 33 THE PAPERS OF THOMAS JEFFERSON 475–76 (Barbara B. Oberg ed., 2006).

[30] WOLFE, *supra* note 7, at 41–62.

[31] *Ogden v. Saunders*, 25 U.S. (12 Wheat.) 213, 332 (1827).

[32] 2 JOSEPH STORY, COMMENTARIES ON THE CONSTITUTION §400 (1833).

[33] *Id.*; *see also* FRANCIS LIEBER, LEGAL AND POLITICAL HERMENEUTICS 23 (1839) ("Interpretation is the art of finding the true sense [of the words] which their author intended to convey, and of enabling others to derive from them the same idea which the author intended to convey.")

contributed to the Constitution's meaning. As summarized by Johnathan O'Neill: "despite disagreement about what the Constitution meant or required and the variety of sources invoked, few at the time thought interpretation was anything other than the ascertainment and application of original intent."[34]

This originalist approach to constitutional interpretation continued until the Progressive Era, with some notable errors along the way,[35] although the originalism of this period was "more tacit and axiomatic than carefully theorized."[36] For instance, in the Commerce Clause context, the Supreme Court consistently hewed to the Clause's original meaning.[37] In the 1869 case of *United States* v. *Dewitt*, the Supreme Court for the first time struck down as beyond Congress' commerce power a federal statute that criminalized intrastate sales of naphtha and illuminating oils.[38] This originalist interpretation of the Commerce Clause held through 1936 where, for instance, in *A. L. A. Schechter Poultry Corp.* v. *United States*, the Supreme Court ruled that intrastate wholesale sale of chickens was beyond Congress' authority.[39]

Late-nineteenth-century commentators reflected the conventional originalist approach to interpretation. Thomas Cooley, in the most prominent constitutional law treatise of the period, *A Treatise on the Constitutional Limitations*, defined constitutional interpretation in originalist terms: "to give effect to the intent of the people adopting it."[40]

Even in cases where the Supreme Court likely departed from the Constitution's original meaning, such as the *Slaughter-House Cases*, it still purported to utilize originalism.[41] Justice Miller ostensibly identified the Privileges or Immunity Clause's fixed and binding meaning through an originalist investigation of the Constitution's text,[42] structure,[43] and history.[44]

---

[34] O'NEILL, *supra* note 7, at 17.

[35] WOLFE, *supra* note 7, at 64–72. The blips included cases such as *Dred Scott v. Sanford*, 60 U.S. (19 How.) 393 (1856), where Chief Justice Taney utilized a substantive due process rationale to claim that the Missouri Compromise violated slave owners' property rights, and *The Legal Tender Cases*, 79 U.S. 457, 531–35 (1870), where the Court likely misinterpreted Congress' power to "coin" money under the Necessary and Proper Clause.

[36] O'NEILL, *supra* note 7, at 23.

[37] Richard A. Epstein, *The Proper Scope of the Commerce Power*, 73 VA. L. REV. 1387, 1409–42 (1987).

[38] *United States v. Dewitt*, 76 U.S. 1 (1869).

[39] *A. L. A. Schechter Poultry Corp.* v. *United States*, 295 U.S. 495, 542–43 (1936).

[40] THOMAS M. COOLEY, A TREATISE ON THE CONSTITUTIONAL LIMITATIONS WHICH REST UPON THE LEGISLATIVE POWER OF THE STATES OF THE AMERICAN UNION 68 (4th ed. 1878) (emphasis deleted).

[41] *Slaughter-House Cases*, 83 U.S. (16 Wall.) 36 (1872).

[42] *E.g.*, *id.* at 72–74.

[43] *Id.* at 82.

[44] *E.g.*, *id.* at 67.

1.3 ORIGINALISM'S ECLIPSE DURING AND AFTER THE NEW DEAL

This convention of originalist constitutional interpretation came under sustained and increasing pressure as the twentieth century progressed, and originalism was ultimately eclipsed during the New Deal. There are many reasons for this change, let me briefly describe three of the most important: (1) a Progressive Era desire for a more powerful federal government; (2) an evolution-inspired conception of science applied to the law; and (3) the Legal Realist attack on legal determinacy.

These reasons show that American legal culture's abandonment of originalism was caused by forces extrinsic to the Constitution. In particular, the abandonment of originalism was caused by related intellectual movements in politics and law that viewed the Constitution's nature differently from originalism and hence needed a different theory of interpretation. Originalism was eclipsed, in other words, because nonoriginalists abandoned the conventional view of the Constitution as an intentional lawmaking act for the sake of the common good under which view the Constitution's original meaning was the mechanism to communicate the Constitution's legal directions among the Framers, Ratifiers, and Americans.

First, the Progressive Era is named after the Progressive Movement, and the Progressive Movement was a big tent, but one of its central tenets was the use of government power to achieve the Movement's goals.[45] Many of the Progressive Movement's key legal successes on the federal level – antitrust legislation (1890), the Federal Reserve System (1913), the federal income tax (1913), and the first wave of modern federal administrative agencies[46] – are well known and remain with us today; many of the Progressive Movement's other legislative attempts did not succeed (at least not until the New Deal).[47]

Many of the Progressive Movement's goals did not fit with the then-standard originalist interpretation of the Constitution.[48] For example, federal administrative agencies, in order to meet progressive goals, needed to exercise significant discretion, embody governmental functions situated outside of the executive branch, and be insulated from political control. The agencies needed to exercise discretion because their congressional mandates to remedy perceived social problems were, and needed to be, nonspecific, because this allowed the agencies to utilize their experience and expertise to remedy problems quickly and efficiently. The agencies employed nonexecutive functions to achieve their congressionally defined goals

---

[45] SAMUEL ELIOT MORISON, THE OXFORD HISTORY OF THE AMERICAN PEOPLE 811–15 (1965).

[46] These included the Food and Drug Administration (1906), and the Federal Trade Commission (1914), among others.

[47] For example, the Supreme Court repeatedly struck down child labor legislation, *Hammer v. Dagenhart*, 247 U.S. 251, 276–77 (1918); *Bailey v. Drexel Furniture Co.*, 259 U.S. 20, 44 (1922); *Hill v. Wallace*, 259 U.S. 44, 68 (1922), until it didn't. *United States v. Darby Lumber Co.*, 312 U.S. 100 (1941).

[48] John O. McGinnis, *Public Choice Originalism: Bork, Buchanan, and the Escape from the Progressive Paradigm*, 10 J. L. ECON. & POL'Y 669, 671 (2014).

through the making of legal norms (legislation) and deciding whether a particular party violated those norms (adjudication). Without the capacity to exercise these legislative and adjudicative powers, agencies would have to rely on the politicized and nonexpert Congress, and the slow and nonexpert judiciary. Agencies needed political insulation to protect the space needed by the agency's experts and to avoid political co-option that would thwart the agencies' social-reform mandate.

However, these three essential agency characteristics bumped into Article I, § 1, cl. 1, Article II, § 1, cl. 1, and Article III, § 1, cl. 1, and Article II, § 3. These clauses delegated specific powers to respective branches of the federal government, and together and along with other constitutional textual provisions, such as the Necessary and Proper Clause,[49] mandated an institutional separation of powers inconsistent with agencies' structure and power.

The Interstate Commerce Commission (ICC), the first modern agency, is representative.[50] The ICC (ostensibly) utilized governmental power to protect farmers, merchants, and consumers from avaricious railroads that unfairly used their bargaining power to raise transportation prices. The ICC exercised significant discretion preventing "unjust and unreasonable" rates for railroads.[51] The ICC exercised powers traditionally associated with the federal judiciary by "trying" alleged violations of the Act.[52] Congress protected the ICC Commissioners from political influence by creating six-year terms and providing protection from presidential removal.[53]

Originalism stood in the way of achieving these politically popular goals through the mechanism of administrative agencies and therefore became a target of criticism. For example, future President Woodrow Wilson argued in 1885 that "[t]he government of a country so vast and various as the U.S. must be strong, prompt, wieldy, and efficient," and that the traditional conception of separation of powers had impeded the federal government's capacity to achieve this goal.[54] Therefore, a new method of interpretation was utilized to constitutionally justify administrative agencies. For example, James Landis argued in *The Administrative Process* that administrative agencies were constitutionally justified by the crucial work they do providing the necessary regulation of an urban, national, industrialized economy in a way that the traditional, separate branches of government could not.[55]

---

[49] Gary Lawson & Patricia B. Granger, *The "Proper" Scope of Federal Power: A Jurisdictional Interpretation of the Sweeping Clause*, 43 Duke L.J. 267 (1993).
[50] The Interstate Commerce Act of 1887, 24 Stat. 379 (1887).
[51] *Id.* § 1.
[52] *Id.* §§ 14, 15.
[53] *Id.* § 11.
[54] Woodrow Wilson, Congressional Government: A Study in American Politics 206–07 (2006 reprint of 1885 ed.).
[55] James Landis, The Administrative Process 39, 69 (1938).

Second, late-nineteenth-century progressive Americans believed that Charles Darwin's theory of evolution was a model for law-as-science.[56] For example, Harvard Law School Dean Christopher Columbus Langdell claimed in the first-ever casebook that he taught students that contract law was a science of classification and relationships of evolving legal doctrines.[57] The scientific model was of organic entities growing and changing, and doing so in response to environmental stimuli, or else dying.[58] As summarized by Dean Langdell: "Each of these [contract] doctrines has arrived at its present state by slow degrees; in other words, it is a growth, extending in many cases through the centuries."[59] These scholars saw themselves as acting in opposition to what they believed was the prior static conception of humanity, human society, and law.[60]

The evolutionary science conception of law meant that the Constitution should adapt to the changing environment; its meaning had to change to suit the new needs of American society.[61] Woodrow Wilson argued in his 1908 book, *Constitutional Government in the United States*, that "the definitions and prescriptions of our constitutional law, though conceived in the Newtonian spirit and upon the Newtonian principle, are sufficiently broad and elastic to allow for the play of life and circumstance."[62]

This conception of law and the Constitution worked in tandem with the Progressive Movement's goals. For instance, proponents of administrative agencies argued that the Constitution's meaning needed to change to permit new governmental arrangements, such as administrative agencies, which were necessary to respond to the new phenomenon of a national industrial economy.[63]

This meant that originalism, with its static and fixed original meaning, would not – could not – work because, by definition, its meaning did not change. The original meaning would prevent the Constitution from adapting to America's changing society. Therefore, originalism had to be jettisoned and a flexible nonoriginalist theory substituted in its place.

A third reason for the abandonment of originalism was Legal Realism. Beginning in the late nineteenth and early twentieth centuries, Realist legal thought argued that the law was indeterminate.[64] The law did not itself determine the outcome of

[56] EDWARD A. PURCELL, JR., THE CRISIS OF DEMOCRATIC THEORY: SCIENTIFIC NATURALISM AND THE PROBLEM OF VALUE 5–6, 11, 74–94 (1973); BRADLEY C. S. WATSON, LIVING CONSTITUTION, DYING FAITH *passim* (2009).

[57] C. C. LANGDELL, ON THE LAW OF CONTRACTS: WITH REFERENCES AND CITATIONS *Preface* (1871).

[58] PURCELL, *supra* note 56, at 75–76.

[59] LANGDELL, *supra* note 57, at *Preface*.

[60] PURCELL, *supra* note 56, at 74.

[61] O'NEILL, *supra* note 7, at 30; WATSON, *supra* note 56, at 10, 15; WOLFE, *supra* note 7, at 205–16.

[62] WOODROW WILSON, CONSTITUTIONAL GOVERNMENT IN THE UNITED STATES 55 (1908).

[63] Stephen Skowronek, Essay, *The Conservative Insurgency and Presidential Power: A Developmental Perspective on the Unitary Executive*, 122 HARV. L. REV. 2070, 2086 (2009).

[64] JEROME FRANK, LAW AND THE MODERN MIND 138 (1930); MORTON J. HORWITZ, THE TRANSFORMATION OF AMERICAN LAW: 1870–1960, at 176–78, 190 (1992).

concrete disputes – certainly not as often or in the way portrayed by traditional legal thought. Instead, factors other than, or in addition to, the law moved judges to make decisions.[65]

Applied to the Constitution, the Realist critique purported to show that the Constitution's meaning could be molded to fit Progressive-New Deal legal goals. The critique did this by showing that, contrary to originalism's claims, the Constitution's meaning was sufficiently indeterminate to be adaptable to the new exigencies of American life. For example, the New Deal Court followed President Roosevelt and the New Deal Congress by deferring to Congress' economic regulations of *intrastate non-*market activity in the Commerce Clause context.[66] The Supreme Court justified its nonoriginalist interpretation perhaps most clearly in the case that made the Contracts Clause a near-nullity, *Home Building & Loan Ass'n v. Blaisdell*:

> It is manifest from this review of our decisions that there has been a growing appreciation of public needs and of the necessity of finding ground for a rational compromise between individual rights and public welfare ... Where, in earlier days, it was thought that only the concerns of individuals or of classes were involved, and that those of the state itself were touched only remotely, it has later been found that the fundamental interests of the state are directly affected; and that the question is no longer merely that of one party to a contract as against another, but of the use of reasonable means to safeguard the economic structure upon which the good of all depends.
>
> It is no answer to say that this public need was not apprehended a century ago, or to insist that what the provision of the Constitution meant to the vision of that day it must mean to the vision of our time. If by the statement that what the Constitution meant at the time of its adoption it means to-day, it is intended to say that the great clauses of the Constitution must be confined to the interpretation which the framers, with the conditions and outlook of their time, would have placed upon them, the statement carries its own refutation. It was to guard against such a narrow conception that Chief Justice Marshall uttered the memorable warning: "We must never forget, that it is a constitution we are expounding" (*McCulloch v. Maryland*, 4 Wheat. 316, 407); "a constitution intended to endure for ages to come, and, consequently, to be adapted to the various crises of human affairs." Id. page 415 of 4 Wheat ....
>
> Nor is it helpful to attempt to draw a fine distinction between the intended meaning of the words of the Constitution and their intended application. When we consider the contract clause and the decisions which have expounded it in harmony with the essential reserved power of the states to protect the security of their peoples, we find no warrant for the conclusion that the clause has been warped by these decisions from its proper significance or that the founders of our government would have interpreted the clause differently had they had occasion to assume that

---

[65] HORWITZ, *supra* note 64, at 176–78, 190.
[66] E.g., *Wickard v. Filburn*, 317 U.S. 111, 128–29 (1942).

responsibility in the conditions of the later day. The vast body of law which has been developed was unknown to the fathers, but it is believed to have preserved the essential content and the spirit of the Constitution. With a growing recognition of public needs and the relation of individual right to public security, the court has sought to prevent the perversion of the clause through its use as an instrument to throttle the capacity of the states to protect their fundamental interests. This development is a growth from the seeds which the fathers planted . . . [67]

The *Blaisdell* Court's justification for its departure from the Constitution's original meaning combined Progressive-New Deal political goals, an evolutionary conception of the Constitution, and legal indeterminacy. These same themes echoed in the opinions of other Progressive and New Deal justices.[68]

Beginning with the New Deal, and continuing through the 1960s, originalism was almost entirely eclipsed. What had once been the consensus, traditional manner of interpreting the Constitution became exotic, even unheard-of during this period. In its place arose a nonoriginalist practice.

First, the Supreme Court's rhetoric and holdings ignored and, in many cases, contradicted the Constitution's original meaning. I already noted *Blaisdell's* nonoriginalist holding and justifications. The New Deal, Warren, and Burger Courts' *United States Reports* volumes are littered with nonoriginalist holdings and reasoning, ranging from important cases, such as *Brown v. Board of Education*[69] and *Roe v. Wade*,[70] to the more mundane.[71]

Second, the various theoretical justifications offered during the period to explain and justify this nonoriginalist practice were also nonoriginalist. The most important early justification was found in *Carolene Products* Footnote 4.[72] There, in the midst of the New Deal Court's otherwise widespread retreat from robust judicial review, the Court suggested a tentative basis for more rigorous judicial review. The Court identified the contours of judicial review in terms other than the Constitution's original meaning.

---

[67] *Home Bldg. & Loan Ass'n v. Blaisdell*, 290 U.S. 398, 442–44 (1934).

[68] Justice Holmes, for instance, argued in *Missouri v. Holland* that "[w]hen we are dealing with words that are a constituent act, like the Constitution of the U.S., we must realize that they have called into life a being the development of which could not have been foreseen . . . It was enough for them to realize or to hope that they had created an organism." *Missouri v. Holland*, 252 U.S. 416, 433 (1920).

[69] *See Brown v. Board of Education*, 347 U.S. 483, 489–91 (1954) (describing the Equal Protection Clause's history as "inconclusive" and consequently resorting to contemporary social science research to conclude that racially segregated primary education is inherently unequal). I am not claiming that *Brown's* result was inconsistent with the original meaning.

[70] *See Roe v. Wade*, 410 U.S. 113, 152 (1973) ("The Constitution does not explicitly mention any right of privacy. In a line of decisions, however . . . .").

[71] *See Wickard v. Filburn*, 317 U.S. 111 (1942) (ruling that the intrastate activity of growing and consuming wheat on a farm was "Commerce . . . among the several States").

[72] *United States v. Carolene Prods.*, 304 U.S. 144, 152 n.4 (1938).

The Warren Court later revived aggressive judicial review in the context of "individual" or "fundamental" rights.[73] The Court's reasoning and results were nonoriginalist. The most (in)famous example, at the initiation of this genre, is Justice Douglas' opinion for the Court in *Griswold* v. *Connecticut*.[74] After "declin [ing] th[e] invitation" to resurrect *Lochner*, the Court went on to identify "penumbras, formed by emanations" from prior cases' interpretations of the Bill of Rights.[75] Indeed, the Warren Court's aggressive nonoriginalist stance challenged legal scholars in what became known as the Legal Process School.

Legal Process had its principal home at Harvard Law School, though it had prominent adherents on the Court and throughout the academy.[76] For my purposes, I will focus on one of Legal Process' key tenets, institutional settlement.[77] Institutional settlement is the idea that legal systems should distribute decision-making authority for particular legal issues to those institutions best suited to make the best decisions, and other legal institutions should treat those decisions as authoritative.[78] The theory did not focus on "correct" interpretive answers; instead, it looked for processes of decision-making to identify who was most likely to make the best interpretive decision. Legal Process was not originalist.

Other than the Legal Process School, there was relatively little theorizing about how to interpret the Constitution, and Legal Process' influence began to wane as the Warren Court's cases became more and more difficult to justify in Legal Process terms. Liberal[79] legal academics associated with the Legal Process School initially expressed significant misgivings about the Court's unprecedented assertions of judicial power.[80] As the 1970s progressed, however, most legal academics defended the Warren and Burger Courts' ambitious rulings,[81] though frequently with apologies for the Court's own weak justifications.[82]

---

[73] Though, not all rights, even enumerated ones, received the Warren Court's solicitous treatment. For example, the right to contract was unprotected from impairing governmental regulation.

[74] *Griswold* v. *Connecticut*, 381 U.S. 479 (1965).

[75] *Id.* at 482, 484.

[76] BRIAN Z. TAMANAHA, LAW AS A MEANS TO AN END 102–04 (2006).

[77] *Id.* at 104.

[78] Ernest Young, *Institutional Settlement in a Globalizing Judicial System*, 54 DUKE L.J. 1143, 1150 (2005).

[79] By the label "liberal," I mean (only) scholars on the liberal or progressive or left end of the American legal and political spectrum who agreed with the substantive outcomes of the Warren Court cases.

[80] Perhaps the most famous example of this was Herbert Wechsler, *Toward Neutral Principles of Constitutional Law*, 73 HARV. L. REV. 1 (1959); O'NEILL, *supra* note 7, at 93.

[81] *See* RONALD DWORKIN, TAKING RIGHTS SERIOUSLY 124–30 (1977) (describing how *Roe* fits Dworkin's conception of law-as-integrity).

[82] John Hart Ely, *The Wages of Crying Wolfe: A Comment on Roe* v. *Wade*, 82 YALE L.J. 920, 922–26 (1973).

In sum, for at least thirty years, originalism was a jurisprudential exile.[83] Only slowly, over the course of the late twentieth and early twenty-first centuries, has it regained credibility. This brief review of originalism's eclipse during the early-through-mid-twentieth century shows that nonoriginalism's dominance of our constitutional practice was a contingent phenomenon that occurred because of several causes extrinsic to the Constitution and our practice. It also suggests that originalism's revival, which I describe in Section 1.4, though also the result of contingent factors, is an attempt to return our legal practice to its initial faithfulness to the written Constitution.

1.4 ORIGINALISM'S REINCARNATION AND EVOLUTION

1.4.1 *Modern Originalism's First Generation*

Originalism's slow resurgence[84] began primarily as a scholarly movement in the 1970s, the aim of which was to criticize the Warren and Burger Courts' excesses.[85] Since it was a critical stance, originalism's characteristics met that need. In particular, originalists claimed that originalism was superior to nonoriginalism because it cabined judicial discretion.[86] Only by tying judges' constitutional interpretations to the meaning intended by the Framers and Ratifiers, argued then-Justice Rehnquist in 1976, would judges remain in their proper – limited – role.[87]

The first key originalist scholars were Robert Bork and Raoul Berger. Both lauded originalism for its ability to constrain judges. In his seminal piece, *Neutral Principles and Some First Amendment Problems*, Bork – consciously acting in the Warren Court's shadow[88] – argued that the Constitution's originally intended meaning was the sole proper source of Supreme Court authority. An originalist Supreme Court that followed this meaning, Bork argued, "need make no fundamental value choices."[89] Instead, the Constitution's originally intended meaning would restrain

---

[83] *Compare* Stephen E. Sachs, *The "Constitution in Exile" as a Problem for Legal Theory*, 89 NOTRE DAME L. REV. 2253 (2014) (arguing that all theories of interpretation suffer from an inability to fully fit extant legal practices).

[84] For a summary of this history see Solum, *What is Originalism?*, *supra* note 2.

[85] RAOUL BERGER, GOVERNMENT BY JUDICIARY: THE TRANSFORMATION OF THE FOURTEENTH AMENDMENT 307–09 (2d ed. 1997); Robert H. Bork, *Neutral Principles and Some First Amendment Problems*, 47 IND. L.J. 1, 1 (1971); *see also* O'NEILL, *supra* note 7, at 66–67, 92–110; Keith E. Whittington, *The New Originalism*, 2 GEO. J. L. & PUB. POL'Y 599, 601–03 (2004).

[86] Paul Brest, *The Misconceived Quest for the Original Understanding*, 60 B. U. L. REV. 204, 204 (1980).

[87] William H. Rehnquist, *The Notion of a Living Constitution*, 54 TEX. L. REV. 693, 696–97 (1976).

[88] And within the Legal Process School tradition. Bork, *supra* note 85, at 7.

[89] *Id.* at 5.

the Court: "The judge must stick close to the text and the history, and their fair implications."[90]

Raoul Berger's 1977 *Government by Judiciary* raised the stakes by arguing that much of the Warren and Burger Courts' controversial constitutional edifice was illegitimate. Berger contended that Supreme Court judicial review was legitimate only when it enforced the Constitution.[91] Effectuating this limited form of judicial review required the Supreme Court to follow the Constitution's original intent.[92] The Warren Court, whose case law greatly deviated from the Fourteenth Amendment's original intent exceeded its proper constitutional role and therefore was undemocratic:[93] "The Constitution represents fundamental choices that have been made by the people, and the task of the Courts is to effectuate them, 'not [to] construct new rights'."[94]

Originalism's advocates also claimed that originalism would cabin judicial discretion by advancing legal norms of relatively narrow, concrete breadth. This resulted from the focus on the constitutional provisions' framers' concrete intentions, including their expectations on how the Constitution would be applied.[95] Bork's 1971 discussion of the Fourteenth Amendment's meaning, for instance, focused on whether the "history ... reveal[ed] detailed choices" by the Framers.[96]

The normative attractiveness of originalism's ability to cabin judicial discretion was tied to a second claim: judges limited by originalism would respect democratic choices.[97] In originalism's infancy, its critical stance meant that it focused on the Warren and Burger Courts' most controversial cases, which involved the Court striking down state and federal laws that purportedly infringed on fundamental constitutional rights.[98] Originalists contended that the Supreme Court acted undemocratically and hence illegitimately when it overturned acts of the elected branches without a clear warrant in the Constitution's text or history.[99] According to Bork, "Courts must accept any value choice the legislature makes unless it clearly runs contrary to a choice made in the framing of the Constitution."[100]

---

[90] *Id.* at 8.

[91] BERGER, *supra* note 85, at 3–4.

[92] *Id.* at 3–4, 402.

[93] *Id.* at 3, 22–23, 308, 458.

[94] *Id.* at 314.

[95] Whittington, *supra* note 85, at 603.

[96] Bork, *supra* note 85, at 13; *see also* BERGER, *supra* note 85, at 17–18, 409–10.

[97] Rehnquist, *supra* note 87, at 696–97.

[98] *Griswold* v. *Connecticut*, 381 U.S. 479 (1965) and *Roe* v. *Wade*, 410 U.S. 113 (1973) were the most prominent examples of this because of the Court's use of unenumerated rights, though the Court's expansive interpretations of more textually rooted criminal procedure rights, such as in *Miranda* v. *Arizona*, 384 U.S. 436 (1966), received significant criticism as well. Whittington, *supra* note 85, at 601–03; *see also* Bork, *supra* note 85, at 7; BERGER, *supra* note 85, at 286–87.

[99] Bork, *supra* note 85, at 6.

[100] *Id.* at 10–11.

A third characteristic of this early conception of originalism, already suggested, was its focus on original intent.[101] The original intent of a constitutional provision was the meaning that the provision's framers intended it to mean.[102] For example, Berger argued that the Equal Protection Clause protected the rights listed in the 1866 Civil Rights Act from unequal treatment, because that is what its drafters in the Reconstruction Congress intended.[103] "[T]he framers meant to outlaw discrimination only with respect to enumerated privileges … [T]he framers chose words which aptly expressed … their limited purposes."[104] Berger's discussion is replete with references to framer purposes and goals, the rhetoric of original intent.

Busied with defending originalism in a hostile legal academy, originalists focused their attention on the basics. Originalists did not initially address subtler issues, such as originalism's response to nonoriginalist precedent. Those discussions began in earnest following nonoriginalist criticism. A second impetus for greater originalist attention to originalism's subtler implications was the Rehnquist Court, which did not pose as good a target for criticism and instead stood in need of a more fully fleshed-out theory to support originalist aspects of its jurisprudence.[105]

1.4.2 *Nonoriginalist Criticisms Engaged*

In the late 1970s and early 1980s, nonoriginalists raised a host of criticisms.[106] The most powerful critique, given originalism's critical stance regarding perceived Warren Court activism, was that originalism did not, upon inspection, limit judicial discretion. Nonoriginalists utilized a variety of arguments to support this criticism; I briefly describe three.

First, nonoriginalists argued that it was either impossible in principle to ascertain the original intent of a multimember body, such as the Philadelphia Convention or state ratification conventions;[107] or, if possible, it was practically so difficult that the endeavor would regularly fail.[108] Ronald Dworkin echoed others when he claimed that "there is no such thing as the intention of the Framers waiting to be discovered, even in principle."[109] If there was no originally intended meaning, then judges could not be cabined by it.

Second, nonoriginalists argued that, even when one could reliably ascertain the Constitution's original intent, it frequently "ran out."[110] This occurred,

---

[101] Berger, *supra* note 85, at 402; Whittington, *supra* note 85, at 603.
[102] Berger, *supra* note 85, at 402.
[103] *Id.* at 201, 207, 219.
[104] *Id.* at 199.
[105] Whittington, *supra* note 85, at 603–04.
[106] Solum, *What Is Originalism?*, *supra* note 2, at 12, 17–19; Whittington, *supra* note 85, at 605–07.
[107] Brest, *supra* note 86, at 214–15, 221–22.
[108] *Id.* at 214, 220.
[109] Ronald Dworkin, *The Forum of Principle*, 56 N. Y. U. L. Rev. 469, 477 (1981).
[110] Brest, *supra* note 86, at 222.

nonoriginalists argued, when societal circumstances changed to such a degree that the original intent's application was underdeterminate.[111] The original intent also "ran out" when, due to the text's high level of generality, it did not determine the outcome of concrete cases.[112] These sources of underdeterminacy left judges adrift and their decisions unmoored from the Constitution's intended meaning, thus fatally undermining originalism.

Nonoriginalists further claimed that originalism was fatally flawed because of its commitment to overrule all, or almost all, nonoriginalist precedent. This was a flaw because it showed that originalism was deeply inconsistent with existing legal practice.[113] Originalism's dramatic inconsistency also raised the specter of legal instability caused by overruling so much existing constitutional doctrine.[114]

Though not related to judicial discretion, nonoriginalists also charged that originalism was unacceptable because of the bad consequences to which its adoption purportedly would lead.[115] Critics had in mind the purported original intent that would reject *Brown v. Board of Education*[116] and require *Plessy v. Ferguson*[117].[118] Nonoriginalists questioned whether even the most committed originalist would push originalism so far. As Professor Paul Brest summarized, originalism "would produce results that even a strict intentionalist would likely reject."[119]

1.4.3 *The Main Outlines of Originalism's Second-Generation Conceptual Changes*

1.4.3.1 Introduction

In response to these and other criticisms, originalists reconceptualized originalism.[120] I describe in this subsection five changes many originalists instituted. First, most originalists moved from original intent to original meaning. Second, most originalists identified a role for constitutional construction within originalism. Third, most originalists explained the continuing viability of some nonoriginalist precedent. Fourth, most originalists acknowledged the existence of discretion within

---

[111] *Id.* at 220.
[112] *Id.* at 216–17.
[113] *Id.* at 223.
[114] *Id.* at 231.
[115] *Id.* at 221, 229 n.96, 230.
[116] *Brown v. Board of Education*, 347 U.S. 483 (1954).
[117] *Plessy v. Ferguson*, 163 U.S. 537 (1896).
[118] Laurence H. Tribe & Michael C. Dorf, On Reading the Constitution 12–13 (1991); Mark V. Tushnet, *Following the Rules Laid Down: A Critique of Interpretivism and Neutral Principles*, 96 Harv. L. Rev. 781, 800 (1983); *see also* Alexander M. Bickel, *The Original Understanding and the Segregation Decision*, 69 Harv. L. Rev. 1, 58 (1955).
[119] Brest, *supra* note 86, at 221.
[120] For a clear, recent summary of the main currents of originalist scholarship, see Lawrence B. Solum, *Originalist Methodology*, 84 U. Chi. L. Rev. 269 (2017).

originalism. Fifth, originalists offered a wide variety of normative justifications for originalism. Then, in Chapter 2, I describe in detail my conception of originalism, one that builds on these five changes.

1.4.3.2 Original Meaning

Most originalists moved away from original intent by adopting an original meaning conception of originalism.[121] Succinctly, the original meaning is the public meaning of the Constitution's text at the time of its authorization. Although the subjective intentions of the Constitution's Framers and Ratifiers continued to be evidence of the Constitution's original meaning, they ceased to be the focus of original meaning inquiry.

As originalists' analysis of originalism has proceeded, their description has become more sophisticated and elaborate. Original meaning originalism has a compound internal architecture.[122] Original meaning originalism identifies the Constitution's communicative content as its meaning.[123] This communicative content is, in turn, composed of the text's semantic meaning, augmented and clarified by "contextual enrichment."[124] The text's semantic meaning is its original conventional meaning supplemented by the rules of syntax and grammar.[125]

Identification of the text's conventional meaning is the first step in articulating the original meaning. The conventional meaning of the Constitution's words and phrases is found in the primary source materials from the various periods of ratification in which the words and phrases were used. For example, the First Amendment includes: "Congress shall make no law respecting an establishment of religion, or prohibiting the free exercise thereof . . .";[126] if one wished to uncover the original meaning of the word "religion," one would have to uncover that word's conventional meaning at the time of ratification.[127]

Attempts to discern the Commerce Clause's conventional meaning exemplify this process. Originalists will test which of a stable of candidates for a term's or phrase's conventional meaning best fits the usages of the term or phrase. Professor Randy Barnett, for instance, surveyed the "use of the term 'commerce'" during the period of framing and ratification, and in the Constitution itself.[128] He sought to find a meaning that fit the numerous instances in which "commerce" was used during this

---

[121] Whittington, *supra* note 85, at 609–10.
[122] The most recent scholarly summary is Solum, *Originalist Methodology, supra* note 120.
[123] Lawrence B. Solum, *The Fixation Thesis: The Role of Historical Fact in Original Meaning*, 91 NOTRE DAME L. REV. 1, 15 (2015); Lawrence B. Solum, *Communicative Content and Legal Content*, 89 NOTRE DAME L. REV. 479, 486–88 (2013).
[124] Solum, *Communicative Content, supra* note 123, at 487–88.
[125] *Id.* at 487, 491, 497.
[126] U.S. CONST. amend. I.
[127] Lee J. Strang, *The Meaning of "Religion" in the First Amendment*, 40 DUQ. L. REV. 181 (2002).
[128] BARNETT, *supra* note 3, at 278–97.

period. For example, in reviewing use of the term during the Constitutional Convention, Barnett found that the terms "'trade' or 'exchange' could be substituted for the term 'commerce'."[129] By contrast, the phrase "any gainful activity" was not a possible substitute.[130]

Second, once one has uncovered a word's or phrase's original conventional meaning, one would next need to apply the rules of syntax and grammar to identify the text's semantic meaning. For the word "religion" in the First Amendment, this is moderately challenging, because "religion" is clearly part of a broader phrase, though it is not entirely clear just how much broader. Is it only part of what is typically called the Establishment Clause ("Congress shall make no law respecting an establishment of religion"), or is it part of a broader Religion Clause ("Congress shall make no law respecting an establishment of religion, or prohibiting the free exercise thereof")? The choice between the two characterizations hinges on the contemporary rules of grammar and syntax, and it likely has an impact on the word's ultimate meaning.

Third, after one has discovered a text's semantic meaning, the next step in uncovering the Constitution's original meaning is contextual enrichment. Contextual enrichment is a complex concept. This is the process by which a text's context both provides richness to and (potentially) modifies semantic meaning in order to facilitate communication in a particular context.[131] Contextual enrichment identifies the effect on the semantic meaning caused by the publicly available information that the constitutional text's framers knew was available to the text's audience. As a general example, the Framers in the Philadelphia Convention knew that Americans in the anticipated state ratification conventions would be familiar with the Articles of Confederation's failures. Contextual enrichment includes the purposes for which a particular text was adopted, the text's placement in the document and its surrounding language, the text's historical background, and the broader milieu in which the text was adopted.

A text's context includes both its physical context – such as its location in the document that begins "We the People of the United States" – and the broader context that the text inhabits, such as the United States in 1787. A text's physical context includes other text adjacent to the text, the text's location in a grammatical structure, such as a clause, sentence, and paragraph, and the text's location in a particular part of the Constitution. Returning to the example of "religion" in the First Amendment: the word appears in one (or two) clause(s), it is a restriction on the federal government, and it appears twice in the Constitution (the other time is the Religious Tests Clause).

---

[129] *Id.* at 280.
[130] *Id.*
[131] Solum, *Communicative Content, supra* note 123, at 488. For example, the context of a private conversation between friends is different – and operates differently upon the words' conventional meaning – than the Framers' communication with their audiences.

The broader context embraced by contextual enrichment is capacious: it embraced the publicly accessible social, cultural, legal, and technological information that the text's audience would consider when understanding the text. For instance, contextual enrichment included, when trying to identify the original meaning of "religion," the Clause's long-term and immediate historical background, and the broader cultural, philosophical, and religious milieu. This included the church-state relationships in the United Kingdom, the colonies, and independent states. It also included the debates in the constitutional ratification conventions that prompted James Madison to introduce the Bill of Rights, along with debates in the First Congress and ratification conventions. This historical inquiry further contains the society's characteristics and engagement with the subject of religion. American society in the late eighteenth century generally embraced Protestant Christianity. Additionally, the context included the fact that the First Amendment's Framers were meeting in New York and were drafting a text that they would propose to the American people up and down the eastern seaboard, and members of state ratification conventions in particular, so that Americans would need to be able to know the Constitution's meaning.

The open-endedness of contextual enrichment may make it more likely that reasonable scholars will disagree over whether and/or how the text's communicative context has modified the text's semantic meaning. A possible example of this may be the word "establishment."[132] Different scholars have pointed to different facets of the Establishment Clause's context to argue for different meanings of establishment.[133] Each of these scholarly positions has a plausible quantity of evidence supporting its position, and the question for originalist scholars is which group's evidence is most persuasive.

Given the thick, though relatively unreflective linguistic practice during the Framing and Ratification period, one does not frequently find an explicit articulation of a text's public meaning. Instead, from reviewing the historical record, it is often clear that the text's word or phrase had a commonly accepted, though unarticulated public meaning. This is clear because usage of the term or phrase was consistent, and this consistency is discerned from the usages' various contexts. In my own research into the original meaning of the term "religion" in the First Amendment, I found that very infrequently did the Framers and Ratifiers, much less members of contemporary society, articulate the term's meaning.[134] This method of making the Constitution's meaning explicit fits with how we use language. Normally, we do not articulate the meaning of terms and phrases we use because we assume that our addressees, as participants in our linguistic practice, know their meanings.

---

[132] U.S. CONST. amend. I.

[133] *See* DONALD L. DRAKEMAN, CHURCH, STATE, AND ORIGINAL INTENT 156–95 (2010) (describing these various interpretations).

[134] Strang, *supra* note 127, at 181.

Thoughtful originalists have continued to advocate for original intent original-ism.[135] These scholars defend an intentionalist approach to originalism and criticize original meaning as both unable to deliver on its promises and as subject to (new) criticisms. They argue, for instance, that public meaning originalism is subject to its own – even more intractable – summing problem: original meaning originalists must defend a nonarbitrary choice of authors as the source of (public) meaning.[136] They also argue that the Constitution's originally intended meaning is its meaning because meaning is a product of human minds, so the Constitution's meaning is the product of the humans who authorized it.[137] This fits the important relationship between the Constitution and its unique authorship.[138] Relatedly, intentionalist originalists also argue that the Constitution's public meaning is too thin to do its appointed work; that public meaning does not have the resources to serve as the means of communication from legal authority to its subjects.[139]

In Section 2.2, I argue for a conception of original meaning originalism that acknowledges the importance of the flesh-and-blood human beings who wrote and authorized our written Constitution. I also connect originalism to the unique role and authority the Framers and Ratifiers hold in our legal system through my law-as-coordination account of originalism in Chapter 4.

Recently, another conception of originalism was articulated by Professors John McGinnis and Michael Rappaport: original methods originalism.[140] They argued that the Constitution's meaning is expressed through application of the methods of inter-pretation in use at the time the Constitution's text was ratified.[141] As part of this argument, they also explained that original methods originalism is consistent with original meaning and original intent originalism,[142] a claim I support in Section 2.2. There, I argue that the "conditions of constitutional communication" show that original meaning, original intent, and original methods are not substantively distinct.[143]

---

[135] *E.g.*, Richard Ekins, *Objects of Interpretation*, 32 CONST. COMM. 1, 8–9 (2016); Larry Alexander, *Simple-Minded Originalism*, in THE CHALLENGE OF ORIGINALISM, 87 (Grant Huscroft & Bradley W. Miller, eds., 2011); Stanley Fish, *The Intentionalist Thesis Once More*, in THE CHALLENGE OF ORIGINALISM, 99 (Grant Huscroft & Bradley Miller, eds., 2011); Larry Alexander, *Telepathic Law*, 27 CONST. COMM. 139 (2010); Richard S. Kay, *Original Intention and Public Meaning in Constitutional Interpretation*, 103 NW. U. L. REV. 703 (2009); Larry Alexander & Saikrishna Prakash, *"Is That English You're Speaking?" Why Intention Free Interpretation is an Impossibility*, 41 SAN DIEGO L. REV. 967, 976 (2004).

[136] Alexander, *Simple-Minded Originalism*, *supra* note 135, at 91.

[137] *Id.*, at 87–88; Alexander & Prakash, *supra* note 135, at 972–82.

[138] Alexander, *Simple-Minded Originalism*, *supra* note 135, at 94.

[139] Ekins, *supra* note 135, at 8–9.

[140] McGINNIS & RAPPAPORT, *supra* note 3.

[141] *Id.* at 14; *see also* John O. McGinnis & Michael B. Rappaport, *The Constitution and the Language of Law*, 59 WM. & MARY L. REV. 1321 (2108) (further explaining and supporting original methods).

[142] McGINNIS & RAPPAPORT, *supra* note 3, at 117.

[143] Professors Baude and Sachs have argued over a series of articles that originalism is the proper way to interpret the Constitution because it is our law, and for three reasons: contemporary law

1.4.3.3 Constitutional Construction

A second major move made by most originalists[144] is the embrace of the concept of constitutional construction.[145] Constitutional construction is the idea that, in at least some cases, the Constitution's original meaning does not resolve a case's outcome.[146] This is because the original meaning is underdetermined.[147] The original meaning may limit the range of possible outcomes, but interpreters are left with discretion to construct constitutional meaning. In the "construction zone,"[148] interpreters possess discretion to create constitutional doctrine, consistent with the original meaning, underdetermined though it is. Originalists have argued that construction involves the exercise of choice that is relatively unbounded by the Constitution's original meaning.[149] In the construction zone, constitutional interpreters must utilize factors other than and in addition to the Constitution's original

---

governing interpretation requires textualism-originalism, William Baude & Stephen E. Sachs, *The Law of Interpretation*, 130 HARV. L. REV. 1079 (2017); because the law is the original law until lawfully changed, Stephen E. Sachs, *Originalism as a Theory of Legal Change*, 38 HARV. J. L. & PUB. POL'Y 817 (2015); and because our constitutional practice fits originalism. Baude, *supra* note 3, at 2349. This is called original law originalism. I employ a similar move in Chapter 3.

[144] Professors McGinnis and Rappaport argue that utilization of interpretive closure rules eliminates all (or almost all) underdeterminacy. MCGINNIS & RAPPAPORT, *supra* note 3, at 752.

[145] *See* KEITH E. WHITTINGTON, CONSTITUTIONAL CONSTRUCTION: DIVIDED POWERS AND CONSTITUTIONAL MEANING (1999) (providing the seminal discussion); BARNETT, *supra* note 3, at 118–30; WHITTINGTON, INTERPRETATION, *supra* note 3, at 7–14; JACK M. BALKIN, LIVING ORIGINALISM 4–5 and footnotes (2011). Professor Solum has done the most work on this concept. *E.g.*, Solum, *What is Originalism?*, *supra* note 2, at 24; Solum, *Originalist Methodology*, *supra* note 120, at 272, 292–96; Solum, *The Fixation Thesis*, *supra* note 123, at 9–12; Solum, *Communicative Content*, *supra* note 123, at 507–17; Lawrence B. Solum, *Originalism and Constitutional Construction*, 82 FORDHAM L. REV. 453 (2013); Lawrence B. Solum, *The Interpretation-Construction Distinction*, 27 CONST. COMMENT. 95 (2010).

[146] WHITTINGTON, INTERPRETATION, *supra* note 3, at 7; BARNETT, *supra* note 3, at 118–30; MCGINNIS & RAPPAPORT, *supra* note 3, at 139; BALKIN, *supra* note 145, at 4–5.

[147] Randy E. Barnett, *Interpretation and Construction*, 34 HARV. J. L. & PUB. POL'Y 65, 67, 68 (2011); *see also* Lawrence B. Solum, *On the Indeterminacy Crisis: Critiquing Critical Dogma*, 54 U. CHI. L. REV. 462 (1987) (identifying the concept of underdeterminacy).

[148] Solum, *Originalism and Constitutional Construction*, *supra* note 145, at 469–72.

[149] BARNETT, *supra* note 3, at 122; WHITTINGTON, INTERPRETATION, *supra* note 3, at 7. It is important to note that Professor Solum, beginning in 2010, began articulating a conception of constitutional construction different from that identified here. Solum, *The Interpretation-Construction Distinction*, *supra* note 145, at 95. Professor Solum argued that constitutional interpretation is the articulation of the Constitution's communicative content while construction is giving legal effect to that content. *Id.* at 95–96. For Professor Solum, construction is the activity of articulating the legal content and effect of the Constitution's original meaning, even when that meaning is determinate and the legal content parrots the original meaning. Solum, *Communicative Content and Legal Content*, *supra* note 123, at 511. Professor Solum's conception of construction, even though different (and more capacious), fits my core point: most originalists today agree that constitutional construction exists and, at least in a significant percentage of cases in the "construction zone," "involve[] judgment or choice." Solum, *The Interpretation-Construction Distinction*, *supra* note 145, at 107–08.

meaning, to construct constitutional meaning. The output of constitutional construction is constitutional doctrine.

Constitutional construction depends on a distinction between constitutional interpretation and constitutional construction. Interpretation is when the Constitution's original meaning provides one right answer to a legal question. For example, the Commerce Clause determinatively authorizes Congress to regulate interstate commercial shipments of goods on railroads.[150] Construction, by contrast, is when the Constitution's original meaning is underdetermined; it does not provide one right answer to a legal question. Returning to the Commerce Clause example, Congress likely has discretion on how to construct its authority over interstate commercial transactions performed via the internet. Since originalism's conception of construction is that construction is something other than constitutional interpretation, originalism cordons-off interpretation from construction. This separation exemplifies and preserves originalism's commitment to the Constitution's original meaning.

Originalists differ on which government officers have authority to definitively construct constitutional meaning when the Constitution's original meaning is underdeterminate.[151] The two ends of the spectrum are the political branches and federal courts, respectively. The first set of originalists contend that federal court constructions of constitutional meaning are defeasible in light of contrary constructions by the elected branches.[152] Professor Michael Stokes Paulsen has argued that the political branches have authority to construct constitutional meaning because the judiciary's power extends only to interpretation.[153]

> [I]mplicit in the structure and logic of written constitutionalism, and in the nature of the governmental arrangements that our Constitution creates, is a corollary rule of construction about what to do when textual meaning runs out: … democratic, republican institutions vested with legislative and executive power concerning such matters get to do the 'constructing,' within the range of any construction zones afforded by a partially indeterminate text.[154]

Also important to note is Professor Barnett's recent intervention where he argued that judges in the construction zone are obligated to follow the Constitution's "spirit." Randy E. Barnett & Evan D. Bernick, *The Letter and the Spirit: A Unified Theory of Originalism*, 107 Geo. L.J. 1 (2018). This has the effect of at least reducing discretion in the construction zone. This is a significant change from Professor Barnett's prior position.

[150] *United States v. Lopez*, 514 U.S. 549, 558 (1995).

[151] *Compare* Whittington, Interpretation, *supra* note 3, at 7, 9, 11, *with* Barnett, *supra* note 3, at 122. *But see* Keith E. Whittington, *Constructing a New American Constitution*, 27 Const. Comment. 119, 125–29 (2010) (modifying his previous position).

[152] Whittington, Interpretation, *supra* note 3, at 5.

[153] Michael Stokes Paulsen, *Does the Constitution Prescribe Rules for Its Own Interpretation?*, 103 Nw. U. L. Rev. 857, fn. 141 (2009).

[154] Michael Stokes Paulsen, *The Text, the Whole Text, and Nothing but the Text, So Help Me God: Un-Writing Amar's Unwritten Constitution*, 81 U. Chi. L. Rev. 1385, 1435 (2014).

On the other end of the spectrum are originalists who have argued that the Supreme Court has the authority to conclusively construct the Constitution's meaning. For example, Professor Barnett claimed that, in situations of constitutional underdeterminacy, federal courts must construct meaning using a presumption of liberty that protects individual liberty,[155] and that the elected branches must respect these constructions.[156]

While most originalists, to a greater[157] or lesser degree, accept constitutional construction, the most prominent exceptions are Professors McGinnis and Rappaport. They argue that the original methods and closure rules eliminate construction.[158] I explain their position further in Section 3.3, where I describe my related conception of construction. There, I argue that constitutional construction exists, as most originalists recognize, but that it is limited in terms of both its frequency and which governmental actors have the authority to construct doctrine.

1.4.3.4 Nonoriginalist Precedent

Third, most originalists have argued that originalism preserves a place for at least some nonoriginalist precedent.[159] Nonoriginalist precedent is precedent that incorrectly articulated the Constitution's original meaning or incorrectly applied that meaning in a case. (I explain the distinction between originalist and nonoriginalist precedent in more detail in Subsection 2.4.2.) Nonoriginalist precedent is potentially a major problem for originalism because it may put our legal practice in tension with what originalism prescribes. In other words, it makes it hard for originalism to fit our practice and, more importantly, pushes originalism into the posture of advocating for upending a lot of precedents, some number of which are normatively attractive.

The originalists who accept the continued viability of nonoriginalist precedent have offered different reasons for this position, and their different accounts of nonoriginalist precedent mean that different quantities of such precedent are preserved under their respective approaches. For example, Professor Lash argued that a popular sovereignty-justified originalism should preserve nonoriginalist

---

[155] Barnett argued that this is necessary to ensure or enhance legitimacy. BARNETT, *supra* note 3, at 126.

[156] *Id.* at 118–30.

[157] Jack Balkin has, in practice, likely the most capacious conception of the construction zone. BALKIN, *supra* note 145, at 21–23.

[158] McGINNIS & RAPPAPORT, *supra* note 3, at 139–40.

[159] Originalists scholarship that argues in favor of preservation includes Baude, *supra* note 3, at 2358–60; Lash, *supra* note 5, at 1441–42; McGINNIS & RAPPAPORT, *supra* note 3, at 154–74; Solum, *The Supreme Court in Bondage*, *supra* note 5, at 155–59; Strang, *supra* note 127, at 419–20.

precedents that facilitate majoritarian actions and reverse those decisions that undermine popular sovereignty.[160]

There are also many originalists who reject all (or nearly all) nonoriginalist precedent.[161] They too present a number of arguments supporting their position. Many focus on the privileged status of the Constitution's original meaning, a status identified by originalism's own theoretical commitments[162] and confirmed by the Constitution's text.[163]

In Subsection 3.4.4, I argue that originalism embraces nonoriginalist precedent when retaining the precedent is important for the common good, which, I argue, occurs when the precedent is deeply entrenched, widely respected, and just.

1.4.3.5 Interpreter Discretion and Judgment

Fourth, most originalists acknowledged that judges possess discretion, in at least some situations. As originalists explored the process of originalist interpretation and adjudication, they emphasized the crucial role that judges – and especially their capacities such as judgment – play in legal practice. "By the 1990s," Professor Keith Whittington noted, "originalists . . . were no longer working so clearly in the shadow of the Legal Realists and the fear of judicial freedom."[164] The originalist concession of judicial interpretive discretion was the result of at least three moves made by many originalists: the move to original meaning, the acceptance of constitutional construction, and the acceptance of the viability of some nonoriginalist precedent. Since I described these three changes earlier, here, I will only describe how these changes acknowledged discretion and judgment.

First, the adoption of original meaning originalism results in relatively more cases where the Constitution's meaning is underdetermined,[165] and this occurs for two possible reasons. First, original meaning originalism opens up the likelihood of underdeterminacy because it limits the data[166] upon which interpretation relies.[167] Original meaning originalism[168] relies on language conventions, and the rules of grammar and syntax. Conventions of language usage are positive human artifacts

---

[160] Lash, *supra* note 5, at 1438–44, 1473–77.

[161] E.g., Lawson, *supra* note 5, at 23; Barnett, *supra* note 5, at 257; Paulsen, *supra* note 5, at 289.

[162] BARNETT, *supra* note 3, at 100–13.

[163] Lawson, *supra* note 5, at 27–28.

[164] WHITTINGTON, INTERPRETATION, *supra* note 3, at 609.

[165] Solum, *Originalist Methodology*, *supra* note 120, at 285.

[166] By "data," I mean the pertinent evidence utilized by the respective originalist camps to articulate the Constitution's meaning.

[167] This claim assumes that interpreters cannot draw upon the interpretive conventions in place when the Constitution's text received authority, as Professors McGinnis and Rappaport have argued.

[168] Until the recent move by Professor Solum to employ contextual enrichment.

often without hard edges and frequently lacking in richness.[169] These language conventions may be vague or ambiguous, and the Constitution's employment of language conventions may contain gaps or contradictions.[170]

By contrast, original intent originalism's "data set" is richer.[171] Prominent original intent originalist, Professor Richard Kay, argued that "public meaning originalism will generate more cases of constitutional indeterminacy than will the originalism of original intentions."[172] In addition to language conventions, an interpreter has access to information that can provide both more definition to a language convention's boundaries and a greater thickness within those boundaries. Most important, original intent originalism included within its interpretive data the framers' originally expected applications, and their purposes or goals including how they wished to change the law.[173] This additional information provided mechanisms to narrow and eliminate vagueness, ambiguity, gaps, and contradictions; mechanisms that original meaning originalism did not possess.

The second possible reason original meaning originalism results in interpretive discretion and burdens on interpretive judgments is because of its move to employ contextual enrichment.[174] This move has occurred more recently and is the result of original meaning originalists' acknowledgement that semantic meaning alone is not the full measure of constitutional meaning.[175] Contextual enrichment is the way in which context both provides richness to and (potentially) modifies conventional meaning (to facilitate communication in a particular context).[176] Contextual enrichment is a relatively complex process. It is the phenomenon where the publicly available context in which the Constitution's text was drafted and ratified provides additional information about the text's meaning, which enhances its meaning. Contextual enrichment includes, among other things, the publicly available purposes for which the text was adopted, the text's immediate and long-term historical background, and the broader milieu in which the text was adopted. For instance, the Commerce Clause's context included: its purpose of eliminating interstate trade disputes and providing for a free trade zone; the lack of national power over interstate commerce in the Articles of Confederation and the interstate

---

[169] *Cf.* PLATO, STATESMAN 294b–c (Robin Waterfield trans., 1995) ("[Law] is like a stubborn, stupid person who refuses to allow the slightest deviation from or questioning of his own rules, even if the situation has in fact changed and it turns out to be better for someone to contravene these rules.").

[170] BARNETT, *supra* note 3, at 118–21; WHITTINGTON, INTERPRETATION, *supra* note 3, at 5–14; Solum, *Originalist Methodology*, *supra* note 120, at 285.

[171] Kay, *supra* note 135, at 720.

[172] *Id.* at 721.

[173] Solum, *What Is Originalism?*, *supra* note 2, at 24–27.

[174] Solum, *Originalist Methodology*, *supra* note 120, at 286–93.

[175] Professor Solum's clear articulation of the necessary role of context in original meaning originalism first appeared in 2013. Solum, *Communicative Content*, *supra* note 123, at 492–506; *see also* Solum, *The Fixation Thesis*, *supra* note 123, at 24–26.

[176] Solum, *Communicative Content*, *supra* note 123, at 488.

trade friction that had recently arisen; and the increasingly commercial nature of the American republic.

In brief, original meaning originalism's underdeterminacy requires interpreters to exercise discretion to construct constitutional meaning, and it also puts significant weight on interpreter judgments to ascertain whether constitutional meaning is in fact underdetermined. The addition of contextual enrichment to original meaning originalism places greater burdens on interpreters' judgments. Interpreters must now access and incorporate a body of historical material into their interpretive judgments. Both learning the historical material and fitting a text's semantic meaning into that context will be challenging activities, in at least some situations.

Second (as I already described), most originalists adopted constitutional construction. For these originalists, interpreters have discretion when they are in the "construction zone."

Third, the adoption by most originalists of an intermediate position toward nonoriginalist precedent – between "get rid of it all" and "keep it all"[177] – required originalists to draw a line between those nonoriginalist precedents a judge should overrule (or distinguish), and those she should retain. As an example, I argue in Subsection 2.4.4 that a judge should utilize three factors to determine whether to overrule a nonoriginalist precedent.[178] Applying these factors will frequently be challenging, and judges will frequently possess discretion in doing so, especially if the factors point in different directions and possess different weights. Even if the factors point to a uniquely correct outcome, the analysis will typically significantly burden judges' judgments.

In addition to acknowledging judicial discretion and the burdens on judicial judgment in the three contexts I identified, originalists also explained that, even in cases where judges do not have discretion – in other words, the original meaning provides a correct answer – they must still utilize their capacity for judgment (along with other human capacities). This move by originalists took many forms, but two facets of originalism in particular are important for my purposes: the process of articulating and applying the Constitution's original meaning, and originalist precedent.

First, originalists have begun to explain in more detail the analytical process judges utilize. This process has many features including, importantly, the articulation of the Constitution's original meaning and application of that meaning.[179]

---

[177] I am not aware of any originalists who have advocated keeping all nonoriginalist precedent. In fact, the "keep it all" position is close to the central characteristic of common law constitutionalism. DAVID A. STRAUSS, THE LIVING CONSTITUTION 3 (2010).

[178] The three factors are: (1) how far does the nonoriginalist precedent deviate from the Constitution's original meaning?; (2) how much, if at all, would overruling the precedent harm Rule of Law values?; and (3) does the precedent instantiate justice?

[179] Lee J. Strang, An Originalist Theory of Precedent: The Privileged Place of Originalist Precedent, 2010 BYU L. REV. 1729, 1767 (2010).

Second, and relatedly, originalists have argued that originalist precedent plays a central role in originalism.[180] Both characteristics frequently place significant burdens on judges' judgment and their other faculties.

In sum, today's originalism has opened a space for judicial discretion and identified an important role for the exercise of judicial judgment. Originalism today explicitly acknowledges judicial discretion. Further, originalism has also embraced the fact that judges exercise judgment, constrained though it may be, in the contexts of originalist precedent and in the paradigmatic work of articulating and applying the Constitution's original meaning. My own description of originalism will take into account these changes by incorporating virtue ethics into originalism. I make this connection in Section 2.6.

1.4.3.6 "External" Normative Justifications

The fifth major move made by many originalists, especially since the late 1990s, is to offer a wide variety of normative foundations for originalism. This is a very significant development, and I return to it in Chapter 4, where I offer my law-as-coordination account of originalism.

Stepping back for a moment, originalists have provided both "internal" and "external" normative justifications for originalism.[181] Internal accounts take for granted our legal practice's facets and argue that originalism best explains those facets. External accounts argue that, consistently followed, use of originalism will lead to a better state of affairs than other forms of interpretation. In this subsection, I summarize originalists' external normative justifications.

Originalists have offered a stunning variety of external normative justifications for originalism that cover the figurative waterfront.[182] These include[183]: assisting popular sovereignty,[184] protecting natural rights,[185] and securing good consequences.[186] Each of these normative justifications for originalism contends that the Constitution's original meaning, consistently followed, will create a state of affairs better than that created by other methods of interpretation. What follows is a brief summary of these existing justifications.

---

[180] Solum, *The Supreme Court in Bondage, supra* note 5, at 185; Strang, *supra* note 181, at 1766–88.

[181] WHITTINGTON, INTERPRETATION, *supra* note 3, at 110.

[182] Professor Solum has recently argued that originalism is, on balance, more normatively attractive than alternatives. Lawrence B. Solum, *The Constraint Principle: Original Meaning and Constitutional Practice*, https://papers.ssrn.com/sol3/papers.cfm?abstract_id=2940215 (visited June 19, 2017).

[183] My list is provided in the order in which these arguments were published in their final scholarly form.

[184] WHITTINGTON, INTERPRETATION, *supra* note 3, at 110–59.

[185] BARNETT, *supra* note 3, at 3–5, 53–54, 116–17.

[186] McGINNIS & RAPPAPORT, *supra* note 3, at 11–18, 33–99.

Professor Keith Whittington argued that originalism is the best theory of interpretation because it best advances popular sovereignty,[187] and it does so in two primary ways. First, it *protects* the American People's constitutional judgments, embodied in the Constitution's original meaning, by privileging those judgments over other meanings; for example, nonoriginalist interpretations, which embody different judgments.[188] Second, Whittington maintained that originalism *preserves* the capacity of the American People to embody their constitutional judgments in the Constitution, because it protects those judgments from subsequent derogation via nonoriginalist precedent, and therefore preserves the possibility of future popular constitutional decision-making.[189]

The axis point of Whittington's argument is the original meaning. No other meaning preserves and protects as well the constitutional judgments of the American People. The Constitution's original meaning is the depository of prior constitutional judgments by the American People, and originalism's continued privileging of the original meaning preserves, protects, and incentivizes constitutional judgments by the American People.

Professor Barnett argued that originalism best protects natural rights, and it does so through two steps. First, the Constitution's original meaning is reasonably protective of natural rights,[190] both because of the original meaning itself[191] and because of rights-protective rules of construction found in the Ninth Amendment and the Privileges or Immunities Clause.[192] Second, constitutional interpreters must utilize originalism to "lock-in" the original meaning's rights-protectiveness.[193] Without the Constitution's writtenness and the resulting locking-in of the Constitution's original meaning, the Constitution's rights-protectiveness would be undermined via nonoriginalist interpretations. For instance, if judges utilized nonoriginalist meanings to craft constitutional doctrine, then they would deviate from the Constitution's rights-protective original meaning and thereby undermine natural rights.

Professors John McGinnis and Michael Rappaport recently argued that originalism leads to the best consequences of any plausible theory of constitutional interpretation.[194] In particular, they argued that the Constitution's original meaning leads to better consequences than nonoriginalist judicial precedent because the original meaning was adopted (and amended) via supermajoritarian requirements by the American people.[195] Their key insight is that the American people are a diverse

---

[187] WHITTINGTON, INTERPRETATION, *supra* note 3, at 110–11.

[188] *Id.* at 111.

[189] *Id.*

[190] For an in-depth exploration of Professor Barnett's theory of justice, see RANDY E. BARNETT, THE STRUCTURE OF LIBERTY: JUSTICE AND THE RULE OF LAW (2000).

[191] BARNETT, *supra* note 3, at 153–190, 274–318.

[192] *Id.* at 191–252.

[193] *Id.* at 89–117.

[194] McGINNIS & RAPPAPORT, *supra* note 3.

[195] *Id.* at 62–138.

group[196] – and have been for a long time, including along important axes, such as religious and political views – so the American People's agreement on a proposition is strong evidence of the proposition's soundness.[197] Nonoriginalist precedent, by contrast, did not go through a similar supermajoritarian process – it was adopted by a relatively small, relatively insular, and relatively homogeneous group – and therefore we have less confidence that its propositions are as substantively good as the original meaning.[198]

McGinnis and Rappaport's argument hinges on the Constitution's original meaning having gone through the rigorous supermajoritarian ratification processes. This meaning, and only this meaning, has the assurances that that process provides.[199]

Though the external normative justifications provided by originalists are many and powerful, some originalists have argued that originalists should *not* provide normative justifications because originalism *just is* how one interprets documents like the Constitution. Originalism is a simply an (accurate) description of constitutional interpretation, and therefore does not need a justification. Professor Gary Lawson, for instance, emphasized this distinction: "to say that originalism is the correct way to ascertain the Constitution's meaning says nothing about whether one ought, as a normative matter, to act in deference to the Constitution's meaning."[200] In fact, these originalists argue, providing such a justification causes originalism to fall into the trap of appearing like it is one contested and contestable theory of interpretation among many when, in fact, it is not.

Another group of scholars has likewise purported to dispense with the need for an external normative justification because their "positive" justifications for originalism do not need a justification independent of the law's own normativity or officials' oaths to the law. These scholars argue that originalism can piggyback on whatever normative justification one has for law-following more generally because the original meaning of the Constitution *is* our law. As Professor Stephen Sachs summarized, "'positive' defenses [are] claims that originalism, as a matter of social fact and legal practice, is actually endorsed by our positive law."[201] Originalism has no need, on this account, for a contested normative justification because, if originalism just is the law, few if any scholars claim that the law generally is without normative force, and nearly all scholars accept the existing legal practice. Taking this line of argument, Professor William Baude has argued that his capacious conception, "Inclusive Originalism," fits our legal practice sufficiently to be our

---

[196] *Id.* at 14, 27, 33–61, 81, 202.
[197] *Id.* at 33–99.
[198] *Id.* at 175–78.
[199] *Id.* at 3.
[200] Gary Lawson, *Originalism Without Obligation*, 93 B. U. L. Rev. 1309, 1312 (2013).
[201] Sachs, *supra* note 3, at 817, 819; *see also* Baude, *supra* note 3, at 2349.

law.[202] Looking at our legal practice's "higher-order" and "lower-order" practices, Professor Baude concluded that "a version of originalism is indeed our law."[203]

Professor Solum's nuanced account of originalism also deserves note here because it analytically separates two facets of originalism: the factual question of the Constitution's original meaning,[204] and the normative question of that meaning's authority.[205] Originalism contains both facets, and Professor Solum acknowledges originalism's need for normative justification.[206]

1.5 PLURALISM WITHIN ORIGINALISM AND ORIGINALISM'S FOCAL CASE

These are the best of times for originalism, as evidenced by this robust body of scholarship along with originalism's popular[207] and judicial valence.[208] But, is originalism's success undermining its long-term coherence? Over the past two decades, originalism has migrated from the periphery of debates on constitutional interpretation, to being one of the main theories and itself being the focus of debate.[209] It has prominent proponents on the bench, and in the legal academy there has been a flowering of originalist scholarship. Even more recently, originalists have institutionalized their approach in blogs,[210] conferences,[211] and centers.[212]

---

[202] Baude, *supra* note 3.

[203] *Id.* at 2352. I couple this "positivist" move in Chapter 3 to my law-as-coordination "external" normative justification for originalism. *See* Solum, *The Constraint Principle*, *supra* note 182, at 83–84 (proposing a similar coupling).

[204] Solum, *The Fixation Thesis*, *supra* note 123.

[205] Solum, *The Constraint Principle*, *supra* note 182.

[206] *Id.* at 15–16.

[207] Donald L. Drakeman, *What's the Point of Originalism?*, 37 HARV. J. L. & PUB. POL'Y 1123, 1133–38 (2014).

[208] *See, e.g., Testimony of Judge Brett M. Kavanaugh*, www.judiciary.senate.gov/meetings/nomination-of-the-honorable-brett-m-kavanaugh-to-be-an-associate-justice-of-the-supreme-court-of-the-united-states (Sept. 5, 2018) ("Originalism, as I see it, means, in essence constitutional textualism, meaning the original public meaning of the constitutional text.") (visited Oct. 10, 2018).

[209] Perhaps the best evidence of originalism's central role in debates over constitutional interpretation is the fact that *Cosmopolitan* magazine contained an article on originalism during the Neil Gorsuch confirmation hearing debates. Jill Filipovic, *9 Reasons Constitutional Originalism is Bullsh*t* (March 21, 2017), www.cosmopolitan.com/politics/a9162680/neil-gorsuch-constitutional-originalism-supreme-court/ (visited June 19, 2017).

[210] *The Originalism Blog*, http://originalismblog.typepad.com/ (visited June 19, 2017).

[211] *Annual Salmon P. Chase Lecture and Colloquium on the Constitution*, www.law.georgetown.edu/academics/centers-institutes/constitution/Annual-Lecture.cfm (visited June 19, 2017; *Annual Originalism Works-in-Progress Conference*, www.sandiego.edu/law/centers/csco/call-for-papers.php (visited June 19, 2017).

[212] *The Georgetown Center for the Constitution*, www.law.georgetown.edu/academics/centers-institutes/constitution/ (visited June 19, 2017); *Center for the Study of Constitutional Originalism*, www.sandiego.edu/law/centers/csco/ (visited June 19, 2017).

At the same time that originalism has had tremendous success, it is also facing a possible fracturing. Originalists disagree on a lot. There is no unanimity on the focus of originalist interpretation, nor is there full agreement on whether construction exists or how it operates, nor is there consensus on nonoriginalist precedent, among other important disagreements.

Professor Jack Balkin's recent work deserves special note because his conception of originalism has stretched the theory's boundaries in such a way that it has exacerbated this concern. Balkin's recent scholarship explicitly attempts to build a bridge between originalism and living constitutionalism. Over a series of articles and books, Balkin argued that originalism and living constitutionalism are compatible.[213] Balkin's key move is to argue that originalism, properly understood, limits the role of interpretation to articulating the Constitution's determinate original meaning, while issues about application of that meaning are the province of constitutional construction.[214] It is here, in construction, that popular constitutionalism holds court.[215] Furthermore, within the construction zone, Balkin claimed that the Supreme Court cooperates with and is a mouthpiece for popular constitutional movements to construct constitutional meaning that corresponds to the movements' contemporary constitutional visions.

Balkin's thin original meaning, coupled with robust construction using popular input, means that he reaches substantive conclusions at odds with the work most originalists had done up to that point. For example, Professor Balkin argued that "[t]he conventional wisdom about *Roe* ... is wrong. The right to abortion ... is in fact based on the constitutional text of the Fourteenth Amendment and the principles that underlie it ... "[216]

Some scholars have wondered whether this pluralism is leading to originalism's fragmentation.[217] Professor Steven Smith, for instance, has suggested that originalism may be entering a period of dissolution as a coherent theory of interpretation.[218]

In response to the greater pluralism within originalism, originalists have identified the central meaning, or focal case,[219] of originalism. As articulated by Professor Solum, originalism is characterized by two propositions: the fixation thesis and the

---

[213] BALKIN, *supra* note 145, at 2.

[214] *Id.* at 4. This claim is supported by another proposition: the Constitution's original meaning is composed of relatively abstract principles. *Id.* at 6–7.

[215] *Id.* at 4–6, 10–12.

[216] Jack M. Balkin, *Abortion and Original Meaning*, 24 CONST. COMM. 291, 292 (2007).

[217] *See also* Jeremy K. Kessler & David E. Pozen, *Working Themselves Impure: A Life Cycle Theory of Legal Theories*, 83 U. CHI. L. REV. 1819, 1844–48 (2016) (arguing that originalism's theoretical evolution toward sophistication cost originalism its prior normative justifications).

[218] Steven Smith, *That Old-Time Originalism* 223–45, *in* THE CHALLENGE OF ORIGINALISM: THEORIES OF CONSTITUTIONAL INTERPRETATION (Grant Huscroft & Bradley W. Miller eds., 2013).

[219] For a discussion of the concept of focal case, *see* NLNR, at 9–11.

constraint principle.[220] The fixation thesis states that the Constitution's meaning was fixed when its text was ratified. The constraint principle holds that the Constitution's meaning contributes to and constrains the content of constitutional law. The fixation thesis and constraint principle fit all or nearly all versions of originalism.

My Constitutional Communication Model of originalism, described in Chapter 2, is solidly within the focal case of originalism. It also contributes to intra-originalism pluralism in a number of ways. Most importantly, I provide a law-as-coordination normative justification for originalism in Chapter 4 and I argue for the Constitutional Communication Model in Chapter 2. My contributions to originalist pluralism, however, merely reflect the broader pluralism within Western philosophy and culture, of which the Aristotelian philosophical tradition is one important part. This book explains how one of the major theories of constitutional interpretation is improved when informed by the Aristotelian tradition, a tradition thus far not mined for use in this context.

1.6 CONCLUSION

Originalism is a robust theory of constitutional interpretation that, in response to sustained criticism, has increased in sophistication to such a point that its proponents worry that it is fracturing.

Originalists still have a lot of work to do; this book is part of that work. In Chapter 2, I describe my conception of originalism. Building on my conception of originalism, in Chapter 3 I argue that originalism fits our constitutional practice's important and widespread facets. Then, in Chapter 4, I provide my law-as-coordination account of originalism.

---

[220] For the most recent discussion of these theses in print see Solum, *The Fixation Thesis, supra* note 123, and Solum, *The Constraint Principle, supra* note 182.

2

The Constitutional Communication Model of Originalism

[A] law is imposed on others by way of a rule and measure. Now a rule or measure is imposed by being applied to those who are to be ruled and measured by it . . . Such application is made by its being notified to them by promulgation. Wherefore promulgation is necessary for the law to obtain its force.

Saint Thomas Aquinas[1]

2.1 INTRODUCTION

In Chapter 1, I described originalism's current status, and I noted the many areas of current debate among originalists. My description was ecumenical because it did not "take sides" in the debates.

In this chapter, I explain the Constitutional Communication Model of originalism. This model takes positions on four interrelated and important aspects of originalism: (1) a conception of original meaning originalism that incorporates the insights of original intent and original methods, what I call the Constitutional Communication Model of originalism; (2) a relatively narrow conception of constitutional construction, the Deference Conception of Construction; (3) a robust role for constitutional precedent, including both originalist and nonoriginalist precedent; and (4) virtue ethics to help originalism accommodate interpreter discretion and respond to burdens on interpreters' capacities, while preserving originalism's faithfulness to the Constitution's original meaning.

The Constitutional Communication Model is a manifestation of the Constitution as an intentional law-making act by the Framers and Ratifiers, the purpose of which was to coordinate American society to overcome coordination problems and secure the common good.[2] The Constitution did so through two main mechanisms. The first

---

[1] ST I-II, q. 90, a. 4.
[2] This jurisprudential claim is defended and explained in Chapter 4.

was its original meaning. The Constitution's original meaning is the primary mechanism of communication of legal directives among the Framers, Ratifiers, government officers, and all Americans, in light of the conditions and the process of constitutional communication in the United States (Section 2.2). However, the bare original meaning, by itself, was insufficient to the task of coordinating Americans. Therefore, the Constitutional Communication Model also explains constitutional construction (Section 2.3) and precedent (Section 2.4) as *additional* means of legally directed coordination to implement the Constitution and secure the common good. Lastly, Section 2.6 shows why the judicial virtues are necessary to make the process of constitutional communication and implementation the best it can be, especially in light of the challenges posed by constitutional underdeterminacy and mistaken precedent.

2.2 THE CONSTITUTIONAL COMMUNICATION MODEL OF ORIGINALISM

2.2.1 *Introduction*

In Section 1.4, I described how originalists occupy three major points on the issue of what it is that originalist interpretation seeks to uncover: original intent, original meaning, and original methods. My claim in this chapter is that, given the circumstances of our written Constitution's Framing and Ratification, these three forms of originalism are not substantively distinct. I argue that original intent (the Constitution means what its authors[3] intended it to mean) is the same as original meaning (the Constitution means the public meaning of its text, when it was ratified) and original methods (the Constitution means the meaning produced by the original methods). I call this the Constitutional Communication Model because it conceives of the Constitution's meaning as the primary mechanism of communication of the Constitution's legal directives among the Framers, Ratifiers, officers, and American citizens.

My key move is to argue that, under the "conditions of constitutional communication"[4] that existed between and among the Framers, Ratifiers, federal and state officers, and American citizens generally: (1) the Framers intended the Constitution to mean the original public meaning, (2) the Ratifiers understood and intended the Constitution to mean the original meaning, and (3) governmental officials and Americans understood it as its original meaning, and (4) the communicating parties utilized the original methods to ascertain that meaning. In other words, to enable effective constitutional communication to happen, all the parties utilized original meaning.

---

[3] Here, I elide the issue of the extent to which the Framers and/or the Ratifiers were the Constitution's authors. My own, tentative view is that they were both authors because both participated as speakers to other audiences.

[4] *See* Lawrence B. Solum, *Originalist Methodology*, 84 U. CHI. L. REV. 269, 272–76 (2017) (describing the analogous concept of "Situation of Constitutional Communication").

I tie the Constitutional Communication Model to original *meaning* originalism by arguing that our Constitution's conditions of constitutional communication were a crucial part of the Constitution's public context.[5] The Constitution's context most importantly included: the Framers' goal and knowledge that, to successfully communicate with the Ratifiers (and federal and state officers, and Americans generally), they needed to use public meaning to create the Constitution; the Ratifiers' goal of understanding the Constitution and knowledge that, to do so, they needed to utilize the public meaning to authorize the Constitution; and federal and state officers' (and American citizens') goal of understanding the Constitution, and knowledge that, to faithfully follow the Constitution's legal directives, they needed to utilize the original meaning to understand and follow the Constitution.

I tie my conception of originalism to original *intent* originalism by arguing that the Framers intended to change the law, overcome coordination problems, and secure the common good, and took into account the conditions of constitutional communication when they crafted the Constitution's text to achieve that goal. The Framers recognized that, for a host of reasons, their audiences would not have access to their individual or collective privately-intended constitutional meaning, so they took great care crafting the Constitution. To take the most obvious reason: the Framers had voted to maintain secrecy surrounding their proceedings during and after the Philadelphia Convention.[6] At the same time, the Framers also knew that the Ratifiers, government officers, and Americans generally, would have relatively robust access to the Constitution's public meaning. The Ratifiers, government officers, and Americans similarly knew that they did not have access to the Framers' private intentions, and *they knew the Framers knew they knew this*. The Framers therefore crafted the Constitution's (public) meaning to accurately convey their intended meaning to audiences who did not know their private intentions, in order to achieve the goal of legal change.

I also tie my conception of originalism to *original methods* by arguing that the conditions of constitutional communication faced by the Framers included a conventional interpretive practice. The Ratifiers' usage of conventional methods of interpretation was anticipated by the Framers because these conventional rules of interpretation were the accepted manner in which to understand legal documents like the Constitution, and they were therefore employed by the Framers to craft constitutional meaning for their audiences. The Ratifiers relied on these same original methods to understand the Constitution's meaning to authorize the Constitution, and government officers and Americans employed them to follow it.

---

[5] I described the concept of contextual enrichment in Subsection 1.4.3.
[6] 1 THE RECORDS OF THE FEDERAL CONVENTION OF 1787, at 15 (M. Farrand ed., 1966); 2 RECORDS OF THE FEDERAL CONVENTION OF 1787, at 648 (M. Farrand ed., 1966); 3 RECORDS OF THE FEDERAL CONVENTION OF 1787, at 81–82, 144–45 (M. Farrand ed., 1966).

My conception of original meaning receives significant payoff from integrating original intent and original methods, while it retains the value of original meaning originalism; I will note four benefits. First, original intent is attractive, in part, because it links constitutional meaning to the actual human beings whose intentional lawmaking actions were the source of constitutional meaning, and because it ties constitutional meaning to the particular human beings whose actions authorized the Constitution.[7] Our written Constitution, which currently resides in the National Archives, was crafted by a specific group of flesh-and-blood humans and authorized by another group of Americans. My conception of originalism maintains the Constitution's ties to the historical authors and authorizers of our Constitution.

Second, original methods is attractive, in part, because it fits the Framers' and Ratifiers' interpretive practice.[8] The Framers who carefully crafted the Constitution's text, and the Ratifiers who vigorously debated and adopted the text, both relied on conventional rules of interpretation to know what the Constitution meant. Original methods is also attractive because it explains how the Constitution's original meaning has the capacity to coordinate American society by providing the needed interpretive resources. The bare semantic meaning of the Constitution's text lacks the resources to effectively coordinate government officers and Americans; the original methods enrich the Constitution's semantic meaning and enable the Constitution to fulfill its important coordination function. The Constitutional Communication Model gains better fit with the Constitution's origins and greater capacity to coordinate Americans.

Third, my conception of originalism retains the theoretical sophistication achieved by original meaning originalism. Original meaning originalism has evolved in response to robust criticism and at the hands of numerous scholars of widely varying theoretical commitments. These scholars have articulated a richly nuanced and multi-faceted theory of constitutional interpretation tied to the philosophy of language.[9] My conception of originalism benefits from this sophistication.

Lastly, and most importantly, the Constitutional Communication Model of originalism benefits from three related normative moves.[10] First, I argue that it is important to include the Framers as agents of the Constitution's meaning – and, hence, the Framers' original intent – because they were the text's creators who encapsulated in the Constitution's original meaning their *prudential* judgments on how best to change the law to overcome coordination problems and secure the

---

[7]   Richard S. Kay, *Original Intention and Public Meaning in Constitutional Interpretation*, 103 Nw. U. L. Rev. 703, 714 (2009); Steven D. Smith, *Law Without Mind*, Correspondence, 88 Mich. L. Rev. 104, 113 (1989); Larry Alexander, *Telepathic Law*, 27 Const. Comm. 139, 140–41 (2010).

[8]   John O. McGinnis & Michael B. Rappaport, *The Constitution and the Language of the Law*, 59 Wm. & Mary L. Rev. 1321 (2018).

[9]   Solum, *supra* note 4, at 277.

[10]   I preview these moves in Subsection 2.2.4, and fully explain them in Chapter 4.

common good. Second, I argue that it is important to include the Ratifiers as both an audience and agent of constitutional meaning – and hence the original methods they employed – because they were the humans that Americans today recognize as *authorized* to adopt the Constitution as our Constitution. Third, I argue that it is important to include government officials and American citizens as the primary audience of constitutional meaning because the Constitution's original meaning *coordinates* government officials and the American People through its legal directives, which operate as exclusionary reasons in the audience's practical deliberations.

2.2.2 *Preliminary Note Distinguishing Face-to-Face Communication*

Before explaining and defending the Constitutional Communication Model of originalism, this subsection briefly argues that originalist interpretation cannot rely on face-to-face communication as its model. Face-to-face communication is different from constitutional communication in a number of ways. First, and most importantly, face-to-face communication conveys more information than constitutional communication, making it more likely to succeed. In face-to-face communication, for example, each communicator has access not just to his interlocutor's words, but also to facial expressions, body language, tone, immediate surroundings, and other immediately perceptible information. This class of communicative information is foreclosed to the Framers, Ratifiers, government officials, and Americans generally. This absence requires the Constitutional Communication Model to look elsewhere for interpretive models and resources.

Relatedly, face-to-face communication frequently has the benefit of the communicators being in long-term relationships, and those relationships bring further information to facilitate communication. Constitutional communication was engaged in by people who were functionally anonymous. Most of the Ratifiers had no or little contact with the Framers and therefore could not draw on a relationship's resources to gain more communicative information. And, certainly, later government officers and Americans had little to no contact with the Framers. This pushed the Ratifiers, government officers, and Americans generally to look elsewhere for interpretive resources, such as the text's public meaning, and it pushes the Constitutional Communication Model to do so as well.

Third, face-to-face communication allows for immediate clarification and correction, such as between spouses when grocery shopping. Text 1: "Honey, please buy milk while you're at the store." Text 2: "What kind of milk?" Text 3: "2%." By contrast, the Ratifiers and the Supreme Court could not ask the Framers, "pardon me, but does Article III mean that a sovereign state could be sued by a private party in federal court for breach of contract, even a state that did not consent?"[11] and receive clarification and correction. Instead, they had to interpret the Constitution's

---

[11] *Chisholm v. Georgia*, 2 U.S. (2 Dall.) 419 (1793).

text as best they could, using the evidence and the legal system's interpretive tools at hand. This requires the Constitutional Communication Model to look to this same evidence and interpretive tools.

Fourth, face-to-face communication typically involves one to several subjects, as well as a way to communicate regarding these subjects, with which the communicators are relatively familiar. This makes communication relatively easy and effective. A parent and teacher speaking about a child's homework have familiarity with the communication's subject. Constitutional communication for a national constitution, by contrast, concerns a wide array of subjects with which the communicators are typically not familiar and also not conversant in how to communicate about the subjects. For example, most Ratifiers likely had little idea what "Letters of Marque and Reprisal"[12] were. This makes communication more challenging and raises the specter of rampant miscommunication. To avoid miscommunication, one mechanism our legal system utilized was to primarily write our Constitution in the "language of the law,"[13] and the Constitutional Communication Model must take into account this fact.

Face-to-face communication cannot serve as the model of constitutional communication. I next describe the conditions that must be met in order for constitutional communication to flourish. I call these the conditions for constitutional communication. These conditions precluded the more-robust information, correction mechanisms, and shared expertise of face-to-face communications.

2.2.3 *The Focal Case of Constitutional Interpretation: The Constitution as Communication*

Constitutional interpretation cannot be modeled on face-to-face communication; what is its model? The focal case of legal interpretation is understanding the lawmaker's intentional act of lawmaking as the communication of the legal reasons in a legal text to guide the conduct of the law's subjects.[14]

My argument here depends on the concept of a focal case.[15] The focal case of something is its best, most robust, fullest version of that thing. A tall, thick oak tree with abundant, large acorns and a broad canopy of green leaves is the focal case of oak trees. A scrawny, leaning, short oak tree with few, small acorns and a thin canopy of yellowing leaves is still an oak tree, but not a healthy example of one.

The concept of the focal case applies to human beings as well. The focal case of a person is a hale, virtuous person, one who possesses physical, emotional, intellectual, and spiritual vitality. A human hand that is paralyzed or missing a digit is still a human hand, but it is not the type of hand one would find in anatomy books

[12] U.S. Const. art. I, § 8, cl. 11.
[13] McGinnis & Rappaport, *supra* note 8, at 1321.
[14] This argument is derived from Richard Ekins, The Nature of Legislative Intent 180–284 (2014).
[15] NLNR, at 9–18.

because it is not fully functional. A person whose character is warped by greed, like Ebenezer Scrooge, is still a human, but that person is defective; he is an unhealthy example of a human.

The focal case of communication is the rational use of language to communicate meaning. Effective communication occurs when a speaker successfully conveys his meaning to the audience. Marginal communication occurs when the audience receives less than the speaker's full intended communication.

The focal case of legal interpretation is ascertaining the lawmaker's communicated reasons to the law's subjects. Legal texts, such as statutes, are created by human beings, and humans act for purposes. Humans in legislatures act to identify and correct legal problems in order to secure the common good. Legal texts contain words, and documents with words are characteristically employed by humans to communicate meaning. Lawmakers correct legal problems by communicating reasons through legal texts to the law's subjects.

For example, the Sherman Anti-Trust Act was passed by Congress in 1890.[16] It was passed in response to a coordination problem caused by large capital trusts. The trusts impeded the common good by improperly ordering the American economy, and impeded the individual American's human flourishing.[17] Congress' purpose crafting and passing the Act was to re-order society to eliminate those trusts. The Act re-ordered how Americans acted by eliminating the interstate trust and monopoly as ways to act. The best way to understand the Act is as a communication by Congress to Americans to re-order society to secure the common good through the elimination of trusts. This understanding requires one to treat the Act as a communication.

The Constitution, I argue in this chapter, is likewise best understood as a communication. The focal case of constitutional interpretation is understanding the Framers' and Ratifiers' intentional act of lawmaking as the communication of their reasons through the Constitution to Americans to guide their conduct, overcome coordination problems, and secure the common good. Good constitutional interpretation captures the Framers' and Ratifiers' intended meaning.

My treatment of the Constitution as a means of communication is unexceptional. This view appears to be widely shared by both originalists,[18] nonoriginalists,[19]

---

[16] 26 Stat. 209 (1890).

[17] PAUL JOHNSON, A HISTORY OF THE AMERICAN PEOPLE 560–69 (1997); HERBERT HOVENKAMP, ENTERPRISE AND AMERICAN LAW: 1836–1937, at 226–67 (1991).

[18] For original intent originalists *see, e.g.*, Larry Alexander, *Originalism, the Why and the What*, 82 FORDHAM L. REV. 539, 540 (2013); Kay, *supra* note 7, at 712. For original meaning originalists *see, e.g.*, Jack M. Balkin, *The New Originalism and the Uses of History*, 82 FORDHAM L. REV. 641, 641 (2013); Lawrence B. Solum, *Communicative Content and Legal Content*, 89 NOTRE DAME L. REV. 479, 486–87 (2013); Gary Lawson, *Originalism without Obligation*, 93 B. U. L. L. REV. 1309, 1316–18 (2013); Randy E. Barnett, *The Misconceived Assumptions about Constitutional Assumptions*, 103 N. W. L. REV. 615, 632 (2009).

[19] *See, e.g.*, Cass R. Sunstein, *Of Snakes and Butterflies: A Reply*, 106 COLUM L. REV. 2234, 2238–39 (2006); PHILIP BOBBITT, CONSTITUTIONAL INTERPRETATION 59–60 (1991).

and others.[20] This consensus should not surprise us because, after all, the Constitution is a collection of words drafted by human beings, and humans in the focal case employ language to communicate.

One note before proceeding: the focal case of constitutional interpretation does not necessarily mean that original meaning originalism is the best way to understand the Constitution's communication. Instead, my argument in the following two subsections is that the circumstances in the United States make original meaning originalism the best mechanism to understand the Constitution's communication.

2.2.4 *The Conditions for Constitutional Communication Support the Constitutional Communication Model of Originalism*

My conception of original meaning originalism identifies the Constitution's original meaning as possessing the same content as its original intent and the meaning derived from the original methods. In part, this is because of the conditions of constitutional communication. In the following text, I describe four conditions of constitutional communication that must be met for constitutional communication to be successful. The key condition is that both the constitutional speaker(s) and audience(s) must be able to create and understand the same meaning in order for communication to occur. The Framers, recognizing this, crafted the Constitution's text utilizing public meaning. Relatedly, both the Framers and Ratifiers utilized conventional rules of interpretation to craft and understand the public meaning, and to better effectuate communication.

The conditions of constitutional communication are the conditions that must exist for communication to successfully occur via a national constitution. The conditions include: (1) a speaker; (2) an audience; (3) a mechanism of communication that (A) is encoded with the communicator's meaning, and (B) which meaning is decipherable by the audience; and (4) a purpose to communicate.[21] In the context of the United States, the major dispute will occur over (3). The Constitution's original meaning meets these conditions of communication.

First, condition (1) was met. The Constitution's Framers, at the Philadelphia Convention, were its speaker. The Framers communicated with the Ratifiers, with government officers, and with Americans generally. Following the Convention's conclusion, the Framers signed the constitution and sent it to the Continental Congress with the request that the Congress request ratification of the constitution by state conventions.[22] The Congress complied, and sent the proposed constitution to the states for ratification by conventions.[23]

---

[20] Jeremy Waldron, Law and Disagreement 83 (1999).
[21] *Compare* Corey Rayburn Young, *Constitutional Communication*, 96 B.U. L. Rev. 303 (2016).
[22] 33 Journals of the Continental Congress: 1774–1789, at 488–501 (Sept. 20, 1787).
[23] *Id.* at 548–49 (Sept. 28, 2015).

The Ratifiers were also constitutional speakers, and the Ratifiers communicated with government officials and Americans. The Ratifiers authorized the document that would direct governmental officials and govern Americans. The state Ratifiers informed the Continental Congress of their authorizations of the proposed constitution.[24] After ratification by the ninth state – and after significant bickering by the Continental Congress on the location of the new government's capital – the Continental Congress issued instructions for the initiation of the Constitution's system of government.[25] The instructions were directed to government officials and Americans in the ratifying states. The instructions instructed electors to select a president, and newly elected congressmen to begin the new federal government's operations pursuant to the newly ratified Constitution.

Condition (2) was also met. The Ratifiers, Americans generally, and government officials were the Framers' audience. Americans generally and government officials were the Ratifiers' audience. These groups received the Framers' and Ratifiers' constitutional communications. The Ratifiers received the Framers' communication as evidenced by their debate over, and ultimate approval of, the Constitution. Government officers received the Framers' and Ratifiers' communication as evidenced by their instituting the new federal government and following the Constitution's legal directives.

Third, condition (4) was met. The participants in the creation of our Constitution – the Framers who drafted the Constitution, the Ratifiers who authorized it, and government officials and Americans generally who were guided by it – participated in the constitutional project with the goal of communicating with each other. The Framers wished to communicate with the Ratifiers with the goal of convincing the Ratifiers to authorize the constitution they had crafted. The Framers came to Philadelphia in a last-ditch effort to save the Union,[26] the constitution they drafted was their means to do so, and the Ratifiers' adoption was necessary for its success.[27] The Ratifiers wished to communicate with the Framers to understand what they had created so they could reasonably decide whether to authorize it.[28] They also wished to communicate with government officials and Americans because they wished the Constitution to change the law and better secure the common good. Government officials wished to communicate with the Framers and Ratifiers to maintain their pledge of faithfulness to the Constitution[29] (when they became officers) and thereby coordinate their actions. The American People wished to understand the

---

[24] 34 Journals of the Continental Congress: 1774–1789, at 521–23 (Sept. 13, 1788).

[25] *Id.*

[26] Jack N. Rakove, Original Meanings 23–56 (1996); Forrest McDonald, E Pluribus Unum: The Formation of the American Republic 1776–1790 227–307 (1979).

[27] U.S. Const. art. VII.

[28] Rakove, *supra* note 26, at 94–160; McDonald, *supra* note 26, at 333–71.

[29] U.S. Const. art. VI, cl. 3.

constitutional communication with the goal of coordinating themselves for the common good.

Condition (3) is the tricky constitutional communication condition. To meet condition (3) – for the mechanism of constitutional communication to be effective – the Framers and Ratifiers had to utilize meaning that they all could access and understand and that later government officials and the American People could also access and understand. An effective mechanism for constitutional communication must possess at least two characteristics: accessibility and determinacy.

The first communication characteristic of successful constitutional communication is that the meaning must be *accessible* to the communication participants. If the communicator cannot encode his meaning, or the audience cannot decipher the communicator's meaning, then communication will not occur. For example, if the Framers wished to employ a new concept – for example, one for which there was not a standard English word or for which there was no legal (or other) term of art – then the Framers would have faced difficulty encoding their meaning in the Constitution. The concept of federalism came close to this, though the Framers were able to encode their meaning through, for instance, Article I, Section 1, Clause 1,[30] and other texts' public meanings.[31]

The Constitution's audiences relied on many tools to decode the Framers' intended meaning. For example, Alexander Hamilton treated "Equity"[32] as a term of art in *Federalist 80* in order to explain that the Supreme Court had jurisdiction over the body of law known as equity, not that it had the power to unreasonably interpret the Constitution.[33] On the other side of the debate, Brutus expressly invoked the conventional rules of legal interpretation to support his argument that federal judicial power would be overly broad.[34]

Accessibility does not mean that the entire encoded meaning must be accessible immediately or by everyone in the audience(s). That would confuse excellent communication with communication *simpliciter*. In these situations, the linguistic division of labor[35] can identify those with the time and skill, such as lawyers, to access the encoded meaning and share it with other audiences. Moreover, even if the Framers and Ratifiers were unable to successfully encode a meaning, the Constitution they created contained sufficient closure rules to account for it.[36]

The second communication characteristic that a mechanism of constitutional communication must possess to be successful is that the meaning must be

---

[30] *See* U.S. CONST. art. I, § 1, cl. 1 ("All legislative Powers herein granted … ").

[31] *E.g.*, *id.* art. I, § 8, cl. 18 ("proper").

[32] *Id.* art. III, § 1, cl. 1.

[33] THE FEDERALIST No. 80 (Alexander Hamilton).

[34] THE ESSAYS OF BRUTUS No. XI, *in* 2 THE COMPLETE ANTI-FEDERALIST 419 (Herbert J. Storing ed., 1981).

[35] John O. McGinnis & Michael B. Rappaport, *Original Methods Originalism: A New Theory of Interpretation and the Case Against Construction*, 103 NW. U. L. REV. 751, 771 (2009).

[36] *Infra* Subsection 2.3.3.

sufficiently *determinate*. Here, I am using determinate to mean that the accessible communication possesses the information necessary to answer constitutional issues. Determinacy is required because (even if, for example, the speaker successfully encodes her meaning and the audience successfully accesses that meaning), the communication can still be ineffective if the meaning cannot answer a pertinent constitutional question. For instance, assume, as is likely the case, that the Second Amendment's congressional authors and its ratifiers used the term "Arms" to identify a class of protected weapons. The term "Arms," however, is vague, so that it admits of borderline cases where, even if the original meaning – "weapons that were not specifically designed for military use and were not employed in a military capacity"[37] – is relatively clear, it leaves underdetermined some classes of weapons that may or may not be "Arms."

Determinacy is important because of the Constitution's character as the product of an intentional law-making act by the Framers and Ratifiers for the purpose of coordinating Americans. Americans need clear answers to fundamental coordination problems to secure the common good. The meaning need not be completely determinate for reasonably successful communication to occur.

Original public meaning[38] possesses these two communication characteristics. First, the original meaning was *accessible* to both the Framers and Ratifiers. The Framers employed public meaning to communicate to Ratifiers, government officials, and Americans generally. They knew that the Constitution's text would not be able to communicate their private original intent because the conditions of constitutional communication blocked access to adequate evidence of the privately intended meaning from their audiences. The Framers, therefore, relied on the additional interpretive resources offered by the text's public meaning to convey their intended meaning to the Ratifiers, officers, and the American People.

Language conventions are the original meaning's foundation. By definition, language conventions are widely shared, including by the Framers, Ratifiers, government officials, and the American People. But the Framers and Ratifiers did not rely only on conventional meaning.

The Framers also employed the text's semantic meaning to faithfully encode their meaning. The Framers chose words, phrases, and punctuation to mold the Constitution's semantic meaning to serve their communicative goals. The Framers took great care to craft the Constitution's text to communicate effectively. They debated both the substance and the grammar and syntax of the document's text to avoid miscommunication. As Professor Robert Clinton noted in his seminal article over thirty years ago, "[i]t is difficult to read the debates of the Constitutional Convention without coming to the conclusion that the framers had a finite sense of the meaning

---

[37] *District of Columbia v. Heller*, 554 U.S. 570, 581 (2008).
[38] A reminder that the original public meaning was the semantic meaning as enriched by the publicly-available context.

of language and that they strove to use language precisely to control the governance of not only the contemporary generation, but also generations to come."[39]

However, the text's semantic meaning alone,[40] no matter how well crafted, would not fully and effectively encode the Framers' meaning. For aspects of the Constitution where the semantic meaning was not adequate, the Framers and Ratifiers employed the linguistic division of labor and conventional rules of interpretation. The linguistic division of labor refers to the widespread phenomenon in linguistic practices where experts in fields of the relevant terms of art explain terms of art to non-experts.[41] This occurred in the Constitution's communication process where experts attempted to explain terms of art to non-experts in both the Philadelphia and state ratification conventions.[42] This allowed the Framers and Ratifiers to more precisely and fulsomely communicate their meaning because experts would access and explain that meaning.

The Framers and Ratifiers both had access to and utilized conventional rules of interpretation that helped make the Constitution's semantic meaning more accessible. The Framers were well versed in public discourse. They were adept at crafting their letters, documents, and speeches to convey as precise a meaning as possible. This skill set included facility with the conventions of interpretation that their audiences would utilize. The Framers were generally well educated; furthermore, many of the Framers were trained as attorneys, and one of an attorney's key skills is knowing the governing rules of interpretation of legal documents. The Framers crafted the Constitution on the assumption that the Constitution's audiences would utilize the conventional rules of interpretation.[43] For example, the Constitution itself utilized conventional legal rules of interpretation. One such rule is found in the Supremacy Clause whose language, "any Thing in the Constitution or Laws of any State to the Contrary notwithstanding,"[44] is a form of *non obstante* clause that prevented the application of a common law presumption against implied repeals.[45]

In sum, the original meaning had significant resources to encode and decode the Framers' and Ratifiers' intended constitutional meaning.

---

[39] Robert N. Clinton, *Original Understanding, Legal Realism, and the Interpretation of "the Constitution,"* 72 Iowa L. Rev. 1177, 1190 (1987).

[40] That is, conventional meaning modified by grammar and syntax.

[41] McGinnis & Rappaport, *supra* note 35, at 771.

[42] For example, in the Philadelphia convention, some of the Framers referenced Blackstone's Commentaries to support their claim that the proposed Ex Post Facto Clause text applied only to criminal laws. 2 Records, *supra* note 6, at 617. In the Virginia ratification convention, Edmund Randolph argued that the Ex Post Facto Clause was a term of art that applied only to criminal laws. Convention of Virginia, *in* 3 The Debates in the Several State Conventions On The Adoption of the Federal Constitution 477–79 (Jonathan Elliot ed., 1836).

[43] John O. McGinnis & Michael B. Rappaport, Originalism and the Good Constitution 13 (2013). I described the existence and nature of these widespread conventional rules of legal interpretation in Section 1.2.

[44] U.S. Const. art. VI, cl. 2.

[45] Caleb Nelson, *Preemption*, 86 Va. L. Rev. 225, 246–48 (2000).

Second, the original meaning was also sufficiently *determinate* to enable effective constitutional communication. Language conventions, and rules of grammar and syntax, are facts of the world and, when they exist, are relatively determinate. Of course, it is the case that the Constitution's semantic meaning, by itself, was under-determined. In many situations, it is vague, ambiguous, and contains tensions and gaps. These underdeterminacies, however, have never been extreme, as evidenced by the Constitution's operation, which shows that most underdeterminacies are reduced or eliminated through additional interpretive resources.

The Framers employed three techniques to reduce semantic underdeterminacy: public meaning, terms of art, and rules of interpretation. First, the Framers utilized the text's public meaning. The publicly-available context in which the Constitution was drafted provided audiences with additional information to clarify the Constitution's meaning. For instance, it is not patent that "executive Power" includes the inherent power to remove executive officers, but in light of the background of the English monarch's and colonial and state governors' examples, it was relatively clearer to the First Congress that the President had the power to remove officials.[46]

Second, the Framers made use of terms of art. These terms of art referenced and incorporated thick descriptions and practices that clarified the Constitution's meaning. For example, Article I, Section 8, Clause 10, authorized Congress to define and punish "Offences against the Law of Nations."[47] The Law of Nations was a term of art that referenced nations' practices and influential writings, such as those by Hugo Grotius, Samuel Pufendorf, and Emerich de Vattel.

Third, the Framers employed conventional rules of interpretation. These rules of interpretation operated as "closure rules" to eliminate underdeterminacy through application of the rules. For instance, the Tenth Amendment makes explicit the constitutional principle of limited and enumerated powers. This principle is a closure rule that interprets the Constitution to *not* authorize a federal governmental action if it is not clear that the action is the product of an enumerated power.[48]

Together, public meaning, terms of art, and rules of interpretation made the Constitution's meaning accessible to the constitutional communication participants and made the original meaning sufficiently determinate to achieve its goal of social coordination.[49] Therefore, the Constitution's original meaning met the conditions of constitutional communication.

By contrast, original intent, though it met conditions (1), (2), and (4), did not possess the two communication characteristics (accessibility and determinacy) and therefore

---

[46] Saikrishna Prakash, *New Light on the Decision of 1789*, 91 CORNELL L. REV. 1021 (2006).

[47] U.S. CONST. art. I, § 8, cl. 1.

[48] Kurt T. Lash, *The Original Meaning of an Omission: The Tenth Amendment, Popular Sovereignty, and "Expressly" Delegated Power*, 83 NOTRE DAME L. REV. 1889, 1954 (2008).

[49] Moreover, the Constitution contains a number of closure rules that operate in those areas of continued underdeterminacy (Section 2.3), and it also contains a theory of precedent that operates to implement the Constitution's determinate and underdeterminate original meaning (Section 2.4).

failed condition (3).[50] The Ratifiers could not, or at least not reliably, access the Framers' privately intended meaning. This was either because there was not one originally intended meaning of the multi-member Philadelphia Convention or the ratification conventions, or because the evidence to uncover the originally intended meaning was insufficiently available. After all, the Ratifiers did not have access to documentary evidence of the Framers' deliberations and their private notes until much later, when the proceedings and Madison's own notes were published. Nor did the Ratifiers have any basis to know whether, if, and when the Framers' intended meaning diverged from the public meaning. The only source of such evidence was the representations by Philadelphia Convention participants at the ratification conventions.

Original meaning originalism has developed to the point where it has the conceptual components to accommodate the Constitutional Communication Model's picture of successful constitutional communication under the conditions and with the characteristics of constitutional communication I outlined. The key is original meaning originalism's adoption of contextual enrichment. The context in which the Constitution was drafted included publicly-known barriers to and tools for communication, which I have identified. For instance, the Framers (and Ratifiers) knew that the Ratifiers would not have access to the Framers' private intentions, and the Ratifiers knew the Framers knew this. Also, the Framers and Ratifiers knew and utilized terms of art and conventional rules of interpretation.

Original meaning originalism's embrace of contextual enrichment also opened the door for reconciliation between different strands of originalism. The Constitution's originally intended meaning and its original methods meaning is its original meaning. This is because the Framers recognized that the conditions and characteristics of constitutional communication dictated that their private intent was not directly accessible to their audiences. Instead, the Framers resorted to the Constitution's public meaning, funneled through terms of art and the conventional interpretive rules, to convey their intended meaning to the Ratifiers and the American People.

2.2.5 *The Process of Creation of the U.S. Constitution Supports the Constitutional Communication Model of Originalism*

2.2.5.1 Introduction

The process by which the Constitution was created and authorized also supports the Constitutional Communication Model of originalism. In this subsection, I point to three important facets of that process and how they support this model. They support my claim that the Constitution's original meaning is its meaning because they require use of the original meaning in order for the Framers' *practical judgments*

---

[50] This was a major reason why critics pummeled original intent originalism in the 1980s and early 1990s.

(embodied in the Constitution), the Ratifiers' *authority* (to authorize the Constitution), and Americans' *coordination* (by the Constitution) to be effective.[51]

2.2.5.2 The Framers' Prudential Judgments, Embodied in the Constitution's Text, Are Effective Only if the Ratifiers, Government Officers, and Americans Utilize(d) Originalism

The Framers employed their prudential judgment to craft the Constitution in order for the United States to overcome coordination problems and pursue the common good. Original meaning was the only mechanism by which the Framers could communicate those prudential judgments to the Ratifiers, government officers, and the American People.

Put concisely, practical reason is the faculty of the human mind that enables one to identify what is good and to identify the best means to pursue those goods, all things considered.[52] Practical reason pertains to action. It helps us know how to act in a given situation in order to achieve a good.

Practical reason develops over a lifetime and, like other human capacities, is honed through experiences.[53] The Framers of our current Constitution possessed significant practical experience. They utilized their practical reason to identify societal problems in need of solution, craft solutions to those problems, and articulate those solutions in the Constitution's carefully crafted text.

To take an easy example, one of the major problems with the Articles of Confederation was that it did not authorize the national government to regulate interstate commerce, and the baleful effects of this lacuna included the erection of trade barriers and interstate disputes over trade.[54] The Framers recognized this problem and crafted a solution: the Commerce Clause. The Commerce Clause embodied the Framers' all-things-considered judgment on how to resolve interstate trade problems, but in a manner consistent with other values, such as federalism and the principle of limited federal government. One can see this by comparing some of the alternatives available to the Framers. At one extreme, they could have given the federal government complete authority over all activities touching on the subject of commerce. However, the Framers declined to do this for a number of reasons, including to preserve a more robust role for states. At the other extreme, the Framers could have limited the federal government's authority over commerce to commercial activity crossing state lines, somewhat like national authority at national borders. The Framers did not take this route either because it would have been inadequate to fully address the problem and

---

[51] These three facets also form the core of my law-as-coordination account of originalism in Chapter 4.

[52] NE, at 1144a; ST I-II, q. 57, a. 5; NLNR, at 59–86, 100–33.

[53] NE, at 1103a–b, 1141b–1142a; ST I-II, q. 51, aa.2, 3.

[54] JOHNSON, *supra* note 17, at 184–85; SAMUEL ELIOT MORRISON, THE OXFORD HISTORY OF THE AMERICAN PEOPLE 301–05 (1965); Clinton, *supra* note 39, at 893–94, 896.

maintain interstate political amity. The Commerce Clause's solution to the Articles of Confederation problem was a reasonable practical judgment.

However, from the Framers' own perspective, their solution to interstate trade disputes – the Commerce Clause – was valueless unless it was authorized by the Ratifiers and also followed by state and federal officials. For the Framers to communicate their solutions to the Ratifiers, government officers, and Americans, and for the Ratifiers and others to access the Framers' practical solution, all parties to constitutional communication need(ed) to utilize an accessible constitutional meaning.

The Framers needed the Ratifiers to access their practical judgment, embodied in the Commerce Clause, for their solution to be effective. Lacking ratification, the Constitution solved no problems and the Articles remained in effect. Relatedly, the Framers needed government officers to access their practical judgment for their solution to be effective. If federal judges, for instance, misunderstood the Commerce Clause, they would nullify the Framers' all-things-considered practical judgment and substitute a different one.

The best way the Ratifiers and government officers could decipher the practical judgment embodied in the Commerce Clause was to employ the Clause's original public meaning. The public meaning was accessible to the Ratifiers and government officers because it was the meaning derived from the text's semantic meaning, augmented by the publicly available context, terms of art, and rules of interpretation, all of which the Ratifiers and officers could utilize.

Before moving on, let me emphasize that tying the original meaning to the Framers' practical reason affirms the fundamental rationality of the constitution-making process. Stepping back for a moment, the point of the process of framing and ratifying the Constitution was to employ practical reason in an authoritative manner to solve the new nation's coordination problems. Otherwise, what would have been the point of having one group of Americans debate and draft, and then having another group of Americans debate and adopt the first group's work product? The key to making the point of the constitutional process effective was that the Framers and Ratifiers (respectively) encoded and deciphered the Framers' practical judgments. The only meaning that could do so was the Constitution's original public meaning.

2.2.5.3 The Ratifiers' Authority, Which Authorized the Constitution's Text, Is Effective Only if the Ratifiers, Government Officers, and Americans Utilize(d) Originalism

Briefly, authority is the capacity of a person or institution to provide exclusionary reasons for action in a subject's practical deliberations.[55] A parent has the capacity to

---

[55] JOSEPH RAZ, THE AUTHORITY OF LAW 28–29 (2d ed. 2009); *see also* YVES SIMON, A GENERAL THEORY OF AUTHORITY 48 (1962) ("The power in charge of unifying common action through rules binding for all is what everyone calls authority.").

change a child's course of conduct by substituting the parent's reason for the child's. Legal authority is a particular type of authority that provides legal reasons that displace reasons for action in the practical reasoning of those subject to the authority's law.[56] A state's department of transportation has the capacity to change a driver's proposed speed while traveling within that jurisdiction.

The Ratifiers comprised the body that was, and still is, recognized as possessing the authority to authorize the Constitution. The document in the National Archives *is* the United States' Constitution because the Ratifiers authorized it.[57] No other people or institution had or has the authority to authorize a U.S. Constitution. For instance, Supreme Court justices have not and do not claim for themselves – nor does our practice recognize for them – the authority to authorize a constitution.[58] Nor does any other document – no matter how much more normatively attractive it may be than the Constitution authorized by the Ratifiers – possess the Constitution's authority. For example, Supreme Court justices do not claim that their opinions are the Constitution.[59]

The Ratifiers exercised their authority by debating whether the proposed constitution was in the country's best interests, and then approving it. Both the Ratifiers' own understanding of the proposed constitution and the Ratifiers' ability to debate among themselves the relative merits and demerits of the proposed constitution depended on their utilizing the Constitution's original public meaning. Moreover, the success of the Ratifiers' authorization of the Constitution was contingent on the Constitution's other audiences – government officers and the American People – understanding the Constitution in the same manner as the Ratifiers, and this depended on the audiences likewise utilizing the Constitution's public meaning.

The Ratifiers had access to the constituent parts of the proposed constitution's public meaning – semantic meaning enriched by context, terms of art, and rules of interpretation – but they had limited access to the Framers' private meaning(s). Similarly, the Ratifiers would not have been able to engage in the robust debates over the proposed constitution's merits in the various conventions unless the debate participants utilized a consistent and accessible meaning. The public meaning was that meaning. For example, the New York ratification debate included the *Federalist Papers*. The *Federalist Papers* did not rely on the Framers' private meaning to support its claims about the Constitution's meaning. Instead, Publius used the semantic meaning, enriched by context, terms of art, and rules of interpretation to ascertain the public meaning.

---

[56] NLNR, at 231–96; RAZ, *supra* note 55, at 29.
[57] Richard S. Kay, *American Constitutionalism, in* CONSTITUTIONALISM: PHILOSOPHICAL FOUNDATIONS 16, 29–33 (Larry Alexander ed., 1998).
[58] *See infra* Subsection 3.4.2 (explaining this claim).
[59] Richard S. Kay, *Original Intention and Public Meaning in Constitutional Interpretation*, 103 NW. U.L. REV. 703, 717 (2009).

Similarly, the public meaning authorized by the Ratifiers provided a meaning accessible to government officials and Americans. Post-Ratification, Americans utilized the Constitution's public meaning to know and follow the Constitution's meaning.[60]

Maintaining the link between constitutional meaning and the Ratifiers is important because it ties the original meaning to the rational human beings who had the authority to give the Constitution its legal status and acted intentionally to do so. Authority is part of law's focal case; law's capacity to displace other reasons for actions (because of its authority) is one of its essential characteristics. Meaning tied to law's authority respects that authority and facilitates its exercise.

Originalism's maintenance of the link between the Ratifiers' authority and constitutional meaning is also important because it highlights a second fundamental aspect of law: law is a reflection, not only of human reason, but also of human will. Therefore, in addition to the fundamental rationality of the American constitution-making process, instantiated via the Framers' practical wisdom, the U.S. Constitution is also the product of human will. The Ratifiers – particular humans in a particular time and in a particular place – exercised their collective will to authorize the Constitution of the United States. Originalism facilitates the Ratifiers' authoritative exercise of will by enabling their exercise of collective will (their debate and ratification) and those subject to the Constitution to follow the Constitution (through coordination).

2.2.5.4 Government Officials' and the American People's Social-Coordination Pursuant to the Constitution Is Effective Only if They Utilize (d) Originalism

Social coordination is a community's unity-of-action towards an end.[61] For example, a family may coordinate its activity at dinnertime by establishing a particular time (*e. g.*, 5 p.m.), delegating particular tasks to family members (*e.g.*, Lucy puts glasses on the table), and the entire family dining together. Law's focal case is the coordination of its subjects toward the community's common good.[62]

The Constitution has coordinated government officers and the American People since its ratification, and it continues to do so today. The Commerce Clause provides an example. One facet of the Commerce Clause was its authorization to Congress to control interstate trade to facilitate trade and to prevent trade barriers. Congress exercised that authority from the initiation of the Republic, and Congress continues to exercise its Commerce Clause authority today, including in situations

---

[60] *Supra* Subsection 1.2.3.
[61] NLNR, at 137–38.
[62] *Id.* at 149–60, 231–96.

when Congress judges that other values, such as federalism, are more important than the free interstate flow of goods and services.[63]

Constitutional communication using the Constitution's public meaning enabled the American people and governmental officials, then and now, to understand the Constitution and order their actions accordingly. Like the Ratifiers, government officials and Americans did not have the ability to access the Framers' privately-intended meaning(s). Instead, officers and other Americans had resort to the text's semantic meaning, modified by contextual enrichment and facilitated by terms of art and rules of interpretation. If government officials followed a meaning other than the Constitution's original meaning, then the Constitution's capacity to authoritatively coordinate would be undermined.

Tying constitutional meaning to social coordination is important because coordination is the Constitution's formal purpose:[64] "in Order to form . . .".[65] The Constitution responds to coordination problems by settling on one mode of coordination. The Constitution's modes of coordination are the product of the Framers' practical wisdom and the Ratifiers' authority, and the Constitution's original meaning most effectively harnesses their reason and authority via the Constitution's solutions to effectuate coordination for the sake of the common good.

2.2.6 *Why Original Meaning, Original Intent, and Original Methods Were Perceived as Distinct*

One potential response to the Constitutional Communication Model of originalism, and its synthesis of original meaning, original intent, and original methods is to ask, "what was all the fuss about?" How were so many intelligent scholars, in good faith, wrong to think that they were not talking about the same thing? There were two main reasons for the perception.

First, on the original meaning side of the equation, original meaning's reason for articulation and theoretical development initially precluded such originalists' ability to see that their position was compatible with original intent. I described originalism's evolution in Chapter 1, and I showed that originalists initially adopted original meaning because it seemed to avoid the theoretical and practical problems of ascertaining Framer or Ratifier intended meaning. Original meaning offered a (more) determinate source of constitutional meaning, and its adoption was simultaneously a rejection of original intent.

Further, original meaning originalism's initial theoretical framework was the text's semantic meaning.[66] This meaning was derived from application of the rules of

---

[63] *See, e.g.*, The McCarran-Ferguson Act, 59 Stat. 33 (1945) (authorizing state regulation of medical insurance despite its effect on interstate commerce).

[64] ARISTOTLE, METAPHYSICS 1013a–b. (Hugh Tredennick trans., 1975).

[65] U.S. CONST. pmbl.

[66] Randy E. Barnett, *An Originalism for Nonoriginalists*, 45 LOY. L. REV. 611, 616 (1999).

grammar and syntax to the text's conventional meaning. This conception of constitutional meaning precluded the original intent conception of meaning.

Later, original meaning originalists came to see that the critique of original intent was not as devastating as once thought,[67] and that it had some purchase on original meaning originalism, in any event. This lessened the need to distance originalism from original intent. Originalists learned to live with a little gray, so to speak. At the same time, original meaning originalism's theoretical sophistication increased, and the resultant inclusion of contextual enrichment provided a space in which original intent could operate. These changes opened original meaning originalism to a reconciliation between it and original intent.

Second, on the original intent side of the spectrum, original meaning's apparent disconnect of constitutional meaning from the flesh-and-blood human beings who created and authorized the Constitution prevented original intent advocates from seeing the necessary role for original meaning in constitutional communication.[68] Original intent originalists focused on the relationship between meaning and intelligence. Marks, words, and texts do not have meaning, they reasoned, without originating from an intelligent being who utilized them to communicate. Original meaning seemed to sever constitutional meaning from the Framers, who carefully drafted the Constitution, and the Ratifiers, who gave it its authority, thereby rendering it unintelligible. The necessary connection between constitutional meaning and authority, and with the humans who created and authorized the Constitution, seemed to preclude original meaning originalism.

These appropriate criticisms of original meaning inhibited original intent originalists from seeing how original meaning facilitated original intent because it provided the mechanism of communication of the Framers' intended meanings while, at the same time, surmounting the critiques of original intent.

Fitting original methods into this narrative is relatively simple. Professors McGinnis and Rappaport have persuasively argued that original methods is not only compatible with original meaning and intent; they also have shown that it facilitates both.[69] The original interpretive conventions advance original intent by effectuating the Framers' communication by helping audiences understand their intended meaning. The original methods also assist original meaning by providing more information for audiences and closure rules. Most importantly, this included conventional rules of interpretation that facilitated constitutional communication among the Framers, Ratifiers, and the American People.

---

[67] Keith E. Whittington, *The New Originalism*, 2 GEO. J. L. & PUB. POL'Y 599, 609 (2004).
[68] Kay, *supra* note 59, at 715–19.
[69] MCGINNIS & RAPPAPORT, *supra* note 43, at 121–26.

2.2.7 *Conclusion*

In this section, I advanced the Constitutional Communication Model of original-ism. This model understands the Constitution as the product of the Framers' and Ratifiers' intentional lawmaking. The Constitution contained legal directives to Americans to overcome coordination problems and secure the common good. The conditions and process of constitutional communication in the United States made communication of the Constitution's reasons via the original meaning suc-cessful, and they also made this meaning the Framers' and Ratifiers' intended meaning, one that employed the conventional methods of interpretation.

2.3 THE DEFERENCE CONCEPTION OF CONSTITUTIONAL CONSTRUCTION

2.3.1 *Introduction*

The debate over constitutional construction is important for four main reasons. First, construction can dramatically affect the Constitution's capacity to answer important constitutional questions and, therefore, its capacity to coordinate Ameri-can society. The greater the scope of construction, the fewer determinate answers the Constitution provides. This could profoundly affect the Constitution's ability to guide government officers and Americans generally. For instance, if the Interstate Commerce Clause is underdetermined on the point of whether, and to what extent, states may not affect interstate commerce (in the absence of congressional action), then state officials and federal judges lack important guidance.

Second, and relatedly, construction affects the scope of federal power and consti-tutional rights. The greater the scope of construction then, depending on one's conception of construction, there is greater or lesser federal power and greater or lesser constitutionally protected rights. For instance, if one's conception of construc-tion includes a "presumption of liberty,"[70] then an underdetermined Commerce Clause is constructed to mean that Congress does not have power; by contrast, if one's conception of construction includes a "presumption of authority," then Congress could construct its commerce power relatively more capaciously.

Third, construction affects the relative power of the judiciary compared to the other federal branches and the states. The greater the scope of construction then, depending on one's conception of construction, the elected or judicial branches may possess relatively greater authority. If one's conception of construction includes federal court primacy in the construction zone, then federal courts are relatively more powerful; if one's conception of construction includes elected

---

[70] RANDY E. BARNETT, RESTORING THE LOST CONSTITUTION 253–73 (2004).

branch and state primacy in the construction zone, then the federal courts are relatively less powerful.

Fourth, originalism's coherence as a theory of interpretation may depend on its ability to identify a place for construction while, at the same time, identifying principled limits to it. If the scholarly consensus that the Constitution's original meaning is underdetermined is based on sound reasons, then originalism should accept construction. At the same time, originalism must explain construction's boundaries so that it does not undermine originalism's distinctive commitment to following the original meaning, and therefore the original meaning's capacity to coordinate American society.

In this section, I argue for a modest conception of constitutional construction, and for three reasons: first, originalism includes closure rules that reduce the constitutional underdeterminacy that is a prerequisite for construction; second, construction occurs only when the Constitution's original meaning is epistemically underdetermined; and, third, in the construction zone, judicial interpreters should defer to elected branch constructions.[71] But first, let me explain the sound reasons for so many scholars' embrace of constitutional construction.

2.3.2 *The* Prima Facie *Plausibility of Constitutional Construction*

The existence of constitutional underdeterminacy, and therefore of constitutional construction in those areas of underdeterminacy, is *prima facie* plausible. This supports the originalist consensus I described in Subsection 1.4.3.

Stepping back for a moment, as a practical matter, linguistic communication regularly fails. Everyday written communication frequently misfires. We write emails and texts that fail to communicate our meaning to their recipients. Legal texts likewise suffer from underdeterminacy. For example, the Supreme Court in *Smith* v. *United States* fractured on whether 18 U.S.C. § 924(c)(1), "during and in relation to ... [a] drug trafficking crime[,] uses ... a firearm," applied to a defendant trading a weapon in exchange for cocaine.[72] The consensus among legal academics is that the law is moderately underdetermined.[73]

In the context of the Constitution, there has been and continues to be disagreement among originalist judges and scholars on the Constitution's original meaning. For instance, there continues to be disagreement over the Establishment Clause's original meaning, with three primary currently contending interpretations.[74] This

---

[71] There are a number of payoffs from the deference conception of construction. For instance, I rely on the deference conception to argue, in Subsection 3.4.5, that constitutional construction helps originalism better fit our existing constitutional practice.

[72] *Smith* v. *United States*, 508 U.S. 223 (1993).

[73] Ken Kress, *Legal Indeterminacy*, 77 CAL. L. REV. 283, 284 (1989); Lawrence B. Solum, *On the Indeterminacy Crisis: Critiquing Critical Dogma*, 54 U. CHI. L. REV. 462, 503 (1987).

[74] DONALD L. DRAKEMAN, CHURCH, STATE, AND ORIGINAL INTENT 156–95 (2010).

disagreement does not itself prove that there is no "truth of the matter," but it does suggest that, at the very least, our legal practice has difficulty identifying the Constitution's determinate original meaning.

Originalists who advocate for constitutional construction have identified at least four causes of underdeterminacy. They include vagueness, ambiguity, gaps, and contradictions.[75] Each of these prevents the original meaning from being fully determinate. For example, the Article IV, Section 4 guarantee of a "Republican" form of government admits of borderline cases and is therefore vague. Some forms of government clearly count as "Republican"; Ohio's general assembly, for instance. Other forms of government clearly do not count as "Republican"; the Soviet Union,[76] for instance. However, there will be borderline cases where it is unclear whether a governmental structure is "Republican" or not. Perhaps state legislatures apportioned on the basis of geography (prior to *Reynolds* v. *Sims*[77]) were examples.

The debates in the early Republic over the Constitution's meaning also suggest that the Constitution's original meaning was underdetermined. Despite the Constitution's recent drafting and ratification, Americans vigorously debated important issues of constitutional meaning including whether the President had the power to remove executive officers unilaterally,[78] and whether Congress could authorize the President to locate a post road.[79]

One of the most vigorous such debates was over whether Congress had the power to charter a national bank. This initial debate began when Secretary of the Treasury Hamilton introduced his *Report on a National Bank* on Dec. 14, 1790,[80] the debate occurred in the House in early 1791,[81] and then continued in the Washington Administration as President Washington deliberated on whether to sign the Act.[82] The House ultimately decided to charter the bank, and Congress passed the Act on Feb. 25, 1791.[83] The debate suggests that the participants appeared to acknowledge that the question was not open-and-shut; they did not appear to believe that arguments were unnecessary to establish the accuracy of their interpretation, nor did they appear to believe that their opponents' arguments were patently false or frivolous.

It is not possible to identify specific portions of the Constitution's text for which there was underdetermined original meaning without significant historical research, which is beyond the scope of this book. However, the everyday failure of language to

---

[75] Solum, *supra* note 4, at 285.

[76] THE UNION OF SOVIET SOCIALIST REPUBLICS CONSTITUTION § 126 (1936).

[77] *Reynolds* v. *Sims*, 377 U.S. 533 (1964).

[78] *Myers* v. *United States*, 272 U.S. 52, 109–36 (1926).

[79] 3 ANNALS OF CONG. 229–36 (1791).

[80] Alexander Hamilton, *Report on a National Bank*, 2 ANNALS 2082 (Dec. 14, 1790).

[81] 2 ANNALS 1940 (Feb. 1, 1791).

[82] *See generally* LEGISLATIVE AND DOCUMENTARY HISTORY OF THE BANK OF THE UNITED STATES 2–114 (M. St. Clair Clarke & D. A. Hall, eds., 1832).

[83] An Act to incorporate the subscribers to the Bank of the United States, 1 Stat. 191 (Feb. 25, 1791).

communicate, coupled with the scholarly consensus of legal underdeterminacy and the preliminary evidence that at least some constitutional provisions did not have a fully determinate original meaning, shows *prima facie* the need for constitutional construction.

This picture, I believe, is incomplete. In the next subsection, I argue that public meaning originalism's incorporation of contextual enrichment has opened it to use of the closure rules that reduce the scope of potential underdeterminacy. Second, I show that construction occurs only when the Constitution's original meaning is epistemically underdetermined (even though the original meaning is metaphysically determined by original closure rules). Third, originalism should utilize judicial deference to elected branch constructions when a case is in the construction zone. Together, these three claims delineate a modest conception of constitutional construction.

2.3.3 A Modest Role for Constitutional Construction

2.3.3.1 Construction Is Modest Because of Closure Rules

Putting to one side, for the moment, the existence and impact of the original methods of interpretation, any theoretically possible construction zone is modest because closure rules reduce its scope. Three originalist closure rules I describe in the following subsections reduce the need for construction: first, a judge should choose that interpretation which is supported by the best legal evidence (the "best-available-evidence" standard); second, if the interpretive question is one of *federal* power, then the party *supporting* federal power bears the burden of proof; and, third, if the interpretive issue involves *state* power, then the party claiming that the Constitution *preempts* the state action through a constitutional limit bears the burden of proof. The first closure rule is a "standard of proof" that identifies the quantum of legal evidence needed to support a constitutional interpretation, and the second and third rules are "burdens of proof" that identify which parties in litigation must meet the standard of proof.[84] These closure rules operate in the realm of *epistemic* underdeterminacy, which I describe in the following subsection. They have the effect of preventing cases from being in the construction zone that would otherwise have been in the zone.

Stepping back for a moment, there is widespread agreement that closure rules exist and that they are employed in our legal practice in a variety of contexts. These rules serve as rules of thumb; they guide interpreters when faced with some level of epistemic underdeterminacy. Closure rules are very common, and one general

---

[84] I have adopted the labels "standard of proof" and "burden of proof" from Gary Lawson, *Legal Indeterminacy: Its Cause and Cure*, 19 Harv. J. L. & Pub. Pol'y 411, 423 (1996). This is nonuniform labeling in this context. *See* 21B Charles Alan Wright et al., Federal Practice and Procedure Evidence § 5122 (2d ed. 2019) (explaining this).

manifestation of closure rules is courts' use of "equitable" constructions of statutes to pursue goals or avoid harms.[85] A common example is the rule of lenity in criminal law, where a court will narrowly interpret criminal statutes.[86] In the constitutional context, the Supreme Court frequently uses rules of construction. The nondelegation doctrine is both a rule of law and also a closure rule following which the Supreme Court will narrowly interpret a congressional delegation to an agency to avoid violation of Article I.[87] Even more analogously to my purposes, the Supreme Court, in *NFIB* v. *Sebelius*, narrowly construed the federal government's Commerce Clause power because of the constitutional principle of limited and enumerated powers.[88]

Before describing the three originalist closure rules that reduce underdeterminacy, let me briefly explain the concept of "legal evidence" upon which these closure rules rely. Legal evidence is the evidence for or against the veracity of a legal proposition. For example, the textual grant of "executive Power" to the President in Article II is (some) legal evidence supporting the legal proposition that the President possesses the power to unilaterally remove executive officers. Like factual evidence, parties marshal legal evidence to support their respective legal claims, and like factual evidence, the legal system assigns burdens of proof and persuasion to parties. For instance, a party relying on foreign law must provide a preponderance of the legal evidence to support the existence of the foreign legal proposition.[89]

Legal evidence, in the context of originalist constitutional interpretation, is evidence for or against a proposition of original meaning. For example, an original language convention that "commerce" meant trade[90] is legal evidence supporting the proposition that the Commerce Clause's original meaning covers the commercial transport of goods and services across state lines. The following three closure rules identify the burden of legal evidence and the party upon whom the burden falls.[91]

2.3.3.1.1 ORIGINALIST CLOSURE RULE 1: THE BEST-AVAILABLE-EVIDENCE STANDARD The first closure rule instructs interpreters to choose that interpretation of the Constitution that is supported by the best-available legal evidence.[92] Imagine

---

[85] Roger A. Shiner, *Aristotle's Theory of Equity*, 27 LOY. L. A. L. REV. 1245 (1994).
[86] *United States v. Gradwell*, 243 U.S. 476, 485 (1917).
[87] *The Benzene Cases*, 448 U.S. 607, 646 (1980).
[88] *See NFIB v. Sebelius*, 567 U.S. 519, 536 (2012) (Roberts, C. J.) ("This case concerns two powers that the Constitution does grant the Federal Government, but which must be read carefully to avoid creating a general federal authority akin to the police power.").
[89] 9A CHARLES ALAN WRIGHT ET AL., FEDERAL PRACTICE AND PROCEDURE §§ 2441–2447 (3d ed. 2019).
[90] Randy E. Barnett, *New Evidence of the Original Meaning of the Commerce Clause*, 55 ARK. L. REV. 847 (2003).
[91] After this point, I discuss these closure rules only in the context of Article III judges.
[92] Some of my arguments follow Professors McGinnis and Rappaport's discussion. MCGINNIS & RAPPAPORT, *supra* note 43, at 141–43.

a judge who is asked to identify the original meaning of the Second Amendment.[93] The parties in the case before the judge would present legal evidence for their respective positions. The parties would marshal arguments from text, structure, history, and precedent for their respective proffered interpretations. Each party may emphasize different types of arguments to the judge. For example, one party may have relatively more historical arguments, while another party may have relatively more precedential arguments. Furthermore (from each party's own perspective and the judge's as well), the weight of the parties' individual arguments would vary. A party may view its historical evidence of the original conventional meaning of "keep and bear Arms" as more powerful than its historical evidence of a legal practice that preambles did not have input into the meaning of texts following the preambles. The judge would evaluate different possible interpretations and adopt the interpretation supported by the best-available legal evidence, taking into account the quantity and weight of the various interpretive arguments.[94]

The best-available-evidence closure rule is a product of the judicial duty "to say what the law is ... If two laws conflict with each other, the courts must decide on the operation of each."[95] Federal judges have no choice: once they accept the office of federal judge and exercise "judicial Power" in cases properly before them, their judicial duty to "say what the law is" requires them to identify the law.[96] The meaning of the Constitution is the constitutional interpretation supported by the most legal evidence.

The standard cannot be lower than the best-available-evidence standard. If the threshold of sufficient evidence were, for instance, 30 percent of the possible evidence, then it could be possible for more than one of the parties' interpretations to meet the threshold. A judge could be faced with a case in which he was required by the hypothetical closure rule to identify both – conflicting – interpretations as the Constitution's meaning. This below-the-best-available evidence rule would prevent the judge from fulfilling his judicial duty to say what the law is.

The standard cannot be higher than the best-available-evidence standard. If the threshold of sufficient evidence for an interpretation were, say, 60 percent of the legal evidence, then there would be cases where judges could not adopt one of the parties' proffered interpretations. Without an additional closure rule that operated in this situation, then judges in such cases would be unable to rule, which is outside of our practice and contrary to judicial duty. Judges *never* say that the Constitution does *not* provide an answer in a case that calls for its interpretation. They always say what the law is.

---

[93] This is an abstract treatment of *District of Columbia* v. *Heller*, 554 U.S. 570 (2008).

[94] STEVEN J. BURTON, JUDGING IN GOOD FAITH 35–68 (1992).

[95] *Marbury* v. *Madison*, 5 U.S. (1 Cranch) 137, 177 (1803).

[96] *See also* Gary Lawson, *Proving the Law*, 86 NW U. L. REV. 859, 890 (1992) (concluding that our legal system's unarticulated standard of proof is "a legal interpretation is correct if it is better than its available alternatives").

In "easy cases,"[97] judges simply choose the clearly correct interpretation, an interpretation that is supported by significantly more than the second-best-available-alternative legal evidence. It is sometimes the case, however, that an interpreter will face a situation where the legal evidence for two alternative interpretations of the Constitution's original meaning is relatively evenly matched. Stated differently, an interpreter will not always face interpretive questions where one interpretation has a significant majority of the legal evidence and another interpretation has a modest amount of evidence supporting it.

This situation is a manifestation of a broader phenomenon in law. For many contested cases, and especially in "hard cases,"[98] there are reasonable legal arguments supporting both parties. Despite the existence of this general legal underdeterminacy, judges *always* make a decision, and they do so on the basis of which side's interpretation of the law is more likely accurate. Judges do so, in close cases, by asking: which party's legal propositions are better supported by the legal evidence than the other's?

The best-available-evidence standard also fits the practice in the early Republic. Both on and off the Supreme Court, Americans engaged in debates and litigation over the Constitution's meaning on contested issues, and they chose the constitutional interpretation (they believed was) supported by the best available legal evidence. Chief Justice John Marshall repeatedly did so, including in cases where the interpretive evidence was relatively evenly matched. In *M'Culloch* v. *Maryland*, for instance, Chief Justice Marshall canvassed the arguments for and against Maryland's and M'Culloch's interpretations of "necessary."[99] He reviewed arguments from text, history, structure, and early practice to support adopting M'Culloch's interpretation of "plainly adapted." Marshall expressly described the issue of congressional power to charter a national bank as involving "a doubtful question, one on which human reason may pause, and the human judgment be suspended."[100] Similarly, the participants in the debate in the First Congress over the constitutionality of the first national bank treated the issue as one with reasonable arguments on both sides that must be sifted and weighed to ascertain the most weighty.[101] As summarized by Christopher Wolfe, after he reviewed the bank debate: "It is the weight or emphasis on each of the different points and, above all, the evaluation of the cumulative impact of them that determined their judgments."[102]

Relatedly, if the best-available-evidence standard was *not* the correct standard, then there should be evidence from early practice of cases where judges decided

---

[97] Frederick Schauer, *Easy Cases*, 58 S. CAL. L. REV. 399 (1985).
[98] Ronald Dworkin, *Hard Cases*, 88 HARV. L. REV. 1057 (1975).
[99] *M'Culloch* v. *Maryland*, 17 U.S. (4 Wheat.) 316, 407–21 (1819).
[100] *Id.* at 401.
[101] 2 ANNALS 1940 (Feb. 1, 1791).
[102] CHRISTOPHER WOLFE, THE RISE OF MODERN JUDICIAL REVIEW: FROM CONSTITUTIONAL INTERPRETATION TO JUDGE-MADE LAW 32 (1986).

hard cases by indicating they were constructing constitutional meaning, which would indicate that the legal evidence was insufficient to provide a determinate constitutional meaning. To my knowledge, there is no such evidence.

More broadly, there is no evidence that the Constitution requires a different standard of evidence. There is nothing in the text or structure that suggests that judges should not choose that interpretation which is most likely correct.

A key facet of our legal system that makes these best-available-evidence determinations relatively easy for judges is that judges are faced with binary interpretive choices.[103] Each party will present an interpretation of the Constitution that supports its position and is supported by legal evidence in favor of its interpretation. For example, in *United States* v. *Morrison*, the United States and Christy Brzonkala argued that the Commerce Clause authorized Congress to regulate intrastate activities, including sexual assault, that substantially affected interstate commerce, while the respondents argued that the Clause did not because the regulated activity, sexual assault, was non-economic.[104] This binary interpretive choice facing the justices asked them to decide: of the two proffered constitutional interpretations, which is supported by the best available evidence? The Supreme Court was not asked to answer the much more difficult question of what the Commerce Clause *in toto* authorized Congress to regulate.

Originalist Closure Rules 2 and 3, described in the following text, are specifications of Rule 1. They identify, in two particular contexts, which party bears the burden of proof supporting its interpretation.

2.3.3.1.2 ORIGINALIST CLOSURE RULE 2: THE FEDERAL POWER BURDEN OF PROOF The second originalist closure rule is: if the interpretive question is one of *federal* power, then the party *supporting* federal power bears the burden of proof.[105] This rules requires a federal judge to adopt an interpretation of the Constitution that supports the exercise of federal governmental power only when the proponent of that interpretation establishes that the legal evidence supporting that interpretation is greater than the evidence against it. In practice, this means that, if the Constitution's original meaning is underdetermined, the proponent of federal power loses.

Imagine judges who are asked to identify the original meaning of the Commerce Clause as a justification for a constitutionally challenged federal statute.[106] One party, the United States, argues that the Commerce Clause's meaning authorized the congressional regulation and provides legal evidence that its interpretation of the

---

[103] Richard S. Kay, *Adherence to the Original Intentions in Constitutional Adjudication: Three Objections and Responses*, 82 Nw. U. L. Rev. 226, 233–34 (1988).

[104] Brief of Petition Christy Bronzkala 26–28, *and* Brief for Respondent Antonio J. Morrison 14, *United States* v. *Morrison*, 529 U.S. 598 (2000).

[105] Lawson, *supra* note 84, at 426.

[106] This is a stylized treatment of *NFIB* v. *Sebelius*, 567 U.S. 519 (2012).

Clause is accurate. It argues, among other things, that the original conventional meaning of "Commerce" was social intercourse.[107] The challenging party offers legal evidence that the Clause's meaning is narrower and does not authorize the regulation. It may utilize a textual argument to show that a congressional regulation of commerce must apply to pre-existing commercial activity in the same manner that congressional regulation of the value of money is distinct from its power to "Coin money."[108] The judges would evaluate the two proffered interpretations and reject the United States' interpretation if its legal evidence failed to show that its interpretation was better than the alternative.

This rule is constitutionally required by the structural constitutional principle of limited and enumerated powers. This principle is that the federal government possess only the powers enumerated to it in the Constitution. There is widespread agreement that there is a constitutional principle that the federal government is one of limited and enumerated powers.[109] This principle is evidenced by the Constitution in many ways. For instance, Article I, § 1, cl. 1., states that Congress has only the powers "herein granted,"[110] Article I, § 8, enumerates Congress' powers,[111] and both Articles II and III each delegate a power to the executive and judicial branches, respectively.[112] Putting to one side its substantive breadth, the mere existence of the principle requires that proponents of the exercise of federal power support that proposition with legal evidence.

Unlike state governments which, in our constitutional system, presumptively possess the police power to act, the federal government presumptively lacks power to act. Instead, any federal government act must be justified by reference to an enumerated power. That justification at least must come in the form of greater legal evidence than the alternative interpretation.

Any different allocation of the burden of proof would result in exercises of federal power without epistemically-warranted belief that the Constitution authorized those exercises. For instance, if a proponent of federal power could succeed even if the opponent's evidence was more powerful, that different allocation would undermine the principle of limited and enumerated powers.

---

[107] Jack M. Balkin, *Commerce*, 109 MICH. L. REV. 1 (2010).

[108] U.S. CONST. art. I, § 8, cl. 5.

[109] *See NFIB v. Sebelius*, 567 U.S. 519, 533 (2012) ("In our federal system, the National Government possesses only limited powers."); *M'Culloch v. Maryland*, 17 U.S. (4 Wheat.) 316, 405 (1819) ("This government is acknowledged by all, to be one of enumerated powers. The principle, that it can exercise only the powers granted to it, would seem too apparent, to have required to be enforced by all those arguments, which its enlightened friends, while it was depending before the people, found it necessary to urge; that principle is now universally admitted."); *compare* Richard Primus, *The Limits of Enumeration*, 124 YALE L.J. 576 (2014).

[110] U.S. CONST. Art. I, § 1, cl. 1.

[111] *Id.* art. I, § 8.

[112] *Id.* art. II, § 1, cl. 1.; *id.*, art. III, § 1.

2.3.3.1.3 ORIGINALIST CLOSURE RULE 3: THE STATE POWER BURDEN OF PROOF The third closure rule is: if the interpretive issue is over *state* power, then the party claiming that the Constitution *preempts* state action through a constitutional limit bears the burden of proof.[113] This requires that a judge adopt an interpretation of the Constitution that limits the exercise of state governmental power only when the proponent of such an interpretation supports it by more evidence than the other party. In practice, this means that, if the Constitution's original meaning is underdetermined, the proponent of restricting state power loses.

Imagine a judge who is asked to identify the original meaning of the Establishment Clause in a constitutional challenge to a Ten Commandments display.[114] The opponent of state power would provide interpretive evidence that the Constitution limited the challenged exercise of state power. The opponent could point to historical evidence that government officials contemporary with the Clause's ratification refused to issue official religious declarations.[115] The proponent of the state's capacity to erect the display would point to other contemporary official public religious statements.[116] The judge would evaluate the two proffered interpretations and reject the state power opponent's interpretation if its legal evidence failed to show that its interpretation was better than the alternative.

This rule is constitutionally required by the structural principle of federalism. Federalism is the division of power between the federal and state governments. Like other structural constitutional principles, there is widespread agreement that the principle of federalism exists.[117] The Constitution evidences this structural principle in many ways. For example, the enumeration of limited powers for the federal government implies the existence of (unenumerated) powers residing elsewhere, because otherwise many important legal subjects – such as contract, tort, and property – would be without a source of legislation. This implication is made explicit by the Tenth Amendment: "The powers not delegated to the United States by the Constitution, nor prohibited by it to the States, are reserved to the States respectively."[118] The Constitution also protects state integrity[119] and autonomy,[120] and specifies numerous important roles for states in the federal government.[121]

Assigning the burden of proof to the opponent of state power is necessary to preserve federalism because, without that assignment, state power would be limited by an epistemically underdetermined warrant in the Constitution. Without this

---

[113] Lawson, *supra* note 84, at 427–28.

[114] This example is based on *McCreary County* v. *ACLU*, 545 U.S. 844 (2005).

[115] *Id.* at 876–80.

[116] *Id.* at 885–89 (Scalia, J., dissenting).

[117] *See Texas* v. *White*, 74 U.S. 700, 725 (1868) ("The Constitution, in all its provisions, looks to an indestructible Union, composed of indestructible States.").

[118] U.S. CONST. amend. X.

[119] *Id.* art. IV, § 3 (protecting a state's territorial integrity).

[120] *Id.* art. V (protecting states from changes to the Constitution without their consent).

[121] *E.g., id.* art. II, § 1, cl. 2.

assignment of the burden, a judge might apply a constitutional limit on states when, in fact, the best-available legal evidence shows that the state should not be limited. There is no principled limit to the extent to which this could occur, once the burden of proof is removed from the proponent of state restriction.

2.3.3.1.4 CONCLUSION Adoption of these closure rules will limit construction by reducing epistemic underdeterminacy. However, the widespread use of closure rules in the legal system coexists with continuing stubborn underdeterminacy, and the same occurs in constitutional interpretation. In those cases where it is clear that the original meaning is underdetermined, even after application of the closure rules, then construction continues to operate.

2.3.3.2 Constitutional Construction Occurs (Only) When the Constitution's Original Meaning Is Epistemically Underdetermined

Almost all originalists agree that the Constitution's original meaning is underdetermined, though they disagree about the relative quantity of construction, a disagreement which, in turn, is driven by different conceptions of construction and original meaning. For instance, the most robust conception of construction is advanced by Professor Balkin, and this follows from his thin conception of original meaning.[122] In this subsection, I argue for a modest conception of construction because, on my account, the Constitution's original meaning is *metaphysically* determined because of the original rules of interpretation identified by Professors McGinnis and Rappaport. However, I also argue that *epistemic* underdeterminacy continues to exist so that constitutional construction will continue to exist when the Constitution's original meaning is epistemically underdetermined.

The first step in my argument is to step back and think about the relative determinacy of areas of human endeavor analogous to constitutional interpretation. One such area is ethics. Like law, it is normative – reason-giving – and it includes application of norms to concrete situations, and fully developed systems of ethics therefore produce doctrines, arguments, precedents, and hard cases. Ethics involves indeterminacy. In fact, one of the challenges to living a principled life is how difficult it is to know, in some situations, what the correct thing to do actually is.

For example, the Aristotelian philosophical tradition includes virtue ethics, one of whose roles in the tradition is to identify how humans resolve difficult ethical situations. Virtue ethics' answer is that a person must have the appropriate character, because ethical indeterminacy is so pervasive that no plausible ethical system can provide a decision-algorithm of rules that will eliminate it. Instead, in areas where the tradition's natural law norms do not determine a course of action, the tradition

---

[122] Jack M. Balkin, Living Originalism 12–13 (2011).

directs a person to utilize his virtue-guided prudential judgment and decide on a course of conduct.

A second such area is language. It is a common occurrence for people in a conversation to misunderstand each other. "Pardon me? Could you say that again?" And the first speaker will restate and clarify with different words what the speaker meant ("What I meant was ..."). It is even more common for people in a textual conversation to misunderstand each other. Think of the widespread use of emoticons to add information to email text to reduce miscommunication and how difficult it is to use irony via email.

Law itself, most scholars agree, contains moderate indeterminacy, also known as underdeterminacy,[123] though there is significant disagreement over how much. Professor Ken Kress expressed the general consensus: "[T]he indeterminacy of the law is no more than moderate."[124] This underdeterminacy manifests itself in many ways, and it is so persistent a phenomenon that our legal system has developed mechanisms to reduce and eliminate underdeterminacy. One example is how our appellate system is structured to present discrete, binary questions to courts of appeals instead of, for instance, the more abstract and difficult question of what interpretation of a contract is the best, all things considered. The appellate court does not say what is the best interpretation of the contract; the court decides which party's interpretation is better. A widespread example of such indeterminacy-reducing mechanisms is our legal system's use of closure rules, which I described in Subsection 2.3.2.

This brief survey of three areas of human endeavor related to constitutional interpretation suggests that we should expect some level of underdeterminacy within constitutional interpretation, unless there are strong reasons for distinguishing constitutional interpretation from other, similar forms of human activity. Professors McGinnis and Rappaport have provided the strongest such argument, which I discuss in the following text. First, I will explain the theoretical reasons why originalist constitutional interpretation contains modest underdeterminacy.

Originalist underdeterminacy might exist in two ways. First, originalist underdeterminacy may exist because of metaphysical underdeterminacy of the Constitution's original meaning. Second, it may exist because of epistemic underdeterminacy. I first explain both concepts abstractly, and then describe more concretely how they apply to originalism.

The distinction between metaphysical and epistemic legal determinacy is, respectively, between whether the law is in fact determinate, and whether participants in our legal practice can ascertain whether the law is determinate.[125] The law

---

[123] Kress, *supra* note 73, at 283; Solum, *supra* note 73, at 503.

[124] Kress, *supra* note 73, at 283.

[125] The best introduction in the law review literature on this distinction remains Ken Kress, *A Preface to Epistemic Indeterminacy*, 85 Nw. U. L. Rev. 134 (1990). I do not address the question of who or what is the relevant standard for determining epistemic determinacy and

is metaphysically determinate when there is one right answer to a legal question. This is true even if participants in our legal practice are unable to ascertain what the law is (that is, the law is epistemically indeterminate).

The law is epistemically determinate when the law is metaphysically determinate and participants in our legal practice can ascertain that the law is determinate.[126] Our legal practice, which aspires toward liberal legality and hence law-governed human activity, aims toward epistemic determinacy.[127] There is a consensus, however, that it does not achieve that goal, at least not always.

The law is epistemically indeterminate when, despite its metaphysical determinacy, participants in our legal practice cannot ascertain the law's content. Stated differently, in some cases, even though there is "one right answer," legal actors cannot discover that answer. Part of the reason for this inability to access the law's determinate content is the limitations imposed by the human condition. Unlike Hercules, legal actors do not have – to pick just one limitation as an example – unlimited time to devote to ascertaining the law's content.

A second reason humans lack the capacity to fully identify the law's metaphysically-determinate content is that law is a practical endeavor. Unlike intellectual investigations that require theoretical reason, which have the goal of certain-truth, practical inquiries often do not offer certainty.[128] Instead, using practical reason, the goal is to determine which course of action is (most likely) correct.

Both the articulation of the Constitution's original meaning and how it governs a particular case will be more or less difficult depending on the subject. It is sometimes clear what the governing original meaning norm is and how it governs a particular case. For example, the original meaning of the Commerce Clause is fairly clear,[129] and its prescription in the case of whether Congress can regulate the railroad transportation of commercial goods from New York to Illinois is also relatively clear.[130] In many other situations, however, things are less clear. And, of course, one of the two processes – *articulating* the original meaning or *applying* that norm – may be clear while the other is less so.

The Constitution's original meaning may be underdetermined in at least four situations: (1) vagueness; (2) ambiguity; (3) gaps; and (4) contradictions.[131] The Constitution's original meaning is vague when it does not clearly cover or not cover

instead use the capacious phrase, "participants in our legal practice," to avoid the issue. I also elide the question of what level of consensus among participants is necessary to qualify for determinacy.

[126] The law can also be epistemically determinate and metaphysically indeterminate. Stated differently, participants in our legal practice know that there is no right answer.

[127] BURTON, *supra* note 94, at 10–11.

[128] NE, at 1109b, 19–23; ST. THOMAS AQUINAS, COMMENTARY ON BOETHIUS' DE TRINITATE AND THE UNICITY OF THE INTELLECT, q. 5, a.1.

[129] BARNETT, *supra* note 70, at 313–15.

[130] *United States* v. *Lopez*, 514 U.S. 549, 552–53, 558 (1995).

[131] Solum, *supra* note 4, at 285.

a particular situation; when there are borderline cases. An instance of where the Constitution's original meaning is likely vague, because of new technology, is whether the Commerce Clause permits Congress to regulate interstate commercial transactions on the Internet. It seems unclear whether the electrons crossing state lines on the Internet,[132] or perhaps the information conveyed by the packages of electrons,[133] constitute "trade or exchange of goods" or "the means of transporting them."[134]

Irreducible ambiguity is where a word or phrase has more than one meaning and where the context will not resolve the ambiguity. Typically, context can clear up ambiguity. For example, the Second Amendment's reference to "Arms" would, without context, be ambiguous. It could have meant either guns or human appendages. Irreducible ambiguity is relatively rare in the Constitution because of the care taken by the Framers when drafting it, along with the relatively thick public context. A possible though unlikely example of irreducible ambiguity, is the Constitution's use of "person" in likely reference to slaves.[135]

Gaps in constitutional meaning are where the Constitution addressed a subject generally but failed to include information necessary to fully address the subject. A possible example of a gap in the Constitution's original meaning is the President's removal power. Article II of the Constitution articulates the procedures for appointment of federal officers, but it does not patently, at least not other than through impeachment, identify how they shall be removed. This gap has existed from when the First Congress debated the issue.

Conflicts are where the Constitution's original meaning provided conflicting information. A possible example of a conflict is between the Recess Appointment Clause and Article III's requirements of life tenure and salary protection. The Recess Appointment Clause authorizes the President to appoint officers during Senate recesses, while Article III prevents removal of federal judicial officers. Like gaps, conflicts are also relatively rare.

The Constitution's original meaning could be metaphysically or epistemically underdetermined in each of these four situations. This occurs when vagueness, ambiguity, gaps, or contradictions exist in the original meaning, *or* when interpreters cannot ascertain the original meaning and, instead, perceive one or more of those four situations as occurring. For example, though the Ninth Amendment's original meaning may be metaphysically determinate, it was epistemically indeterminate for

---

[132] *See Fed. Energy Regulatory Comm'n v. Mississippi*, 456 U.S. 742, 757 (1982).

[133] *See FCC v. League of Women Voters*, 468 U.S. 364, 376 (1984).

[134] BARNETT, *supra* note 70, at 315; *compare Adair v. United States*, 208 U.S. 161, 177 (1908) (summarizing the Supreme Court's then-contemporaneous understanding of Congress' Commerce Clause power as including the power to regulate "the transmission of messages by telegraph").

[135] U.S. CONST. art. I, § 2, cl. 3; § 9, cl. 1; Barnett, *supra* note 18, at 615, 648–50.

most of its history because an imperfect historical record prevented our legal practice from accurately accessing the original meaning.[136]

It is an empirical question how frequently originalist underdeterminacy exists. To fully evaluate its scope, one would have to work through the Constitution's text to ascertain when a particular text's meaning is underdetermined.

Up to this point I have argued that, conceptually, the Constitution's original meaning may be metaphysically or epistemically underdetermined. This underdeterminacy opens the possibility of analytical space for constitutional construction by creating a construction zone within which interpreters must construct constitutional doctrine. Next, I argue that the original rules of interpretation at the time of the Framing and Ratification create metaphysical determinacy. At the same time, they do *not* eliminate epistemic underdeterminacy. This move – adding the rules of interpretation – reduces, but does not eliminate, the space for constitutional construction.

Professors John McGinnis and Michael Rappaport have published the most robust arguments against constitutional construction (from an originalist perspective).[137] They argued that constitutional construction does not exist because originalist underdeterminacy does not exist. The Constitution's original meaning is determinate, they claimed, because of closure rules. "[T]he original meaning need not run out when constitutional language is ambiguous or vague [because] ... interpretive rules can provide a resolution to that ambiguity or vagueness."[138] In particular, they identified two closure rules that reduce or eliminate underdeterminacy: (1) the interpreter must choose the interpretation that is better than alternative interpretations[139]; and (2) if there is an area of original underdeterminacy, the legislature has some authority to authoritatively construct constitutional meaning.[140] Professors McGinnis and Rappaport then argued that these closure rules were part of the Constitution's original meaning because they were the rules of interpretation in use at the time – what they call the original methods.[141]

Professors McGinnis and Rappaport's solution to originalist underdeterminacy is powerful, and it has the theoretical potential to significantly reduce or even eliminate originalist underdeterminacy. It would do so, though, in a particular way, as I understand originalism. Professors McGinnis and Rappaport's use of original methods as closure rules transforms what are typically epistemic-underdeterminacy-reducing rules into metaphysical-underdeterminacy-reducing rules. By that, I mean,

---

[136] Kurt T. Lash, The Lost History of the Ninth Amendment xiv–xv (2009).

[137] McGinnis & Rappaport, supra note 43, at 139–53; *see also* McGinnis & Rappaport, *supra* note 8, at 1321.

[138] McGinnis & Rappaport, *supra* note 43, at 140.

[139] *Id.* at 141.

[140] *Id.* at 143–44. McGinnis and Rappaport appear less certain both of this rule's existence and its scope.

[141] *Id.* at 142–43.

we typically think of closure rules as taking what is otherwise (metaphysically) under-determined and making it (epistemically) determinate. That is how I presented closure rules in my earlier discussion of indeterminacy in the legal system generally. Closure rules take what is metaphysically indeterminate and, for purposes of the legal system – for example, to facilitate the Rule of Law, or to provide more-than-adequate notice of the criminal law's proscriptions – create epistemic determinacy. This also occurs in ethics. If a person is facing a difficult choice, one in which the correct course of action is not clear, a common response is to "take the path most likely to cause the least harm."[142] This rule of thumb does not make the ethical choice determinate; instead, it acknowledges the ethical indeterminacy and utilizes the closure rule to create epistemic determinacy.

Professors McGinnis and Rappaport treat the closure rules as *metaphysical-underdeterminacy-reducing* rules by arguing that the closure rules were part of the Constitution's text's *context*. "If the Constitution were written with the assumption that these interpretive rules would be applied," they argued, "then the resolutions of ambiguity and vagueness that these rules effect would be properly deemed part of the original meaning."[143] The Framers when drafting and the Ratifiers when authorizing the Constitution's text relied on the contemporaneous rules of interpretation to understand the text. These rules of interpretation, what Professors McGinnis and Rappaport call the original methods, were an important part of the Constitution's context. As I described in Subsection 1.4.3, contextual enrichment is the information that context provides to textual communication, and it may result in the context modifying the text's semantic meaning. This modified semantic meaning is the text's communicative content, and it *is* the original meaning. Therefore, following Professors McGinnis and Rappaport's argument, the original methods made the original meaning more (or even fully) metaphysically determinate.

This potentially powerful conclusion depends on the existence, use, and lexical ordering of the original methods by the Framers and Ratifiers. These are empirical and historical questions, and they have yet to receive full answers. Professors McGinnis and Rappaport,[144] and others, including Christopher Wolfe[145] and Jonathan O'Neill,[146] have provided evidence supporting the existence and usage of the original methods by the Framers and Ratifiers. The legal culture contemporaneous with the Framing and Ratification was originalist. For example, Blackstone's *Commentaries* contained a list of interpretive rules.[147] Some of these interpretive rules appear in the Constitution itself. For example, the Ninth Amendment instructs

---

[142] Albert R. Jonsen & Stephen Toulmin, The Abuse of Casuistry: A History of Moral Reasoning 8, 73–74, 118, 252–53 (1989).
[143] McGinnis & Rappaport, *supra* note 43, at 141.
[144] McGinnis & Rappaport, *supra* note 8, at 1355–1400.
[145] Wolfe, *supra* note 102, at 17–89.
[146] Johnathan O'Neill, Originalism in American Law and Politics 12–20 (2005).
[147] I William Blackstone, Commentaries on the Laws of England *59–*62 (1769).

interpreters to construe delegated federal power narrowly.[148] However, as McGinnis and Rappaport acknowledge, their evidence for the original methods' existence and usage, at least at this point in their research, is not fully explained.[149]

Evidence on the lexical ordering of the original methods is also important and needed because, if the original methods are merely a grab bag of rules, the choice of which rule to utilize first, then second, etc., will affect the outcome of the interpretive enterprise.[150] If one interpreter initially utilizes method [1], while another employs method [5], they will reach inconsistent results. Furthermore, if different interpreters ascribe different weights to the methods, they will reach inconsistent results.

In short, the current evidence does not identify how widespread the use of interpretive rules was, the uniformity of the rules, their weight, nor the lexical ordering of the rules. However, even when more robust evidence of the original methods comes to light, and (by hypothesis) it supports Professors McGinnis and Rappaport's claims, then that will have established (only) that the Constitution's original meaning was *metaphysically* determinate.

Even if or when the use and lexical order of interpretive closure rules are established, that will not address whether the metaphysically-determinate original meaning is *epistemically* determinate. Recall from my previous discussion that epistemic determinacy is distinct from metaphysical determinacy. The existence of one does not guarantee the other. Because the original methods are facets of the original meaning's context, they have the capacity to make that original meaning metaphysically determinate; they do not necessarily make that meaning epistemically determinate.

Therefore, even embracing Professors McGinnis and Rappaport's original methods, as I did in Section 2.2, it is likely that the Constitution's original meaning will remain epistemically underdetermined, and for three main reasons. First, both the original meaning (understood as semantic meaning modified by contextual enrichment) and the original methods (understood as part of the publicly available context) require the use of information, some of which may not be fully available. If this information is lacking – either temporarily or permanently – then the original methods will have insufficient information to operate effectively. For instance, we currently do not have adequate information to be confident that we know all of the original methods and the order in which they apply.

Second, original meaning and original methods require the exercise of human judgment, which will fail, on occasion. Questions of interpretation will present themselves that, even after application of the original methods, remain unclear. For instance, Professors McGinnis and Rappaport's proffered closure rule – choose the

---

[148] McGINNIS & RAPPAPORT, *supra* note 43, at 126–27.
[149] *Id.* at 117, 129, 133.
[150] Larry Alexander, *Telepathic Law*, 27 CONST. COMMENT. 139, 146–47 (2010).

interpretation with the "stronger evidence in its favor"[151] – will be applied in situations in which an interpreter does not know which interpretation has the stronger evidence. One reasonable interpreter may believe that Interpretation 1 has more robust evidentiary support than Interpretation 2, but another interpreter may reasonably disagree.

Or, the case may be "too close to call," so that the interpreter just does not know which interpretation is favored by "stronger evidence." This situation does not encompass just those cases where the evidence for respective interpretations is 49 percent versus 51 percent. Human judgment is not so fine. Instead and in addition, the evidence will be such that the interpreter may have a difficult time even knowing how to designate the relative weight of the evidence for different interpretations. Is it 53 percent versus 47 percent, or 55 percent to 45 percent? Along these same lines, an interpreter may tentatively believe that the evidence is 60 percent versus 40 percent, but may lack confidence in that judgment.

Third, the original methods themselves may cause epistemic underdeterminacy. Even though we are assuming for the sake of argument that it is clear what the original methods are and how they are ordered, epistemic underdeterminacy will arise because of the interaction of the individual and groupings of methods. The methods may push in different directions, leading an interpreter to a situation where methods 1 and 5, push for interpretation A, while methods 2, 3, and 4 push for interpretation B. It may not be clear to the interpreter how the combinations of and interactions between methods and groups of methods cash out, causing epistemic indeterminacy.[152]

There is strong historical evidence to support the continued existence of epistemic underdeterminacy despite the assumed operation of the original methods during and after the period of the Framing and Ratification. During the Framing and Ratification debates, one operative assumption of participants on all sides of the various debates was that the Constitution would not – could not – eliminate all underdeterminacy. This occurred during the Philadelphia Convention in a number of ways. One, more general manifestation of this assumption, was the care with which the Framers discussed the fine details of the proposed constitution with the goal to reduce underdeterminacy.[153] For example, during the debates over what became the Article I, § 8, cl. 1, taxing power regarding duties and imposts, the delegates raised the potential lack of clarity.[154]

This expectation by both sides of the debate – that the Constitution would retain ineliminable underdeterminacy – also occurred during the Ratification debates.

[151] McGinnis & Rappaport, *supra* note 43, at 142.
[152] *Compare* Burton, *supra* note 94, at 50–51, 54–62.
[153] Philip A. Hamburger, *The Constitution's Accommodation of Social Change*, 88 Mich. L. Rev. 239, 306 (1989).
[154] James Madison, Notes of Debates in the Federal Convention of 1787, at 466–69 (Aug. 16, 1787).

There, the Constitution's opponents argued that the Constitution's underdeterminacy would permit federal aggrandizement at the expense of the states.[155] For example, Brutus argued that Article III's grant of judicial power to future federal judges was vague, and that it therefore empowered them to utilize an equitable interpretation of the Constitution's delegation of powers to the federal government at the states' expense.[156]

The Federalists responded in two ways. First, they tried to minimize the scope of purported indeterminacy. For instance, James Madison argued that the Constitution was drafted as clearly as possible.[157] Second, the Federalists acknowledged that the Constitution was underdeterminate. Madison stated that "no language is so copious as to supply words and phrases for every complex idea, or so correct as not to include many equivocally denoting different ideas."[158] However, whatever underdeterminacy that remained would be subsequently "liquidated" or fixed through interpretive practice. Madison argued that parts of the Constitution must be "considered as more or less obscure and equivocal, until their meaning be liquidated and ascertained by a series of particular discussions and adjudications."[159] This acknowledgement by the Federalists is evidence that the Framers and Ratifiers believed – despite the original methods existence and utilization – that the methods were by themselves insufficient to eliminate underdeterminacy. Historical episodes in the early Republic bear this out.

Two controversies in the First Congress showed that the Constitution's original meaning, despite the existence and use of the original methods, did not eliminate underdeterminacy:[160] first, presidential removal of executive officials, and second, the national bank question. The Constitution did not, at least expressly, identify a presidential power to remove federal officers. It identified Congress' power to impeach officers,[161] and stated that " . . . all civil Officers of the United States, shall be removed from Office on Impeachment,"[162] which suggests that impeachment was the sole mechanism of removal. One potential – though not patent – source of a presidential removal power was the grant of "executive Power."[163] The members of the First Congress engaged in a thoughtful and thorough discussion over whether the President possessed the "executive Power" to unilaterally remove federal officers.[164] The members used the standard tools of interpretation and ultimately arrived

---

[155] Hamburger, *supra* note 153, at 307.
[156] THE ESSAYS OF BRUTUS NO. XI, *in* 2 THE COMPLETE ANTI-FEDERALIST 419–20 (Herbert J. Storing ed., 1981).
[157] THE FEDERALIST NO. 37 (James Madison).
[158] *Id.*
[159] *Id.*
[160] Unless one argues that these, and other controversies were the result of bad faith, which is implausible.
[161] U.S. CONST. art. I, § 2, cl. 5; *id.* art. I, § 3, cl. 6.
[162] *Id.* art. II, § 4.
[163] *Id.* art. II, § 1, cl. 1.
[164] 1 ANNALS 474–608 (1789) (Joseph Gales ed., 1834).

at what is called The Decision of 1789.[165] However, the length of the debate,[166] the robust arguments employed by the various sides in the debate, the non-unanimous result, and the continued uncertainty regarding the scope of the President's removal power[167] suggest that the original methods did not resolve epistemic underdeterminacy.

Second, the dispute over whether Congress had the authority under the Necessary and Property Clause to charter a national bank exercised Americans more than any other constitutional question in the early Republic.[168] The key point for our purposes is that intelligent Americans, in good faith, made reasonable arguments for and against the power, using the original methods. James Madison opposed the bank in Congress on constitutional grounds using the Blackstonian rules of interpretation.[169] Similarly, those who supported the bank, like Alexander Hamilton, also used rules of interpretation.[170] The parties to the debate did not dispute the other parties' use of rules of interpretation; instead, they disagreed on the import of those rules.[171] This suggests that the original methods did not eliminate epistemic underdeterminacy.

Up to this point I have argued that, though the original methods may eliminate metaphysical underdeterminacy, they do not eliminate epistemic underdeterminacy. Here, let me briefly note why epistemic underdeterminacy may occur at each of the three analytically distinct stages of originalist constitutional interpretation. The first step of originalist interpretation is identifying the text's original conventional meaning. For most of originalism's modern history, and still to a large degree today, this step in originalist interpretation required a scholar or judge to review a large body of documents contemporary with the constitutional text's ratification, to identify uses of the word or phrase in question and to ascertain from the word or phrase's repeated usage in different contexts, whether there was an original conventional meaning and what that conventional meaning was. This process was time-consuming, detail-oriented, and subject to error of the researchers and/or limited data. For example, an interpreter working to uncover an original language convention may utilize a stable of conventions that does not include the actual convention. The actual language convention existed; the interpreter failed to evaluate the evidence to ascertain whether the correct convention fit the historical data.

---

[165] David P. Currie, The Constitution in Congress: The Federalist Period 1789–1801, at 40–43 (1997); Saikrishna Prakash, *New Light on the Decision of 1789*, 91 Cornell L. Rev. 1021, 1029–34 (2006).

[166] The debate lasted over a month.

[167] Patricia L. Bellia, *PCAOB and the Persistence of the Removal Puzzle*, 80 Geo. W. L. Rev. 1371, 1378 (2012).

[168] Daniel A. Farber, *The Story of* McCulloch: *Banking on National Power, in* Constitutional Law Stories 33 (Michael C. Dorf ed., 2009).

[169] 2 Annals 1944 (James Madison) (Feb. 2, 1791); Wolfe, *supra* note 102, at 25–27.

[170] Wolfe, *supra* note 102, at 28–32.

[171] *Id.* at 31.

The second step in originalist constitutional interpretation is ascertaining the text's semantic meaning. This requires an interpreter to place the text's conventional meaning in the context of the clause, sentence, article, and entire document, and to apply the rules of grammar and syntax to the text. This too is subject to epistemic underdeterminacy. For instance, there is scholarly debate on the meaning of the Constitution because of the punctuation utilized.[172]

The third step in originalist interpretation is contextual enrichment. Contextual enrichment takes the publicly available information related to and contemporaneous with the text's semantic meaning and uses it to elucidate the semantic meaning and to potentially modify that meaning. For example, part of the context available to the Framers, Ratifiers, and other Americans, was common legal rules of interpretation. Contextual enrichment may place relatively significant burdens on an interpreter's judgment. First, there is potentially a large amount of information an interpreter must master. Second, the interpreter must decide whether and, if so, how the context modified the text's semantic meaning.

In sum, because originalist interpretation requires skill and judgment, applied to a sometimes large and sometimes unruly data set, interpreters will occasionally fail, and the metaphysically determinate original meaning will go undiscovered. A possible example of this epistemic underdeterminacy in originalism is the Second Amendment. The Amendment's original meaning is metaphysically determinate on the point of an individual right to keep and bear arms.[173] From the perspective of judges prior to the early 1980s, however, there was little readily available evidence of the Second Amendment's original meaning. At this point, the Second Amendment's original meaning was metaphysically determinate and epistemically indeterminate on whether "the people" referred to individuals or a collective. Then, beginning with Don Kates' groundbreaking 1983 article, *Handgun Prohibition and the Original Meaning of the Second Amendment*,[174] a wealth of scholarship explored the Amendment's original meaning. This explosion of scholarship opened the evidentiary door to the Amendment's original meaning and made determinate what was once epistemically underdeterminate.

2.3.3.3 Construction Is Modest Because of Judicial Deference to Elected Officials' Constructions in the Construction Zone

In the prior two subsections, I argued that the quantity of underdeterminate original meaning – and hence the construction zone's scope – is relatively small because of

---

[172] *See, e.g.,* U.S. CONST. art. III, § 2, cl. 2 ("with such Exceptions, and under such regulations as the Congress shall make"); Robert N. Clinton, *A Mandatory View of Federal Court Jurisdiction: A Guided Quest for the Original Understanding of Article III*, 132 U. PA. L. REV. 741, 780 (1984).

[173] Randy E. Barnett & Don B. Kates, Jr., *Under Fire: The New Consensus on the Second Amendment*, 45 EMORY L.J. 1139, 1141 (1996).

[174] Don B. Kates, Jr., *Handgun Prohibition and the Original Meaning of the Second Amendment*, 82 MICH. L. REV. 204 (1983).

closure rules and the elimination of metaphysical underdeterminacy. Here, I advance the deference conception of constitutional construction. Under this conception, when the Constitution's original meaning is underdetermined, federal courts should defer to elected official constructions of the Constitution's meaning within those areas of constitutional underdeterminacy.[175]

Assume that the Commerce Clause's original meaning[176] does not determine the outcome of a case in which Congress' regulation of commercial interstate transactions conducted via the Internet is challenged.[177] In this case, Congress would have the authority to construct the Clause's meaning to either include or exclude regulation of the Internet. So, if the Supreme Court had previously constructed the Commerce Clause to exclude congressional regulation of some class of Internet transactions, a later – contrary – federal statute would control.

Currently, originalists diverge on which branch of the federal government has the authority to authoritatively construct the Constitution's meaning in the construction zone. They fall into two general camps: (1) federal courts should utilize their independent judgment to construct authoritative constitutional doctrine[178]; or (2) federal courts should defer, either presumptively or conclusively, to elected branch constructions.[179] The deference conception falls into the latter category.

The deference conception of construction is supported by at least three related reasons. First, the Constitution does not authorize federal judges to exercise judicial review in the construction zone. Second, Congress is the primary constitutionally-identified mechanism to pursue the common good. Third, Congress is more institutionally capable of pursuing the common good.

2.3.3.3.1 NO AUTHORITY FOR JUDICIAL REVIEW IN THE CONSTRUCTION ZONE   First, in the construction zone, federal judges should defer to elected branch constitutional constructions because the justification for constitutional judicial review is inapplicable and our constitutional social ordering provides that Congress has the authority to legislate for our society towards the common good (within its sphere of authority). Let me first describe the standard originalist justification for judicial review and then explain why Congress possesses such authority.

The standard originalist justification for constitutional judicial review is that the Constitution authorizes and requires federal courts to exercise this power as a

---

[175] The focus of my arguments is Congress. My arguments also apply to the President to the extent the President is faithfully executing the law or lawfully employing the President's constitutional powers. I have not evaluated how my arguments apply to state constructions.

[176] BARNETT, *supra* note 70, at 313.

[177] *Cf. Am. Libraries Ass'n v. Pataki*, 969 F. Supp. 160, 172–73 (S.D.N.Y. 1997) (ruling that the Internet was an instrumentality of commerce).

[178] BARNETT, *supra* note 70, at 122.

[179] KEITH E. WHITTINGTON, CONSTITUTIONAL INTERPRETATION 7, 9, 11 (1999); *but see* Keith E. Whittington, *Constructing a New American Constitution*, 27 CONST. COMMENT. 119, 125–29 (2010).

manifestation of federal judges' constitutionally-prescribed duty to say what the law is.[180] This originalist argument is a relatively uncomplicated application of one of our legal system's basic premises: the Constitution's legal prescriptions are our legal system's most authoritative norms. The originalist argument is that federal courts exercising the "judicial Power of the United States" must prefer the Constitution over other contrary sources of law in the exercise of that power: "If then the courts are to regard the constitution; and the constitution is superior to any ordinary act of the legislature; the constitution, and not such ordinary act, must govern the case to which they both apply."[181] Three sources of the Constitution's original meaning support this.

First, the original meaning of "judicial Power" in Article III is focally a case-deciding power.[182] The essence of federal court case-deciding is ascertaining what the law is and applying that law to the case before the court. The Supremacy Clause mandates that the Constitution is more authoritative than other laws.[183] Putting together these two propositions, originalists conclude that, in the performance of its case-deciding function, a federal court must privilege the Constitution over other law, including federal and state statutes and executive actions.[184] Alexander Hamilton summarized this conclusion:

> The interpretation of the laws is the proper and peculiar province of the courts. A constitution is in fact, and must be, regarded by the judges as a fundamental law. It therefore belongs to them to ascertain its meaning as well as the meaning of any particular act proceeding from the legislative body. If there should happen to be an irreconcilable variance between the two, that which has the superior obligation and validity ought of course to be preferred.[185]

Second, originalists argue that the related constitutional principles of separation of powers and checks and balances require judicial review. First, the principle of checks and balances describes how each branch of the federal government checks the others and therefore limits concentrations of governmental power and preserves liberty. This principle's functionality requires that each branch of the federal government have tools to check the other branches.[186] The judiciary's primary means to do so is constitutional judicial review. Second, the principle of separation of powers describes how the Constitution delegated to each branch of government a separate type of government power and authorized each branch to utilize only that

---

[180] Philip Hamburger, Law and Judicial Duty 2,17–18 (2008).

[181] *Marbury v. Madison*, 5 U.S. (1 Cranch) 137, 178 (1803).

[182] Hamburger, *supra* note 180, at 587–605; Gary Lawson, *The Constitutional Case Against Precedent*, 17 Harv. J. L. & Pub. Pol'y 23, 29–30 (1994).

[183] U.S. Const. art. VI, cl. 2.

[184] Saikrishan B. Prakash & John C. Yoo, *The Origins of Judicial Review*, 70 U. Chi. L. Rev. 887 (2003).

[185] The Federalist No. 78 (Alexander Hamilton).

[186] The Federalist No. 51 (James Madison).

branch's power.[187] Constitutional judicial review is both a manifestation of this principle and a premise. Judicial review is a manifestation of the principle because, as I argued previously, the power exercised by federal judges, coupled with the Supremacy Clause, results in judicial review. Judicial review is also a premise because, without judicial review, federal judges would not be able to exercise fully the type of power allocated to the federal judiciary. In an important subset of federal court cases, federal judges would not be able to properly decide what the applicable law is – a core function of judicial power.

Third, constitutional judicial review is also supported by the concept of popular sovereignty. Popular sovereignty is the idea that the American People are the ultimate political authority in the United States. The American People authorized the Constitution and made it the ultimate legal authority in the country.[188] Judicial review is a mechanism to prevent non-sovereigns, such as Congress, from displacing the American People's constitutional judgments. This was Alexander Hamilton's argument for judicial review in *Federalist 78*. The Supreme Court protects the American People's sovereign judgment when it privileges the Constitution over inconsistent laws. "It only supposes that the power of the people is superior to both; and that where the will of the legislature declared in its statutes, stands in opposition to that of the people declared in the constitution, the judges ought to be governed by the latter."[189]

At the same time that the Constitution authorizes judicial review, the Constitution also delegates powers to Congress via Article I, Section 8, to superintend the national common good.[190] This goal was identified by James Madison in *Federalist 10*, where he argued that the federal legislature was structured in such a way as to help it identify "the permanent and aggregate interests of the community."[191] Chief Justice Marshall's justification for judicial review rested on a similar premise: "the people have an original right to establish, for their future government, such principles as, in their opinion, shall most conduce to their own happiness, is the basis on which the whole American fabric has been erected."[192] Later, Justice Story reiterated the Constitution's orientation toward "the common good" in his *Commentaries on the Constitution of the United States*.[193]

Tying together these two moves: The only warrant possessed by the federal judiciary to override Congress' judgment about how to exercise its delegated powers – about how best to pursue the common good – is the Constitution itself.

---

[187] The Federalist Nos. 48, 49 (James Madison).

[188] U.S. Const. pmbl; *id.* art. VI, cl. 2; *McCulloch v. Maryland*, 17 U.S. (4 Wheat.) 316, 403–04, 405–06 (1819).

[189] The Federalist No. 78 (Alexander Hamilton).

[190] U.S. Const. pmbl. ("general Welfare").

[191] The Federalist No. 10 (James Madison).

[192] *Marbury v. Madison*, 5 U.S. (1 Cranch) 137, 176 (1803).

[193] 1 Joseph Story, Commentaries on the Constitution of the United States § 325, 325 n. 2 (1987 ed.) (1858).

The Constitution commands federal courts, while engaged in their case-deciding function, to prefer the Constitution over congressional action inconsistent with the Constitution. Beyond that constitutional mandate, federal courts possess no constitutional authority to second-guess Congress' judgments about how best to pursue the common good through the (by hypothesis) constitutional exercise of its enumerated powers. *local courts should also adhere to this*

Therefore, when the Constitution's original meaning is underdetermined, federal courts have no authority to second-guess congressional actions. The federal judiciary's only authority is that given it by the Constitution and, by definition, if the original meaning of the Constitution has been exhausted, there is no determinate answer to a question. In its case-deciding function then, Congress' determination of what the common good requires – its construction – prevails because there is nothing in the Constitution that is superior to and inconsistent with it.

There is no natural law norm that authorizes American federal judges, exercising only the power delegated to them via Article III, Section 1, to reject Congress' actions. The natural law is typically not sufficiently specific to identify how American federal judges should rule in a particular case. For example, there is no particularized natural law norm directing Congress to enact (or not enact) specific laws governing the delivery of healthcare. Instead, and as I explain further in Subsection 4.4.3, the natural law is underdetermined on many practical issues. Furthermore, the natural law does not authorize judges to overrule legislative action. The question of judicial power generally, and of American judicial power in particular, is itself underdetermined. As Robert P. George has noted on this subject: "[the] natural law itself does not settle the question of whether it falls ultimately to the legislature or the judiciary in any particular polity to insure that the positive law conform to natural law and respect natural rights."[194] So, answers must be found, if anywhere, in the positive conventions of our society, and I have argued that the Constitution does not authorize federal judges to exercise judicial review when a statute is in the construction zone.

In sum, Article I granted to Congress the authority to determine how best to pursue the common good. The Constitution authorized federal judges to authoritatively interpret the Constitution during constitutional judicial review as part of their case-deciding function. Constitutional construction, by contrast, goes beyond the meaning of the Constitution. Federal judges' constitutional authority does not extend there, leaving Congress' legal judgment intact.

2.3.3.3.2 CONGRESS IS THE PRIMARY CONSTITUTIONAL MECHANISM TO PURSUE THE COMMON GOOD Second, the law-as-coordination account of originalism, which I explain in detail in Chapter 4, supports the deference conception of

---

[194] Robert P. George, *Natural Law, the Constitution, and the Theory and Practice of Judicial Review*, 69 FORDHAM L. REV. 2269, 2279 (2001).

construction. The law-as-coordination account argues that the Constitution contains the solutions to fundamental coordination problems that had and would otherwise have continued to prevent the United States from effectively pursuing the common good. One prominent illustration of this was the Commerce Clause, the purpose of which was to remedy the lack of national power to regulate interstate commerce in the Articles of Confederation, and to empower the federal government to prevent interstate trade disputes, preserve interstate political amity, and encourage interstate free trade.

In addition to granting the federal government power over particular subjects of national life, one of the Constitution's key solutions to coordination problems was to identify which federal officers performed which roles and functions in service of the common good. The three branches of the federal government were each designated a particular role and power that was both authorized and limited by the Constitution. The federal legislature was entrusted, through Article I, with the primary care of the national common good. The Constitution's text delegated to Congress most of those facets of the common good that were national in character.[195] Congress decides, for instance, how to staff the Army.[196]

The federal judiciary, through Article III, was entrusted with a different and narrower slice of the common good: adjudicating disputes under the Constitution (and other laws as well).[197] "The courts must declare the sense of the law; and if they should be disposed to exercise Will instead of Judgement, the consequence would be the substitution of their pleasure to that of the legislative body."[198] Federal judges possess authority from Article III to interpret the Constitution, and they must apply the Constitution, trumping inconsistent congressional statutes if need be. The Framers and Ratifiers structured the federal judiciary in this manner to preserve the Constitution's limits on the federal government.[199] However, in the Constitution's allocation of authority to pursue the common good, the office of federal judge does not include the authority to trump congressional statutes beyond inconsistency with the original meaning.[200] In other words, under our Constitution's social ordering, Congress' judgments on what the common good requires are authoritative, and federal courts cannot thwart those decisions absent a mandate in the source of our nation's social-ordering itself – the Constitution – because the Constitution did not empower the office of federal judge to do so.

---

[195] THE FEDERALIST No. 23 (Alexander Hamilton).

[196] U.S. CONST. art. I, § 8, cl. 14.

[197] *Id.* art. III, § 1.

[198] THE FEDERALIST No. 78 (Alexander Hamilton).

[199] *See id.* ("It is far more rational to suppose, that the courts were designed to be an intermediate body between the people and the legislature, in order, among other things, to keep the latter within the limits assigned to their authority.").

[200] STORY, *supra* note 193, §836.

This argument is bolstered by and related to the democratic legitimacy of Congress and the non-democratic nature of federal courts. Congress is elected by the American People, unlike the federal judiciary. This makes sense because Congress has care for the vast bulk of the United States' national common good, while federal courts play an important, though subsidiary role of dispute resolution and Rule of Law maintenance.

In our society, absent a compelling reason, judgments of the democratically elected legislature are entitled to greater authority than judgments by unelected entities.[201] This primacy of the legislature has repeatedly been acknowledged by the Supreme Court: the legislature is "the appropriate representative body through which the public makes democratic choices among alternative solutions to social and economic problems."[202] The weight of democratic pedigree also plays a pervasive role in constitutional doctrine. For instance, in the administrative law context, one of the justifications for federal court deference to agency statutory interpretations is that Congress delegated that authority to the agencies.[203]

In conclusion, the Constitution's allocation of power designated that Congress would possess primary authority to pursue the national common good. Federal judges pursue the common good via their case-deciding function. The office of federal judges does not include the authority to reject Congress' exercises of power outside of its case-deciding function: outside of the original meaning.

2.3.3.3.3 CONGRESS IS MORE INSTITUTIONALLY CAPABLE OF PURSUING THE COMMON GOOD

Third, Congress has a greater capacity to understand the problems of society – what is impeding the effective pursuit of the common good – and of formulating effective measures to better order society for effective pursuit of the common good.[204] Congress has constant contact with its constituents, while the courts are isolated. Congress can proactively address problems, while courts must wait for a judicial case. Congress has the resources to study problems, while the courts are dependent on the efforts of the parties before it. The courts are "institutionally unsuited to gather the facts upon which economic predictions can be made."[205] Congress can proactively address issues, while the courts must wait for a party to initiate litigation. Congress has the ability to make compromises that balance competing goods and move society forward, while the courts are restrained by precedent and legal principles.

A more general way to think about this is through the mechanism of the focal case. The best congressmen are characterized by the possession of political wisdom, while the best judges possess the capacity of legal wisdom. Political wisdom is the

[201] JOHN HART ELY, DEMOCRACY AND DISTRUST: A THEORY OF JUDICIAL REVIEW 5 (1980).

[202] *Schweiker* v. *Wilson*, 450 U.S. 221, 230 (1981).

[203] *Chevron, U.S.A., Inc.* v. *Natural Res. Defense Council, Inc.*, 467 U.S. 837, 844 (1984).

[204] RICHARD ELKINS, THE NATURE OF LEGISLATIVE INTENT 11–12 (2012).

[205] *General Motors Corp.* v. *Tracy*, 519 U.S. 278, 308 (1997).

species of prudence that allows the legislator to make and change law: to make the natural law effective for an entire society through positive law. Legal wisdom includes the qualities of a good lawyer: mastery of the existing law. This distinction has a long lineage stretching back to England.[206] Limiting federal judges to enforcing the determinate original meaning leverages their legal wisdom while, at the same time, privileging Congress' political wisdom.

In sum, when the original meaning of the Constitution is determinate, courts are warranted in overriding the determinations of the elected branches. However, when the meaning of the Constitution is underdeterminate and the situation is one of constitutional construction, courts should defer to the constructions of the other branches. This division of labor maximizes each branch's respective competences.

2.3.3.4 Judges Continue to Exercise Modest Discretion Crafting Judicial Doctrine that Fits Elected Branch Constructions

I argued that constitutional construction exists, but that it is modest and, in particular, it is modest from the perspective of federal judges who must defer to elected branch constructions. This argument does not entail, however, that these same judges are mere ciphers. Instead, they will exercise modest discretion. When the elected branches construct constitutional meaning, it will be in the form of a statute or executive enforcement action. The constructions will be on particular concrete points. For instance, assuming that the question of whether Congress' regulation of the intrastate market of marijuana is necessary and proper to its prohibition of an interstate market of marijuana[207] was in the construction zone, Congress' construction of its commerce power is on a discrete point of constitutional meaning.

American courts' decisions, however, do not operate that way; they do not (only) pronounce on one point of constitutional meaning. Instead, their decisions have implications for other cases, and together and over time they form doctrines that themselves later govern future cases. Both the crafting of this doctrine and the resulting doctrine itself will not mimic the elected branches' particular constructions. It will account for them, but it will go beyond them because of the different institutional manner in which courts operate.

2.3.4 *Constitutional Construction Is a Subsidiary Mechanism of Constitutional Communication*

The Constitution's original meaning is the primary mechanism by which the Constitution's legal directives are communicated to Americans to coordinate American life and secure the common good. However, the original meaning "runs out."

---

[206] Hamburger, *supra* note 180, at 159–78.
[207] This hypothetical is based on *Gonzales v. Raich*, 545 U.S. 1 (2005).

The deference conception of construction is therefore an important, though subsidiary mechanism of constitutional communication. It picks up where the original meaning leaves off. It provides the needed social coordination when the original meaning itself cannot. The deference conception does so by identifying the elected branches as the primary means of social coordination in the construction zone through their sub-constitutional positive laws, and judicial doctrine that fits and justifies it.

2.3.5 *Conclusion*

The deference conception of construction identifies a narrow scope for constitutional construction because of closure rules and metaphysical determinacy of the original meaning. For cases within the modest construction zone, federal courts should defer to elected branch judgments.

2.4 AN ORIGINALIST THEORY OF PRECEDENT: ORIGINALIST AND NONORIGINALIST PRECEDENT SERVING THE COMMON GOOD

2.4.1 *Introduction*

Originalism has had an uneasy relationship with precedent, unnecessarily so, I will show.[208] Most of the focus of both originalists and their critics has been on originalism's ability – or purported lack thereof – to account for nonoriginalist precedent. This focus was so intense that originalists lost sight of the large and crucial role that *originalist* precedent plays within originalism.

This section fills that gap and explains the important place that both originalist and nonoriginalist precedent hold in originalist interpretation. Originalist precedent is relatively understudied. I provide a detailed discussion of originalist precedent in Subsection 2.4.3, where I describe how originalist precedent is the key mechanism that the Constitution employs to put itself into practice.

Thereafter, I explain the place of nonoriginalist precedent within originalism. From an originalist perspective, nonoriginalist precedent is mistaken. Originalists are divided over whether originalism has a role for nonoriginalist precedent. I argue that originalism has space for some nonoriginalist precedent. I show that the original meaning of "judicial Power" in Article III mandates that federal judges give significant respect to precedent, including nonoriginalist precedent. I also show that this descriptive claim makes originalism more normatively attractive.

Later, in Section 3.4, I capitalize on originalism's robust role for precedent and I argue that originalism's privileging of originalist precedent and preservation of nonoriginalist precedent enables originalism to better fit our existing practice.

---

[208] For a thoughtful theory of precedent that is intentionally not committed to a particular theory of constitutional interpretation, see RANDY J. KOZEL, SETTLED VERSUS RIGHT: A THEORY OF PRECEDENT (2017).

2.4.2 *Distinguishing Originalist from Nonoriginalist Precedent: The Originalism in Good Faith Standard*

2.4.2.1 Introduction

But first, I show how to distinguish originalist from nonoriginalist precedent. Differentiating originalist from nonoriginalist precedent is crucial because of originalism's different treatment of the two types of precedent.

2.4.2.2 Originalism in Good Faith

The standard interpreters should utilize to distinguish originalist from nonoriginalist precedent is Originalism in Good Faith. Originalism in Good Faith requires courts to distinguish between those cases where the Supreme Court properly *interpreted* – articulated – and properly *applied* the Constitution's original meaning, and those precedents where it did not.

For a precedent to merit the label originalist, it must first correctly express the Constitution's original meaning. There are a variety of ways in which the precedent could do this, ranging from an explicit statement of the original meaning, to an inarticulate expression of that meaning. Examples of the first sort are relatively easy to spot. In *Crawford* v. *Washington*, the Supreme Court clearly stated, following its review of the history of the Confrontation Clause, the Clause's original meaning: the Clause prohibited "admission of testimonial statements of a witness who did not appear at trial unless he was unavailable to testify, and the defendant had had a prior opportunity for cross-examination."[209]

Examples of precedents that state the Constitution's original meaning opaquely are, by definition, more difficult to identify. In these cases, the Court does not explicitly articulate the Constitution's meaning, leaving one to gather the meaning from other aspects of the opinion. For example, *Printz* v. *United States'* articulation of the original meaning is not perspicacious.[210] Instead, Justice Scalia's opinion draws on the rather ill-defined "historical understanding and practice, . . . [and] the structure of the Constitution."[211]

Additionally, there are examples where the Court articulates the Constitution's meaning without identifying it as original meaning, requiring one to determine whether the articulated meaning is the Constitution's original meaning. Much of the Court's case law in the antebellum period fits this description. The Court's articulation of the Constitution's meaning in the early Republic accorded with the

---

[209] *Crawford* v. *Washington*, 541 U.S. 36, 53–54 (2004).

[210] *Printz* v. *United States*, 521 U.S. 898, 905 (1997); *see also* Michael B. Rappaport, *Reconciling Textualism and Federalism: The Proper Textual Basis of the Supreme Court's Tenth and Eleventh Amendment Decisions*, 93 Nw. U. L. Rev. 819, 821 (1999).

[211] *Printz*, 521 U.S. at 905.

originalist interpretive norms of the period and hence was unreflectively original-ist.[212] Chief Justice Marshall's interpretation of the Contracts Clause in *Sturges v. Crowninshield* provides a good example.[213] To ascertain the "meaning of words in common use," he relied on the federal structure of the United States, he reviewed the history surrounding the Framing and Ratification of the Clause, and he noted past practices by both the states and the federal government.

Precedents that opaquely articulate the original meaning are relatively rare today. This is the result of the movement toward originalism in response to the previous hegemony of nonoriginalist methodologies. Consequently, originalism was and remains controversial on the Court. Its use by its proponents is explicit as a way to show that the proponent's result is principled (in its proponent's eyes) and to contrast that principled result with the unprincipled result reached using nonoriginalist methods.

Second, in order to be an originalist precedent, it must accurately apply the original meaning to the facts presented in the case. Ascertaining whether a court properly applied the original meaning falls on a continuum, with clearly correct and incorrect applications on each end, and in-between many cases where reasonable disagreement exists.

The Constitution's original meaning takes the form of legal norms – rules, standards, and principles – that are more abstract than the given facts of a case. If the original meaning of a particular constitutional clause is a rule, for example, then that rule provides a norm more general than the class of fact situations to which it is potentially applicable. Consequently, a judge deciding whether and/or how to apply the rule must exercise judgment.

Generally, the more abstract the norm a judge is applying, the greater the burden on the judge's capacities to apply the norm correctly.[214] The relative ease of correctly applying the Presidential Age Clause, compared with the relative difficulty of accurately applying the Fourth Amendment's prohibition on unreasonable searches and seizures, exemplifies this.

2.4.2.3 Originalism in Good Faith Is an Objective Standard

Originalism in Good Faith is the standard interpreters should utilize to determine whether a precedent is originalist or nonoriginalist. A precedent meets this standard if it is an objectively good faith attempt to articulate and apply the Constitution's original meaning.

Originalism in Good Faith's core inquiry is: does the precedent in question show an objectively good faith attempt to articulate and apply the Constitution's original

---

[212] O'NEILL, *supra* note 146, at 12–18; WOLFE, *supra* note 102, at 17–72.
[213] *Sturges v. Crowninshield*, 17 U.S. (4 Wheat.) 122, 191–208 (1819).
[214] ST I-II, q. 94, a. 4.

meaning? The inquiry's focus is primarily on the precedent itself. Therefore, a precedent is an originalist precedent even if later in the author's personal papers it came to light that the author deceitfully, though plausibly, used originalist arguments to reach what, in the author's mind, was a nonoriginalist result. The precedent remained an originalist precedent because *it* plausibly articulated and applied the original meaning.

The inquiry is focused on a precedent's meeting the objective standard of Originalism in Good Faith, not on the subjective beliefs of the precedent's author. Continuing the previous example, a precedent whose author subjectively believed that the precedent did not accurately articulate or apply the original meaning, when in fact the precedent plausibly did so, is an originalist precedent.

Originalism in Good Faith's objective standard is more appropriate than a subjective standard for a number of reasons. Most importantly, courts rarely delve into the subjective views of judges who authored precedents, either in the context of vertical stare decisis or horizontal stare decisis. Instead, a precedent is taken at face value, as standing or falling on its own merits. Originalism in Good Faith fits this deeply-entrenched practice.

Originalism in Good Faith's objective inquiry is relatively easy to perform because the primary data – the precedent – is readily available. By contrast, a subjective inquiry would open the possibility of scholars and litigants delving into the nonjudicial utterances of judges to try to show subjective bad faith. This broadening of the inquiry would undermine Rule of Law values by undermining (what reasonably appears to be) an originalist precedent based on a judge's subjective views and by including in the relevant data materials that are less accessible than the originalist precedent itself.[215]

Relatedly, inquiry into judges' subjective views would prove disruptive to the judicial process because judges could be reversed and overruled based on claims of bad faith. It would also discourage qualified personnel from accepting judicial office because of this sort of intrusive search into judges' nonjudicial writings and statements. The day-to-day interactions of the judicial office itself would become more like the contentious and invasive confirmation process.

There is also little need for a subjective standard because the error rate of Originalism in Good Faith will be low. An objective standard will "catch" many precedents motivated by subjective bad faith. At the same time, the objective standard is protective of precedents that evince a plausible attempt to articulate and apply the original meaning.

Originalism in Good Faith's objective standard is also one that judges can meet. Although the level of effort needed to meet the standard will vary based on the accessibility of the original meaning and the difficulty of applying the original meaning to the question of the case, judges have the resources to do so. Even in

---

[215] The judge's personal papers, for example.

these more challenging cases, so long as a precedent's author shows a good faith attempt to investigate and grapple with the original meaning, then that precedent will meet the standard.

Judges are also "not on their own." Part of the "intellectual division of labor" in originalism is that judges have access to originalist scholarship. This scholarship can assist judges in two basic ways. First, it may directly evaluate a precedent and whether it is originalist or not. Second, scholarship may investigate the original meaning of the same constitutional text that the precedent applied, and a later judge may use the scholarship to evaluate the precedent's interpretation of the text.

Lastly, an objective standard fulfills Originalism in Good Faith's goal of providing a workable benchmark to differentiate originalist precedents from nonoriginalist precedents. For Originalism in Good Faith to be practicable – to preserve precedents' intellectual work – the effort required to differentiate originalist precedents from nonoriginalist precedents must be lower than that required to conduct a de novo review of the Constitution's original meaning. Originalism in Good Faith avoids this pitfall by adopting an objective good faith standard that permits participants in the legal practice to relatively easily identify originalist precedents.

2.4.2.4 Measuring the Objective Good Faith of Originalist Precedent

There is no algorithm to ascertain whether a particular precedent is a good faith attempt to articulate and apply the Constitution's original meaning. Instead, one must look for key indications that the judge acted in good faith when authoring the opinion and justifying the precedent. For example, did the judge plausibly review the pertinent data to articulate the Constitution's original meaning? If not, that is a significant warning that the judge was not in good faith articulating the original meaning. Or, did the judge plausibly respond to credible counter-arguments put forward by the dissent that the original meaning's application led to a contrary result? If not, that is a significant indication that the judge did not in good faith apply the original meaning.

Originalism in Good Faith operates analogously to the administrative review standard labeled "hard look" review.[216] To receive enforcement of its action by a federal court, an administrative agency must show that its decision-making process was reasoned: the agency took into account all pertinent data, responded to reasonable counter-arguments, and explained why it reached its conclusion.[217] Similarly, for a precedent to merit the label "originalist," it should take into account the data regarding the constitutional provision's original meaning, explain what original

---

[216] *Motor Vehicle Mfrs. Ass'n of the U.S., Inc.* v. *State Farm Mut. Auto. Ins. Co.*, 463 U.S. 29 (1983).

[217] 3 CHARLES H. KOCH, JR., ADMIN. L. & PRAC. *Hard Look* § 10.5 (2d ed. 1997).

meaning results from that data, then, apply that original meaning to the facts of the case and, in doing so, respond to plausible counterpoints.

2.4.2.5 Originalism in Good Faith Is the Appropriate Standard to Distinguish between Originalist and Nonoriginalist Precedent

Originalism in Good Faith is the appropriate standard to distinguish originalist from nonoriginalist precedents. First, Originalism in Good Faith meets the mandate of originalism because it accords the Constitution's original meaning authoritative status. The interpreter's final purpose[218] is the original meaning's accurate description and application. The interpreter tests pertinent precedents against the original meaning to ascertain whether the precedent is an originalist precedent.

In practice, judges that strive in good faith to articulate and apply the Constitution's original meaning will regularly succeed. For this reason, it is significantly more likely that opinions written by originalists, such as Justice Scalia[219] or Justice Thomas,[220] in a self-consciously originalist manner, will respect the original meaning, than are opinions written in a self-consciously nonoriginalist manner by nonoriginalists, such as Justice Douglas.[221]

Second, Originalism in Good Faith accepts that precedents that meet the good faith standard it embodies will sometimes be mistaken. Since, as I describe in the following subsection, originalist precedent receives only a presumption of bindingness (which can be overcome), good faith mistakes will be corrected. This prevents precedent from permanently displacing the authoritative original meaning.

Third, Originalism in Good Faith sets the standard at what we should expect of judges. If originalism is the correct method of interpreting the Constitution, then judges must utilize it to fulfill their oaths. And their good faith efforts to articulate and apply the original meaning are necessary to utilize originalist interpretation.

Relatedly, Originalism in Good Faith sets the standard at what we may, as a practical matter, expect of judges. It is futile to require the unerring articulation of the Constitution's original meaning and the unerring application of that meaning, because that standard is unattainable. This is why Ronald Dworkin had to create the hypothetical judge to exemplify his theory of law.[222] By contrast, a judge's good faith attempt to articulate and apply the original meaning is attainable. Indeed, our legal

---

[218] ARISTOTLE, *supra* note 64, at 1013a.

[219] *District of Columbia v. Heller*, 554 U.S. 570 (2008).

[220] *United States v. Lopez*, 514 U.S. 549, 584 (1995) (Thomas, J., concurring).

[221] *See Griswold v. Connecticut*, 381 U.S. 479, 484 (1965) ("The foregoing cases suggest that specific guarantees in the Bill of Rights have penumbras, formed by emanations from those guarantees that help give them life and substance.").

[222] RONALD DWORKIN, TAKING RIGHTS SERIOUSLY 105 (1977).

practice already demands good faith by judges.[223] Supplementing originalism, as I do, with the judicial virtues, facilitates this good faith standard.[224]

Of course, to meet the standard set by Originalism in Good Faith, the mantle of "originalist judge" will not, by itself, suffice. Instead, the authoring judge must "do the work." There are cases where well-known originalist justices have authored arguably nonoriginalist opinions. Randy Barnett, for instance, has argued that Justice Scalia's concurrence in *Gonzales* v. *Raich*[225] fits this description.[226]

Originalism in Good Faith hinges on judges exercising good faith judgment. Like any theory of precedent, the substantive content of precedents will hinge on the authors' judgment of what the original meaning required. For instance, in *District of Columbia* v. *Heller*, Justice Stevens' dissent plausibly reviewed the Second Amendment's original meaning and plausibly applied that meaning to the facts of the case.[227] Thus, Justice Stevens' dissent meets Originalism in Good Faith's requirements. If Justice Stevens could have garnered one more vote, his dissent, and not Justice Scalia's opinion, would have received the deference due under Originalism in Good Faith. This possibility is an unavoidable part of practical human institutions. It also afflicts all plausible interpretive methodologies that depend on fallible human judgment.

2.4.3 *The Interpretive and Constructive Modes of Originalist Precedent*

2.4.3.1 Introduction

Having provided the analysis to distinguish originalist from nonoriginalist precedent, in this subsection I describe the two important roles played by originalist precedent. I argue that originalist precedent is the crucial tool utilized by the Constitution to put the Constitution into the effect and secure the common good. My conception of originalist precedent imparts to it a substantial role in later courts' decision-making, without making it determinative.

2.4.3.2 Stepping Back for a Moment: Three Possible Conceptions of Originalist Precedent

From an originalist perspective, there are three basic possible conceptions of the role of originalist precedent in constitutional adjudication: (1) originalist precedent plays

---

[223] CODE OF CONDUCT FOR UNITED STATES JUDGES Canon 2A, 3A (2009).

[224] *Infra* Section 2.6.

[225] *Gonzales* v. *Raich*, 545 U.S. 1, 33–42 (2005) (Scalia, J., concurring).

[226] Randy E. Barnett, *Scalia's Infidelity: A Critique of "Faint-Hearted" Originalism*, 75 U. CIN. L. REV. 7, 14–15 (2006); *see also* ERIC J. SEGALL, ORIGINALISM AS FAITH 124–25 (2018) (making a similar claim regarding Justice Thomas).

[227] *District of Columbia* v. *Heller*, 128 S. Ct. 2783, 2822 (2008) (Stevens, J., dissenting).

no role in later courts' analyses (the "get rid of it all" conception); (2) originalist precedent plays a significant role in later courts' analyses – it influences the later courts' decisions (the "interpretive and constructive modes"); and (3) originalist precedent entirely or substantially determines the outcomes of later courts' analyses (the "common law constitutionalism" conception). According to the "get rid of it all" conception, in each case presenting a question of constitutional meaning, the court must de novo re-evaluate the Constitution's original meaning and de novo apply that meaning to the case. The "common law constitutionalism" conception requires a court to decide later cases on the basis of originalist precedent without regard for the Constitution's original meaning. In other words, originalist precedent's authority is not subject to rebuttal in light of evidence that the precedent incorrectly articulated or applied the Constitution's original meaning.

These first and third conceptions have reasonable proponents.[228] However, I argue in the following subsections that the second conception is the correct originalist stance. The second conception, what I label the interpretive and constructive modes of originalist precedent, requires federal judges to give significant respect to originalist precedent in the form of presumptive authority in later cases. I label this position the interpretive and constructive modes because of the primary roles originalist precedent plays under this conception; the first is in the context of constitutional interpretation and the second is in the context of constitutional construction. The first role is epistemic: originalist precedent bridges the analytic gap between the Constitution's determinate original meaning and the facts presented in a concrete case; the second role is metaphysical: originalist precedent makes determinate the content of the Constitution's norms when the Constitution's original meaning is metaphysically determinate and epistemically underdetermined.

2.4.3.3 Originalist Precedent's Two Modes of Operation

Earlier, I introduced the concept of constitutional construction, and I then described the deference conception of constitutional construction in detail. These descriptions depended on the fundamental distinction between determinate original meaning and underdetermined original meaning. Here, I take that distinction and use it to describe originalist precedent's two modes of operation.

---

[228] *Compare* Michael Stokes Paulsen, *Does the Supreme Court's Current Doctrine of Stare Decisis Require Adherence to the Supreme Court's Current Doctrine of Stare Decisis?*, 86 N. C. L. Rev. 1165, 1210–11 (2008) (arguing that precedent can play a limited informational role, but that it does not have independent authority), *with* Kurt T. Lash, *Originalism, Popular Sovereignty, and Reverse Stare Decisis*, 93 Va. L. Rev. 1437, 1441–42 (2007) (arguing that an originalism justified by popular sovereignty maintains a role for precedent), *and* Lawrence B. Solum, *The Supreme Court in Bondage: Constitutional Stare Decisis, Legal Formalism, and the Future of Unenumerated Rights*, 9 U. Pa. J. Const. L. 155, 186–201 (2006) (advocating a "neoformalist" conception of constitutional stare decisis that significantly binds the Supreme Court).

Originalist precedent's interpretive mode is when originalist precedent – again, that is, precedent that meets the Originalism in Good Faith standard – provides the presumptively correct articulation and application of the Constitution's determinate original meaning. Originalist precedent operates in its interpretive mode when the Constitution's original meaning is determinate; that is, when the meaning is both metaphysically and epistemically determinate. Originalist precedent in this context does not create the Constitution's governing norms and instead it is only an explication of the Constitution's determinate original meaning in a particular factual context.

Under the interpretive mode, originalist precedent governs later cases so long as the presumption in its favor remains unrebutted. If later judges, litigants, or scholars rebut the presumption, then the precedent loses its bindingness on later cases, and later judges should use their own good faith judgment to articulate and apply the Constitution's original meaning de novo.

As with the interpretive mode, originalist precedent in the constructive mode – precedent that constructs constitutional meaning – is protected by a rebuttable presumption. If later judges, litigants, or scholars show that the Constitution's original meaning – underdetermined though it is – excludes the precedent's construction, then the presumption is overcome. Similarly, if later arguments are offered showing that the precedent's application of the constructed meaning is wrong, then the presumption is overcome.

However, the constructive mode toward originalist precedent also treats originalist precedent as providing the *defeasibly* correct construction of the Constitution's meaning. Judges should utilize the constructive mode when the Constitution's original meaning is epistemically indeterminate. Originalist precedent, in this context, creates – determines – the Constitution's governing norms. However, the precedent's determination of the Constitution's meaning is defeasible in light of a differing constitutional construction by the elected branches, for reasons I explained in Subsection 2.3.3.

2.4.3.4 Tying the Interpretive and Constructive Modes of Originalist Precedent to Deeper Understandings of Law

The arguments here regarding the interpretive and constructive modes of originalist precedent draw on the validity of the distinction between interpretation and construction. The distinction between interpretation and construction, in turn and as I understand it, flows from the distinction between determinate and indeterminate law. This distinction, in turn, is tied to the concepts of epistemic and metaphysical legal determinacy.[229]

---

[229] *Supra* Subsections 2.3.2–2.3.3.

Originalist precedent has an epistemic role in the context of interpretation, and it plays a metaphysical role in the context of construction. The interpretive mode of originalist precedent is appropriate when the law is metaphysically and epistemically determinate. The constructive mode applies when the Constitution's original meaning is epistemically indeterminate.

The interpretive mode operates when the Constitution's original meaning is metaphysically and epistemically determinate. In these cases, an originalist precedent will articulate the determinate original meaning that governs the legal questions raised by the case. The precedent does not create constitutional meaning.

In this situation, originalist precedent is playing an epistemic role by articulating, in good faith, the Constitution's original meaning and, in good faith, applying that meaning to the facts presented by a case. The precedent is putting into practice the original meaning. These precedents provide evidence of how the original meaning controls concrete situations. Originalist precedents operating in the interpretive mode show how the gap between the Constitution's authoritative meaning and the conduct it governs is bridged.

Originalist precedent operating in the interpretive mode explains the Constitution's resolution of particular issues presented in cases by specifying how the Constitution resolves discrete legal questions, by making implicit constitutional norms explicit, by resolving perceived tensions in the Constitution's meaning, and by embedding these resolutions in precedent. These resolutions, preserved in originalist precedent, embody the authoritative norms that govern social activity in the class of situations analogous to the originalist precedent. Giving originalist precedent significant respect preserves these accomplishments and avoids leaving all questions open to re-evaluation.

By contrast, the interpretive mode does not operate when the Constitution's original meaning is epistemically underdetermined. Instead, the constructive mode applies, and later judges will give deference to originalist precedents that construct constitutional meaning. The constructive mode operates when the Constitution's original meaning is metaphysically determinate but epistemically indeterminate. This is because, though the Constitution's meaning is metaphysically determinate so that, in principle, there is a right answer, there are obstacles to accessing that right answer. Therefore, from our legal practice's perspective, the original meaning is underdetermined. Originalist precedent in this context creates constitutional meaning and applies that meaning.

Originalist precedent in the constructive mode is playing the metaphysical role of creating constitutional law and then applying those norms to the facts of the case. It crafts legal norms that resolve particular issues presented in cases. These constructed constitutional norms coordinate social activity. Giving the constructions embodied in originalist precedent significant respect protects the work done by the prior court in constructing the norms, and it prevents continual attack on the precedential resolution of issues.

I explain in more detail originalist precedent's interpretative and constructive modes in Subsection 3.4.4, where I show that originalist precedent's robust role fits the Supreme Court's practice of employing constitutional doctrine.

2.4.3.5 Originalist Precedent Is Presumptively – and Rebuttably – Binding

Originalist precedent that meets the Originalism in Good Faith standard is protected by a rebuttable presumption. Litigants, scholars, and judges may rebut the presumption by showing that (1) there is not substantial evidence that the originalist precedent in question correctly articulated the original meaning and/or (2) there is not substantial evidence that the precedent correctly applied that meaning.

The presumption in favor of originalist precedent is strong enough that it protects originalist precedents from destabilizing challenges and thereby prevents my conception of originalist precedent from collapsing into the "get rid of it all" conception. At the same time, the presumption is low enough that litigants, scholars, and judges can effectively challenge precedents. This prevents my conception from sliding into the "common law constitutionalism" conception of precedent and thereby preserves the primacy of the Constitution's original meaning.

The presumption gives originalist precedent its privileged place in constitutional adjudication. It protects originalist precedent from subsequent scrutiny and challenge. It also ensures that originalist precedent receives the constitutionally mandated "significant respect," described in Subsection 2.4.4.

One possible challenge to my theory of originalist precedent is that it will result in precedential drift. Precedential drift occurs when, over time, precedent builds upon itself, with the result that the operative legal meaning of the Constitution, as articulated by the precedent, diverges from the Constitution's original meaning. This would not occur immediately. Instead, it would happen over a series of cases. Indeed, there need be no bad faith; only judges doing their level-best to faithfully apply the applicable precedent to different factual scenarios.

A possible instance of precedential drift occurred in the Supreme Court's Commerce Clause case law in the late nineteenth and early twentieth centuries.[230] During this period, most Supreme Court Commerce Clause precedent met the standard of Originalism in Good Faith. For example, in *United States* v. *E. C. Knight Co.*, the Court ruled that Congress' Commerce Clause power did not extend to manufacturing.[231] The Supreme Court there applied the Clause's original meaning. Yet, during this period, the Court's precedent slowly expanded the operative legal meaning of what Congress could regulate.[232] For instance, the

[230] Richard A. Epstein, *The Proper Scope of the Commerce Power*, 73 VA. L. REV. 1387, 1408–42 (1987).

[231] *United States* v. *E. C. Knight Co.*, 156 U.S. 1, 12 (1895).

[232] Epstein, *supra* note 230, at 1408–42.

Supreme Court permitted federal regulation of intrastate activity that was in the "stream" of commerce.[233]

The primary check on precedential drift is the rebuttability of the presumption protecting originalist precedent. The presumption is low enough that litigants, scholars, or judges can effectively challenge precedents. This limits precedential drift and preserves the primacy of the Constitution's original meaning.

2.4.3.6 This Conception of Originalist Precedent Meets Article III's Mandate

This conception of originalist precedent is originalist because it comports with Article III's requirement that federal judges give precedent "significant respect."[234] Here, I tie Article III's mandate to the interpretive and constructive modes of originalist precedent. In doing so, I show how judges can be faithful to the Constitution's original meaning and, at the same time, follow precedent.

First, utilizing the interpretive and constructive modes is faithful to the Constitution's determinate original meaning. These approaches give the original meaning pride of place by aspiring to accurately articulate and apply the original meaning. As a practical matter, judges who in good faith strive to articulate and apply the Constitution's original meaning will regularly succeed. Further, since originalist precedent receives only a presumption of bindingness, mistakes will be corrected.

Second, the interpretive and constructive modes require judges to follow precedent and, consequently, Article III's requirement. When federal judges give originalist precedent significant respect, they preserve the interpretive and constructive work done by those precedents. Regarding originalist precedent operating in the interpretive mode, giving those precedents significant respect ensures that they perform their evidentiary work of articulating the Constitution's original meaning and explaining how that meaning governs particular fact patterns. For originalist precedent operating in the constructive mode, significant respect preserves their creative articulation and application of constitutional meaning.

Another way of looking at my resolution of the quandary is that my explanation of the interpretive and constructive modes shows why Article III's command that federal judges give precedent significant respect makes sense. One could argue that, in every case, an originalist judge should retire to the original meaning and skip any pertinent precedent; the critic could say that the originalist precedent is adding nothing to the judge's analysis. In response, my conception of originalist precedent shows that originalist precedent has two important roles: evidentiary and creative. I have also argued that these roles are effectuated by according originalist precedent

---

[233] *Swift & Co. v. United States*, 196 U.S. 375 (1905).
[234] *Infra* Subsection 2.4.4.

a presumption of correctness. Therefore, the originalist judge acts intelligently when he utilizes originalist precedent in constitutional adjudication.

2.4.4 *Originalism Preserves Some Nonoriginalist Precedent for the Sake of the Common Good*

2.4.4.1 Introduction

Nonoriginalist precedent is precedent that incorrectly articulated the Constitution's original meaning or incorrectly applied the original meaning. For example, the Supreme Court incorrectly articulated the Commerce Clause's meaning in *Wickard* v. *Filburn*.[235] The New Deal Court claimed that the Interstate Commerce Clause governed intrastate agricultural activity.

Nonoriginalist precedent is a potential problem for originalism for three primary reasons. First, to the extent nonoriginalist precedent is pervasive and to the extent that originalism rejects nonoriginalist precedent, originalism could cause instability by eliminating precedent and doctrines upon which significant legal reliance has been placed. Second, on the same conditions, originalism may fail to fit our constitutional practice because legal officials appear to believe the nonoriginalist precedent is legally authoritative and constitutionally valid. Third, on the same conditions, originalism could result in substantively suboptimal constitutional law.

In the following subsections, I argue that originalism is able to adequately respond to these problems because it requires the continued viability of some nonoriginalist precedent.

2.4.4.2 We Should Not Be Surprised That Nonoriginalist Precedent Exists

Nonoriginalist precedent is one manifestation of a broader phenomenon in constitutional law, law generally, and human life more generally still: mistakes. Both unintentionally and intentionally, humans take actions that are mistaken, even by their own lights.

The practice of constitutional judicial review in the United States is old, deep, and rich. For over 200 years, the Supreme Court has been ruling statutes unconstitutional. This vast span of time presents great difficulties for any institution that requires the exercise of fallible human judgment for its functioning. Over time, mistakes will inevitably occur (regardless of one's interpretive methodology).

Relatedly, the central institution in the practice of constitutional judicial review is the Supreme Court. The Court has periodic changes in personnel, appointed and approved by political actors whose jurisprudential views have varied over the vast span of the Court's existence. These personnel changes bring new views on the

---

[235] *Wickard* v. *Filburn*, 317 U.S. 111 (1942).

correctness of past precedents, which in turn were based on different understandings of the nature of the Constitution. For example, between 1948 and 2016, the party affiliation of the president changed nine times. Many of these changes brought with it a president with different views on the meaning of the Constitution and the role of the Supreme Court. In turn, the presidents attempted to appoint justices in line with their views. The result is a slow change in the jurisprudential views of members of the Court.

Similarly, the general current of legal thought has changed over the course of the Court's history. Judges were first lawyers who came of age in a particular jurisprudential climate. As young law students (or, in an earlier era, legal apprentices), they imbibed the understanding of law presented to them. Accordingly, as new judges replace old, the legal views of the judges – especially with respect to past cases – change as well.

Further, what Alexis de Tocqueville wrote in 1835 is more pertinent than ever: "There is almost no political question in the United States that is not resolved sooner or later into a judicial question."[236] For a substantial period of its history, the Supreme Court has waded into the most contentious issues in our social life including racial issues, economic issues, abortion, euthanasia, marriage, gun rights, the size and power of the federal government, and religion in public life, among many, many others. These issues cause emotions to run high and implicate our most deeply held beliefs. This could impair the judgment of judges as to whether and/or how the Constitution is implicated. Some may be tempted to rule in a manner they know is not in accord with what the Constitution requires. Others may unknowingly be swayed. In either case, mistaken precedent is created.

Lastly, the interpretive issues faced by the Supreme Court are often not easy. Judges must both identify the pertinent constitutional meaning and then determine whether the government action in question contravenes that meaning. Well-intentioned, intelligent judges can err in making these determinations and thereby create a mistaken precedent.

2.4.4.3 Article III Requires the Preservation of Some Nonoriginalist Precedent

Article III authorizes federal judges to exercise "judicial Power."[237] The original meaning of "judicial Power" requires federal judges to give precedent significant respect. This duty extends to all constitutional precedent, both originalist and nonoriginalist.

---

[236] ALEXIS DE TOCQUEVILLE, DEMOCRACY IN AMERICA 257 (Harvey C. Mansfield & Delba Winthrop eds., trans., 2000) (1840).
[237] U.S. CONST. art. III, § 1.

To establish that "judicial Power" includes the duty to give precedent significant respect, in the following subsections, I provide a summary of the historical evidence from the English practice up to the early Republic. This survey shows that Article III incorporated the contemporary practice and understanding of precedent into the judicial power exercised by federal judges.

Although there is disagreement among scholars regarding when and in what manner precedent was incorporated into the concept of judicial power, the evidence shows that the understanding of precedent evolved over time and that, by 1787–1789, the concept of judicial power included significant respect for precedent. The core determinate understanding was that judicial power included significant respect for precedent and that judges would be bound by precedent such that they would have to follow analogous precedent or give significant reasons for not doing so.[238]

This approach to precedent is thoroughly originalist because it is rooted in the Constitution's determinate original meaning. Though some may find it counter-intuitive that originalism requires the retention of some nonoriginalist precedent, I argue that doing so fits our broader practice regarding legal mistakes and makes good sense.

2.4.4.4 The Practice and Understanding of Precedent in the United Kingdom

The American understanding of judicial power has its roots in the English common law.[239] Though the English doctrine changed over time,[240] by 1787 the British understanding and practice of precedent required significant respect for prior analogous cases. As two British legal scholars noted, "[t]he importance of case-law has been emphasized since the days of the year books, and there are signs that the [English doctrine of precedent] was becoming rigid in the eighteenth century."[241]

There were three features of the English common law system out of which developed the English doctrine of stare decisis. First was "the judges' practice of reasoning by analogy" from cases.[242] As long ago as the thirteenth century, Lord Bracton articulated the rule that courts should rely on analogy in making their decisions when confronted with new issues: "If, however, any new and unaccustomed cases shall emerge, and such as have not been usual in the realm, if, indeed any like cases should have occurred, let them be judged after a similar case, for it is a

---

[238] Polly J. Price, *Precedent and Judicial Power after the Founding*, 42 B. C. L. REV. 81, 92–93 (2000); *see also* McGINNIS & RAPPAPORT, *supra* note 43, at 154 ("[T]he constitution, as a matter of judicial power, incorporates a minimal notion of precedent.").

[239] HAMBURGER, *supra* note 180, at 281.

[240] *Cf.* SIR CARLETON KEMP ALLEN, LAW IN THE MAKING 187 (7th ed. 1964).

[241] RUPERT CROSS & J. W. HARRIS, PRECEDENT IN ENGLISH LAW 24 (4th ed. 1991).

[242] *Id.* at 25.

good occasion to proceed from like to like."[243] Bracton himself exemplified this principle: his treatise referred to some five hundred decided cases.[244] Bracton did not invent the practice of reasoning by analogy, however, because it is evident from many of the cases that he cited in his treatise that "judges were seeking the guidance of precedent as early as the thirteenth century."[245] The Year Books, which began during the reign of Edward I and ended during the reign of Henry VIII, contain many examples of arguments and decisions guided by precedents.[246]

In the mid-sixteenth century, the practice of according binding status to precedent began to solidify.[247] Sir Edward Coke was central to this change. Coke produced the most complete set of law reports to date, and he used precedent extensively in his conflicts with the Stuarts and to limit the authority of the King and other courts.[248]

This leads to a second feature of the English legal system that contributed to the rise of the doctrine of stare decisis: the increasing availability of reliable law reports.[249] Before such reports were available, attorneys and judges were reluctant to rely on precedent for fear of inaccuracy[250] and because of the simple fact that many past cases became lost to history. By the mid-eighteenth century, relatively reliable reports first became available,[251] though, as noted, reports were in existence prior to this time.

A third characteristic of the English common law that contributed to the development of the doctrine of precedent was its "declaratory theory" of precedent: courts do not make the law, but merely declare and apply the principles of the common law in concrete cases – thus, the decisions of courts did not say what the law was, but rather provided "evidence of the law."[252] The declaratory theory was used by contemporaries to explain the pervasive practice of precedent.[253]

This was the tradition articulated by Coke, Hale, and Blackstone. For example, Lord Coke stated that "the function of a judge" was not to make law, "but to declare the law, according to the golden mete-wand of the law and not by the crooked cord

---

[243] 1 Henrici De Bracton, On the Laws and Customs of England 9 (Sir Travers Twiss ed., William S. Hein & Co. 1990) (1878).

[244] Allen, *supra* note 240, at 188.

[245] *Id.* at 189.

[246] *Id.* at 190–203.

[247] Thomas Healy, *Stare Decisis as a Constitutional Requirement*, 104 W. Va. L. Rev. 43, 60–62 (2001); *see also* Harold J. Berman & Charles J. Reid, Jr., *The Transformation of English Legal Science: From Hale to Blackstone*, 45 Emory L.J. 437, 444–51 (1996).

[248] Healy, *supra* note 247, at 62–66.

[249] *Id.* at 72–73.

[250] *Id.* at 63.

[251] *Id.* at 69.

[252] Cross & Harris, *supra* note 241, at 25, 27–34.

[253] Healy, *supra* note 247, at 68.

of discretion."[254] As Chief Justice from 1613 to 1617, Lord Coke exemplified the philosophy he espoused; he frequently relied on precedent to guide his decisions.[255] Lord Coke's writings had an enormous influence on several generations of jurists and likely inspired John Vaughan, the Chief Justice of the Court of Common Pleas from 1668 to 1674, to attempt "to develop a systematic theory of the authority of precedents."[256] Sir Matthew Hale, another seventeenth-century influential legal scholar, also drew on the declaratory theory in *The History and Analysis of the Common Law of England*:

> [T]he Decisions of Courts of Justice, tho' by Vertue of the Law do not make a Law properly so called, (for that only the King and Parliament can do); yet they have a great Weight and Authority in Expounding, Declaring, and Publishing what the Law of this Kingdom is, especially when such Decisions hold a Consonancy and Congruity with Resolutions and Decisions of former Times; and tho' such Decisions are less than a Law, yet they are a greater Evidence thereof, than the Opinion of any private Persons, as such, whatsoever.[257]

In Hale's view, like his predecessors', individual judges were constrained by prior decisions: they were not empowered to ignore decisions they found disagreeable.

Of course, no discussion of the declaratory theory of precedent would be complete without reference to Sir William Blackstone's seminal *Commentaries*. Blackstone summarized the declaratory theory, which is that "judicial decisions are the principal and most authoritative evidence, that can be given, of the existence of such a custom as shall form a part of the common law."[258] Blackstone's noted exception to the rule of following prior analogous decisions – "where the former determination [was] most evidently contrary to reason"[259] – shows that stare decisis in 1760s England was not an iron-clad rule.

The practice of precedent, justified by the declaratory theory, was a crucial component of the English legal system's conception of the office of judge because stare decisis was a necessary tool for judges to fulfill their judicial duty, "[t]he duty of common law judges ... to decide in accord with the law of the land."[260] As described by Professor Philip Hamburger, English common law judges had a judicial duty to evaluate legal claims based solely on the law.[261] This duty originated from a number of sources, including judges' oaths and the philosophical distinction

---

[254] 1 Edward Coke, The Second Part of the Institutes of the Laws of England 51 (London, E&R Brooke 1797) (1642).

[255] Healy, *supra* note 247, at 63.

[256] Allen, *supra* note 240, at 209.

[257] Sir Matthew Hale, The History and Analysis of the Common Law of England 68 (Legal Classics Library 1987) (1713).

[258] 1 Blackstone, *supra* note 147, at *69–*70.

[259] *Id.* at *69.

[260] Hamburger, *supra* note 180, at 101.

[261] *Id.* at 103–47.

between human will, exercised by lawmakers like the king, and reason (or judg-ment) exercised by judges.[262] This judicial duty directed judges to apply the existing law; however, in a positive law–poor environment, common law custom was the primary focus of judges' duty.[263] Judicial precedent was evidence of the common law and, therefore, absent good reasons, later judges' judicial duty required them to follow precedent.[264] "The exposition of the law [by judges] ... was a matter of judgment, and thus when, in the course of their duty, the judges had to explain their decisions, their expositions of the law ... enjoyed the authority of their office."[265]

The bindingness of precedent – including for advocates of the declaratory theory – was prominently displayed in *Perrin v. Blake*, where Blackstone reversed Chief Judge Mansfield's refusal to follow the Rule in Shelley's Case established by Coke.[266] In his opinion for the Exchequer Chamber, Blackstone wrote:

> There is hardly an ancient rule of real property but what has in it more or less of a feudal tincture.[B]ut whatever their parentage was, they are now adopted by the common law of England, incorporated into its body, and so interwoven with its policy, that no court of justice in this kingdom has either the power or (I trust) the inclination to disturb them.[267]

Stare decisis was applied more vigorously in cases involving property or contract. The predominant view was that, for property and contractual reliance issues, it was better that the law "be settled than that it be settled right."[268] One frequently cited case that illustrates this principle is *Morecock v. Dickins*, argued before the High Court of Chancery in 1768.[269] In issuing his opinion, Lord Camden stated that, although he was inclined to agree with the logic of the plaintiff's claim, he was bound by precedent to rule against him.[270]

As the foregoing analysis demonstrates, by 1787 in England there was a coherent theory and practice of precedent. The eighteenth-century system of precedent practiced by British courts was largely based on the declaratory theory. Judges were bound in real and meaningful ways – they were not free to simply ignore prior decisions, as demonstrated by cases where judges ruled in ways contrary to their preferences.

---

[262] *Id.* at 106–12, 159–61.

[263] *Id.* at 90–95.

[264] *Id.* at 218.

[265] *Id.*

[266] *See* David Lieberman, The Province of Legislation Determined: Legal Theory in Eighteenth-Century Britain 135–42 (1989).

[267] *Id.* at 139–40.

[268] Healy, *supra* note 247, at 69; Thomas R. Lee, *Stare Decisis in Historical Perspective: From the Founding Era to the Rehnquist Court*, 52 Vand. L. Rev. 647, 688 (1999).

[269] *Morecock v. Dickins* (1768) 27 Eng. Rep. 440 (Ch.).

[270] *Id.* at 441 (citation omitted).

2.4.4.5 The Practice and Understanding of Precedent in the United States

American understanding and practice of precedent developed over time from the colonial era to the Ratification of the Constitution. By the time of the Ratification, the Framers and Ratifiers understood judicial power to include stare decisis: judges must give significant respect to prior analogous cases and must give significant reasons for overruling precedents.

2.4.4.5.1 PRECEDENT IN COLONIAL AMERICA: CREATING THE NECESSARY CON-DITIONS FOR PRECEDENT In order to understand how the doctrine of precedent developed in the United States, it is necessary first to explore some of the factors that influenced the American legal system in its formation. When the colonists came to the New World, they brought with them and created legal norms rooted in the British common law.[271] Of course, as scholars have pointed out, labeling the colonial laws a legal "system" or "systems" is something of a misnomer.[272] In the seventeenth century, the colonists had only just begun the process of taming the New World, and so it is not surprising that their legal system was simple. There were several obstacles that the colonists had to overcome to establish a practice of precedent. Three of these obstacles included: (1) the animosity that many colonists felt for lawyers; (2) the lack of adequate legal training in the early colonies; and (3) the scarcity and poor quality of early court reports.

Ill-will directed at lawyers by the colonists was fairly widespread.[273] In many locations, lawyers were forbidden to practice their craft, and there was often a great deal of ill-will directed at anyone who professed training in or knowledge of the law.[274] The colonists' enmity lacked longevity, however, and there was a dramatic reversal of public opinion in the late seventeenth and early eighteenth centuries. The colonists began to accept lawyers as a "necessary evil," and "as soon as a settled society posed problems for which lawyers had an answer or at least a skill, the lawyers appeared in force, and flourished despite animosity."[275] By the mid-eighteenth century, lawyers had gained respect and prestige, and many held public office.[276]

The second obstacle that the colonists had to overcome was the lack of good-quality, consistent legal training. There were no American law schools in the seventeenth century; the first formal law school in America was not established until nearly the end of the eighteenth century, when the Litchfield Law School was

---

[271] LAWRENCE M. FRIEDMAN, A HISTORY OF AMERICAN LAW 4–5, 15 (3d ed. 2005). After the Revolutionary War, most colonies officially adopted the common law by statute. MORTON J. HORWITZ, THE TRANSFORMATION OF AMERICAN LAW: 1780–1860 4 (1977).

[272] Stanley N. Katz, *Explaining the Law in Early American History*, 50 WM. & MARY Q. 3, 6 (1993); FRIEDMAN, *supra* note 271, at xiii.

[273] DANIEL J. BOORSTIN, THE AMERICANS: THE COLONIAL EXPERIENCE 197 (1958).

[274] FRIEDMAN, *supra* note 271, at 53–59.

[275] *Id.* at 83–84.

[276] *Id.* at 84–85.

founded in Connecticut in 1782.[277] To fill the vacuum, some lawyers came over from England to practice in the colonies.[278] Many colonists also began to take up the practice of law through self-instruction or apprenticeship.[279] In the eighteenth century, an increasing number of would-be lawyers were able to secure apprentice-ships, where, in theory at least, they would learn the law from an established practitioner.

Similar to England, the third obstacle the colonists faced in establishing their legal system was the lack of case reports. As one historian bluntly stated, "[t]here were no American reports to speak of in the colonial period."[280] Colonial lawyers had to rely chiefly on English casebooks or on what they could decipher about the cases included in English legal treatises.[281] A few lawyers made their own reports. Some used only cases to which they were a party; some collected cases tried by the local courts, on their own or with the assistance of sitting judges; most had to rely on their memory, but a few had access to notes written by the lawyers or judges involved in the case. For the most part, these lawyers did not publish the reports they made; they seem to have made them simply for their own use.[282]

Some reports were published, however, such as Ephraim Kirby's *Connecticut Reports*, which began in 1789, and Alexander Dallas's *Reports of Cases Ruled and Adjudged in the Courts of Pennsylvania, Before and Since the Revolution*, which was published in 1790 and contained cases going back as far as 1754.[283] These reports proved to be quite popular and "lawyers were eager for a supply of reported cases; and were willing to pay for such reports."[284] Notwithstanding the efforts of these enterprising lawyers, the few private reports that were available were inadequate for the needs of the burgeoning colonial legal system.

Given these conditions, it is not surprising that the doctrine of precedent was slow to develop in the colonial legal system. Nevertheless, such a system did develop over time. The doctrine of stare decisis was at its weakest in the seventeenth century, when the colonists were still focused on eking out an existence in their new land and did not have the time or resources necessary for a system of precedent to function. As colonial society grew more populous and more sophisticated, the services of skilled lawyers became more in demand.[285] Lawyers came in ever greater numbers from

---

[277] Craig Evan Klafter, Reason over Precedents: Origins of American Legal Thought 133 (1993).

[278] Friedman, *supra* note 271, at 55.

[279] Richard J. Ross, *The Legal Past of Early New England: Notes for the Study of Law, Legal Culture, and Intellectual History*, 50 Wm. & Mary Q. 28, 40 (1993).

[280] Friedman, *supra* note 271, at 241; *see also* Frederick G. Kempin, Jr., *Precedent and Stare Decisis: The Critical Years, 1800 to 1850*, 3 Am. J. Legal Hist. 28, 34 (1959).

[281] Friedman, *supra* note 271, at 241–42.

[282] Kempin, *supra* note 280, at 34–35; Friedman, *supra* note 271, at 241–45.

[283] Friedman, supra note 271, at 242.

[284] *Id.*

[285] *Id.* at 22.

England and brought a strong respect for precedent with them, which was inculcated in subsequent generations of lawyers. In the early- to mid-eighteenth century, lawyers and judges began to develop and apply a system of precedent.[286] The declaratory theory became even more popular in the colonies after the publication of Blackstone's *Commentaries* in 1765–69.[287]

While the colonial courts of the seventeenth century seemed to favor flexibility and innovation over certainty, in the eighteenth century these values were reversed. "Americans of the prerevolutionary period expected their judges to be automatons who mechanically applied immutable rules of law to the facts of each case."[288] John Adams exemplified the growing respect for precedent. He regarded precedent as an absolute necessity to prevent courts from encroaching upon the rights of the citizens. Adams wrote that "the Laws of every State ought always to be fixed, [and] certain,"[289] and that "every possible Case [should be] settled in a Precedent, leav[ing] nothing, or but little to the arbitrary Will or uninformed Reason of Prince or Judge."[290]

As in England, stare decisis in the colonies was especially strong in cases involving property or commercial reliance interests. In *Somerville* v. *Johnson*,[291] for example, a Maryland judge wrote an opinion reminiscent of the language found in the early English case of *Morecock* v. *Dickins*.[292] The *Somerville* Court was confronted with a question involving the interpretation of a will in which William Deacon granted a life estate in land and four slaves to Mary Johnson. The main issue was whether children born to one of the slaves after Deacon's death were also part of the life estate.[293] The judge believed that the better argument was that the children should be part of the life estate,[294] but ruled against Johnson because of precedent: "I apprehend the present rule must be stare decisis, a rule founded on great convenience. [As] Lord Talbot observed, that the rules of property being certain and known, it is not of great consequence what they are."[295] The language used by the court was very similar to that of the English *Morecock* case: both judges were expressing similar concepts based on a long-standing tradition of increased deference to precedents involving property and commercial reliance issues.

---

[286] Lawrence Friedman, A History of American Law 50 (1st ed. 1973).

[287] William D. Bader, *Some Thoughts on Blackstone, Precedent, and Originalism*, 19 Vt. L. Rev. 5, 6, 8 (1994).

[288] William E. Nelson, Americanization of the Common Law: The Impact of Legal Change on Massachusetts Society, 1760–1830 19 (1975).

[289] *Id.*

[290] 1 Diary and Autobiography of John Adams 167 (L. H. Butterfield ed., 1961).

[291] *Somerville* v. *Johnson*, 1 H. & McH. 348 (Md. Ch. 1770).

[292] *Morecock* v. *Dickins* (1768) 27 Eng. Rep. 440 (Ch.).

[293] *Somerville*, 1 H. & McH. at 348–49.

[294] *Id.* at 353.

[295] *Id.* at 353–54.

From the foregoing analysis, it is clear that there was a discernible doctrine and practice of precedent in the later American colonial legal system. During the seventeenth century such a doctrine was weak, but in the eighteenth century, as the colonial legal system became increasingly mature and influenced by English practice, the doctrine of precedent came to resemble its English counterpart. Stare decisis was particularly strong in cases involving property or commercial reliance issues.

2.4.4.5.2 PRECEDENT IN STATE COURTS AFTER THE REVOLUTION Americans continued their practice of precedent following the Revolution. As one might expect, however, the Revolution caused some disruption in how newly independent state courts followed stare decisis. American courts, after Independence, developed a set of principles that governed when courts would disregard precedents. These principles developed out of the growing reluctance of American courts to be bound by English precedents.[296]

Connecticut was possibly the first state to begin to reject English precedents. In 1786, the Superior Court of Connecticut decided *Wilford* v. *Grant*, where the court was confronted with the problem of whether to grant a new trial for two minors who had been sued for and found guilty of assault and battery, along with four other men.[297] Requesting a new trial, the minor defendants appealed, but common law precedents did not permit a new trial to be granted for some co-defendants and not for others.[298] The court granted the new trial for the minors, and in so doing, articulated a modified version of stare decisis that afforded less weight to English precedent because English common law precedent accorded with English custom which, although frequently the same as Connecticut's, was not always the same.[299] Hence, when the customs of the two differed, Connecticut was justified in rejecting the English precedent.[300]

Not all states were so quick to embrace a modified doctrine of stare decisis. Virginia, for example, demonstrated reluctance in abrogating English precedents.[301] Part of this reluctance probably stemmed from the fact that the Virginians' "preferred method of modifying the common law was to redact it into codes."[302] Even in Virginia, however, some judges felt that English precedents were no longer binding after the Revolution. In the case of *Commonwealth* v. *Posey*, for example, Judge Tazewell argued that

---

[296] KLAFTER, *supra* note 277, at 67.
[297] *Wilford* v. *Grant*, 1 Kirby 114 (Conn. 1786).
[298] *Id.* at 114–16.
[299] *Id.* at 116–17.
[300] Richard W. Murphy, *Separation of Powers and the Horizontal Force of Precedent*, 78 NOTRE DAME L. REV. 1075, 1092 (2003).
[301] *E.g.*, *Boswell* v. *Jones*, 1 Va. (1 Wash.) 322 (1794).
[302] KLAFTER, *supra* note 277, at 71.

[p]recedents, like many other things, may be carried too far; and, although adjudications upon statutes are often to be considered, as valuable expositions of the
grounds and extent of the enactments, yet, in a case of life and death, I cannot be
bound by the dictum of a British judge, upon a written law; for, although I venerate
precedents, I venerate the written law more.[303]

Judge Tazewell was in the minority, however, and the court declined the opportunity to reject the English precedents on point.

Some states went farther than Connecticut in modifying the doctrine of stare
decisis. New York, for example, demonstrated a particular zeal for casting off
English precedents.[304] In 1799, the New York Supreme Court of Judicature ignored
an English precedent because "a strict adherence to English common law principles
could on occasion be incompatible with New York's notions of justice and rationality."[305] By 1802, the New York High Court declared that English precedents no
longer bound New York courts.[306]

Many state courts in the post-Revolutionary era grew increasingly willing to depart
from English precedents based on a systematic method that was incorporated into a
modified doctrine of stare decisis that gave English precedent less weight than
domestic precedent. State courts were less likely to deviate from their own precedents. As a result, a two-tiered doctrine of stare decisis developed in which English
precedents were not accorded as much weight as American precedents. Moreover,
in many states, the unmodified doctrine of stare decisis remained the rule.[307]
Finally, even in the cases where courts did depart from precedent, they still felt
the need to address those precedents, and they offered reasons for abandoning them.

2.4.4.5.3 ARTICLE III "JUDICIAL POWER" INCLUDED THE CONCEPT OF STARE
DECISIS Up to this point, I have shown that there was a practice of precedent in the
United Kingdom and that, over time, the American colonies came to follow a
similar practice. Following the Revolution, the American practice of precedent
continued, with the exception that, in some states, English precedent received less
weight because of the Revolution and the different circumstances faced by the
American states. Here, I show that the meaning of "judicial Power" in Article III
included significant respect for precedent.

There is not a great deal of direct evidence to draw from in this period. Professor
Norman Williams has discussed the difficulty regarding the sparse historical record
on this subject: "The Framers never engaged in a focused discussion of the role of

---

[303] *Commonwealth v. Posey*, 8 Va. (4 Call) 109, 116 (1787).
[304] KLAFTER, *supra* note 277, at 74.
[305] *Id.* at 75 (discussing *Silva v. Low*, 1 Johns. Cas. 184 (N. Y. Sup. Ct. 1799)).
[306] HORWITZ, *supra* note 271, at 27.
[307] *See, e.g., Oliver v. Newburyport Ins. Co.*, 3 Mass. (2 Tyng) 37 (Mass. 1807); *Fisher v. Morgan*, 1
N. J. L. 125 (N. J. 1792); *Young v. Erwin*, 2 N. C. (1 Hayw.) 323 (N. C. 1796); *Hannum v. Askew*,
1 Yeates 25 (Pa. 1791).

precedent in federal court adjudication, much less whether Article III required some respect for precedent and, if so, in what form."[308] I am not aware of any mention of the doctrine of stare decisis in the Constitutional Convention. Instead, most of the references made regarding the judicial branch of the federal government were concerned with whether that branch should possess a power of judicial review of all statutes passed by the legislature, how long federal judges should serve, whether the Supreme Court should be involved in impeachment proceedings, and what method should be used to appoint the judges.[309] Likewise, there does not appear to be any mention of the doctrine of stare decisis in the records of the state ratifying conventions.[310]

However, and tellingly, both opponents and proponents of the new Constitution argued for their respective positions based on the premise that judicial power included stare decisis. As one scholar has summarized the evidence, "they all expected the new federal courts to adhere to something like the declaratory theory's doctrine of precedent."[311] The participants who utilized this premise did not dispute the other participants' use, nor did they justify their own use of the premise. Instead, this premise was unarticulated, inchoate. This strongly suggests that the original meaning of "judicial Power" included stare decisis.

One of the earliest references to the doctrine of precedent in the debates leading up to Ratification of the Constitution appeared in *The Anti-Federalist Papers*. The Federal Farmer was concerned about the lack of precedents to guide the federal courts, especially with regard to decisions that in England had been left to courts of equity: "[W]e have no precedents in this country, as yet, to regulate the divisions in equity as in Great Britain; equity, therefore, in the supreme court for many years will be mere discretion."[312] This comment reveals both an understanding that precedent acts as a binding limitation on a federal court's decision-making power, and also a recognition that the judicial power exercised by federal courts would, in time, create binding precedents. The complaint by the Federal Farmer – "mere discretion" – exemplifies a concern of many of the Framers and Ratifiers (along with Blackstone earlier) about judges exercising arbitrary discretion. The theme of cabining judicial discretion through the practice of precedent crossed party lines, as I show in the discussion of the Federalists.

---

[308] Norman R. Williams, *The Failings of Originalism: The Federal Courts and the Power of Precedent*, 37 U. C. Davis L. Rev. 761, 766 (2004).

[309] *See* James Madison, The Debates in the Federal Convention of 1787 Which Framed the Constitution of the United States of America 51, 56–58, 67–69, 97, 274–77, 294, 300–303, 405, 472–74, 535–36 (Gaillard Hunt & James Brown Scott eds., int'l ed. 1999).

[310] *See generally* 1–5 Jonathan Elliot, The Debates in the Several State Conventions, On the Adoption of the Federal Constitution, as Recommended by the General Convention at Philadelphia, in 1787 (William S. Hein & Co. 1996) (2d ed. 1861).

[311] Murphy, *supra* note 300, at 1096.

[312] *Letter from the Federal Farmer III* (Oct. 10, 1787), *in* 2 The Complete Anti-Federalist 234, 244 (Herbert J. Storing ed., 1981).

Unlike the Federal Farmer, who was concerned about the lack of binding precedent, another important Anti-Federalist writer, Brutus, feared the opposite danger, namely, too many precedents. Brutus feared that the federal courts' precedents would metastasize and eventually swallow the freedom of states and citizens:

> Perhaps nothing could have been better conceived to facilitate the abolition of the state governments than the constitution of the judicial. They will be able to extend the limits of the general government gradually, and by insensible degrees, and to accommodate themselves to the temper of the people. Their decisions on the meaning of the *constitution* will commonly take place in cases which arise between individuals, with which the public will not be generally acquainted; one adjudication will form a precedent to the next, and this to a following one. These cases will immediately affect individuals only; so that a series of determinations will probably take place before even the people will be informed of them.[313]

Brutus believed that federal courts would issue binding constitutional precedents. And, although Brutus did not express a fear of uncabined judicial discretion as did the Federal Farmer, his premise – precedent binds federal judges – remained.

Alexander Hamilton penned *Federalist 78* in response to the concerns similar to those expressed by the Federal Farmer and Brutus. In Hamilton's view, the judiciary was the "least dangerous" of the three federal branches because its power was limited by the Constitution in several ways.[314] One of these limits identified by Hamilton was the requirement of following precedent. In Hamilton's words:

> It has been frequently remarked, with great propriety, that a voluminous code of laws is one of the inconveniences necessarily connected with the advantages of a free government. To avoid an arbitrary discretion in the courts, it is indispensable that they should be bound down by strict rules and precedents, which serve to define and point out their duty in every particular case that comes before them; and it will readily be conceived, from the variety of controversies which grow out of the folly and wickedness of mankind, that the records of those precedents must unavoidably swell to a very considerable bulk, and must demand long and laborious study to acquire a competent knowledge of them.[315]

Hamilton raised the subject of precedent as part of an argument in favor of lifetime appointment for federal judges: only men who were engaged in the craft for life would have the experience and time to study the "considerable bulk" of precedents that would bind them. This shows that Hamilton presumed that federal judges would, like the common law judges with whom he was familiar, create and work with binding precedents. Indeed, Hamilton followed the common theme of tying an accumulation of precedent to limiting judicial discretion, a value central to

---

[313] *Brutus XV* (Mar. 20, 1788), *in* THE ANTI-FEDERALIST PAPERS AND THE CONSTITUTIONAL CONVENTION DEBATES 308 (Ralph Ketcham ed., 1986) (emphasis added).
[314] THE FEDERALIST NO. 78 (Hamilton).
[315] *Id.*

Hamilton's broader claim in *Federalist 78* of the limited role of judges as exercising *judgment*—discerning the law—and not *will*—not creating law.

James Madison likewise had a relatively clear understanding that the doctrine of precedent was part of judicial power. In a letter to Samuel Johnston in the months preceding Ratification, he lamented that, at times, the meaning of certain parts of the Constitution was difficult to determine conclusively.[316] Contrary to Brutus, Madison welcomed the accumulation of precedents because such precedents would help to settle the meaning of the Constitution: "Among other difficulties, the exposition of the Constitution is frequently a copious source, and must continue so until its meaning on all great points shall have been settled by precedents."[317] Madison presented these same thoughts publicly during the period of Ratification, in *Federalist 37*, arguing that precedents are necessary to "liquidate []" the meaning of the Constitution.[318] For precedent to serve the settlement function Madison saw in it, precedent would have to be binding on later interpreters.[319]

Thus, Madison, like Hamilton, understood that judicial power included the doctrine of binding precedent. And like his contemporaries, Madison saw binding precedent as a means to limit judicial discretion, which was consistent with his broader vision of the limited role of the judiciary.

In the period following Ratification, William Cranch, the second reporter for the Supreme Court, began his first edition of the Supreme Court Reports with a preface discussing the importance of precedents:

> In a government which is emphatically styled a government of laws, the least possible range ought to be left for the discretion of the judge. [A]nd perhaps, nothing conduces more to that object than the publication of reports. Every case decided is a check upon the judge: he cannot decide a similar case differently, without strong reasons, which, for his own justification, he will wish to make public.[320]

According to Cranch, limited judicial discretion was central to the Rule of Law, and precedent was key to constraining federal judges in their exercise of the judicial power.

---

[316] *See Letter from James Madison to Samuel Johnston* (June 21, 1789), *in* 12 THE PAPERS OF JAMES MADISON 249, 250 (Charles F. Hobson et al. eds., 1979).

[317] *Id.*

[318] *See* THE FEDERALIST No. 37 (James Madison) (arguing, in the context of discussing the difficulties the Constitutional Convention faced in forming "a proper plan," that "[a]ll new laws" must have "their meaning liquidated and ascertained by a series of adjudications").

[319] More than forty years later, Madison again touched on the importance of the doctrine of precedent. Madison described the "authoritative force" of "judicial precedents" as stemming from the "obligations arising from judicial expositions of law on succeeding judges." *Letter from James Madison to Charles Jared Ingersoll* (June 25, 1831) *in* JAMES MADISON, THE MIND OF THE FOUNDER: SOURCES OF THE POLITICAL THOUGHT OF JAMES MADISON 390, 391 (Marvin Meyers ed., rev. ed. 1981).

[320] 1 WILLIAM CRANCH, REPORTS OF CASES ARGUED AND DECIDED IN THE SUPREME COURT OF THE UNITED STATES iii (1804).

Given the common law background, which was pervasive in the legal education, legal practice, and thought of the Framers and Ratifiers,[321] it is not surprising that all of the evidence we have of the Framers' and Ratifiers' understanding of the nature of judicial power is consistent with the pre-existing declaratory theory of precedent. This connection was made explicit in James Wilson's writings. Wilson argued that "[j]udicial decisions are the principal and most authentic" proof of what the law is and "every prudent and cautious judge will appreciate them [because] his duty and his business is not to make the law, but to interpret and apply it."[322] This view of precedent required courts to follow reasonable precedents, even if the court itself would not have reached that result.[323] For instance, Chief Justice of the Connecticut Supreme Court, Zephaniah Swift, argued that "when a court ha[s] solemnly and deliberately decided any question or point of law, that adjudication bec[omes] a precedent in all cases of a similar nature, and operate[s] with the force and authority of a law."[324]

The evidence discussed in this subsection shows that the Framers and Ratifiers possessed a coherent and widespread understanding of the role precedent would play in the judicial power exercised by federal judges: federal judges would create and, in turn, be bound by precedents. The doctrine of precedent was one of the assumptions involved in the formation of the federal judiciary. Further, the direct evidence coincides with what one would expect to find given the broader historical legal context discussed earlier: stare decisis was part of the background of their Anglo-American lawyerly understanding of judicial power. The binding nature of federal precedent was also a product of, and consistent with, the Framers' and Ratifiers' goal of constraining judicial discretion to accord with the judges' limited role in a republic.

Indeed, the very *lack* of a comprehensive discussion of stare decisis by the Framers and Ratifiers makes it *more* likely that they understood and accepted it as a basic foundation of a workable judiciary. After all, the simple fact is that there are many topics regarding which the Framers never had a detailed discussion, but about which we are relatively certain they had a coherent understanding. For instance, the nature of "Court" is not defined in Article III, nor was it extensively discussed at the time of the Framing and Ratification. The most plausible reason is that, to the Framers and Ratifiers, with their Anglo-American legal background, the term "Court" referred to the institution of courts as defined by existing and historical social practice. This suggests that if the Framers and Ratifiers thought that the doctrine of precedent was something altogether mysterious, or that it was a new concept, then they likely would have discussed it in great detail.[325] This is especially

---

[321] *See* FORREST McDONALD, NOVUS ORDO SECLORUM: THE INTELLECTUAL ORIGINS OF THE CONSTITUTION (1985) (arguing that the intellectual lives of the Framers and Ratifiers was formed by the common law, among other things).

[322] 1 THE WORKS OF JAMES WILSON 502 (Robert Green McClosky ed., 1967); *see also id.* at 524.

[323] Murphy, *supra* note 300, at 1086–87.

[324] 1 ZEPHANIAH SWIFT, A SYSTEM OF THE LAWS OF THE STATE OF CONNECTICUT 40 (1795).

[325] The Framers did, after all, discuss the nature and powers (and implications of those powers) of the federal judiciary itself. *E.g.*, THE FEDERALIST Nos. 78–82 (Alexander Hamilton).

true since both opponents and proponents based arguments on the assumption that federal judges would create and be bound by precedents. The fact that in each of the instances when one of the Framers or Ratifiers mentioned the doctrine of precedent it was to draw on it as a supporting argument for a different, more controversial claim, leads to the conclusion that such a doctrine was a background principle that needed no further explanation.

It is also significant that so many of the Framers and Ratifiers were lawyers.[326] As I demonstrated, a doctrine of precedent was part of the basic structure of the English, colonial, and post-Independence conception of judging and law. It would be remarkable if Americans did not share an understanding of the doctrine of precedent, which was so central to the common law.

Relatedly, the fact that so many of the participants in the Framing and Ratification debates were lawyers is a key facet of the relevant public context. The Framing Convention, which consisted of many lawyers, knew that the ratifying conventions would also be composed of many lawyers. This allowed the Framers to utilize terms like "judicial Power" with the knowledge that the ratifying conventions contained lawyers who knew how judges exercised their power in the Anglo-American legal tradition, including the use of stare decisis. The Ratifiers, in turn, knew that the Framers knew this, so they were able to access this thicker legal meaning of "judicial Power," in place of the thinner conventional meaning of the phrase. Non-lawyer Ratifiers, and Americans generally, accessed this term's meaning from lawyers.[327]

Finally, many historians who do not find a doctrine of stare decisis during the period of the Framing and Ratification are forced to claim that a "strict" view of precedent suddenly appeared early in the nineteenth century.[328] Based on the evidence I provided, the more plausible description of the history is that the Framers and Ratifiers had a conception of binding precedent and that – instead of its appearance out of whole cloth – later courts employed a stricter conception of stare decisis that evolved out of this earlier understanding.

2.4.4.5.4 THE PRACTICE AND UNDERSTANDING OF PRECEDENT IN FEDERAL COURTS AFTER THE RATIFICATION OF THE CONSTITUTION UNTIL 1800 CON-TINUED TO EMPLOY STARE DECISIS In this subsection, I conclude with a discussion of the understanding and practice of the doctrine of precedent in the newly created federal courts.[329] My focus is on the earliest federal court decisions, beginning with the Judiciary Act of 1789 until the dawn of the nineteenth century.

---

[326] Thirty-one of the fifty-five delegates to the Constitutional Convention were lawyers. FRIEDMAN, *supra* note 271, at 59.

[327] This is an example of the linguistic division of labor.

[328] Price, *supra* note 238, at 84.

[329] Although I do not discuss state court practice following ratification, it is clear that state courts, like their federal counterparts, continued the practice of following precedent. For example, in the Pennsylvania Supreme Court decision, *Kerlin's Lessee* v. *Bull*, 1 U.S. (1 Dall.) 175, 178–79.

A review of the reports reveals that the legal practice in the early federal courts included frequent citation to, discussion of, and reliance upon precedent. For example, in *United States v. Callender*,[330] the United States was attempting to prosecute Callender for seditious libel against President Adams. The defendant's attorney, Hays, argued that the allegedly libelous book could not be introduced as evidence supporting the indictment because the indictment failed to name the book itself.[331] Hays argued that he had reviewed "fifteen or twenty cases" that supported his argument and explained three such cases in more detail.[332] After doing so, Hays argued that "the attorney for the United States cannot give a single case" against his position.[333] Circuit Justice Chase then distinguished Hays' cases and relied on a contrary case (drawn from his memory) to overrule Hays' objection.[334] There are countless similar examples showing that stare decisis was a ubiquitous feature of early federal court legal practice as employed by litigants,[335] the courts,[336] and even the reporters.[337]

(Pa. 1786), the Court described the declaratory theory of precedent it followed and then followed a prior case even "though some may not [have] be[en] satisfied in their private judgment," because it enunciated a "rule of property." Further, the legal practice in the state courts was heavily focused on precedent. For instance, in *Commonwealth v. Coxe*, where the Pennsylvania Supreme Court evaluated a dispute over tracts of land located along the Ohio and Allegheny Rivers, an attorney relied on a number of authorities supporting his argument. 4 U.S. (4 Dall.) 170 (Pa. 1800). Alexander Dallas, the reporter, summarized the arguments: "Stare decisis, is a maxim to be held forever sacred, on questions of property; and, in the present instance, applies with peculiar force, as the rule was given by the state herself, through the medium of her officers." *Commonwealth v. Coxe*, at 192.

[330] *United States v. Callender*, 25 F. Cas. 239 (C. C. D. Va. 1800) (No. 14,709).

[331] *Id.* at 246.

[332] *Id.* at 247.

[333] *Id.*

[334] *Id.* at 249.

[335] *E.g., United States v. Maunier*, 26 F. Cas. 1210, 1211 (C. C. D. N. C. 1792) (No. 15,746) (defense counsel citing precedent); *Harvey v. Harvey*, 1 Del. Cas. 342 (C. C. D. Del. 1793), available at 1793 WL 618 (both parties' counsel citing precedent); *United States v. Ravara*, 27 F. Cas. 714, 715 (C. C. D. Pa. 1794) (No. 16,122a) (government counsel citing precedent); *Parasset v. Gautier*, 2 U.S. (2 Dall.) 329, 331 (C. C. D. Pa. 1795) (defense counsel citing precedent); *Geyger's Lessee v. Geyger*, 2 U.S. (2 Dall.) 332 (C.C.D. Pa. 1795) (defense counsel citing precedent); *United States v. Insurgents of Pa.*, 2 U.S. (2 Dall.) 334, 339 (C. C. D. Pa. 1795) (government counsel citing precedent); *United States v. Stewart*, 2 U.S. (2 Dall.) 343, 344 (C. C. D. Pa. 1795) (defense counsel citing precedent).

[336] *E.g., Georgia v. Brailsford*, 2 U.S. (2 Dall.) 402, 407 (1792) (opinion of Wilson, J.); *id.* at 408 (opinion of Cushing, J.); *Georgia v. Brailsford*, 2 U.S. (2 Dall.) 415, 417 (1793) (opinion of Iredell, J.); *Chisholm v. Georgia*, 2 U.S. (2 Dall.) 419, 429, 437–39, 442–44 (1793) (opinion of Iredell, J.); *Vanhorne's Lessee v. Dorrance*, 2 U.S. (2 Dall.) 303, 317 (C. C. D. Pa. 1795); *Dixon v. The Cyrus*, 7 F. Cas. 755, 756, 757 (D. C. D. Pa. 1789) (No. 3,930); *Weeks v. The Catharina Maria*, 29 F. Cas. 579, 579 (D. C. D. Pa. 1790) (No. 17,351); *Findlay v. The William*, 9 F. Cas. 57, 60 (D. C. D. Pa. 1793) (No. 4,790); *Tunno v. Preary*, 24 F. Cas. 323, 323 (D. C. D. S. C. 1794) (No. 14,238); *Jansen v. The Vrow Christina Magdalena*, 13 F. Cas. 356, 359 (D. C. D. S. C. 1794) (No. 7,216).

[337] *E.g., Rice v. The Polly & Kitty*, 20 F. Cas. 666, 667 n.2 (D. C. D. Pa. 1789) (No. 11,754).

The earliest explicit discussion of the doctrine of stare decisis as its own concept in the federal courts appears to have occurred in *Jennings* v. *Carson*,[338] three years after the birth of the federal judiciary. In *Jennings*, the District Court of Pennsylvania evaluated a claim under admiralty law regarding a challenge to the capture of a Dutch sloop and her cargo during the Revolutionary War.[339] The sloop was captured by a privateer schooner owned by Joseph Carson.[340] Carson maintained that the Dutch sloop was carrying goods "belonging to the subjects of Great Britain, contrary to the regulations and laws of the then congress."[341] The sloop was condemned after a jury trial in the state court of admiralty of New Jersey.[342] Jennings, representing the interests of the owner of the Dutch sloop, brought suit against Carson's executors, claiming that the sloop had been taken in violation of the law of the sea.[343] Carson's executors defended the capture and relied on the decision by the New Jersey state court of admiralty.[344] Jennings countered by arguing that the decision of the New Jersey state court had been reversed by the Court of Appeals of the United States in 1780.[345]

The district court first looked to the English case of *Case of Lindo and Rodney* – brought to the court's attention by counsel – to evaluate whether it had jurisdiction to hear prize appeals.[346] It then examined the history of admiralty courts in the United States and the American colonies.[347] Judge Peters determined that the rule of admiralty law created by Lord Mansfield in *Case of Lindo and Rodney* was not found in any American admiralty courts – it was unique to the English courts.[348] He concluded that the United States was no longer bound by English precedent in admiralty cases and held that the Constitution granted jurisdiction to federal courts to hear all admiralty cases: "Acting as we now do in a national, and not a dependent capacity, I cannot conceive that we are bound to follow the practice in England, more than that of our own, or any other nation."[349]

This case is instructive because it shows that the earliest federal courts were familiar with the requirements of the doctrine of stare decisis. Even though the court did not follow the *Case of Lindo and Rodney*, the fact that the advocates before the court argued from precedent, and that the judge felt the requirement to

---

[338] *Jennings* v. *Carson*, 13 F. Cas. 540 (D. C. D. Pa. 1792) (No. 7,281).
[339] *Jennings*, 13 F. Cas. at 540.
[340] *Id.* at 540–41.
[341] *Id.*
[342] *Id.* at 541.
[343] *Id.* at 540–41.
[344] *Id.* at 541.
[345] *Id.*
[346] *Case of Lindo and Rodney, discussed in LeCaux* v. *Eden* (1781) 99 Eng. Rep. 375, 385 n.1 (K. B.).
[347] *Jennings*, 13 F. Cas. at 542.
[348] *Id.*
[349] *Id.*

articulate his reasons for departing from that precedent, demonstrates that federal judges understood their judicial power to include a respect for precedent.

Eight years later, the Circuit Court for the District of Pennsylvania considered the requirement of following precedent. In the famous *Case of Fries*, the Circuit Court evaluated the conviction of John Fries for treason.[350] Fries had been the "ringleader" of a group of men who had resisted enforcement of federal tax statutes requiring property owners to pay taxes on the value of their slaves and lands.[351] Fries was charged with treason for levying war against the United States.[352] Fries argued that he was not guilty of treason as defined by the Constitution.[353] Specifically, Fries complained that the judge had given an incorrect instruction to the jury that resisting enforcement of a federal statute constituted treason.[354] In essence, Fries argued that the judge had misconstrued the constitutional definition of treason.[355]

Justice Chase began by pointing out that the Constitution defined treason in Article III.[356] Justice Chase then outlined how previous federal courts had interpreted the Constitution's definition of treason in two cases of insurrection in Pennsylvania from 1795.[357] Justice Chase concluded, based on this precedent:

> The[se] decisions, according to the best established principles of our jurisprudence, became a precedent for all courts of equal or inferior jurisdiction; a precedent which, though not altogether obligatory, ought to be viewed with great respect, especially by the court in which it was made, and ought never to be departed from, but on the fullest and clearest conviction of its incorrectness.[358]

Justice Chase believed himself bound by precedents on the constitutional definition of treason.[359] Chase "considered the law as settled by those decisions, with the correctness of which on full consideration he was entirely satisfied; and by the authority of which he should have deemed himself bound, even had he regarded the question as doubtful in itself."[360] Hence, from its earliest days, the federal courts gave significant respect to precedent.

Contrary to the claims of some scholars,[361] the Supreme Court, from its inception, frequently looked to precedent to guide it. One study evaluated the reliance on

---

[350] *Case of Fries*, 9 F. Cas. 924 (C. C. D. Pa. 1800) (No. 5,127).

[351] *Id.* at 935.

[352] *Id.* at 924.

[353] *Id.* at 935.

[354] *See id.* at 930.

[355] *Id.* at 935.

[356] *Id.* at 930 (citing U.S. Const. art. III, § 3, cl. 1).

[357] *Id.* at 931 (discussing *United States* v. *Mitchell*, 26 F. Cas. 1277 (C. C. D. Pa. 1795) (No. 15,788); *United States* v. *Vigol*, 28 F. Cas. 376 (C. C. D. Pa. 1795) (No. 16,621)).

[358] *Id.* at 935.

[359] *See id.* at 936 ("[I] considered [my]self and the court as bound by the authority of the former decisions.").

[360] *Id.* at 936.

[361] HEALY, *supra* note 247, at 85.

precedent by the early Supreme Court.[362] From 1787 to 1815, the Supreme Court decided 706 cases. Of those, 275 included "references to legal citations,"[363] most of which relied on common law precedents to reach their decisions.[364]

From 1787 to 1800, the Supreme Court relied on common law precedents 667 times and cited its own precedent eight times.[365] However, there was a marked shift in the pattern of the Court's reliance beginning in 1801. From 1801 to 1805, the Court relied on common law precedents seventeen times and cited its own precedents nine times.[366] From 1806 to 1815, the Court relied on common law precedents forty-five times, and cited its own precedents forty-three times.[367] Thus, beginning around 1801, the Court began to rely on its own precedents with greater relative frequency than common law precedents.[368] This shift is attributable to a critical mass of its own precedent as the most recent authority on legal issues, which replaced citation to earlier, and less authoritative, English common law and other sources.[369] Further, during this same period, the Court also frequently cited lower federal court precedent and state court precedent.[370]

In sum, the federal judiciary followed precedent from its formation, including on the Constitution's meaning. In the beginning, the federal courts looked to the precedents of the colonial and early state courts, along with the precedents of the English common law. As time passed and the courts developed their own corpus of case law, they increasingly relied on their own precedents.

2.4.4.6 Retaining Nonoriginalist Precedent Is Important for the Sake of the Common Good and Human Flourishing

It is important for originalism to preserve nonoriginalist precedent for three primary reasons. First, originalism should preserve some nonoriginalist precedent because it helps originalism fit our constitutional practice. I describe why this is important and how this occurs in Subsection 3.4.6, so I bracket this claim until then. Second, originalism should do so because stare decisis serves Rule of Law values. These Rule of Law values are central to any plausible account of how a society may effectively

---

[362] Timothy R. Johnson, James Spriggs II, & Paul J. Wahlbeck, *The Origin and Development of Stare Decisis at the U.S. Supreme Court* (Nov. 9, 2015), http://lawexplores.com/the-origin-and-development-of-stare-decisis-at-the-u-s-supreme-court/#tab9_2 (visited July 11, 2017); *see also* James F. Spriggs et al., *The Political Development of a Norm Respecting Precedent in the American Judiciary* (Apr. 15–18, 2004) (unpublished paper presented at the annual meeting of the Midwest Political Science Association).

[363] *Id.* at 12.

[364] *Id.*

[365] *Id.*

[366] *Id.*

[367] *Id.*

[368] *Id.*

[369] *Id.*

[370] *Id.*

pursue the common good and human flourishing. Third, some nonoriginalist precedents, despite the fact that they misinterpreted the Constitution, reached otherwise substantively just results. Therefore, originalism is better able to serve the common good.

The Rule of Law is both intrinsically and instrumentally valuable. Something has intrinsic value when it is good in itself; when it is pursued for its own sake and not for the sake of another good. Something is instrumentally valuable when one pursues it for the sake of some other good that the instrumental good procures.

The Rule of Law is intrinsically valuable because, "[w]here it is observe[d], people are confronted by a state which treats them as rational agents due some respect as such."[371] Human beings grasp and act based on practical reasons and, at the same time, exclude acting upon other practical reasons.[372] "Laws," in turn, "provide beings capable of grasping and acting on reasons with (additional) reasons for action"[373] because laws enable social cooperation without which members of a society could not achieve many corporate and individual goods.[374] Therefore, the Rule of Law, which provides members of a society with reasons for action, treats the members respectfully, as rational beings – as beings that act based on reasons and not force – and is valuable as a result.

Stare decisis treats the law's subjects as rational beings. Stare decisis identifies[375] the law, and this as-identified law provides legal reasons for action. Doing so treats humans with the respect they deserve.

Instrumentally, the Rule of Law provides the necessary environment so that members of a society can pursue goods constitutive of themselves free from arbitrary manipulation. John Finnis summarized eight commonly accepted characteristics of the Rule of Law:

> A legal system exemplifies the Rule of Law to the extent that (i) its rules are prospective, not retroactive, and (ii) are not in any other way impossible to comply with; that (iii) its rules are promulgated, (iv) clear, and (v) coherent one with another; that (vi) its rules are sufficiently stable to allow people to be guided by their knowledge of the content of the rules; that (vii) the making of decrees and orders applicable to relatively limited situations is guided by rules that are promulgated, clear, stable, and relatively general; and that (viii) those people who have authority to make, administer, and apply the rules in an official capacity (a) are

---

[371] Neil MacCormick, *Natural Law and the Separation of Law and Morals*, in NATURAL LAW THEORY: CONTEMPORARY ESSAYS 105, 123 (Robert P. George ed., 1992).

[372] ROBERT P. GEORGE, IN DEFENSE OF NATURAL LAW 116 (1999).

[373] *Id.* at 120.

[374] NLNR, at 155.

[375] Here, I am eliding the two basic conceptions of the common law: the declaratory theory and the positive law theory. Under either conception, stare decisis provides reasons to rational beings.

accountable for their compliance with rules applicable to their performance and (b) do actually administer the law consistently and in accordance with its tenor.[376]

Stare decisis advances these values.

Members of society know that the proposition decided in Case X will govern their conduct into the future and are thereby given reasons to prospectively direct their conduct. The legal norms announced in Case X, in our legal practice, are realistically possible to follow. The publication of opinions, announcement of opinions in open court, discussion in the media, and inclusion in Westlaw and LexisNexis effectively alert attorneys, and (via the division of labor) the populace, to the content of a precedent. Courts strive mightily to assimilate a case with past precedent and with other pertinent areas of law. The result is that precedents are generally clear and cohere with other decisions.

The doctrine of stare decisis also ensures that the rule announced in a precedent will govern conduct into the future without sudden or drastic changes. A doctrine of precedent allows members of society to plan their lives, to make decisions that will have an impact into the future, and to be confident that their plans will not be harmed because of radical change. A doctrine of precedent serves the value of stability by limiting change in the law. Change is not eliminated, but its pace is slowed. Members of society know that decisions affecting their lives will do so in a predictable manner. Accordingly, they will be able to order their private and public lives with faith that their plans will not be thwarted unexpectedly.

Lastly, a value advanced by adherence to precedent is that judicial discretion is constrained. As case law builds up around authoritative texts, the open legal questions that remain diminish in importance and number because legal solutions to such questions have been authoritatively identified through adjudication. This process advances the other interests supported by stare decisis (for example, predictability) as it constrains judges through the law.

The harmful impact on Rule of Law values caused by the Supreme Court's failure to adhere to constitutional precedent can be seen by looking at its death penalty jurisprudence. The Eighth Amendment of the U.S. Constitution prohibits "cruel and unusual punishments."[377] When the Eighth Amendment was ratified in 1791, the death penalty was regularly used. Further, the text of the Constitution appears to recognize the constitutionality of the death penalty in the Fifth Amendment by permitting the deprivation of "life" with due process of law. Therefore, it came as no surprise when, in the 1971 case of *McGautha* v. *California*, the Supreme Court upheld the constitutionality of the challenged death penalty regimes.[378]

---

[376] NLNR, at 270–71; *see also* LON L. FULLER, THE MORALITY OF LAW 39 (rev. ed. 1969) (offering eight criteria of the Rule of Law similar to Finnis); Joseph Raz, *The Rule of Law and Its Virtue*, 93 LAW Q. REV. 195 (1977) (offering a formulation of the Rule of Law). For an earlier and influential formulation of the components of the Rule of Law, *see* A. V. DICEY, INTRODUCTION TO THE STUDY OF THE LAW OF THE CONSTITUTION 202–03 (10th ed. 1960).

[377] U.S. CONST. amend. VIII.

[378] *McGautha* v. *California*, 402 U.S. 183, 196 (1971).

However, the very next year, in *Furman* v. *Georgia*, the Court ruled that the death penalty, as practiced in most states, was unconstitutional.[379] *Furman* caused enormous disruption in the nation both culturally and legally. The immediate legislative result was that at least thirty-five states re-enacted death penalty statutes trying to conform to *Furman's* mandates.[380]

A mere four years after *Furman*, in *Gregg* v. *Georgia*, the Supreme Court reversed course again, this time concluding that the death penalty was not unconstitutional in all applications, and upholding Georgia's revised capital punishment statute.[381] The result of the Supreme Court's death penalty jurisprudence has been, as Justice Scalia later wrote, to "destroy[] stability and make[] our case law an unreliable basis for the designing of laws by citizens and their representatives, and for action by public officials."[382]

In earlier subsections, I described how the Framers and Ratifiers of Article III recognized the crucial role stare decisis plays protecting Rule of Law values, such as through limiting judicial discretion. One of the ways that they integrated this value for the United States was by incorporating it into "judicial Power."

Third, stare decisis is valuable because it preserves some nonoriginalist precedents that reach substantively just results. Regardless of one's perspective, there are nonoriginalist precedents the results of which one believes are substantively just. For example, progressive Americans tend to laud the constitutional right to abortion identified in *Roe* v. *Wade*,[383] while conservative and libertarian Americans tend to embrace the anti-commandeering rule articulated in *Printz* v. *United States*.[384] From different perspectives, all Americans can identify nonoriginalist precedents that create justly-ordered relationships and which consequently contribute to the common good and human flourishing. By preserving some nonoriginalist precedent, originalism preserves their contributions to the common good. I explain further this reason in the following subsection.

2.4.4.7 Analysis to Evaluate Nonoriginalist Precedent

Up to this point, I showed that the original meaning of "judicial Power" requires federal courts to provide significant respect for precedent. I then explained in the prior subsection how this meaning was normatively attractive because it helped secure Rule of Law values and justice, which are central to securing the common good and human flourishing. Here, I describe the analysis federal judges should utilize when evaluating nonoriginalist precedent.

---

[379] *Furman* v. *Georgia*, 408 U.S. 238, 239–40 (1972).
[380] *Gregg* v. *Georgia*, 428 U.S. 153, 179–80 (1976).
[381] *Id.* at 187, 206–07.
[382] *Roper* v. *Simmons*, 543 U.S. 551, 630 (2005) (Scalia, J., dissenting).
[383] *Roe* v. *Wade*, 410 U.S. 113 (1973).
[384] Assuming *Printz* is nonoriginalist. *But see* Rappaport, *supra* note 210.

Stepping back for a moment to first think about nonoriginalist precedent, a judge in a typical constitutional case following an originalist methodology must attempt to discern and apply the Constitution's original meaning. However, when faced with a nonoriginalist precedent purporting to interpret the Constitution, a judge's duty is more complicated. In these situations, a judge is faced with a mistake. My claim, up to this point, is that originalism, like our legal system more generally, contains a mechanism to deal with these mistakes: it preserves some, but not all nonoriginalist precedent.

Next, I argue that, when faced with nonoriginalist precedent, federal judges should employ three factors to decide how to proceed: (1) the extent to which the precedent deviates from the Constitution's original meaning; (2) the extent to which overruling the precedent would affect Rule of Law Values; and (3) the extent to which the precedent is just.[385] Making these determinations requires judges with the judicial virtues, described more fully in Section 2.6.

2.4.4.7.1 DEGREE OF DEPARTURE The first factor is the degree to which the nonoriginalist precedent departs from the original meaning. This factor is necessary because nonoriginalist precedent is not all created equal. Some are slight deviations, and others are major. In some cases, it is easy to see that a decision greatly deviates from the original meaning. For example, few scholars argue that the Supreme Court's current doctrine of substantive due process is faithful to the original meaning of the Fourteenth Amendment's Due Process Clause, and most scholars agree that the doctrine is a significant departure from the Clause's original meaning.[386] However, many potentially nonoriginalist decisions are not so clear-cut. Do cases holding that the Equal Protection Clause governs all racial classifications, including so-called benign classifications, depart from the original meaning of the Clause, and, if so, how far?[387] Or, what about cases that extend the protection of the Religion Clauses of the First Amendment beyond monotheistic beliefs to non-theistic beliefs?[388]

This first factor is also important because it addresses the legitimacy of the Supreme Court's prior action(s) and the nonoriginalist precedent's legal authority. The Supreme Court may legitimately overrule an act of the elected branches only if

[385] I am using "just" in a manner I explain shortly.

[386] ELY, *supra* note 201, at 18 ("[T]here is simply no avoiding the fact that the word that follows 'due' is 'process.'"); RAOUL BERGER, GOVERNMENT BY JUDICIARY: THE TRANSFORMATION OF THE FOURTEENTH AMENDMENT 248–82 (2d ed. 1997); Ryan C. Williams, *The One and Only Substantive Due Process Clause*, 120 YALE L.J. 408, 460–99 (2010).

[387] *See City of Richmond v. J. A. Croson Co.*, 488 U.S. 469, 493 (1989) (holding that all racial classifications are subject to strict scrutiny).

[388] *See United States v. Seeger*, 380 U.S. 163, 165–66 (1965) (defining religion in the draft-exemption statute to include nontheistic beliefs purportedly to avoid the constitutional issue of an establishment); *Torcasco v. Watkins*, 367 U.S. 488, 495 (1961) (defining religion to include theistic and nontheistic beliefs, such as "Secular Humanism").

the elected branches contravene the (determinate) original meaning of the Constitution. A Supreme Court justice's duty is to enforce the authoritative, prudential, social ordering that has enabled our society to effectively pursue the common good, embodied in the Constitution's original meaning.[389] The more a precedent deviates from the original meaning, the stronger is the judge's obligation to correct the deviation because, by definition, the greater the precedent pulls away from the Constitution's identified path of pursuit of the common good.

To get a handle on this, consider the Supreme Court's pre-New Deal expansions of its interpretation of the Commerce Clause. In *Swift & Co. v. United States*, and *The Shreveport Rate Cases*, the Supreme Court interpreted the Clause to authorize Congress to regulate intrastate activities that were part of the stream of commerce and an instrumentality of commerce, respectively.[390] These cases may be deviations from the Constitution's original meaning[391] but, if they are, they are substantially smaller deviations than *Wickard v. Filburn*,[392] which fully enunciated the substantial effects test.

Relatedly, the judge's obligation to reverse nonoriginalist decisions varies proportionately with the decision's variation from the original meaning because, the greater the variation, the more harm it causes to the common good. The Constitution's original meaning is the meaning that coordinates our society's members toward to the common good, which enables them to pursue their own flourishing. The more a nonoriginalist precedent deviates from the original meaning, the more it detracts from the coordination created and maintained by the original meaning. For example, Article IV, Section 4 requires the federal government to protect state governments when those state governments are subject to "domestic violence." The Clause's original meaning is a fine-tuned federalism balance that respects state autonomy while, at the same time, protecting them. A different interpretation will detract from that federalism balance, and the greater the deviation – to one extreme or the other – the more grievous the harm will be to the original meaning's social coordination. If, for instance, the Clause were interpreted to authorize federal intervention in cases of spousal abuse, that would be a greater upsetting of the social ordering than if the Clause were interpreted to authorize federal action when a state experiences peaceful protests.

A third reason why a judge's duty is variable is that the perceived legitimacy of the exercise of judicial review varies depending on the clarity and extent to which a decision deviates from the original meaning. The more a decision deviates, the more likely it jeopardizes the valuable role the proper exercise of judicial review plays in preserving our constitutional social ordering. Constitutional judicial review

---

[389] *Infra* Section 4.5.
[390] *Swift & Co. v. United States*, 196 U.S. 375 (1905); *The Shreveport Rate Cases*, 234 U.S. 342 (1914).
[391] Epstein, *supra* note 230. at 1411–21, 1439–40.
[392] *Wickard v. Filburn*, 317 U.S. 111 (1942).

is essential to our society's ability to govern itself by keeping the elected branches within their delegated powers. Since the average American's view of the proper exercise of constitutional judicial review is roughly characterized as originalism,[393] deviations from the original meaning threaten public acceptance of judicial review and therefore threaten our society's ability to abide by our constitutional social ordering. This is because, absent following the original meaning, most Americans believe that the Supreme Court is merely imposing its own policy preferences on society. Leaving other factors aside, the greater a decision deviates from the original meaning, the more suspicious Americans will be of the Supreme Court's exercise of judicial review.

2.4.4.7.2 RULE OF LAW VALUES The second factor judges must consider when addressing nonoriginalist precedent is the impact on Rule of Law values caused by overruling or limiting a nonoriginalist precedent. Impact on Rule of Law values is a necessary factor to consider because of its central role in the justification for stare decisis and its necessary role in the common good.

There is no single, easy-to-apply rule governing how a judge should address the Rule of Law values implicated by a nonoriginalist precedent because the circumstances regarding nonoriginalist cases are myriad. On one end of the spectrum are cases where it is relatively clear that overruling a precedent would cause great harm to Rule of Law values. For example, Article I, Section 8, Clause 5 of the Constitution authorizes Congress to "coin money."[394] There is scholarship showing that Congress was not authorized by this provision to issue paper money.[395] However, the Supreme Court held in the *Legal Tender Cases* that acts passed by Congress making notes issued by the Federal Government legal tender were constitutional.[396] Today, however, over 130 years later, paper money is ubiquitous. "[I]n our age of checks, credit cards and electronic banking, the issue is off the agenda: no Supreme Court would now reexamine the merits, no matter how closely wedded it was to the original intent theory and no matter how certain it was of its predecessor's error."[397] A return to the original meaning – the Supreme Court overruling the *Legal Tender Cases* – would dramatically harm Rule of Law values.

---

[393] Donald L. Drakeman, *What's the Point of Originalism?*, 37 HARV. J. L. & PUB. POL'Y 1123 (2014); RICHARD H. FALLON, JR., IMPLEMENTING THE CONSTITUTION 13, 123 (2001); ELY, *supra* note 201, at 12.

[394] U.S. CONST. art. I, § 8, cl. 5.

[395] *E.g.*, Kenneth W. Dam, *The Legal Tender Cases*, 1981 SUP. CT. REV. 367, 389; Claire Priest, *Currency Policies and Legal Development in Colonial New England*, 110 YALE L.J. 1303, 1399 n.358 (2001); *but see* Robert G. Natelson, *Paper Money and the Original Understanding of the Coinage Clause*, 31 HARV. J. L. & PUB. POL'Y 1017 (2008).

[396] *The Legal Tender Cases*, 110 U.S. 421 (1884).

[397] Henry Paul Monaghan, *Stare Decisis and Constitutional Adjudication*, 88 COLUM. L. REV. 723, 744 (1988).

On the other end of the spectrum are cases where overruling would not significantly harm Rule of Law values, either because the overruling itself would not harm the values or because the nonoriginalist precedent itself harms Rule of Law values and overruling the precedent would eliminate those baleful effects. An example of this is *Crawford* v. *Washington*.[398] There, the Court overruled a 1980 case, *Ohio* v. *Roberts*, which had held that the Confrontation Clause of the Sixth Amendment did not bar admission of an unavailable witness' statements against a criminal defendant if the statements bore "adequate 'indicia of reliability'."[399] The majority in *Crawford* found that the original meaning of the Confrontation Clause prohibited admission of unavailable witness' statements that were "testimonial" absent the opportunity for cross-examination by the criminal defendant.[400]

The overruling of nonoriginalist precedent in *Crawford* likely advanced Rule of Law values. This is because the rule announced in *Crawford*, unlike the "indicia of reliability" rule from *Roberts*, is relatively easy to apply and applies in a more predictable manner, so defendants and the government can plan more accurately. Also, the rule in *Crawford* better accords with the Court's case law in surrounding areas, which improved legal coherence, itself a Rule of Law value.[401] Furthermore, there are few reliance interests harmed by overruling *Roberts* because it does not affect previously existing property or contract interests, and because only the relatively small number of criminal defendants who had not yet had a trial before *Crawford* was announced (and prosecutors prosecuting these defendants) could conceivably have relied on *Roberts*.

The two ends of the spectrum are relatively easy to identify. By contrast, the area between the ends requires sound practical wisdom. The duty of the judge in the middle area is to determine whether and/or how overruling a nonoriginalist precedent will harm the Rule of Law values so central to society's effective pursuit of the common good. Unlike those cases where the original meaning is determinate and judges have no discretion, here judges are relatively unconstrained and must make practical judgments drawing on the judicial virtues.

Originalism also contains two mechanisms to minimize harm to Rule of Law values caused by overruling nonoriginalist precedent. First, the Supreme Court could slowly turn the law in an area away from its nonoriginalist orientation and re-orient it toward the original meaning. This is a three-step and relatively long-term process that I explain in Subsection 3.4.6. This process has the virtue of signaling the law's slow evolution back to the original meaning, which helps the legal system plan for the changes and maximizes protection of reliance interests. This slow evolution and eventual overruling permits individuals and society to conform to the shift

---

[398] *Crawford* v. *Washington*, 541 U.S. 36 (2004), *overruling in part Ohio* v. *Roberts*, 448 U.S. 56 (1980).
[399] *Roberts*, 448 U.S. at 66.
[400] *Crawford*, 541 U.S. at 53–54.
[401] *See id.* at 57.

towards the original meaning of the Constitution and away from the nonoriginalist precedent with relatively little harm to Rule of Law values.

A second manner by which the potential harm to Rule of Law values caused by overruling nonoriginalist precedent may be reduced is through the exercise of federal courts' inherent equitable power.[402] Courts could utilize their equitable power to tailor a ruling so that it reduced harm to Rule of Law values. For example, a court could determine that, to allow society time to adjust to an overruling, the court's ruling would take effect at a point in the future. Or, a court could issue an order implementing its ruling in stages over a period of time. The most prominent example of this equitable tailoring of an order is *Brown* v. *Board of Education*, where the Court tailored the implementation of its ruling taking into account the systemic obstacles facing desegregation.[403]

One additional point is worth emphasizing. The Framers and Ratifiers chose to (re)order American society through a written Constitution coupled with the originalist linguistic conventions of the day. One of the key benefits of this choice is that it provides relatively robust determinacy compared to common law constitutionalism.[404] Common law constitutionalism, at least as practiced by the United States Supreme Court and its scholarly advocates, contains disagreement about how to interpret particular precedents and precedent generally, what "modalities" justices should employ, what level of respect to give to precedent before it can be overruled, and disingenuous distinguishing and overruling of precedent by justices.

2.4.4.7.3 THE PRECEDENT'S JUSTNESS The last factor a judge must consider when faced with a nonoriginalist precedent is the justness of the decision. This is the characteristic of a precedent to rightly order the relationships of persons and institutions even though the judicial act of ordering – the precedent – was itself illegal because it was not in accord with the governing law. This characteristic is exemplified by the common expression, "I like the result of the case," where one believes that the ruling in the case contributes to just relationships but, at the same time, one believes that the judge was not authorized by the existing law to reach the desirable result. In any system of law, including ours, that does not employ animate justice[405] – in other words,

---

[402] *See generally* Robert J. Pushaw, Jr., *The Inherent Powers of Federal Courts and the Structural Constitution*, 86 IOWA L. REV. 735 (2001) (arguing that the grant of "judicial Power" to "Courts" included inherent judicial powers).

[403] *Brown* v. *Board of Education*, 349 U.S. 294, 299–301 (1955).

[404] Jeffrey A. Pojanowski & Kevin C. Walsh, *Enduring Originalism*, 105 GEO. L.J. 97, 156 (2016).

[405] Perhaps the most prominent example of animate justice is King Solomon, who had received from God the power of wise judgment: "Behold I have done for thee according to thy words, and have given thee a wise and understanding heart, insomuch that there hath been no one like thee before thee, nor shall arise after thee." 1 KINGS 3:12. And perhaps the most well-known example of Solomon's solomonic exercise of judgment occurred when two women appeared before Solomon both claiming to be the mother of the same child. *Id.* at 3:24–27.

where the law making and law applying functions are separated – this phenomenon will occur.[406]

Aristotle defined justice, broadly understood, as justice-as-lawfulness because of the central role law plays in enabling a society to effectively pursue the common good.[407] Justice-as-lawfulness identified justice as law-following, which was crucial to the common good and human flourishing because of law's capacity to coordinate the members of society.[408] Aristotle also described a narrower facet of justice: justice-as-fairness, or giving each his due.[409] Modern scholars often employ the label "general" justice for justice-as-lawfulness, and "particular" justice for justice-as-fairness.[410]

There are occasions when the correct application of a positive law norm leads to an ordering of relationships that, absent the positive law norm, would have been unjust in the sense of justice-as-fairness. In other words, the characteristic of justice-as-fairness can be in tension with the characteristic of justice-as-lawfulness: judgment in accord with the positive law.

This result arises from the hardness – the posited-ness – of positive law coupled with the limited nature of the authority of the particular law-application office. Positive law is made for the generality of cases. It can result in suboptimal results on the margins. Judges receive their authority to judge – to apply the law – from their office, which is a creation of the judge's particular society.[411] If a judge acts beyond that authority, the judge has wrongfully usurped authority.[412] In a society such as ours that employs inanimate justice, a federal judge's authority extends to enforcement of the law: "Hence, it is necessary to judge according to the written law."[413]

So, there will be occasions when the proper application of a legal norm (*i.e.*, justice-as-lawfulness) would lead to what, absent the law (*i.e.*, justice-as-fairness) would be an unjust ordering of relationships. However, because judges in our legal system may not misapply the law – because to do so would exceed the limits of their office's authority – they will be pushed to issue decisions that put justice-as-lawfulness in tension with justice-as-fairness. Some judges may, because of this tension, misapply the law to achieve a just (justice-as-fairness) result at the expense of justice (justice-as-lawfulness).

---

[406] *See* PLATO, THE STATESMAN 294b–c (Robin Waterfield trans., 1995) (describing inanimate law as "a stubborn, stupid person who refused to allow the slightest deviation from or questioning of his own rules, even if the situation has in fact changed and it turns out to be better for someone to contravene these rules").

[407] NE, at 1129a–1129b.

[408] ST II-II, q. 58, aa. 5, 7.

[409] NE, at 1129b.

[410] *See, e.g.*, AQUINAS, at 130 n.e; RICHARD KRAUT, ARISTOTLE 102 n.6 (2002).

[411] ST II-II, q. 60, a. 2.

[412] *Id.*

[413] *Id.* II-II, q. 60, a. 5.

A poignant example of this phenomenon is *DeShaney* v. *Winnebago County Department of Social Services.*[414] There, the mother of Joshua, a four-year old boy who had been left profoundly mentally retarded after being severely beaten by his father, sued the county social services department and local government officials. "Poor Joshua!"[415] Prior to the beating, the county officials had good reason to know that Joshua's father was abusing him. Joshua's mother argued that the failure of the county officers to intervene to stop the abuse deprived Joshua of his liberty without due process in violation of the Fourteenth Amendment.

The Supreme Court ruled, consistent with the text, history, and purpose of the Due Process Clause, that the officials had not deprived Joshua of due process.[416] The Court acknowledged the "undeniably tragic" facts of the case[417] and how "[j]udges and lawyers[were] moved by natural sympathy in a case like this to find a way for Joshua and his mother to receive adequate compensation for the grievous harm inflicted upon them."[418] Despite the injustice dealt to Joshua and his mother, the Court refused to incorrectly interpret or apply the positive law norm (the Due Process Clause) to rightly order the relationships between Joshua, his mother, and the government officials. The Court, in other words, acted justly (justice-as-lawfulness) and refused to effect – through a legally unwarranted decision – just relationships among the parties (justice-as-fairness).[419]

Some nonoriginalist decisions rightly order the relationships of persons and institutions despite their inconsistency with the original meaning. In fact, this is frequently identified by critics as a or the primary reason to reject originalism. For instance, *Brown* v. *Board of Education* is probably the most prominent example identified by critics.[420] *Brown*, decided in 1954, ruled that racial segregation in public schools was unconstitutional.[421] The Court appeared to suggest that the original meaning of the Equal Protection Clause of the Fourteenth Amendment did not outlaw racially segregated schools.[422] There is scholarly support for this view of the Clause's meaning.[423] Thus, *assuming* for the sake of argument that the

---

[414] *DeShaney* v. *Winnebago County Department of Social Services*, 489 U.S. 189 (1989).

[415] *Id.* at 213 (Blackmun, J., dissenting).

[416] *Id.* at 195–96.

[417] *Id.* at 191.

[418] *Id.* at 202–03.

[419] My claim does not entail that DeShaney should not have prevailed under another provision, such as the Equal Protection Clause.

[420] To be clear, this analysis is not evidence that I agree with these critics.

[421] *Brown* v. *Board. of Educ.*, 347 U.S. 483, 493 (1954).

[422] *Id.* at 489–90.

[423] There has been significant scholarly research into whether the original meaning of the Equal Protection Clause prohibited segregated public schools. Some scholars have concluded that it did not. *See, e.g.*, BERGER, *supra* note 386, at 132–54 (arguing that segregation was not precluded by the Fourteenth Amendment); ROBERT H. BORK, THE TEMPTING OF AMERICA: THE POLITICAL SEDUCTION OF THE LAW 75 (1990) ("The inescapable fact is that those who ratified the amendment did not think it outlawed segregated education."); LAURENCE H. TRIBE

original meaning of the Equal Protection Clause did not outlaw segregated public schools, the ruling in *Brown* was not just (justice-as-lawfulness), though it was just (justice-as-fairness).

The result in *Brown* is lauded for helping create rightly ordered relationships among persons and institutions in states with previously-segregated public schools. Black Americans were no longer accorded and denied benefits solely on the basis of race, which is rarely an appropriate basis for such decisions.[424] The result in *Brown* was just (justice-as-fairness).

The fact that a precedent possesses the characteristic of justice-as-fairness is something, *ceteris paribus*, that a society and judge should prefer. Remember, the situation about which we are concerned is not whether, prior to the deciding of a case, a society and judge should prefer rightly ordered relationships between persons and institutions. Given a judge's duty to enforce the positive law norms of a society, the judge must strive for justice (justice-as-lawfulness), even when it comes at the cost of justice (justice-as-fairness) – even if following the law would result in (or allow to persist) what, absent the legal norm, would be an unjust ordering of the relationships of the parties to the case. The situations about which we are concerned are nonoriginalist precedents – precedents that, when issued, violated the law – and our only question is what a judge should do regarding such precedents. One potential characteristic of such precedents, which makes retention of them more desirable, is justice-as-fairness.

Return again to *Brown*: assuming that the other two factors are in equipoise, a judge is left with two possible worlds – one in which *Brown* is overruled and one in which *Brown* is not overruled. The fact that not overruling *Brown* would more likely lead to a society in which relationships, relative to the world where *Brown* is overruled, are more rightly ordered is a reason to not overrule *Brown*.

& MICHAEL C. DORF, ON READING THE CONSTITUTION 12–13 (1991) ("There is very little doubt that most of the [Framers of the Fourteenth Amendment] assumed that segregated public schools were, at the time, entirely consistent with the Fourteenth Amendment."); Alexander M. Bickel, *The Original Understanding and the Segregation Decision*, 69 HARV. L. REV. 1, 58 (1955) (finding that the Fourteenth Amendment, "as originally understood, was meant to apply neither to jury service, nor suffrage, nor antimiscegenation statutes, nor segregation"); *see also* Jack M. Balkin, *Original Meaning and Constitutional Redemption*, 24 CONST. COMM. 427, 450 (2008) ("Before McConnell's article, most people accepted Alexander Bickel's conclusion that the framers of the Fourteenth Amendment did not intend to prohibit segregated public schools."). The most powerfully argued scholarship to the contrary is Michael W. McConnell, *Originalism and the Desegregation Decisions*, 81 VA. L. REV. 947 (1995). For responses to Professor McConnell's thesis see Earl M. Maltz, *Originalism and the Desegregation Decisions – A Response to Professor McConnell*, 13 CONST. COMMENT. 223 (1996); Michael J. Klarman, *Response: Brown, Originalism, and Constitutional Theory: A Response to Professor McConnell*, 81 VA. L. REV. 1881 (1995).

[424] Perhaps in the context of race riots in prison, for example, government could legitimately act based on the race of rioters.

2.4.4.8 Application of Analysis to Two Prominent Precedents

In this subsection, I apply the three-factor analysis described in the prior subsections to two of the most important Supreme Court decisions in the twentieth century: *Brown* v. *Board of Education* and *Roe* v. *Wade*. These are the two decisions against which constitutional interpretive methodologies are often measured by individuals in light of their deeply held beliefs and by scholars for intellectual consistency.

Application of these three criteria calls for judges with the judicial virtues, which I describe in Section 2.6. The judge must accurately apply and balance these criteria to determine whether to overrule the nonoriginalist precedent. The following applications are preliminary in nature. Of course, reasonable people may have legitimate differences on the conclusion of this complex process.

2.4.4.8.1 BROWN V. BOARD OF EDUCATION As previously stated, the first factor judges should utilize to decide what to do with nonoriginalist precedent is the extent of deviation from the original meaning. Many scholars have argued that *Brown* deviated from the original meaning of the Equal Protection Clause. Even Michael McConnell, who has provided the most powerful argument that *Brown* is an originalist precedent, has noted:

> An impressive array of academic authorities, from across the ideological and jurisprudential spectrum – including such figures as Alexander Bickel, Laurence Tribe, Richard Posner, Mark Tushnet, Raoul Berger, Ronald Dworkin, and Walter Burns – had come to the conclusion that under the original understanding of the Fourteenth Amendment, racial segregation of public schools was constitutionally permissible.[425]

However, even if *Brown* violated the original meaning of the Clause, its ruling was not significantly contrary to the Clause's original meaning. For instance, the Clause's overall purpose was to remove the incidents of slavery of black Americans,[426] a purpose with which *Brown* comports. Furthermore, there is good reason to believe that that the Privileges or Immunities Clause, whose meaning the *Brown* Court was prevented from following by the nonoriginalist *The Slaughter-House Cases*,[427] prohibits racially segregated schools and would support *Brown*'s result.[428]

---

[425] Michael W. McConnell, *The Originalist Case for Brown v. Board of Education*, 19 HARV. J. L. & PUB. POL'Y 457, 457 (1996).

[426] *See* 3 RONALD D. ROTUNDA & JOHN E. NOWAK, TREATISE ON CONSTITUTIONAL LAW: SUBSTANCE AND PROCEDURE § 18.7, at 310 (3d ed. 1999) ("Their central concern throughout the debate was securing some rights for freed blacks which state governments (or a future Democratic Congress) could not disregard.").

[427] *The Slaughter-House Cases*, 83 U.S. 36 (1872).

[428] Steven G. Calabresi & Michael W. Perl, *Originalism and Brown v. Board of Education*, 2014 MICH. ST. L. REV. 429, 436–37 (2014); Christopher R. Green, *Originalism and the*

Brown is not like other applications of the Clause that deviated further from the Clause's original meaning. For example, Justice Kennedy argued in *Obergefell v. Hodges* that the challenged Ohio statute, which defined marriage as between one man and one woman, violated the Clause.[429] Justice Kennedy relied on the claim that "the marriage laws enforced by the respondents are in essence unequal: same-sex couples are denied all the benefits afforded to opposite-sex couples and are barred from exercising a fundamental right" to find that Ohio's law "serves to disrespect and subordinate them," and hence violated the Equal Protection Clause.[430] This string of claims is only remotely related to the original meaning of the Clause. Indeed, Justice Kennedy expressly stated that "history is the beginning of these cases."[431] In sum, if *Brown* deviated from the original meaning of the Constitution, its deviation was relatively minor.

The second factor is whether overruling the nonorginalist precedent would harm Rule of Law values. The no-segregation rule announced in *Brown* is easy to apply and it was clearly stated.[432] The no-segregation rule of *Brown* has been consistently applied by the Supreme Court, lower federal courts, and state courts. The rule is now, nearly seventy years later, deeply embedded in our law, not only in the case law following and implementing *Brown*, but through federal and state statutes, such as the Civil Rights Act of 1964,[433] which enforces and expands upon the *Brown* rule. Further, state and federal institutions, such as schools and public accommodations, premise their mode of operation on the *Brown* rule, and many federal and state institutions are charged with ensuring the implementation of *Brown*. In sum, overruling *Brown* would cause great harm to the Rule of Law values served by precedent.

Last is the question of the justness of the precedent. As explained in my previous discussion concerning the third factor, *Brown* is a clear example of a precedent creating rightly ordered relationships. In conclusion, assuming that *Brown* is a nonoriginalist precedent, the constitutionally mandated significant respect calls for a judge to affirm *Brown*.

2.4.4.8.2 *ROE V. WADE* AND ITS PROGENY *Roe* held, in 1973, that there is a constitutionally protected right to abortion.[434] The constitutional right announced in *Roe* is a significant departure from the original meaning of the Due Process Clause of the Fourteenth Amendment. First, the Due Process Clause did not have

---

Sense-Reference Distinction, 50 ST. LOUIS U. L.J. 555, 593–627 (2006); John Harrison, *Reconstructing the Privileges or Immunities Clause*, 101 YALE L.J. 1385, 1462–63 (1992).

[429] *Obergefell v. Hodges*, 125 S. Ct. 2584, 2602–05 (2015).

[430] *Id.* at 2604.

[431] *Id.* at 2594.

[432] The only substantial question was the breadth of the rule, which was relatively quickly resolved by the Court in subsequent cases. 3 ROTUNDA & NOWAK, *supra* note 426, § 18.8, at 332–33.

[433] 1964 Civil Rights Act, 42 U.S.C. §§ 2000e–e17 (2000).

[434] *Roe v. Wade*, 410 U.S. 113, 164–65 (1973).

substantive content when enacted,[435] or its substantive content was limited.[436] Therefore, finding a substantive right to abortion in the term "liberty" is contrary to the original meaning. Second, when the Due Process Clause was ratified in 1868, all states had limits on abortion, many states strictly limited abortion, and the trend was toward complete prohibition of abortion except in rare cases.[437] Therefore, the original meaning of "liberty" did not encompass a right to abortion. Further, the primary goal of the Due Process Clause was to ensure that newly-freed black Americans were protected from arbitrary deprivations because of race.[438] This concern is far from preventing states from prohibiting the killing of unborn human beings.

In contrast to *Brown*, overruling *Roe* would likely not harm Rule of Law values, although there are factors pointing in both directions. The rule announced initially in *Roe* and its companion case of *Doe v. Bolton*[439] was clear and relatively easy to apply. However, *Planned Parenthood v. Casey*, though it salvaged *Roe*'s result, also substituted a vague test in its place.[440] *Casey*'s "undue burden" standard is much more difficult to apply in a principled manner than the alternative offered by federalism: states may regulate abortion as much, or as little, as they wish. Rejection of the *Casey* test will therefore aid legal clarity.

It is true that the principle of individual autonomy that *Roe* utilized from *Eisenstadt v. Baird*[441] remains embedded in parts of the Court's case law.[442] Still, there is also case law that limits the individual autonomy principle relied upon by *Roe*,[443] including an express narrowing of *Roe* and *Casey*'s conception of reproductive autonomy.[444] Similarly, there are numerous federal and state laws that limit *Roe*, along with several attempts at overruling it. These include: partial birth abortion bans[445]; protection of children born after failed

---

[435] ELY, *supra* note 201, at 98.

[436] Williams, *supra* note 386, at 460–99.

[437] The key source for the history of abortion regulation is JOSEPH W. DELLAPENNA, DISPELLING THE MYTHS OF ABORTION HISTORY (2006).

[438] 3 ROTUNDA & NOWAK, *supra* note 426, § 18.8, at 309–10.

[439] *Doe v. Bolton*, 410 U.S. 179 (1973).

[440] *See Planned Parenthood v. Casey*, 505 U.S. 833, 878 (1992) ("An undue burden exists, and therefore a provision of law is invalid, if its purpose or effect is to place a substantial obstacle in the path of a woman seeking an abortion before the fetus attains viability.").

[441] *Eisenstadt v. Baird*, 405 U.S. 438 (1972).

[442] *E.g., Obergefell v. Hodges*, 135 S. Ct. 2584, 2597–98 (2015); *Lawrence v. Texas*, 539 U.S. 558, 565 (2003); *Romer v. Evans*, 517 U.S. 620 (1996).

[443] *Washington v. Glucksberg*, 521 U.S. 702, 721 (1997) (quoting *Moore v. E. Cleveland*, 431 U.S. 494, 503 (1977)); *Michael H. v. Gerald D.*, 491 U.S. 110, 124 (1989); *see also* Michael Stokes Paulsen, *Abrogating Stare Decisis by Statute: May Congress Remove the Precedent Effect of Roe and Casey?*, 109 YALE L.J. 1535, 1557–62 (2000).

[444] *Gonzales v. Carhart*, 550 U.S. 124 (2007).

[445] *See* Partial-Birth Abortion Ban Act of 2003, Pub. L. No. 108–105, 117 Stat. 1201 (codified at 18 U.S.C.A. § 1531 (West Supp. 2005)). States have also imposed partial-birth abortion bans. For

abortions;[446] unborn-child pain prevention acts;[447] bills banning abortions after an unborn child's detectable heartbeat;[448] repeated attempts at a constitutional amendment to end abortion;[449] the annual introduction of the Hyde Amendment, which prohibits federal funding for abortions;[450] restrictions on the use of military facilities to provide abortions;[451] attempts to restrict federal court jurisdiction over abortion cases;[452] recognition that unborn children are victims of crimes;[453] recognition that unborn children are human beings;[454] regulation of abortion facilities;[455] and requirements for parental notification,[456] among others.[457] Overruling *Roe* would bring the Supreme Court's interpretation of the Constitution into alignment with these numerous other facets of the law.

an updated summary of the approximately twenty states that ban partial-birth abortion, see Guttmacher Institute, *Bans on Specific Abortion Methods Used after the First Trimester*, www .guttmacher.org/state-policy/explore/bans-specific-abortion-methods-used-after-first-trimester (visited July 18, 2017).

[446] Born-Alive Infants Protection Act of 2002, Pub. L. No. 107–207, 116 Stat. 926.

[447] *See* National Right to Life Committee, Inc., *Pain-Capable Unborn Child Protection Act*, www .nrlc.org/uploads/stateleg/PCUCPAfactsheet.pdf (visited July 18, 2017) (identifying sixteen states with such acts as of Jan. 9, 2017).

[448] *See* Ann Sanner & Julie Carr Smyth, *Abortion Foes Push Fetal Heartbeat Bills in States*, www .nbcnews.com/id/44879242/ns/politics-more_politics/t/abortion-foes-push-fetal-heartbeat-bills-states/#.WW4IYRXyuUk (Oct. 12, 2011) (summarizing this legislation).

[449] *See, e.g.*, S. J. Res. 12, 96th Cong. (1980).

[450] *See, e.g.*, Act of Nov. 20, 1979, Pub. L. No. 96–123, § 109, 93 Stat. 923, 926; Act of Oct. 12, 1979, Pub. L. No. 96–86, § 118, 93 Stat. 656, 662; Act of Oct. 18, 1978, Pub. L. No. 95–480, § 210, 92 Stat. 1567, 1586; Act of Dec. 9, 1977, Pub. L. No. 95–205, § 101, 91 Stat. 1460, 1460; Act of Sept. 30, 1976, Pub. L. No. 94–439, § 209, 90 Stat. 1418, 1434.

[451] *See, e.g.*, 10 U. S. C. § 1093(b) (2000); National Defense Authorization Act for Fiscal Year 1996, Pub. L. No. 104–106, § 738, 110 Stat 186, 384; *see generally* DAVID BURRELLI, CONG. RESEARCH SERV., 7-5700, ABORTION AND MILITARY MEDICAL FACILITIES (2012).

[452] *See, e.g.*, H. R. 867, 97th Cong. (1981); S. 158, 97th Cong. (1981).

[453] *See, e.g.*, Unborn Victims of Violence Act (Laci and Conner's Law) of 2004, Pub. L. No. 108–212, 118 Stat. 568 (codified at 18 U.S.C.A. § 1841 (West Supp. 2005)); Cal. Penal Code § 187 (a) (West 1999); Fla. Stat. Ann. § 782.09 (West 2000); 720 Ill. Comp. Stat. Ann. 5/9–1.2, –2.1, – 3.2 (West 2002); Mich. Comp. Laws Serv. § 750.322 & n.2 (LexisNexis 2003); N.Y. Penal Law § 125.00 (McKinney 2004); Ohio Rev. Code Ann. §§ 2903.01–.05, .09 (LexisNexis 2003); 18 Pa. Cons. Stat. Ann. §§ 2601–05 (West 1998); Tex. Penal Code Ann. § 1.07 (a)(26) (Vernon Supp. 2004); *Commonwealth* v. *Cass*, 467 N.E.2d 1324, 1325 (Mass. 1984).

[454] *See* Sanctity of Human Life Act, H.R. 586 (115th Congress, Jan. 17, 2017) (stating that "each human life begins with fertilization, cloning, or its equivalent . . . at which time every human has all the legal and constitutional attributes and privileges of personhood").

[455] Guttmacher Institute, *Targeted Regulation of Abortion Providers*, www.guttmacher.org/state-policy/explore/targeted-regulation-abortion-providers (visited July 18, 2017).

[456] Guttmacher Institute, *Parental Involvement in Minors' Abortions*, www.guttmacher.org/state-policy/explore/parental-involvement-minors-abortions (visited July 18, 2017); *e.g.*, La. Rev. Stat. Ann. § 40:1299.33 (2001); N.H. Rev. Stat. Ann. §§ 132.24–.28 (2006); Tex. Fam. Code Ann. §§ 33.001–.011 (Vernon 2002 & Supp. 2005).

[457] For an updated summary of the various state abortion restrictions see Guttmacher Institute, *State Laws and Policies*, www.guttmacher.org/state-policy/laws-policies (visited July 18, 2017). For an updated summary of federal and state legislation see National Right to Life Committee, Inc., *Take Action*, www.nrlc.org/takeaction/ (visited July 18, 2017).

Unlike *Brown*, there are no governmental institutions built to ensure widespread acceptance and compliance with *Roe*. Instead, federal and state governments have taken action to ensure that their governmental apparatuses do not promote – and instead often act to limit – abortion. Abortion, unlike racial discrimination, continues to be what is likely the most divisive issue in American legal and social life. *Roe*, unlike *Brown*, has also been incredibly harmful to the institutional integrity of the Supreme Court and the Rule of Law, as the plurality in *Casey* recognized.[458]

Scholars have severely criticized the broad conception of reliance used by the *Casey* plurality, which makes the ability to procure abortion the nexus of people's lives.[459] A more traditional understanding of reliance would recognize that women who are pregnant (and those by whom they became pregnant) may have acted in reliance on *Roe*.[460] There are relatively few such persons, and their reliance interests dissipate in the short term.

Reducing the dispute over the nature of reliance is the fact that overruling *Roe* would return the legal landscape to the state-by-state regime that existed prior to *Roe*, with some states permitting and some prohibiting abortion. Thus, reliance by individuals on the right announced in *Roe* could be met in states that permit abortion. In sum, although the conclusion is not as clear as with *Brown*, it is likely that Rule of Law values would at least not be significantly harmed by overruling *Roe*, and would be advanced in some ways by overruling *Roe*.

Lastly, *Roe* is unjust. In the United States since *Roe*, over 59 million abortions have occurred.[461] The result has been the death of those aborted, the broken lives of women who aborted their children,[462] the development and growth of a multimillion-dollar industry that profits from the fears of women who are pregnant

---

[458] *Casey v. Planned Parenthood of Se. Pa.*, 505 U.S. 833, 855, 861, 866–67, 869 (1992).

[459] Paulsen, *supra* note 443, at 1554.

[460] *Id.* at 1553.

[461] *See* NAT'L RIGHT TO LIFE, *Abortion in the United States: Statistics and Trends*, www.nrlc.org/uploads/factsheets/FS01AbortionintheUS.pdf (visited July 18, 2017).

[462] The negative effects of abortion include increased physical and mental health problems, *see* Huang Y. et al., *A Meta-Analysis of the Association between Induced Abortion and Breast Cancer Risk among Chinese Females*, 25 CANCER CAUSES CONTROL 227 (2014) (concluding that "[induced abortion] is significantly associated with an increased risk of breast cancer among Chinese females, and the risk of breast cancer increases as the number of [induced abortions] increases"); P. K. Coleman et al., *Reproductive History Patterns and Long-Term Mortality Rates: A Danish, Population-Based Record Linkage Study*, 23 EUR. J. PUB. HEALTH 569 (2013) (finding that "increased risks of death were 45%, 114% and 191% for 1, 2 and 3 abortions, respectively, compared with no abortions after controlling for other reproductive outcomes and last pregnancy age"); P. K. Coleman, *Abortion and Mental Health: Quantitative Synthesis and Analysis of Research Published 1995–2009*, 199 BR. J. PSY. 180 (2011) (finding that "[w]omen who had undergone an abortion experienced an 81% increased risk of mental health problems, and nearly 10% of the incidence of mental health problems was shown to be attributable to abortion"); Philip G. Ney et al., *The Effects of Pregnancy Loss on Women's Health*, 38 SOC. SCI. MED. 1193, 1196–98 (1994) (finding that abortion has a greater negative impact on women's health than miscarriages); David C. Reardon et al., *Depression and Unintended Pregnancy in the National Longitudinal Survey of Youth: A Cohort Study*, 324

in unfortunate circumstances,[463] targeting of minority communities,[464] and a coarsening culture that increasingly devalues human life.[465] Unlike *Brown*, the

BRIT. J. MED. 151, 152 (2002) ("Among married women, those who aborted were significantly more likely to be at 'high risk' of clinical depression compared to those who delivered unintended pregnancies."); increased rates of suicide and homicide, *see* Mika Gissler et al., *Injury Deaths, Suicides and Homicides Associated with Pregnancy, Finland 1987–2000*, 15 EUR. J. PUB. HEALTH 459, 462 (2005) ("In the year after undergoing an abortion, a woman's mortality rate for unintentional injuries, suicide and homicide was substantially higher than among non-pregnant women in all age groups combined."); David C. Reardon et al., *Deaths Associated with Pregnancy Outcome: A Record Linkage Study of Low Income Women*, 95 S. MED. J. 834, 837–38 (2002) (finding the same); increased maternal substance abuse, *see* Priscilla K. Coleman et al., *Substance Use Among Pregnant Women in the Context of Previous Reproductive Loss and Desire for Current Pregnancy*, 10 BRIT. J. PSYCHOL. 255, 261 (2005) ("[H]istory of one induced abortion compared with no history of abortion was associated with a significantly higher likelihood of using substances of all forms during pregnancy."); Priscilla K. Coleman et al., *A History of Induced Abortion in Relation to Substance Use during Subsequent Pregnancies Carried to Term*, 187 AM. J. OBSTETRICS & GYNECOLOGY 1673, 1677 (2002) ("[T]he results revealed significantly higher rates of consumption associated with a previous abortion, compared with previous birth relative to the use of any illicit drugs and alcohol."); and increased risk of complications in future pregnancies and births, *see* Jean Bouyer et al., *Risk Factors for Ectopic Pregnancy: A Comprehensive Analysis Based on a Large Case-Control, Population-Based Study in France*, 157 AM. J. EPIDEMIOLOGY 185, 192 (2003) (finding an increased risk of ectopic pregnancy from prior induced abortions); Brent Rooney et al., *Induced Abortion and Risk of Later Premature Births*, 8 J. AM. PHYSICIANS & SURGEONS 46, 46 (2003) (finding an increased risk of low birth weight and premature birth from prior induced abortions); *see also* PAUL C. REISSER & TERI REISSER, A SOLITARY SORROW (2000) (summarizing harms); Lynne Marie Kohm, *Roe's Effects on Family Law*, 71 WASH. & LEE L. REV. 1339 (2014) (summarizing the negative effects of the right to abortion on families).

[463] Planned Parenthood, the largest abortion provider, itself had revenue of $1.14 billion, in 2015–2016. Planned Parenthood, *2015–2016 Annual Report*, www.plannedparenthood.org/uploads/filer_public/18/40/1840b04b-55d3-4c00-959d-11817023ffc8/20170526_annualreport_p02_singles.pdf (visited July 18, 2017).

[464] *See* Susan W. Enouen, New Research Shows Planned Parenthood Targets Minority Neighborhoods, LIFE ISSUES CONNECTION (Oct. 2012), www.protectingblacklife.org/pdf/PP-Targets-10-2012.pdf (visited July 18, 2017) ("Our analysis [of the 2010 Census) shows that 102 out of 165, or 62% of the Planned Parenthood abortion facilities are located in areas with relatively high African American populations, or in "targeted neighborhoods." An abortion facility is considered to be in a targeted neighborhood if at least one census tract within walking distance has an African American population that is at least 50%, or 1.5 times the percentage of the surrounding county."); Susan A. Cohen, *Abortion and Women of Color: The Bigger Picture*, 11 GUTTMACHER POL. REV. 2 (2008), www.guttmacher.org/gpr/2008/08/abortion-and-women-color-bigger-picture (visited July 18, 2017) ("In the United States, the abortion rate for black women is almost five times that for white women.").

[465] Perhaps the best example of this is the Kermit Gosnell murders of children born alive from Gosnell's botched abortions. *See* Samuel W. Calhoun, *Stopping Philadelphia Abortion Provider Kermit Gosnell and Preventing Others Like Him: An Outcome that Both Pro-Choicers and Pro-Lifers Should Support*, 57 VILL. L. REV. 1 (2012) (describing Gosnell's actions); *see also* NAT'L CONFERENCE OF CATHOLIC BISHOPS, *Abortion and the Supreme Court: Advancing the Culture of Death*, 30 ORIGINS 405, 407 (Dec. 7, 2000) (noting the coarsening of American culture because of *Roe*). For an example of the coarsening of American culture, *see* MTV, *Yo Mamma*, www.mtv.com/onair/dyn/yo_momma/about.jhtml (last visited May 4, 2006) ("Yo Momma is a no-holds-barred competition that pits toughest trash-talkers against one another.").

injustices wrought by *Roe* counsel in favor of its overruling. In conclusion, a judge faced with the question of whether to follow *Roe* should probably overrule it.[466]

2.4.4.9 Preserving (Some) Nonoriginalist Precedent Fits Our Practice of Preserving (Some) Legal Mistakes and Is Normatively Attractive

Originalism's preservation of some nonoriginalist precedent fits well with our broader legal practice's approach to mistakes: sometimes it rejects them, and sometimes is keeps them. Within this broader picture, accepting nonoriginalist precedent appears not only less exotic, it is the conventional way our legal practice operates.

Our legal practice is operated by humans who make mistakes. Sometimes this occurs intentionally, though usually in good faith. Stepping back for a moment, a legal system could make any of three general responses to mistakes: reject all mistakes, accept some mistakes, and accept all mistakes. Our legal practice as a whole takes the middle-of-the-road position,[467] though in particular areas of the law it occasionally makes the first response. For example, in property law, if parties failed to formally identify an easement upon the division of a parcel with a pre-existing use, courts may "fix" the parties' mistake through the doctrine of easements by implication.[468] In the public law context, if a legislature mangles a statute through its "slip of the pen," courts can "correct" that error.[469] Even in the constitutional context, our practice acknowledges and works with mistakes. For instance, the law-of-the-case doctrine requires a subsequent judge to treat an earlier judge's ruling as correct even if it was mistaken.[470]

Our legal system permits the continued existence of mistakes and has developed doctrines to do so, and for good reasons. The reasons include, for instance, protection of reliance interests[471] and rewarding valuable activity,[472] all the while policing these doctrines to ensure that these exceptions do not swallow the Rule of Law.[473] Our legal practice generally charts a prudent middle-of-the-road approach to

---

[466] This analysis leaves out of the equation the constitutionally required norm of vertical stare decisis that binds lower federal court judges to the Supreme Court's precedent.

[467] Stephen E. Sachs, *Originalism as a Theory of Legal Change*, 38 Harv. J. L. & Pub. Pol'y 818, 858–60 (2015).

[468] 25 Am. Jur. 2d: *Easements and Licenses* § 18 (2017).

[469] Antonin Scalia, Matter of Interpretation: Federal Courts and the Law 20 (1997).

[470] Federal Judicial Center Manual for Complex Litigation §20.133 (2004).

[471] The Law of Easements & Licenses in Land §§ 11:7, 11.9 (J. W. Bruce & J. W. Ely Jr. eds., 2017).

[472] Am. Jur. Proof of Facts 3d: *Acquisition of Title to Property by Adverse Possession* § 2 (2017).

[473] *See, e.g.*, The Law of Easements & Licenses in Land, *supra* note 471, § 8.14 (identifying continued court resistance to forcing transfer of right to serve nondominant land to dominant tenant that abused the easement by servicing nondominant land).

mistakes by accepting those mistakes that are either most valuable or most likely to significantly harm the common good if corrected.

Originalism's acceptance of some nonoriginalist precedent is of a piece with our broader practice's approach to mistakes. Originalism does not accept all nonoriginalist precedent, nor does it reject all nonoriginalist precedent. Instead, using the three-factor analysis I described previously, originalism tries to filter out those nonoriginalist precedents especially worthy of preservation, either because they are valuable in their own right or because overruling them would cause significant harm. By doing so, originalism preserves its integrity, protects Rule of Law values, and maintains the just social relations created by some nonoriginalist precedents.

2.4.5 *Precedent Is a Key Means by Which the Constitution's Original Meaning Is Effectively Communicated*

The Constitution's original meaning is the primary mechanism by which its legal directives to Americans are communicated. The original meaning, however, is not perspicacious, and I argued in this section that the Constitution identified judicial precedent as a key means by which the original meaning is implemented, thus making its communication effective.

Originalist precedent is a key means of implementing the Constitution, through its interpretive and constructive modes. Even nonoriginalist precedent is a means of implementing the Constitution, and not just Article III's mandate of "significant respect." Nonoriginalist precedent secures the common good by accounting for mistaken precedent and, in doing so, maximizing the Rule of Law and substantive justice.

2.4.6 *Conclusion*

In this subsection, I argued that originalism gives pride of place to the practice of precedent. Originalist precedent is articulated, protected, and followed, because of the valuable epistemic and constructive work it does. Nonoriginalist precedent is preserved because of its own justness and/or because overruling it would cause major harm to the common good. Originalism's treatment of both originalist and nonoriginalist precedent is a manifestation of the Constitution's command to give precedent significant respect, and this respect will both help originalism fit our existing constitutional practice (Section 3.4) and make that practice normatively attractive (Chapter 4).

2.5 THE DEFERENCE CONCEPTION OF CONSTRUCTION AND THE ORIGINALIST THEORY OF PRECEDENT ARE BOTH MANIFESTATIONS OF JUDICIAL LEGAL DEFERENCE TO OTHER INTERPRETERS

Up to this point, I argued that originalism incorporates a modest conception of constitutional construction, what I called the deference conception of construction.

Then, I showed that originalism privileged precedent. Though I justified each of these moves separately, they also represent a common manifestation of a broader practice of deference.

Deference in the context of constitutional interpretation occurs when one interpreter subordinates her own best judgment on what the Constitution means to another interpreter's judgment. Interpretive deference may occur in one of two forms: epistemic deference and legal deference.[474] Epistemic deference is where an interpreter defers to another's interpretive judgment because the interpreter believes that the other interpreter has greater access to the true meaning. For example, in the Necessary and Proper Clause context, the Supreme Court defers to Congress' judgment about whether a particular means is necessary to properly utilize an enumerated power.[475]

Legal deference occurs when one interpreter defers to another's interpretive judgment because he is required by law to do so: because of the other interpreter's legal status. This is likely the rationale for (some of) the political question doctrine cases where the justification for the doctrine rests on a textual commitment of interpretive authority to Congress or the President.[476]

With these different conceptions of deference in mind, it is now clear that I argued that both judicial deference in the construction zone and to precedent was legally required by the Constitution. Judicial deference to elected branch constructions was legally required because of the lack of legal warrant for constitutional judicial review coupled with Article I's authorization to Congress to make authoritative legal determinations for the United States. Even if the Supreme Court believed that an alternative construction of the Constitution was wiser, it is constitutionally required to defer to Congress' constitutional construction. I similarly showed that the original meaning of "judicial Power" in Article III requires federal judges to defer to prior federal judicial interpretations embodied in precedent. Even if the current Supreme Court believes that a prior Court interpretation was wrong, it may be required to defer to that prior interpretation. The plausibility of any one instance of legal deference is bolstered if it is part of a broader practice of deference, as I argued is the case with originalism.

2.6 VIRTUE'S HOME IN ORIGINALISM: ORIGINALISM IS FORTIFIED BY JUDGES WHO POSSESS JUDICIAL VIRTUE

2.6.1 *Introduction*

Originalism is not a machine or algorithm into which one feeds interpretive data and out of which spits constitutional meaning. Instead, it is a theory of interpretation

---

[474] Gary Lawson & Christopher D. Moore, *The Executive Power of Constitutional Interpretation*, 81 Iowa L. Rev. 1267, 1271, 1278–79, 1300–02 (1996).

[475] *NFIB v. Sebelius*, 567 U.S. 519, 559 (2012).

[476] *Baker v. Carr*, 369 U.S. 186, 216 (1962). The meaning of "sole Power to try all Impeachments" in Article I, § 3, cl. 6, is an example. *United States v. Nixon*, 506 U.S. 224 (1993).

that requires humans to engage in sometimes-demanding research and make sometimes-challenging judgments. Like any other human practice, certain characteristics, habits, and skills help originalist interpreters perform these tasks in the best way possible. In this section, I describe the virtues necessary to practice originalism well. My description relies on the Aristotelian tradition's conception of virtue ethics.

My incorporation of virtue ethics into originalism produces two important payoffs. First, it gives originalism greater explanatory power for common practices, like precedent. Second, it makes originalism more normatively attractive by identifying how the principal actors in our practice of constitutional interpretation may perform their function excellently. This section's use of virtue ethics to facilitate originalism is of-a-piece with my law-as-coordination account of originalism in Chapter 4 because both are grounded in the Aristotelian philosophical tradition.

2.6.2 *An Introduction to Virtue Ethics*

Virtue ethics is one of the key components of the Aristotelian philosophical tradition, and I discuss it in more detail in Section 4.4. At this point, suffice it to say that virtue ethics is a part of practical philosophy; it is a branch of ethics that is concerned with guiding human action.[477]

Virtue ethics is primarily characterized by its focus on the concept of virtue in the ethical life.[478] In answer to what is usually taken as the fundamental ethical question of "what sorts of action should I do?," a virtue theorist answers, "what a virtuous agent would characteristically ... do in the circumstances."[479] However, virtue ethics pushes back against the question itself. In virtue ethics, the fundamental subject of study is not action: it is character.[480] Virtue theorists argue that the focus of ethical inquiry should be the instantiation and exercise of virtue, not an algorithm of right action.[481]

Virtue is a habit[482] – an entrenched disposition of character[483] – to perform a human function well. For example, the virtue of fortitude enables one to ascertain what courage requires in concrete situations and to – willingly – act accordingly.[484] A person who possesses fortitude will know what courage requires in particular situations, have the intellectual disposition to act courageously when called to do so, be emotionally disposed to act courageously, and will reliably act courageously.

---

[477] ST I-II, q. 55, a.1.
[478] ROSALIND HURSTHOUSE, ON VIRTUE ETHICS 1–3 (1999).
[479] *Id.* at 26, 28.
[480] *Id.* at 29.
[481] *Id.* at 2–3.
[482] ST I-II, q. 56, a. 3.
[483] HURSTHOUSE, *supra* note 478, at 10–12.
[484] JOSEF PIEPER, THE FOUR CARDINAL VIRTUES: PRUDENCE, JUSTICE, FORTITUDE, TEMPERANCE 115–41 (1965).

Virtues are conventionally divided into two categories:[485] intellectual virtues and moral virtues.[486] The intellectual virtues perfect our reasoning faculties. They include theoretical wisdom[487] and practical wisdom.[488] The moral virtues perfect our appetites and most prominently include justice, temperance, and fortitude.[489]

2.6.3 *The Key Judicial Virtues*

The central players in constitutional interpretation today are federal judges and, in particular, Supreme Court justices. Judging, as a general activity – in other words, not confined to constitutional interpretation – requires a number of virtues for its successful execution.[490] The principal judicial virtues include: theoretical wisdom, practical wisdom, justice-as-lawfulness, temperance,[491] and fortitude. Next, I describe each virtue in more detail.

A judge is excellent only if she has the theoretical wisdom – the intellectual "firepower," we might say – to perform the relatively abstract legal tasks necessary to judging. Judges must possess this capacity in order to know and understand the law that bears on a given case. In some cases, especially hard cases,[492] this task places tremendous burdens on the judge's faculties and, depending on one's theory of adjudication, judges may have to utilize theoretical wisdom on a regular basis.[493]

Theoretical wisdom first enables the judge to master the law's "data": the cases, statutes, regulations, legal principles, doctrines, history, traditions, and practices that are pertinent to the case before the judge. This mastery has two components: the judge's pre-existing knowledge of the law in the judge's jurisdiction, and the knowledge of the law that the judge gathers in the context of a particular case. Building on this knowledge of the legal data, the judge must then uncover the relationship between and among the pertinent legal materials – the judge must

---

[485] ST I-II, q. 56, aa. 3, 4.

[486] *Id.* at I-II, q. 56, aa. 3–4.

[487] *Id.* at I-II, q. 57, a. 2.

[488] Ralph McInerny, Ethica Thomistica 96 (rev. ed., 1997).

[489] *Id.* at 97–98.

[490] Professor Lawrence Solum identified and described the primary virtues required for judging, and my discussion parallels his excellent scholarship. *See* Lawrence B. Solum, *The Aretaic Turn in Constitutional Theory*, 70 Brook. L. Rev. 475, 491–520 (2005); Lawrence B. Solum, *Natural Justice*, 51 Am. J. Juris. 65, 76–92 (2006); Lawrence B. Solum, *Virtue Jurisprudence: A Virtue-Centered Theory of Judging*, 34 Metaphilosophy 178 (2003); *see also* Colin Farrelly & Lawrence B. Solum, An Introduction to Aretaic Theories of Law, in Virtue Jurisprudence 1–23, 142–92 (Colin Farrelly & Lawrence B. Solum eds., 2008).

[491] Professor Solum identified the virtue of judicial temperament. *See* Solum, *Virtue Jurisprudence, supra* note 490, at 191.

[492] Ronald Dworkin, Taking Rights Seriously 81–130 (1977).

[493] *See* Solum, *Virtue Jurisprudence, supra* note 490, at 182–83 (making this point regarding Dworkin's theory of law as integrity).

ascertain which of the legal data structures the other pieces, and how the data is structured.[494] Theoretical wisdom permits the judge to arrive at the structure of legal norms governing a case.

For instance, to understand how the Fifth Amendment's Public Use Clause governs a particular case, a judge would have to grasp the Clause's original meaning, read and understand originalist precedent applying the Clause, and ascertain any authoritative practices under the Clause.[495] Then, the judge would synthesize this data into a coherent legal structure. Most frequently, this takes the form of the legal rules, standards, or principles tailored to the factual context presented by the case.[496] At each step, without significant intellectual capabilities, the judge will perform poorly. Consequently, judges need theoretical wisdom to perform these tasks well.

Practical wisdom is the intellectual virtue that enables its possessor to perform two tasks well: first, identify those goods that are valuable and therefore worth pursuing; and second, perceive the means most conducive to pursuing those identified goods.[497] Practical wisdom, in the context of judging, is primarily concerned with the second task.[498] Practical wisdom provides the capacity to articulate legal doctrine that mediates legal meaning and the facts presented in cases.

Using the Commerce Clause as an example, once a judge has mastered the Clause's meaning, the judge must still apply that meaning in a case. In doing so, the judge will articulate legal doctrines that connect the meaning to the facts. In the Commerce Clause context, the pre-New Deal Supreme Court created a series of doctrines, such as the original packages doctrine[499] and the instrumentalities of commerce doctrine,[500] among others,[501] to do just that. These legal doctrines bridged the analytical space between the Clause's original meaning and the recurring factual situations presented by the cases in which the Court articulated those doctrines.

Justice-as-lawfulness is the virtue of giving one's society's laws their due.[502] Justice-as-lawfulness is *the* excellence that defines a good judge qua judge.[503] Without the

---

[494] BURTON, *supra* note 94, at 54–59.

[495] *E.g.*, *Kelo v. City of New London*, 545 U.S. 469, 505–14 (2005) (Thomas, J., dissenting).

[496] *See Kelo*, 545 U.S. at 514 (Thomas, J., dissenting) ("[T]he Public Use Clause is most naturally read to authorize takings for public use only if the government or the public actually uses the taken property.").

[497] ST I-II, q. 57, a. 5.

[498] Practical wisdom in the context of judging is primarily concerned with the second task because the judge's ends are, in the focal case of judging, set for the judge by the pertinent law. HAMBURGER, *supra* note 180, at 2. As I describe below, however, practical wisdom, in situations when judges exercise discretion, also plays the first role of identifying goods worth pursuing. This occurs in the context of nonoriginalist precedent.

[499] *Brown v. Maryland*, 25 U.S. (12 Wheat.) 419, 441–42 (1827).

[500] *Shreveport Rate Cases*, 234 U.S. 342, 351 (1914).

[501] *Swift & Co. v. United States*, 196 U.S. 375, 399 (1905); *Stafford v. Wallace*, 258 U.S. 495, 517 (1922).

[502] NE, at 1095a; KRAUT, *supra* note 410, at 102–03, 106.

[503] Solum, *Virtue Jurisprudence*, *supra* note 490, at 194. Saint Thomas Aquinas recognized this when he described the etymology of "judge." ST II-II, q. 60, a. 1.

virtue of justice-as-lawfulness, a judge's incredible intellect, stout courage, and measured temperament would only make the judge capable of more wickedness,[504] like a Professor Moriarty with robes.[505] A just judge is one who exercises judgment[506] "according to the written law."[507] The link between justice-as-lawfulness and a society's positive law flows from the essential role positive law plays securing a society's common good.[508]

The virtue of justice-as-lawfulness has the most "bite" when a judge faces a law that the judge does not think – at least in that instance – advances the common good. For example, in *Herrera v. Collins*, the Supreme Court denied Herrera's habeas petition that alleged that he was actually innocent.[509] The Court acknowledged that "we have held that a petitioner otherwise subject to defenses of abusive or successive use of the writ may have his federal constitutional claim considered on the merits if he makes a proper showing of actual innocence."[510] The Court ruled, despite the substantive attractiveness of petitioner's claim, that it did not fit in the existing categories upon which habeas relief could be granted, and in doing so it exemplified justice-as-lawfulness.[511]

In the context of originalism, justice-as-lawfulness has its most critical bite because of the deviations from the Constitution's original meaning that have occurred, especially since the New Deal. There are many post–New Deal nonoriginalist precedents and doctrines that reasonable judges would find normatively attractive. Furthermore, much of the Constitution's original meaning arose in contexts when Americans possessed different (*e.g.*, more limited) factual knowledge and held different normative convictions. This leads to a disjunction between what the original meaning requires and what a reasonable modern judge might believe is normatively attractive. Judges express justice-as-lawfulness when they possess an initial disposition to follow the original meaning and ultimately do so, even in these cases.

Temperance and fortitude describe two facets of judicial character that a judge must possess to rule according to the law. A temperate judge will hold in check his sensual appetites.[512] A temperate judge will be resistant to the allure of, for instance,

---

[504] Solum, *Virtue Jurisprudence, supra* note 490, at 194.
[505] *See* 1 Sir Arthur Conan Doyle, The Memoirs of Sherlock Holmes 219 (1894) ("A criminal strain ran in his blood, which, instead of being modified, was increased and rendered infinitely more dangerous by his extraordinary mental powers.").
[506] ST II-II, q. 60, a. 1.
[507] *Id.* at II-II, q. 60, a. 5.
[508] *Id.* at I-II, q. 96, a. 4; Kraut, *supra* note 410, at 102–11. I explain this link in detail in Subsection 4.4.3.
[509] *Herrera v. Collins*, 506 U.S. 390 (1993).
[510] *Id.* at 404.
[511] *Id.* at 404–07.
[512] ST II-II, q. 141, aa. 1–2.

the "good life" that a bribe could buy.[513] A temperate judge will also be calm, unlike the Queen of Hearts.[514]

Originalist judges need temperance to resist the allures offered by the nonoriginalist legal establishment. Supreme Court justices in particular, and other judges to a lesser degree, are offered the blandishments of elite legal culture, which is nonoriginalist, *so long as they are* nonoriginalist. These inducements do not come in the form of money or positions; instead, they trade on the "coin of the realm": respect. One piece of evidence supporting this is the dramatic disparity between the number of Ivy League honorary degrees given to Supreme Court justices. As of 2015, Ivy League schools had granted twelve honorary degrees to nonoriginalist justices, and zero such honors to originalist justices.[515] Receiving praise from the most respected members of American culture is attractive, and faithful judges need the strength to resist that allure.

Courage is the firmness of mind that enables one to react appropriately to danger,[516] and a courageous judge will rule according to the law even in the face of potential harm to his reputation, career, or even his family and life.[517] The federal judges in the South who implemented *Brown* v. *Board of Education* and other civil rights laws during the Civil Rights Era possessed courage in the face of threats.[518]

Originalist judges need courage. Originalist decisions and opinions subject one to criticism and vitriol.[519] Most humans, and most judges, do not wish to be criticized or verbally castigated, and writing originalist opinions will subject the author to robust criticism. Courage helps judges do so.

To make these and other important judicial habits of character effective, our legal culture needs to cultivate and select for them. For example, during the judicial confirmation process, the President should identify nominees who are faithful to the Constitution's original meaning, and the Senate should screen nominees for their courage to follow the original meaning.

---

[513] *See United States* v. *Nixon*, 816 F.2d 1022, 1023 (5th Cir. 1987) (describing how Judge Nixon had "been dissatisfied with his modest judicial salary, and had looked for means of augmenting it").

[514] "Let the jury consider their verdict," the King said, for about the twentieth time that day. "No, no!" said the Queen. "Sentence first – verdict afterwards." "Stuff and nonsense!" said Alice loudly. "The idea of having the sentence first!" "Hold your tongue!" said the Queen, turning purple. "I won't!" said Alice. "Off with her head!" the Queen shouted at the top of her voice.

Lewis Carroll, Alice's Adventures in Wonderland 99 (1898).

[515] John O. McGinnis, *Ivy Honors and the Justices*, www.libertylawsite.org/2015/07/20/ivy-honors-and-the-justices/ (visited Dec. 1, 2015).

[516] ST II-II, q. 123, aa. 1–2.

[517] With due regard, of course, for the judge's family's safety and flourishing.

[518] J. W. Peltason, Fifty-Eight Lonely Men: Southern Federal Judges and School Desegregation (1971).

[519] *See, e.g.*, Maureen Dowd, Opinion, *Could Thomas Be Right?*, N.Y. Times (June 25, 2003), www.nytimes.com/2003/06/25/opinion/could-thomas-be-right.html (visited July 18, 2017) (stating that Justice Thomas' *Grutter* dissent "is a clinical study of a man who has been driven barking mad by the beneficial treatment he has received").

Of course, judges are not the only actors in our constitutional system for whom virtues help perform their roles. For instance, legislative prudence is needed by legislators. All federal and state officers – and citizens – also need the necessary habits of character to follow the Constitution's original meaning.

Next, I describe how incorporating virtue ethics into originalism makes it a better theory of interpretation.

2.6.4 *Incorporating Virtue Ethics into Originalism Makes It More Descriptively Accurate and Normatively Attractive*

2.6.4.1 Introduction

In this subsection, I show some of the many ways in which concepts from virtue ethics contribute to a richer originalism. First, I show that an originalism that takes on virtue ethics' insights is more descriptively accurate. Second, I describe the virtues' roles at key steps in the interpretive process and show how virtue ethics makes originalism more normatively attractive. I end by summarizing virtue ethics' contribution to originalism: it preserves originalism's core faithfulness to the Constitution, while facilitating its transformation toward a sophisticated theory of constitutional interpretation that fits the important and widespread facets of our constitutional practice.

2.6.4.2 Virtue Ethics Gives Originalism Greater Explanatory Power

Originalism's incorporation of virtue ethics makes originalism more descriptively accurate in at least four ways: (1) originalism is more hospitable to, and paints in a better light, common practices; (2) originalism is able to embrace the widespread and attractive conception of judging-as-craft; (3) originalism is able to take on board the fact that constitutional interpretation is a human practice; and (4) originalism better fits the Framers' and Ratifiers' plan of constitutional government, which reflected their virtue-infused assumptions.

First, originalism is more hospitable to, and paints in a better light, common practices. I will use nonoriginalist precedent as my example. Virtue ethics helps originalism incorporate the practice of nonoriginalist precedent. It does so by ensuring that judges who face nonoriginalist precedent will still regard themselves as bound by the Constitution's original meaning, and therefore nonoriginalist precedent is less likely to erode the original meaning's pride of place. A judge with the virtue of justice-as-lawfulness will seek to give the Constitution's original meaning its full due. A virtuous judge will not overrule (or limit) a nonoriginalist precedent only for good reasons. Accepting the continued viability of some nonoriginalist precedent will not, therefore, undermine originalism, and originalism can more easily fit this facet of our legal practice.

More importantly, originalism's picture of practices, such as nonoriginalist precedent, will also be more attractive because it will have the tools to explain how to
make judges engaging in the practices the best they can be. Judges' decisions on
whether and to what extent to overrule or limit a nonoriginalist precedent will
frequently be hard. Judges have to evaluate and weigh a number of factors, each of
which has a hard-to-quantify weight. For instance, it may be challenging to evaluate
the harm to Rule of Law values caused by overruling a precedent. An originalism
that incorporates the lessons of virtue ethics can show how judges faced with those
difficult choices can make the best determinations, all things considered. For
example, a judge with practical wisdom will, by definition, have the best insight
into the extent to which overruling a nonoriginalist precedent would harm Rule of
Law values.

Relatedly, an originalism that incorporates concepts from virtue ethics will produce the judges most capable of accurately evaluating nonoriginalist precedent
because originalism will have the tools to identify and/or educate judges best suited
to the practice. For example, originalism will have the resources to suggest that
potential judges "acquire judicial intelligence, integrity, and wisdom" from "train
[ing] in the law [and] experience [in] legal practice."[520] With its ability to identify,
inculcate, and select for virtuous judges, originalism will produce better results.

Second, by incorporating virtue ethics' insights, originalism also better fits the
widespread judging-as-craft account of judging.[521] The core insight of this account is
that judges are participants in a human practice with internal standards, and that, to
be excellent in the craft, a judge must master those standards. Hence, some judges,
more than others, are excellent writers, construct elegant analyses of the law,
powerfully articulate the law's meaning and import, possess a judicial disposition,
and so on.

Virtue ethics helps originalism incorporate this judging-as-craft account. Originalism can emphasize, for instance, the theoretical wisdom a judge needs in order to
fashion a persuasive presentation of the Constitution's original meaning.

Third, giving virtue a place in originalism emphasizes, in a way that is often
missed by scholars of all stripes, the key fact that our legal system generally, and
constitutional interpretation in particular, is a human practice.[522] Virtue helps
originalism explain that law is a process, with human actors at each critical step in
the process. Law begins when an authorized person or group of people identifies a

---

[520] Lawrence B. Solum, *The Virtues and Vices of a Judge: An Aristotelian Guide to Judicial
Selection*, 61 S. Cal. L. Rev. 1735, 1755 (1988).

[521] Some of the more prominent judging-as-craft scholarship includes Benjamin N. Cardozo,
The Nature of the Judicial Process (1921); Frank M. Coffin, The Ways of a Judge:
Reflections from the Federal Appellate Bench (1980); and Karl N. Llewellyn, The
Common Law Tradition: Deciding Appeals (1960).

[522] Paul Horwitz, *Book Review, Judicial Character (and Does It Matter)*, 26 Const. Comm. 97,
106–07 (2009).

societal problem they believe is susceptible to legal solution. These lawmakers craft a law, the goal of which is to re-order society to solve the identified problem. In our system, congressmen must ascertain whether the law is authorized by an enumerated power and whether it violates a constitutional limit, and both of these judgments require constitutional interpretation. The next step in the process is when the executive branch enforces the law, and doing so in our system requires the executive to ascertain, in its own judgment, whether the law is constitutional or, how to enforce the law in a manner consistent with the Constitution, processes that both require constitutional interpretation. In some instances, enforcement of the law also requires judicial resolution of whether, to what extent, and how the law applies to discrete parties. Our system's federal judges' judicial duty mandates that they ascertain whether the law is consistent with the Constitution. Citizens governed by the law internalize the law in their practical deliberations and act according to its dictates, and they form judgments about whether the law is consistent with the Constitution that they then bring to the political and legal arenas.[523]

At each step in the process of law, human actors perform their roles more or less well depending upon whether they possess the requisite virtues, and the paradigmatic virtues necessary for each participant in the process will be different as well. The judicial virtues I described in the previous text are key to describing and evaluating the performance of our processes' judicial participants.

Fourth, originalism, bolstered by virtue ethics, better fits the historical record surrounding the Framing and Ratification, and the Constitution itself. The Framers and Ratifiers believed in virtue ethics and relied on that belief when constructing the Constitution.[524] Historical and legal scholarship, though differing on the degree to which virtue ethics was part of the intellectual climate during the Framing and Ratification, generally agrees with my modest claim that, among other intellectual commitments, the Framers and Ratifiers believed in virtue ethics and relied on that

---

[523] *E.g.*, Larry D. Kramer, The People Themselves: Popular Constitutionalism and Judicial Review 139 (2004).

[524] The literature on the Framers' and Ratifiers' intellectual commitments is vast. *See generally* Daniel T. Rodgers, *Republicanism: The Career of a Concept*, 79 J. Am. Hist. 11 (1992) (describing the intellectual history of scholarly views on the Framing and Ratification period). The foundational sources for the proposition that a commitment to virtue ethics was at least one major current during the Framing and Ratification are Bernard Bailyn, The Ideological Origins of the American Revolution (1967); J. G. A. Pocock, The Machiavellian Moment (1975); and Gordon S. Wood, The Creation of the American Republic: 1776–1787 (1969). These sources generated a "Republican Revival" in legal scholarship in the mid-1980s to early 1990s. *E.g.*, Frank I. Michelman, *Forward: Traces of Self-Government*, 100 Harv. L. Rev. 4 (1986); Cass R. Sunstein, *Interest Groups in American Public Law*, 38 Stan. L. Rev. 29 (1985). *See also* Lawrence B. Solum, *Book Review, Republican Constitutionalism our Republican Constitution: Securing the Liberty and Sovereignty of We the People*, 32 Const. Comm. 175, 185–96 (2017) ("[T]he notion that virtue is a means to the effectiveness of republican constitutionalism is part of a family of republican theories that includes members from the Founding era.").

belief when constructing the Constitution.[525] An instance of this emphasis on virtue – though by no means an isolated example – is James Madison's observation, in *Federalist 57*, that

> [t]he aim of every political constitution is, or ought to be, first, to obtain for rulers men who possess most wisdom to discern, and most virtue to pursue, the common good of the society; and in the next place, to take the most effectual precautions for keeping them virtuous, whilst they continue to hold their public trust.[526]

Madison argued that the proposed constitution capitalized on the good character available to it while, at the same time, not falling into the trap of earlier republics, which placed inordinate weight on human virtue to sustain republican freedom.

> As there is a degree of depravity in mankind which requires a certain degree of circumspection and distrust, so there are other qualities in human nature which justify a certain portion of esteem and confidence. Republican government presupposes the existence of these qualities in a higher degree than any other form. Were the pictures which have been drawn by the political jealousy of some among us faithful likenesses of the human character, the inference would be, that there is not sufficient virtue among men for self-government; and that nothing less than the chains of despotism can restrain them from destroying and devouring one another.[527]

This conception of representation, which was a premise of the Constitution's structure of representation,[528] incorporated virtue ethics.

Originalism's embrace of virtue ethics gives it a greater ability to appreciate this and similar historical facts, and to better understand the Constitution itself.

2.6.4.3 Virtue Ethics Makes Originalism More Normatively Attractive

For each of the following facets of originalist constitutional interpretation, I describe how virtue ethics provides the tools originalism needs to make originalism the best it can be in those contexts. The virtues' roles differ depending on which of two situations the judges are in: first, where judges exercise discretion; and second, where ascertaining and applying the Constitution's determinate original meaning places significant burdens on judges' faculties. The first category occurs primarily in the contexts of nonoriginalist precedent and constitutional construction, while the

---

[525] E.g., Sunstein, *supra* note 524, at 38–45.
[526] THE FEDERALIST No. 57 (James Madison).
[527] THE FEDERALIST No. 55 (James Madison).
[528] For instance, the President is elected by electors. U.S. CONST. art. II, § 1, cl. 2; *see also* THE FEDERALIST No. 64 (John Jay) ("As the select assemblies for choosing the President ... will, in general, be composed of the most enlightened and respectable citizens, there is reason to presume, that their attention and their votes will be directed to those men only who have become the most distinguished by their abilities and virtue.").

second takes place in the contexts of originalist precedent and articulating and applying the original meaning. The key contribution virtue ethics makes in each instance is that the judicial virtues enable judges to give the original meaning its due, while also giving other interpretive factors their due, all in their proper proportion.

2.6.4.3.1 VIRTUE'S ROLE WHEN JUDGES EXERCISE DISCRETION: NONORIGIN-ALIST PRECEDENT AND CONSTITUTIONAL CONSTRUCTION Here, I describe the various ways the judicial virtues operate when judges possess discretion. The two main instances of this are the contexts of nonoriginalist precedent and constitutional construction.

Large swaths of American constitutional law are populated or, in some instances, dominated by nonoriginalist precedent. Many originalists, including myself, have argued that federal judges must retain at least some nonoriginalist precedent. In particular, I argued that a judge must utilize three factors to decide whether to overrule a nonoriginalist precedent: (1) the extent of the precedent's deviation from the Constitution's original meaning; (2) harm to the Rule of Law caused by overruling the precedent; and (3) the extent to which the precedent creates a just social ordering.[529] However, this opens originalism to the criticism that originalism gives judges too much discretion. In particular, a critic could argue that a purport-edly originalist judge may – intentionally or otherwise – follow a nonoriginalist meaning when he should have followed the original meaning, and thereby under-mine originalism's distinctive commitment to the original meaning. Virtue ethics enables originalism to adequately address this critique.

Originalists can respond that a judge with the judicial virtues will appropriately evaluate the three factors and come to the correct conclusion – the conclusion that gives the Constitution's original meaning its due regard while, at the same time, taking into account the other important values of the Rule of Law and substantive justice. First, the virtuous judge will possess the virtue of theoretical wisdom, which will enable the judge to accurately ascertain the Constitution's original meaning. For instance, when faced with a case that requires a judge to ascertain the Com-merce Clause's meaning, this virtue will permit the judge to perform the necessary research into the historical data. The judge will also review pertinent originalist precedent. Then, the judge will synthesize those legal materials into the authorita-tive constitutional meaning. At the same time, the judge will ascertain the import of the nonoriginalist precedent in question.

Second, a judge with the virtue of justice-as-lawfulness has the disposition to give the Constitution's original meaning and binding originalist precedent their due regard: to treat them as controlling. This means, among other things, that the virtuous judge will be inclined to overrule nonoriginalist precedent, especially

---

[529] *Infra* Subsection 2.4.4.

precedent that deviates greatly from the Constitution's original meaning. For example, *Wickard v. Filburn* is a nonoriginalist precedent because it incorrectly articulated the Commerce Clause's original meaning.[530] Coming to this conclusion will incline the virtuous judge to overrule *Wickard*.

Third, the virtuous judge will utilize the virtue of practical wisdom to ascertain the extent of harm to Rule of Law values (if any) that the judge would cause if she overruled a precedent. This will frequently be a difficult task. For instance, in evaluating whether to overrule (or limit) *Wickard*, the judge faces the daunting challenge of calculating the reliance interests built on *Wickard*; for instance, in the form of numerous federal statutes premised on the substantial effects test.

Additionally, practical wisdom empowers a judge to articulate legal doctrine that will accurately connect the Constitution's meaning to the facts presented by a case.[531] In the context of nonoriginalist precedent, this will frequently be a challenging task if the judge determines not to overrule the precedent but, instead, to limit it. The judge will then have to modify existing (nonoriginalist) doctrine in a way that moves constitutional law toward the original meaning, while at the same time ensuring that the doctrine is as coherent as possible. The challenge to doctrinal coherence is caused by the dichotomous commitments made by the hypothetical doctrine: on the one hand, the nonoriginalist precedent remains viable, pulling the doctrine in one direction; and on the other hand, the original meaning pulls the doctrine in another direction. Practical wisdom gives a judge the ability to make the best of this difficult though common situation.

This was arguably the situation faced by the justices inclined to limit *Wickard* in *United States v. Lopez*.[532] *Wickard*'s substantial effects test, the majority acknowledged, could justify upholding the challenged law.[533] To preserve – and limit – *Wickard*, while at the same time moving the Court's Commerce Clause case law toward the original meaning – toward "first principles," as the majority stated[534] – the majority articulated the commercial-noncommercial distinction as an added limit to *Wickard*'s reach.[535]

Fourth, in evaluating whether the nonoriginalist precedent in question creates a just ordering, a judge must utilize the virtue of justice-as-fairness. While the virtue of justice-as-lawfulness inclines the judge toward overruling the nonoriginalist precedent – because of its illegality – the virtue of justice-as-fairness enables the judge to determine whether the precedent otherwise – that is, despite its inconsistency with

---

[530] BARNETT, *supra* note 70, at 315.

[531] In the context of judges constructing constitutional doctrine, this form of practical wisdom is legal wisdom. Gerard V. Bradley, *Beguiled: Free Exercise Exemptions and the Siren Song of Liberalism*, 20 HOFSTRA L. REV. 245, 251–56 (1991).

[532] *United States v. Lopez*, 514 U.S. 549 (1995).

[533] *Id.* at 563–68.

[534] *Id.* at 552.

[535] *Id.* at 563–68.

the original meaning – properly orders relations. Again, taking a constitutional challenge to *Wickard* as our example, the virtuous judge will decide whether the increased scope to Congress's Commerce Clause authority increases or decreases just relationships. One place where this inquiry has bite is the federal antidiscrimination laws that are premised on *Wickard's* expansive reading of the Commerce Clause. Would overruling *Wickard* cause the demise of the Civil Rights Act, which helped eliminate one form of unjust ordering?[536]

Each of the decisions made by a judge in the process of evaluating the continued vitality of a nonoriginalist precedent is augmented by a virtue. Having these virtues, by hypothesis, makes it more likely that these decisions are the best they can be. Therefore, although a judge has discretion, that discretion does not undermine the originalist project because the Constitution's original meaning continues in its pride of place,[537] consistent with other values. Indeed, the virtuous judge's discretion provides the opportunity to arrive at the best (humanly possible) decision, all things considered. The virtuous judge will not be the perfect judge, however, and this is especially true when the burdens on the judge's capacities are at their highest; for instance, in ascertaining possible harm to Rule of Law values.

Constitutional construction is another part of originalism that explicitly acknowledges judicial discretion. As with nonoriginalist precedent, originalism augmented by virtue ethics can incorporate the concept of construction without undermining originalism. This is because a judge who possesses the judicial virtues will, so far as possible, respect the Constitution's original meaning and, by hypothesis, construct the best constitutional meaning within the original meaning's parameters. Before proceeding to identify how the judicial virtues augment originalism's employment of constitutional construction, let me pause to note how the deference conception of construction impacts this inquiry.

Recall that the deference conception of construction identified a narrow quantity of construction and that, within this relatively small construction zone, the federal judiciary should defer to constitutional constructions by the other federal branches (and possibly the states, in appropriate circumstances). This is not a lot of discretion, but it is not *de minimus* either. This conception of construction does not eliminate judicial discretion because the Supreme Court must construct constitutional doctrine that fits these other-branch constructions. Federal judges will craft constitutional doctrine that fits and justifies the other-branch constructions. For

---

[536] This determination, in turn, involves a significant number of subsidiary determinations that require legal and practical wisdom for their proper resolution: Are there other plausible constitutional bases for the Act? Do state and local antidiscrimination laws adequately ensure just relationships in the absence of federal law? Are popular mores such that federal antidiscrimination laws are no longer necessary? Are federal antidiscrimination laws themselves sufficiently harmful in their collateral consequences that their elimination is, on balance, good?

[537] Because of the virtue of justice-as-lawfulness.

instance, the constitutional doctrine may identify principled limits to other-branch constructions, such as where the constructions bump up against determinate original meaning.

As with nonoriginalist precedent, the judicial virtues of theoretical wisdom and justice-as-lawfulness will enable the virtuous judge to correctly decide what the original meaning is, allow the judge to recognize that the original meaning does not determine the outcome of the case, and give the judge the disposition to follow, so far as possible, that original meaning. These virtues prevent the judge from seeing underdeterminacy when the original meaning is determinate and thereby prevents the judge from ruling that government actions are consistent with the underdetermined original meaning when they are, in fact, inconsistent with the determinate original meaning. This preserves the original meaning's primacy in constitutional interpretation.

Practical wisdom, unlike in the context of nonoriginalist precedent, performs on a more "open field" here. In the nonoriginalist precedent context, the judge's practical wisdom is limited to the task of ascertaining whether, and to what extent, overruling would harm the Rule of Law.[538] That is frequently a difficult task, though it is focused. By contrast here, within the known original meaning, the judge's task is to facilitate the legislative role of constructing constitutional meaning that will best advance the common good. The judge must create doctrine that fits the legislature's construction and explains why it is consistent with the Constitution. All of the variables that a legislator would take into account, the judge should also utilize crafting this doctrine. By contrast, constitutional interpretation, discussed in the following subsection, does not place as significant a burden on judges' practical wisdom because the original meaning determines those cases' outcomes.

2.6.4.3.2 VIRTUE'S PLACE IN DETERMINATE LAW: CONSTITUTIONAL INTERPRETATION AND ORIGINALIST PRECEDENT In this subsection, I spell out how virtue ethics makes originalism a better theory even in those run-of-the-mill situations where judicial decisions are fully constrained by the original meaning. The common theme here is that there are hard cases that place significant burdens on judges' faculties, and that to bear those burdens well, judges need the judicial virtues.

The core process of constitutional interpretation includes both articulating the Constitution's meaning and applying that meaning in the context of a case. Constitutional interpretation differs from construction and nonoriginalist precedent because judges do not have discretion. Consequently, the virtues' roles are different, though still significant.

A judge engaged in constitutional interpretation will need the intellectual virtue of theoretical wisdom. The need for theoretical wisdom will vary depending on,

---

[538] If a judge determines that limiting a nonoriginalist precedent is appropriate, then the judge's task will be analogous to that in the construction zone.

among other variables, how patent the text's original meaning is. As with other facets of originalism, judges will also need the moral virtue of justice-as-lawfulness. This ensures that the judges follow the original meaning.

A judge will utilize practical wisdom to bridge the distance between the Constitution's original meaning and the facts of a case. The greater the distance, the larger the burden practical wisdom must carry. For instance, in the late nineteenth century, the Supreme Court faced the challenge of articulating consti-tutional doctrine that, faithful to the Commerce Clause's original meaning, speci-fied how that meaning governed a changing economy and society. In particular, the challenge included properly mediating the Clause's application to new or newly common phenomena. The Court met this challenge by articulating a number of constitutional law doctrines.

The original packages doctrine is one such doctrinal move. In a series of cases, beginning in 1827 with *Brown v. Maryland*,[539] the Supreme Court fashioned the doctrine to mediate two constitutional commitments: (1) Congress' authority over interstate commerce; and (2) the states' reserved police power over in-state commer-cial transactions. The doctrine's function was to find a doctrinal line that accom-plished this purpose and fit the facts of the world. For example, in *Austin v. Tennessee*, the Supreme Court decided whether the doctrine applied to cigarettes imported from other states in relatively small packages.[540] To reach its conclusion, the Court reviewed the doctrine's seventy-year history and how the doctrine advanced its purpose of mediating between the constitutional commitments identi-fied above.[541] Practical wisdom facilitated this.

Originalist precedent is another, particularly important facet of constitutional inter-pretation where judges do not have discretion. To properly understand, synthesize, follow, and apply originalist precedent, a judge will need theoretical wisdom, justice-as-lawfulness, and practical wisdom. Using the pre-New Deal Commerce Clause case law as an example, the Supreme Court had crafted a number of interrelated doctrines that formed a complex body of law. These included: the original packages doctrine,[542] mentioned previously, the instrumentalities of commerce doctrine,[543] the streams of commerce doctrine,[544] the doctrinal distinction between commerce and manufactur-ing,[545] and the related doctrinal distinction between direct and indirect effects.[546] These doctrines represented the Court's attempt to follow the twin constitutional commit-ments to federal commerce power and state police power. To master this intricate body

[539] *Brown v. Maryland*, 25 U.S. (12 Wheat.) 419, 443 (1827).
[540] *Austin v. Tennessee*, 179 U.S. 343, 350 (1900).
[541] *Id.* at 351–63.
[542] *Brown*, 25 U.S. at 441–42.
[543] *Shreveport Rate Cases*, 234 U.S. 342, 351–52 (1914).
[544] *Swift & Co. v. United States*, 196 U.S. 375, 398–99 (1905); *see also Stafford v. Wallace*, 258 U.S. 495, 515–16 (1922).
[545] *United States v. E.C. Knight Co.*, 156 U.S. 1, 12 (1895).
[546] *A. L. A. Schechter Poultry Corp. v. United States*, 295 U.S. 495, 546–48 (1935).

of law, a judge would have needed theoretical wisdom, and to follow it faithfully would have required justice-as-lawfulness.

In sum, incorporating virtue ethics into originalism makes originalism more normatively attractive. Originalists can embrace the discretion wielded by judges because virtue ethics provides the tools to preserve intact originalism's core commitments. Theoretical wisdom helps judges accurately ascertain the original meaning, and the original meaning retains its privileged position because of justice-as-lawfulness, which inclines judges to follow it. In those situations where judges wield discretion, practical wisdom, and the moral virtues of temperance and fortitude, ensure that judges reach the humanly-best result within the scope of the judge's discretion. When judges do not have discretion, the virtues ensure that judges construct the best legal doctrines.

2.6.5 *Conclusion*

Originalism is a complex human enterprise. Like all such human practices and institutions, the people who staff it need the character and skills to perform their parts in the enterprise well. Virtue ethics identifies the types of people who possess the skills to be excellent originalist judges. Virtue ethics therefore allows originalism to successfully navigate the shoals of constitutional construction and nonoriginalist precedent and maintain its heading toward the original meaning.

2.7 CONCLUSION

In this chapter, I described a new conception of originalism. Originalism, on my reading, has a number of important facets. It embraces the Constitutional Communication Model of originalism, the deference conception of construction, a robust role for constitutional precedent, and virtue ethics. Under the Constitutional Communication Model, the Constitution's original meaning is the primary mechanism to communicate the Constitution's legal directions to Americans to overcome coordination problems and secure the common good. Constitutional construction is a subsidiary mechanism of social coordination, identified by the Constitution, that operates when the original meaning itself is underdetermined. Precedent is a key means by which the Constitution's original meaning is implemented and makes the original meaning effective. Originalism is complex, and virtue ethics is the toolkit originalism needs to make it work effectively.

My conception of originalism draws on the Aristotelian tradition's resources, especially its conception of law, legal authority, and virtue. This conception of originalism supports my arguments in Part II that originalism best fits our existing constitutional practice (Chapter 3), and it also supports my claim that originalism is the most normatively attractive theory of constitutional interpretation (Chapter 4).

Originalism Is the Best Explanation of Our Existing Constitutional Practice and the Most Normatively Attractive Theory of Constitutional Interpretation

3

Originalism Best Explains Our Existing Constitutional Practice

That the people have an original right to establish, for their future government, such principles as, in their opinion, shall most conduce to their own happiness, is the basis, on which the whole American fabric has been erected.

Chief Justice John Marshall[1]

3.1 INTRODUCTION: WHY IT IS IMPORTANT FOR ORIGINALISM TO FIT IN

It is important for originalism to fit our constitutional practice. Most importantly, originalism needs to fit our practice because positive law itself is crucially important.[2] Positive law is the primary mechanism by which members of a society (of any significant complexity) work together to achieve their corporate common good and individual human flourishing. Positive law must play this role because the natural law cannot because it underdetermines how societies coordinate their members' actions. Societies therefore create positive law to coordinate toward the common good.

This positive law is an artifact of the society that created it. It has its own independence and integrity. In this sense, it is like other human artifacts. Not only do we have copies of Justinian's *Corpus Juris Civili*, we also have structures built by him, such as the Hagia Sophia. If one wished to understand Roman law in the sixth century, one would have to know Justinian's *Code*, the central facet of Roman Law at the time; if one wished to learn about Byzantine architecture during the same period, one would study the Hagia Sophia, the most powerful example of its kind.

---

[1]   *Marbury* v. *Madison*, 5 U.S. (1 Cranch) 137, 176 (1803).
[2]   The Aristotelian philosophical tradition, as I explain in Section 4.4 and contrary to popular accounts, prescribes an important – indeed, crucial – role for positive law.

Positive law's independent integrity means that a society's positive law is a given. Its existence and, in a healthy legal system, its content is not up for grabs. As a result, American legal practice is what it is. Any interpreter must find a place for the most important facets of our constitutional practice, including our written Constitution, the Supreme Court's role, and the bulk of constitutional law, in his theory of interpretation. Like Byzantine architecture, one can criticize or praise (parts of) America's constitutional practice, but to claim that one is interpreting it, one must fit the important and widespread facets of the practice.

Because of positive law's crucial function securing the common good and its "givenness," fit is a powerful argument in law.[3] The more "data" of a legal practice that a purported "interpretation" of that practice can satisfactorily explain, the more powerful the theory. A proffered interpretation of a legal practice that accounts for only twenty percent of the practice's data does not fit and, therefore, cannot be an interpretation of that practice. However, the quantity of data fit by an interpretation is only one axis upon which to evaluate interpretations. Interpretations also vary on the axis of the quality of their fit. For instance, some interpretations are more elegant than others; they may fit the data more cleanly. The result is that one should prefer an interpretation that paints a practice in a better light, even if that interpretation fits slightly less of the data than a competing interpretation.

The claim that fit is an important part of legal argument is not controversial. Scholars across the spectrum embrace it. Most famously, Ronald Dworkin made fit the first of the two-step analysis for his law-as-integrity theory. Originalists as well characteristically make fit arguments. For example, Professors McGinnis and Rappaport argued that it was important for originalism to contain a doctrine of precedent to avoid "it becom[ing] a theory with limited appeal and usefulness. Originalism would then require ignoring precedent even when doing so has enormous costs. It would also be in conflict with the practice of almost every justice and judge in the nation's history."[4] Professor Barnett's "writtenness" argument for originalism focuses on the fact that our Constitution is written and from that key facet of our practice, draws out originalism.[5] Other originalists make similar moves.[6]

Legal practices surrounding the Constitution are complex. The most important facet is the United States Constitution itself and its character as a written document, one that is changeable via the Article V amendment process. This Constitution originated in and from a particular context. And it remains the center of American

---

[3] Ronald Dworkin, Law's Empire 230 (1986).

[4] John O. McGinnis & Michael B. Rappaport, Originalism and the Good Constitution 154 (2013).

[5] Randy E. Barnett, Restoring the Lost Constitution: The Presumption of Liberty 91–117 (2004); *see also* Keith E. Whittington, Constitutional Interpretation: Textual Meaning, Original Intent & Judicial Review 47–61 (1999) (making a similar move).

[6] William Baude, Essay, *Is Originalism our Law?*, 115 Colum. L. Rev. 2349, 2352 (2015); Stephen E. Sachs, *Originalism as a Theory of Legal Change*, 38 Harv. J. L. & Pub. Pol'y 817, 820 (2015).

constitutional practice. Another important aspect is the Supreme Court's role interpreting and applying the Constitution through constitutional doctrine articulated in its cases. The Supreme Court's actions, and its explanations for its actions, are a second central aspects of our practice.

Our legal practice's complexity includes multiple levels of convention and agreement regarding those various conventions. The higher-level conventions are located at or near the apex of our practice. These higher-level conventions have the most authority within the legal system, and they form and structure the lower-level conventions. Our practice's higher-level conventions include our written Constitution and the Supreme Court's legally authoritative actions, such as its practices of constitutional law, forms of argument, and holdings. Lower-level conventions include, for example, particular holdings, tests, and precedents, the number of Supreme Court justices, and rhetoric regarding the Constitution. My key move in this chapter is to argue that originalism's strong fit with our practice's most important conventions (such as our written Constitution), coupled with its fit of widespread lower-level practices (such as constitutional doctrine articulated in precedent), shows that the practice's departure from originalism in some of it particular lower-level aspects of the practice (such as some nonoriginalist precedent) are marginal.

This sets up two possibilities. First, originalism's fit of our current practice is sufficiently tight to make it the best description of our practice, so that inconsistent aspects should be marginalized. Or, second, originalism's fit is less tight, but still roughly equal to other methods of interpretation, in which case my normative argument for originalism in Chapter 4 suggests that participants in our legal practice should move the practice more fully toward originalism.

Originalism, I show in this chapter, provides a reasonable and, in many ways, elegant description of our constitutional practice, a more elegant description than competing interpretive methodologies. My claim is that originalism fits both the key and widespread facets of our constitutional practice. This enables originalism to meet many criticisms lodged against it by nonoriginalist critics, particularly dealing with nonoriginalist precedent, constitutional doctrine, and constitutional change.

At the same time, I do not oversell originalism's capacity to fit our current practice. I describe the ways in which some facets of our practice are mistakes. Some of these mistakes, originalism retains; others, it rejects. This means that, to some – I argue modest – extent, originalism is a reform project. Though, originalism is relatively less of a reform effort than other interpretive theories – in particular, it does *not* require changing our practice's central facets – and I argue in Chapter 4 that originalism has strong normative reasons to support its reforms of other marginal facets of our practice.

My claim is not that our current constitutional practice univocally requires originalism. My claim is that originalism fits well with our practice's most fundamental aspects and with its widespread or common aspects. This high level of fit, when coupled with the law-as-coordination normative account in Chapter 4, provides two payoffs. First, it provides sound reasons for Americans to follow originalism intra-systemically, including when the practice does not prescribe originalism and when it prescribes nonoriginalism. It justifies reform of those marginal aspects of the practice that originalism does not currently fit. Second, it justifies originalism and shows that it is a normatively valuable project for Americans to pursue.

My argument in this chapter proceeds in three parts. First, I show that originalism fits well with our constitutional practice's central and most important facet: the written Constitution. Second, I describe how originalism adequately fits Supreme Court practice. Third, I explain originalism's capacity to accommodate social and constitutional change.

3.2 SUMMARY OF CLAIMS THAT ORIGINALISM DOES NOT FIT OUR CONSTITUTIONAL PRACTICE

Before moving to my positive argument, let me first summarize the nonoriginalist criticisms to which this chapter responds. My argument in this chapter is contrary to one of the powerful and commonly-made arguments against originalism. This criticism claims that originalism is deeply in tension with our constitutional practice. This claim has been advanced since the modern rise of originalism,[7] and it has recently been reiterated.[8]

This claim has three main components, which I will describe in a moment. Before this, let me note that each of the three criticisms shares this common move: the American Constitution is defined by official (and, for some, public) acceptance of legal norms and practices.[9] The American Constitution, on this account, is identified by current conventions of acceptance. To the extent that originalism identifies constitutional meaning that is inconsistent with the meaning identified by these conventions, critics conclude, it is not a theory of interpretation; it is a reform project.

---

[7] Paul Brest, *The Misconceived Quest for the Original Understanding*, 60 B.U. L. Rev. 204 (1980).

[8] David A. Strauss, The Living Constitution 12–17 (2010); Peter J. Smith, *Originalism and Level of Generality*, 51 Ga. L. Rev. 485, 490 (2017); Richard H. Fallon, Jr., *How to Choose a Constitutional Theory*, 87 Cal. L. Rev. 535, 548–49 (1999); *see also* Mitchell N. Berman, *Reflective Equilibrium and Constitutional Method: Lessons from John McCain and the Natural-Born Citizenship Clause*, in The Challenge of Originalism, Theories of Constitutional Interpretation 246, 258–69 (Grant Huscroft & Bradley W. Miller eds., 2013).

[9] *E.g.*, Richard H. Fallon, Jr., implementing the Constitution 18 (2001); *see also* H. L. A. Hart, The Concept of Law 117 (2d ed., Oxford University Press, 1994).

First and most prominently, critics have argued that originalism cannot account for the role nonoriginalist precedent plays in constitutional adjudication.[10] Critics argue that much of constitutional law is composed of nonoriginalist precedent. They couple that claim to the further claim that originalism's call to overrule nonoriginalist precedent would cause tremendous harm to the Rule of Law and reliance interests. Professor Michael Gerhardt has argued along these lines: "[F]aithful adherents to original understanding face an inescapable dilemma. They either can strive to overrule the better part of constitutional doctrine and thereby thrust the world of constitutional law into turmoil, or they must abandon original understanding in numerous substantive areas in order to stabilize constitutional law."[11]

A second, similar claim is that originalism does not fit our practice because it does not have the capacity to develop and account for the practice of constitutional doctrine, which structures constitutional law and implements the Constitution. American constitutional practice abounds in constitutional doctrine. The claim is that originalism's fixation on the Constitution's original meaning does not leave sufficient analytical room for constitutional doctrine, which is ubiquitous in our practice, and that originalism therefore does not fit our practice.

The group of scholars who make this claim as part of a broader project is known as the New Doctrinalists.[12] They argue that: (1) there is a distinction between propositions about the Constitution's meaning and propositions implementing or putting into effect the Constitution's meaning[13]; and (2) there is a permissible disparity between these two sorts of propositions.[14] New Doctrinalists scholars argue that these two key points are not only an accurate description of our practice[15]; they claim that these points are necessary to any plausible theory of constitutional interpretation.[16]

Third, nonoriginalist critics argue that originalism's inability to fit our practice is also manifested in its resistance to societal change and its related inability to account for the robust changes in constitutional doctrine. One of the most oft-repeated criticisms of originalism is that it is not a viable interpretive methodology because it would bind today's society to the legal norms of the vastly different society that enacted the Constitution. Professor Daniel Farber, for instance, argued that "[w]hat

---

[10] FALLON, *supra* note 9, at 15–17; Henry Paul Monaghan, *Stare Decisis and Constitutional Adjudication*, 88 COLUM. L. REV. 723, 739 (1988).

[11] Michael J. Gerhardt, *The Role of Precedent in Constitutional Decisionmaking and Theory*, 60 GEO. WASH. L. REV. 68, 133–34 (1991).

[12] The most prominent New Doctrinalists are Professors Mitchell Berman, Richard Fallon, and Kermit Roosevelt.

[13] Kermit Roosevelt III, *Constitutional Calcification: How the Law Becomes What the Court Does*, 91 VA. L. REV. 1649, 1652 (2005).

[14] Richard H. Fallon, Jr., *Judicially Manageable Standards and Constitutional Meaning*, 119 HARV. L. REV. 1274, 1317 (2006).

[15] Mitchell N. Berman, *Constitutional Decision Rules*, 90 VA. L. REV. 1, 35 (2004).

[16] FALLON, *supra* note 9, at 37–42.

is wrong with originalism is that it seeks to block judges from even considering these later developments, which on their face seem so clearly relevant to the legitimacy of [statutes under constitutional challenge]."[17] Farber found that the Second Amendment provided a good example of originalism's inability to meet the challenge of change.[18]

These three claims purport to fundamentally undermine originalism's claim to adequately describe our practice of constitutional interpretation. This is a potentially devastating claim for originalism because its failure to adequately fit our constitutional practice would mean that it could not account for the posited human legal "artifacts" that make up our practice and therefore it would not be a theory of interpretation. It would instead be a theory of dramatic reform or change or creation which, in turn, would require a robust normative justification for the disruption such reform would cause, a claim that is *prima facie* implausible. As summarized by Professor Sachs,

> Many sophisticated opponents of originalism have claimed (and some of its supporters have accepted) that originalism offers a deeply inaccurate picture of our law. It can't explain changes to our practice over time; in fact, it doesn't even try. Without an adequate theory of our legal system, originalism becomes merely a political effort — flawed or welcome, depending on your view — to change American law into something else.[19]

In the following section, however, I argue that originalism fits well with our constitutional practice.

3.3 OUR WRITTEN CONSTITUTION FITS ORIGINALISM

3.3.1 *Introduction*

The most important facet of our constitutional practice is our written Constitution. It is the focal point of the practice. Americans of all stripes, whatever their place in society, their religious views and their ideology, appeal to it. Citizens point to it as supporting their legal and political claims. Lawyers rely on it to advance their clients' claims. Legislators raise it to justify their actions. And judges explain that their decisions are justified by the written Constitution. This Constitution – its text, is provenance, and its amendment process – is consistent with originalism and in tension with other theories of interpretation.

---

[17] Daniel A. Farber, *Disarmed by Time: The Second Amendment and the Failure of Originalism*, 76 CHI-KENT L. REV. 167, 192 (2000).

[18] *Id.* at 189–92.

[19] Stephen E. Sachs, *The "Constitution in Exile" as a Problem for Legal Theory*, 89 NOTRE DAME L. REV. 2253, 2255 (2014).

3.3.2 *The Constitution's Text Identifies Originalism as the Correct Mode of Interpretation*

The written Constitution itself – which all or nearly all members of our constitutional practice acknowledge is at least part of the constitution[20] – identifies originalism as the appropriate manner of interpretation. The written Constitution is the foundational element of our constitutional practice. As summarized by Professor Richard Fallon, "Judges and Justices always purport to reconcile their rulings with the written Constitution and have never claimed authority to displace it."[21]

Even nonoriginalist scholars identify the written Constitution as (at least) part of the authoritative American constitution. For example, according to Philip Bobbitt, two of the six "modalities" of American constitutional law are facets of the written Constitution: text and structure.[22] Similarly, Ronald Dworkin identified the written Constitution as a "basic piece of interpretive data"[23] that forms, for Dworkin, the larger body of practices that constitute the constitution.[24]

This written Constitution identifies originalism as the appropriate theory of constitutional interpretation. In particular, the Constitution's indexicals, coupled with the Constitution's text that indicates the Constitution's point of chronological expression, show that originalism is the correct theory of constitutional interpretation.[25] This argument has three parts. First, constitutional indexicals are the Constitution's text's identification of what the U.S. Constitution is. The U.S. Constitution contains many indexicals, beginning with the Preamble's identification of the document of which it is a part as "this Constitution,"[26] and ending with the Ratification Clause, at the book-end of the original Constitution, which confirms

---

[20] I use the small-c constitution to designate the set of practices and documents identified by some nonoriginalist scholars as the authoritative American constitution, and to distinguish it from the big-C Constitution located in the National Archives. *See* AKHIL REED AMAR, AMERICA'S UNWRITTEN CONSTITUTION: THE PRECEDENTS AND PRINCIPLES WE LIVE BY x–xi (2012); Kenneth Einar Himma, *The U.S. Constitution and the Conventional Rule of Recognition* 111, *in* THE RULE OF RECOGNITION AND THE U.S. CONSTITUTION (Matthew D. Adler & Kenneth Einar Himma eds., 2009).

[21] Richard H. Fallon, Jr., *Precedent-Based Constitutional Adjudication, Acceptance, and the Rule of Recognition* 55, *in* THE RULE OF RECOGNITION AND THE U.S. CONSTITUTION (Matthew D. Adler & Kenneth Einar Himma, eds., 2009).

[22] PHILIP BOBBITT, CONSTITUTIONAL INTERPRETATION 12 (1991).

[23] RONALD DWORKIN, JUSTICE IN ROBES 128–29 (2006).

[24] *See also* STRAUSS, *supra* note 8, at 99.

[25] Christopher R. Green, *"This Constitution": Constitutional Indexicals as a Basis for Textualist Semi-Originalism*, 84 NOTRE DAME L. REV. 1607, 1641–65 (2009); Michael Stokes Paulsen, *Does the Constitution Prescribe Rules for its Own Interpretation?*, 103 NW. U. L. REV. 857, 864–72 (2009).

[26] U.S. CONST. pmbl.

that "this Constitution" is the written Constitution that went through the ratification process.[27] Therefore, both the Constitution's enactment and ratification texts refer only to the written Constitution. In between the Preamble and Article VII are further numerous identifications of the Constitution as the written Constitution; for instance, Article V describes how changes to the text of "this Constitution" may occur.[28]

Second, the Constitution's text makes explicit that the Constitution was temporally expressed at the points in time when it was ratified.[29] In other words, "this Constitution['s]" meaning was fixed at those chronological points. For example, the Constitution distinguished between "We the People" and "our Posterity."[30] Article VII identified the discrete point in time at which "We the People" "Establish[ed]" the Constitution.[31] The Constitution's text repeatedly references "now," showing that the Constitution was chronologically fixed.[32] Lastly, the text limiting those eligible to the presidency to natural born citizens or citizens "at the time of the Adoption of this Constitution" likewise chronologically identified the Constitution.[33]

Third, the Article VI Supremacy Clause confers on "This Constitution" (that is, the document identified by the constitutional indexicals as the U.S. Constitution – the one that was "ordain[ed] and establish[ed]" by "We the People"[34] – which chronologically identified the Constitution at the time of Ratification) the status of "supreme Law of the Land."[35] The Constitution's indexicals and chronology-identifiers, coupled with the Supremacy Clause, identify the Constitution's original meaning – and only it – as the Constitution's meaning, and therefore the proper method of constitutional interpretation.

The written Constitution's fixing of its meaning at the time it was given authority by the American People has widespread appeal. This appeal is so pervasive in our practice that nonoriginalists regularly lament the fact that prominent actors in our practice publicly – though, in the nonoriginalists' eyes, falsely – justify their (sub-rosa nonoriginalist) claims with reference to the original meaning of the

---

[27] *Id.* art. VII.
[28] *Id.* art. V.
[29] Green, *supra* note 26, at 1657–66.
[30] U.S. Const. pmbl.
[31] *Id.* art. VII.
[32] *See* Green, *supra* note 26, at 1663 n.177 (listing the key uses of "now" by the Constitution).
[33] U.S. Const. art. II, § 1, cl. 5.
[34] *Id.* pmbl.
[35] *Id.* art. VI, cl. 2.

Constitution. For example, nonoriginalists lamented that, even progressive Supreme Court nominees[36] (not to mention the conservative nominees![37]) during their confirmation hearings purported to invoke the written Constitution's time-limited meaning.[38] Another example is the Supreme Court's "rhetoric" that its decisions are compelled by the Constitution, which nonoriginalists attempt to show is a facade, or screen, for the truth (of nonoriginalism).[39] The existence of the standard non-originalist move of "pulling back the curtain"[40] itself testifies how strongly our practice focuses on only the written Constitution.

This appeal is nothing new, either. It fits the interpretive conventions at the time of the Framing and Ratification. The Framers deliberately chose a written Constitution, and the Ratifiers deliberately adopted our written Constitution because it, when coupled with those conventional rules of interpretation, provided fixed law.[41]

Only originalism fits the Constitution's identification of originalism as the correct theory of interpretation. This means that originalism precisely fits the most important facet of our existing constitutional practice: our written Constitution.

3.3.3 *The Constitution's Provenance Identifies Originalism as the Correct Mode of Interpretation*

Our constitutional practice identifies our Constitution by its unique provenance. This provenance identifies only the written Constitution as the Constitution and only its original meaning as its authoritative meaning.[42]

Constitutional provenance is the origin of a constitution. Constitutional provenance is crucial because it is the characteristic that explains why a particular document, and not another, is a polity's constitution. For example, in the United States, not only our current Constitution purports to be our constitution, but the Articles of

---

[36] *E.g.,* The Nomination of Elena Kagan to be an Associate Justice of the Supreme Court of the United States: Hearing Before the S. Comm. on the Judiciary, 111th Cong. (2010), www.gpo .gov/fdsys/pkg/CHRG-111shrg67622/html/CHRG-111shrg67622.htm.

[37] *E.g.,* Confirmation Hearing on the Nomination of John G. Roberts, Jr. to Be Chief Justice of the United States: Hearing Before the S. Comm. on the Judiciary, 109th Cong. 56 (2005) (statement of Judge John G. Roberts, Jr.), www.gpo.gov/fdsys/pkg/GPO-CHRG-ROBERTS/ pdf/GPO-CHRG-ROBERTS.pdf.

[38] Or Bassok, *The Court Cannot Hold*, 30 J.L. & Pols. 1, 40–41 (2014); Todd E. Pettys, *Judicial Discretion in Constitutional Cases*, 26 J.L. & Pols. 123 (2011).

[39] *See, e.g.,* III Bruce Ackerman, We the People: The Civil Rights Revolution 32–33 (2014) ("[T]he official canon is composed of the 1787 Constitution and its subsequent formal amendments."); Strauss, *supra* note 8, at 29 ("Constitutional law is supposed to consist in the interpretation of a written text.").

[40] *Compare* Barnett, *supra* note 5, at 2.

[41] The Federalist No. 78 (Alexander Hamilton); The Essays of Brutus No. XI, *in* 2 The Complete Anti-Federalist 419 (Herbert J. Storing ed., 1981).

[42] This argument is drawn from Richard Kay in Richard S. Kay, *American Constitutionalism* 29–33, *in* Constitutionalism: Philosophical Foundations (Larry Alexander ed., 1998).

Confederation's text likewise claims for itself the title of our constitution. These documents' different provenances enable Americans today to identify which document is actually our governing Constitution.

A constitution's provenance is identified by the "constituent authority" that possessed the authority to designate a document as the constituent authority's polity's constitution.[43] The identification of which document – the U.S. Constitution or the Articles of Confederation, for example – is our Constitution depends on what the United States' constituent authority designated. The constituent authority in a given society is the person or entity that the members of that society recognize as having such authority. The relevant people *today* must recognize the constituent authority's authority.

A society's constituent authority may be identified in a number of ways. Typically, in the modern West, a constituent authority is the person or entity identified by the society's current legal officials as having authority to identify the constitution. In other cultures or times, identification could proceed by identification by a subset of the population – the nobility, for example – or even brute force in many cases, including the Norman Conquest, the Roman Empire, and the Soviet Union.

The U.S. Constitution is identified by its provenance. Only the Constitution of the United States originated from the Philadelphia Convention on September 17, 1787, and was ratified by nine state ratification conventions by 1788. Americans of all stripes then – and today – recognize(d) that the unique Ratification process is the United States' constituent authority. This authority designated the document now located in the National Archives as the U.S. Constitution: the Framers in Philadelphia crafted the written Constitution, and the Ratifiers in the state ratification conventions possessed the authority to empower it.[44] No matter how much more normatively attractive another document is, it is not the U.S. Constitution if it did not go through that Framing and Ratification process.

For this reason, for instance, Supreme Court precedent is not (part of) the Constitution: no Supreme Court case was drafted in the Philadelphia Convention and authorized in state ratification conventions. Nor is the Supreme Court recognized by Americans today as a constituent authority with the power to identify new parts of the Constitution. Our society recognizes only one constituent authority. This also explains why the other self-proclaimed best candidate for the role of current American constitution, the Articles of Confederation, is not our Constitution. The U.S. Constitution's provenance identifies – includes – only one item: the written Constitution in the National Archives' Rotunda. As recently summarized by Professor Scott Shapiro:

---

[43] Richard S. Kay, *Constituent Authority*, 59 Am. J. Comp. L. 715 (2011).
[44] Strauss, *supra* note 8, at 10; Richard S. Kay, *Original Intention and Public Meaning in Constitutional Interpretation*, 103 Nw. U.L. Rev. 703, 717 (2009).

[T]he United States legal system strongly resembles an authority system. The reverence in which the 'Founding Fathers' are held, the privileging of democracy to the exclusion of all other modes of political legitimization, the political impossibility of criticizing the Constitution, and the veneration with which the text is treated all bespeak a belief that the authority of the Constitution stems from its special provenance.[45]

This same provenance identifies the Constitution's original meaning as the document's meaning. The Framers who drafted and the Ratifiers who authorized the Constitution – our constituent authority – created and empowered the Constitution using its original meaning.[46] As I described in Section 2.2, the Framers wished to pursue the common good by re-ordering American society to overcome the Articles of Confederation's defects. The Framers knew that, to achieve this goal, the Constitution needed adoption by the state ratification conventions, and it needed to direct and control future federal and state officers. The Constitution's original meaning was the mechanism the Framers employed to communicate their prudential, coordinating decisions on how to pursue the national common good. The Ratifiers similarly, to understand the Constitution sufficiently in order to rationally authorize it, and to understand how the Constitution would ultimately direct and control future federal and state officers, needed to understand its authoritative, prudential, coordinating decisions. The meaning that permitted them all to effectively participate in the process was its public meaning.[47] American citizens then, and today, in order to understand the Framers' and Ratifiers' communications, likewise utilize(d) the Constitution's original meaning. Therefore, the constituent authority that adopted the U.S. Constitution adopted its original meaning.

Bolstering this conclusion is the fact that the Framers and Ratifiers utilized the then-relatively unique tool of a written constitution to achieve their goals. One of constitutionalism's primary goals is legal and (ultimately) social stability: stable limits on a government to protect liberty, and stable authorizations to the government to empower it.[48] The Framers' and Ratifiers' choice to employ a written constitution chooses the benefits of constitutionalism (primarily permanency) over its costs (primarily flexibility). This choice, as a practical matter,[49] excludes nonoriginalist

---

[45] Scott J. Shapiro, Legality 351 (2011).
[46] Barnett, *supra* note 5, at 94–100; McGinnis & Rappaport, *supra* note 4, at 126–38; Christopher Wolfe, The Rise of Modern Judicial Review: From Constitutional Interpretation to Judge-Made Law 17–38 (1986); Johnathan O'Neill, Originalism in American Law and Politics 12–21 (2005); Howard Gillman, *The Collapse of Constitutional Originalism and the Rise of the Notion of the "Living Constitution" in the Course of American State-Building*, 11 Studies in Am. Pol. Dev. 191, 197–203 (1997).
[47] McGinnis & Rappaport, *supra* note 4, at 13, 116–32.
[48] Kay, *supra* note 43, at 17–22.
[49] A written constitution is not logically inconsistent with nonoriginalist interpretive methodologies because the text could serve functions other than coordination and achieve goals other

interpretation methodologies.[50] It does so because a nonoriginalist method would authorize government officials to vary constitutional interpretations using different modalities, and these government officials would do so in unpredictable ways at unpredictable times, and this would undermine stability, potentially expand their power, and potentially reduce liberty.

Nonoriginalism is in tension with the Constitution's provenance in one of two ways. On the one hand, nonoriginalists frequently privilege documents, traditions, and practices other than the written Constitution over the written Constitution.[51] For example, David Strauss claimed that nonoriginalist precedent possesses a constitutional status like the written Constitution.[52] These documents, traditions, and practices did not originate from the same constitutional provenance, nor is there an alternative constituent authority that authorized these documents, traditions, or practices.

One oft-cited source of authoritative coordination that is clearly *excluded* by the Constitution's provenance is United States Supreme Court nonoriginalist precedents. Constitutional provenance in the United States is and is only the Framing and Ratification process (and subsequent amendments). Supreme Court precedents do not originate from that process. Moreover, neither the precedents themselves, nor the Supreme Court, nor our constitutional practice, identify nonoriginalist Supreme Court precedents as possessing an alternative constitutional provenance.[53]

On the other hand, nonoriginalists reject the original meaning's authority. The Constitution's original meaning, according to nonoriginalism, is one factor among many in constitutional interpretation, and other modalities may displace the Constitution's original meaning. These other modalities, such as current policy preferences, were not authorized by our constituent authority and do not possess the appropriate provenance, as does the Constitution's original meaning. For instance, the Framers did not employ current (2019) policy preferences to communicate the Constitution's directives to the Ratifiers.

Originalism, by contrast, fits well the Constitution's provenance because it was employed by the United States' constituent authority. Originalism privileges the written Constitution and its original meaning over all other sources of law.

---

than stability. For example, a nonoriginalist written constitution could be a focal point for political discussions and provide relatively flexible constitutional meaning.

[50] WHITTINGTON, INTERPRETATION, *supra* note 5, at 47–61.

[51] STRAUSS, *supra* note 8, at 3; BOBBITT, *supra* note 23, at 12–13; Fallon, *supra* note 8, at 545–48.

[52] STRAUSS, *supra* note 8, at 3.

[53] I show in Subsection 3.4.2 that the Supreme Court's own practice identified its precedent as subordinate to the Constitution's original meaning.

3.3.4 *The Amendment Process Identifies Originalism as the Correct Mode of Interpretation*

The Constitution's amendment process likewise shows that the Constitution's original meaning is its authoritative meaning, and in two main ways. First, the amendment process shows that the original meaning is the Constitution's meaning when amendments displace meaning contrary to the original meaning. Second, the amendment process shows that the original meaning is the Constitution's authoritative meaning because originalism is a necessary condition for the Article V amendment process to be substantively valuable.

Our written Constitution includes, not just its original text, but also amendments, and those amendments became part of the Constitution through an amendment process. The Constitution's text authorizes changes to itself.[54] The Constitution also recognizes that these changes – amendments – are equivalent to and part of the written Constitution. These amendments are sufficiently authoritative that they may replace the Constitution's previously existing text, which had been, up to that point, authoritative.

The existence of constitutional amendments shows that only originalism is the correct theory of constitutional interpretation. It does so by identifying constitutional amendments as having the authority to displace all other facets of our legal practice – including, importantly for our purposes, Supreme Court precedent that utilized nonoriginalist meaning – contrary to the amendment.

The Supreme Court recognizes that amendments displace its contrary holdings, and this has occurred repeatedly,[55] including in situations where the amendment makes clear that the Supreme Court had previously *mis*interpreted the Constitution, such as occurred in the context of state sovereign immunity. There, the American People rejected *Chisholm* v. *Georgia's* incorrect interpretation of Article III and restored the correct interpretation of Article III through the Eleventh Amendment. "The Judicial power of the United States shall not be construed to extend . . . ."[56] As the Court explained in *Alden* v. *Maine*, "Congress acted not to change but to restore the original constitutional design."[57] Moreover, the Supreme Court has never "overruled" an Article V amendment, and scholarly calls to do so are exotic. This shows an asymmetry between amendments and Supreme Court precedent: the former may correct the latter, but not vice versa. The Constitution's authorization

---

[54] U.S. CONST. art. V.

[55] The Eleventh Amendment abrogated *Chisholm* v. *Georgia*, 2 U.S. (2 Dall.) 419 (1793), the Thirteenth and Fourteenth Amendments abrogated *Dred Scott* v. *Sandford*, 60 U.S. 393 (1857), the Sixteenth Amendment abrogated *Pollock* v. *Farmers' Loan & Trust Co.*, 157 U.S. 429 (1895), the Nineteenth Amendment abrogated *Minor* v. *Happersett*, 88 U.S. 162 (1875), and the Twenty-Sixth Amendment abrogated *Oregon* v. *Mitchell*, 400 U.S. 112 (1970).

[56] U.S. CONST. amend. XI (1798).

[57] *Alden* v. *Maine*, 527 U.S. 706, 722 (1999).

of amendments and our legal practice surrounding them shows that meanings inconsistent with the written Constitution's original meaning are not the Constitution's meaning.

Second, originalism is a necessary condition for the amendment process to produce substantively valuable results.[58] The Amendment process was the exclusive manner by which the Framers and Ratifiers channeled change to constitutional meaning.[59] This process is identified and contained in its own article in the Constitution, and amendments are thereafter part of the Constitution.[60] The amendment process requires multiple supermajorities of Americans to agree that a proposition should be embodied in the Constitution's text.

The Article V amendment process produces at least four major benefits. First, it incentivizes and protects the constitutional judgments made by the American People and embodied in the Constitution's text.[61] Second, this supermajoritarian process has the benefit of making it relatively more likely that constitutional amendments will have substantively valuable content.[62] Third, the Article V process strikes a reasonable balance between stability and plasticity of constitutional meaning.[63] Fourth, it forces Americans to exercise their "civic muscles" to persuade their fellows in order to alter the Constitution.[64]

Originalism complements the amendment process because it preserves the Constitution's meaning until a consensus of the American People has emerged to change it. Originalism "locks-in" the Constitution's original meaning, as Professor Barnett has argued, and prevents judicial "updating" using a nonoriginalist methodology.[65] Originalism thereby preserves a space for and gives time within our democratic republic for Article V to operate and the American People to debate and come to constitutional judgments. Originalism's lock-in also preserves the supermajoritarian benefits of the Article V process, which are more likely to produce substantively attractive constitutional meaning than nonoriginalist judicial meaning. Originalism maintains the Constitution's reasonable balance between stability and change, and

---

[58] WHITTINGTON, INTERPRETATION, *supra* note 5, at 111; McGINNIS & RAPPAPORT, *supra* note 4, at 2, 90–93.

[59] Some scholars have argued that Article V is not the exclusive means of constitutional amendment, based on originalist-type arguments. *See, e.g.,* 2 BRUCE ACKERMAN, WE THE PEOPLE: TRANSFORMATIONS, 81, 92 (1998); Akhil Reed Amar, *The Consent of the Governed: Constitutional Amendment Outside Article V,* 94 COLUM. L. REV. 457, 458–59 (1994); Akhil Reed Amar, *Philadelphia Revisited: Amending the Constitution Outside Article V,* 55 U. CHI. L. REV. 1043, 1044 (1988). In my view, Professor Henry Monaghan rebutted these claims. Henry Paul Monaghan, *We the People[s], Original Understanding, and Constitutional Amendment,* 96 COLUM. L. REV. 121 (1996).

[60] U.S. CONST. art. V.

[61] WHITTINGTON, INTERPRETATION, *supra* note 5, at 110–11, 128–59.

[62] McGINNIS & RAPPAPORT, *supra* note 4, at 62–80.

[63] *Id.* at 76.

[64] *Id.* at 201–02.

[65] BARNETT, *supra* note 5, at 100–09.

avoids nonoriginalism's facility of change. Lastly, originalism pushes the American People to persuade their fellow citizens to favor (and oppose) direct constitutional change via amendment.

Contrast this with nonoriginalism. Nonoriginalism permits – indeed, is almost defined by – constitutional change through judicial updating. Judicial updating is typically easier and speedier than constitutional change through amendment because it only needs the nomination of five Supreme Court justices willing to employ judicial updating. This relative ease of use means that those seeking constitutional change can achieve it more easily through focusing their efforts on molding the Supreme Court's personnel and persuading it to update the Constitution's meaning using nonoriginalism.

Nonoriginalist judicial updating has caused and continues to cause the Article V amendment process to fall into disquietude. The American People vigorously debated important issues of substance, and embodied them in the Constitution's text, until the New Deal. Prior to then, major changes in the American Constitution were embodied in the Constitution's text, because that was the only (legitimate) way to change the Constitution's meaning. The pre-New Deal amendments were very weighty: taxation,[66] representation,[67] voting,[68] and numerous protections from state abuse.[69] After the New Deal, Americans ceased to embody their major constitutional changes in the Constitution's text, and instead focused on the judicial nomination process. The post-New Deal textual amendments that have occurred are less weighty: congressional compensation, lowering the voting age by three years, executive succession, a prohibition on poll taxes, District of Columbia presidential voting, and presidential term limits.

Without originalism to cabin the Supreme Court – to maintain the amendment process as the means of constitutional change – the amendment process has been reduced to relatively minor changes. All the real action occurs at the Supreme Court. Think of all the major constitutional issues over which Americans debate—abortion, marriage, flag burning, the size of government, gun rights, executive power – and how those debates are Court-centered and not geared toward the amendment process. One way to get at this is to ask yourself how often you try to convince other Americans to work toward a constitutional amendment compared to how frequently you try to convince them to vote for a presidential candidate who will appoint justices who will interpret the Constitution in a particular way. Nearly no-one does the former; nearly everyone does the latter.

---

[66] U.S. Const. amend. XVI (1913).
[67] *Id.* amend. XVII (1913).
[68] *Id.* amend. XIX (1919).
[69] *Id.* amends. XIII–XV (1865–1870).

Originalism would restore the amendment process to its proper place as the exclusive mechanism of constitutional change. This would, in turn, preserve that process' four key benefits.

3.3.5 *Conclusion*

Originalism fits well with the fundamental facet of our constitutional practice: the Constitution itself. Moreover, the Constitution's provenance and amendment process all identify originalism as uniquely the means to interpret the Constitution.

3.4 SUPREME COURT PRACTICE FITS ORIGINALISM

3.4.1 *Introduction*

Originalism also fits well the Supreme Court's practice. Supreme Court practice consists primarily of the Supreme Court's reasoning and arguments, its creation and employment of constitutional doctrine, and holdings in cases. Supreme Court practice is an important part of our constitutional practice because of the central role the Court possesses in our constitutional system.

My claim is that originalism fits this complex practice. The fit, however, is not perfect; it is less clean than with the written Constitution. Therefore, I argue at the end of this section that originalism's fit is still sufficient and relatively better than alternative methodologies because it fits the most important facets of our constitutional practice.

3.4.2 *The Supreme Court's Reasoning and Arguments*

The Supreme Court provides reasons and arguments to justify its holdings. This facet of the practice is frequently pointed to as one of the key distinguishing characteristics of the judiciary compared to the other branches.[70]

The Supreme Court's reasoning and arguments reflects both the widespread use and priority of originalism and originalist arguments. This is important because our constitutional practice is, among other things, an argumentative practice. The lack of originalist arguments, therefore, would be powerful evidence against it fitting the practice. Similarly, the widespread use of originalist arguments, including the prioritization of such arguments, shows that originalism fits the practice.

---

[70] HENRY M. HART, JR. & ALBERT M. SACKS, THE LEGAL PROCESS: BASIC PROBLEMS IN THE MAKING AND APPLICATION OF LAW 143–52 (William N. Eskridge, Jr. & Philip P. Frickey, eds., 1994); Lon L. Fuller, *The Forms and Limits of Adjudication*, 92 HARV. L. REV. 353, 363 (1978); Herbert Wechsler, *Toward Neutral Principles of Constitutional Law*, 73 HARV. L. REV. 1 (1959).

First, the Supreme Court regularly uses originalist arguments to support its rulings.[71] Perhaps most prominently, in *District of Columbia* v. *Heller*, the Supreme Court justified its controversial holding in terms of fealty to the Constitution's original meaning: "[t]here seems to us no doubt, on the basis of both text and history, that the Second Amendment conferred an individual right to keep and bear arms."[72]

Second, the Supreme Court also justifies changes in its constitutional doctrine – including, importantly, rejecting nonoriginalist precedent – by reference to the Constitution's original meaning. In *Crawford* v. *Washington*, for instance, the Court rejected its governing rule from a nonoriginalist precedent (*Ohio* v. *Roberts*[73]) and defended this change with reference to the Constitution's original meaning: "The legacy of *Roberts* in other courts vindicates the Framers' wisdom in rejecting a general reliability exception."[74]

Third, the Supreme Court defends even its most controversial decisions as mandated by the Constitution's original meaning. *INS* v. *Chada* involved the constitutionality of the popular legislative veto.[75] The legislative veto permitted Congress, or one of its houses or committees, to "veto" agency action in statutorily specified situations. These legislative vetoes did not go through Article I's legislative process. Legislative veto proponents claimed that it was a necessary check on administrative agencies empowered through broad congressional delegations.[76] Nonetheless, the Supreme Court ruled that the legislative veto was unconstitutional, invoking the original meaning:

> The choices we discern as having been made in the Constitutional Convention impose burdens on governmental processes that often seem clumsy, inconvenient, even unworkable, but those hard choices were consciously made by men who had lived under a form of government that permitted arbitrary governmental acts to go unchecked. There is no support in the Constitution or decisions of this Court for the proposition that the cumbersomeness and delays often encountered in complying with explicit Constitutional standards may be avoided, either by the Congress or by the President. With all the obvious flaws of delay, untidiness, and potential for abuse, we have not yet found a better way to preserve freedom than by making the exercise of power subject to the carefully crafted restraints spelled out in the Constitution.[77]

---

[71] Baude, *supra* note 6, at 2370–91 (elaborating on this and related claims); *see also* SOTIRIOS A. BARBER & JAMES E. FLEMING, CONSTITUTIONAL INTERPRETATION: THE BASIC QUESTIONS 19 (2007) (arguing that there is "no case in which the Court fails to connect its answer to a provision of the constitutional text").

[72] *District of Columbia* v. *Heller*, 554 U.S. 570, 595 (2008).

[73] *Ohio* v. *Roberts*, 448 U.S. 56 (1980).

[74] *Crawford* v. *Washington*, 541 U.S. 36, 62 (2003).

[75] *INS* v. *Chada*, 462 U.S. 919 (1983).

[76] *Id.* at 968–74 (White, J., dissenting).

[77] *Id.* at 945.

The *Chada* Court's use of originalism was especially powerful because it occurred in the face of very attractive pragmatic reasons to reject the Constitution's original meaning.

Fourth, the Supreme Court, even when it is implausible, identifies the Constitution's original meaning as a reason for its actions. The Court's *Obergefell v. Hodges* opinion provides an example.[78] The Supreme Court ruled that the Fourteenth Amendment required states to issue marriage licenses to opposite and same-sex couples. To justify its ruling, the Court argued that

> The generations that wrote and ratified the Bill of Rights and the Fourteenth Amendment did not presume to know the extent of freedom in all of its dimensions, and so they entrusted to future generations a charter protecting the right of all persons to enjoy liberty as we learn its meaning. When new insight reveals discord between the Constitution's central protections and a received legal stricture, a claim to liberty must be addressed.[79]

This is an originalist argument, though an implausible one.[80] The fact that the Court made it, despite is fantastic character, shows originalism's pull on the Court's argumentative practice and constitutional doctrine.[81]

Fifth, the Supreme Court prioritizes originalism over other potential sources of constitutional law, even when it would be plausible to use these other forms of argument autonomously of the original meaning.[82] For example, in *NLRB v. Noel Canning*, the Court refused to rely on a long-standing constitutional tradition, even though it was invited to do so by the administration,[83] to supplant the original meaning.[84] Instead, the Court first found that the phrase "Recess of the Senate"[85] was ambiguous,[86] and relied on the originalist interpretive method of "liquidation"[87] to argue that constitutional tradition had fixed the meaning of the phrase to permit intra-recess appointments.[88]

Sixth, dissenting justices regularly appeal to the Constitution's original meaning against existing doctrine. For example, Justice Ginsburg worked hard to show why

---

[78] *Obergefell* v. *Hodges*, 135 S. Ct. 2584 (2015).

[79] *Id.* at 2598.

[80] Baude, *supra* note 6, at 2382–83.

[81] *See also Dickerson* v. *United States*, 530 U.S. 428, 432, 438, 440, 444 (2000) (affirming that *Miranda* v. *Arizona* "announced a constitutional rule," was a "constitutional decision," was "constitutionally based," and was "constitutionally required").

[82] *See* Sachs, *supra* note 6, at 856 (identifying the substance of this claim).

[83] Transcript of Oral Argument 6–8 (January 13, 2014), *in NLRB* v. *Noel Canning*, 134 S. Ct. 2550 (2014).

[84] *NLRB* v. *Noel Canning*, 134 S. Ct. 2550, 2559–60 (2014).

[85] U.S. Const. art. II, § 2, cl. 3.

[86] *Noel Canning*, 134 S. Ct. at 2560–61.

[87] McGinnis & Rappaport, *supra* note 4, at 128–38.

[88] *Noel Canning*, 134 S. Ct. at 2561–64.

her dissent was consistent with the Commerce Clause's original meaning in *NFIB* v. *Sebelius*:

> The Commerce Clause, it is widely acknowledged, "was the Framers' response to the central problem that gave rise to the Constitution itself." Under the Articles of Confederation, the Constitution's precursor, the regulation of commerce was left to the States. This scheme proved unworkable, because the individual States, understandably focused on their own economic interests, often failed to take actions critical to the success of the Nation as a whole. See Vices of the Political System of the United States, in James Madison: Writings 69, 71, ¶ 5 (J. Rakove ed. 1999) (As a result of the "want of concert in matters where common interest requires it," the "national dignity, interest, and revenue [have] suffered.").
>
> What was needed was a "national Government ... armed with a positive & compleat authority in all cases where uniform measures are necessary." See Letter from James Madison to Edmund Randolph (Apr. 8, 1787), in 9 Papers of James Madison 368, 370 (R. Rutland ed. 1975) ... The Framers' solution was the Commerce Clause, which, as they perceived it, granted Congress the authority to enact economic legislation "in all Cases for the general Interests of the Union, and also in those Cases to which the States are separately incompetent." 2 Records of the Federal Convention of 1787, pp. 131–132, ¶ 8 (M. Farrand rev. 1966).
>
> The Framers understood that the "general Interests of the Union" would change over time, in ways they could not anticipate. Accordingly, they recognized that the Constitution was of necessity a "great outlin[e]," not a detailed blueprint, see McCulloch v. Maryland, 4 Wheat. 316, 407, 4 L.Ed. 579 (1819), and that its provisions included broad concepts, to be "explained by the context or by the facts of the case," Letter from James Madison to N.P. Trist (Dec. 1831), in 9 Writings of James Madison 471, 475 (G. Hunt ed. 1910). "Nothing ... can be more fallacious," Alexander Hamilton emphasized, "than to infer the extent of any power, proper to be lodged in the national government, from ... its immediate necessities. There ought to be a CAPACITY to provide for future contingencies[,] as they may happen; and as these are illimitable in their nature, it is impossible safely to limit that capacity." The Federalist No. 34, pp. 205, 206 (John Harvard Library ed. 2009). See also McCulloch, 4 Wheat., at 415 (The Necessary and Proper Clause is lodged "in a constitution[,] intended to endure for ages to come, and consequently, to be adapted to the various crises of human affairs.") .... Consistent with the Framers' intent .... [89]

This same move was made by Justice Scalia, on the other end of the Court's ideological spectrum, to justify his dissent:

> The Constitution, though it dates from the founding of the Republic, has powerful meaning and vital relevance to our own times. The constitutional protections that this case involves are protections of structure. Structural protections—notably, the restraints imposed by federalism and separation of powers—are less romantic and

---

[89] *NFIB* v. *Sebelius*, 567 U.S. 519, 599–603 (2012) (Ginsburg, J., dissenting in part).

have less obvious a connection to personal freedom than the provisions of the Bill of Rights or the Civil War Amendments. Hence they tend to be undervalued or even forgotten by our citizens. It should be the responsibility of the Court to teach otherwise, to remind our people that the Framers considered structural protections of freedom the most important ones, for which reason they alone were embodied in the original Constitution and not left to later amendment. The fragmentation of power produced by the structure of our Government is central to liberty, and when we destroy it, we place liberty at peril. Today's decision should have vindicated, should have taught, this truth; instead, our judgment today has disregarded it.[90]

Seventh, the Supreme Court *never* claims that its conclusions are at variance with the Constitution's original meaning. Despite the widespread belief in different versions of nonoriginalism – which, on many accounts, permit trumping the written Constitution with other modalities of constitutional argumentation[91] – both on and off the Supreme Court, no Supreme Court opinion or justice's opinion states that it is contrary to the Constitution's original meaning. This includes cases where the consensus is that the Supreme Court's *holding* was contrary to the paradigm example of what the text was meant to do, such as *Home Building and Loan v. Blaisdell*,[92] where the Supreme Court purported to follow the Contracts Clause.[93]

3.4.3 *Originalism Accounts for the Practice of Constitutional Doctrine*

3.4.3.1 Introduction

In this subsection, I show that originalism fits well with our constitutional practice's creation and application of constitutional doctrine. Before making that claim, I first describe constitutional doctrine and then the practice of precedent that gives rise to it.

3.4.3.2 Constitutional Doctrine

Constitutional doctrine is the body of norms produced by the Supreme Court in its cases interpreting and applying the Constitution. Constitutional doctrine consists of rules, standards, principles, tests, and forms of analysis ostensibly derived by

---

[90] *Id.* at 706–07 (Joint Dissent).

[91] *E.g.*, BOBBITT, *supra* note 23, at 12–13; STRAUSS, *supra* note 8, at 34, 44, 101; Ian Bartrum, *Two Dogmas of Originalism*, 7 WASH. U. JURIS. REV. 157, 181 (2015); Mitchell N. Berman & Kevin Toh, *Pluralistic Nonoriginalism and the Combinability Problem*, 91 TEX. L. REV. 1739, 1751 (2013).

[92] *Home Building & Loan v. Blaisdell*, 290 U.S. 398 (1934).

[93] *See* Baude, *supra* note 6, at 2376–77 (arguing that *Blaisdell's* holding may have been contrary to the original meaning, but that its reasoning was "anodyne"); JED RUBENFELD, REVOLUTION BY JUDICIARY: THE STRUCTURE OF AMERICAN CONSTITUTIONAL LAW 67–68 (2005).

the Court from the Constitution and utilized by the Court to implement the Constitution in its cases.

Constitutional doctrine is ubiquitous. It is the main "stuff" learned in constitutional law classes, like "strict scrutiny" or the "substantial effects test." It is a lawyer's bread-and-butter in constitutional litigation, like discriminatory purpose or intent prongs of various tests. And it populates Supreme Court opinions. The Supreme Court's constitutional law cases teem with doctrine that appears to govern its cases' outcomes. Doctrine is so important that there is even a group of "New Doctrinalist" scholars.

There are good and sound reasons for constitutional doctrine's pervasive and important place in our constitutional practice. Most importantly, it is the primary connection between the Constitution and the real world. The Constitution's original meaning itself resolves few issues without at least modest inquiry, and though there are many, many easy constitutional cases, there remain many constitutional cases where people in good faith – and even more where people who wish to win – can make plausible arguments that threaten the original meaning's capacity to coordinate Americans' conduct. Constitutional doctrine, embodied in precedent, is the Constitution's primary mechanism to overcome this problem.

Originalism must be able to account for this pervasive and important facet of our constitutional practice. If originalism required eliminating the use of constitutional doctrine, or if it required a drastic change in how constitutional doctrine was created and employed, it would fail to adequately fit our constitutional practice and run against the good reasons for constitutional doctrine.

The Supreme Court's constitutional doctrine is articulated, elaborated, synthesized, and applied in its cases. In the following subsections, I show that, through both originalist precedent and nonoriginalist precedent, originalism requires the continued practice of constitutional doctrine. Because of the central role of precedent to constitutional doctrine, I next discuss precedent generally.

3.4.3.3 The Practice of Precedent

The practice of following precedent is pervasive in our society, and not only in the legal realm.[94] To take just one example: those of us who are parents recognize that the mere fact that we decided an issue in one manner for one child will give rise to our other children asserting that they should be treated likewise in future similar situations. In the legal realm, American lawyers have been inculcated from our first law class in the common law method, a central aspect of which is precedent. Even as our legal system has become dominated by statutory and administrative law, the common law case method and precedent remain the central focus of legal education and our legal practice.

[94] Frederick Schauer, *Precedent*, 39 STAN. L. REV. 571, 572 (1987).

The situation is the same in our constitutional practice. From the beginning of the Republic, and with increasing robustness, the Supreme Court has created a body of precedent that interprets and applies the Constitution. After nearly 230 years, the Supreme Court's case law is a vast and complex body. In current practice, the role of precedent in constitutional adjudication is relatively clear. Although not always consistent, the Court's rhetoric is that it will follow incorrect constitutional precedents absent a "special justification" otherwise.[95] The most prominent example and explanation of the role precedent has played in American constitutional practice is found in *Planned Parenthood of Southeastern Pennsylvania v. Casey*, where the Supreme Court declined to overrule *Roe v. Wade* largely on the basis of stare decisis.[96]

Playing such a central role in our legal system means that the practice of precedent is a given; it cannot be changed. The practice of precedent is like positive law more generally. It is a human convention that exists. One may argue that the convention is bad or good, but to show that one's theory of interpretation is not a not-so-subtly-disguised reform effort, one must show that one's theory can account for the conventions. Therefore, like any interpretive methodology, originalism has to show that it has a robust place for precedent. It does.

Most scholars believe that stare decisis is normatively attractive,[97] and its prominence in our legal practice suggests that its participants do as well[98]; consequently, theories of constitutional interpretation will be more normatively attractive if they maintain a place for stare decisis. Originalism as well, is relatively more normatively attractive because it provides a role for stare decisis.

I will first show in Subsection 3.4.4, that originalism robustly employs originalist precedent. Originalist precedent's function is to put the Constitution into effect. This use of precedent by originalism accounts for the phenomenon of constitutional doctrine and much of the Supreme Court's existing precedent. Second, in Subsection 3.4.5, I demonstrate how constitutional construction facilitates originalism's congruence with our practice because it allows for the creation of constitutional doctrine that comports with elected branch constructions. Third, in Subsection 3.4.6, I show that, contrary to claims that originalism is rejected by our practice because of pervasive nonoriginalist precedent, originalism's capacity to preserve nonoriginalist precedent maintains its fit with current practice.

---

[95] *See Dickerson v. United States*, 530 U.S. 428, 443 (2000); *United States v. IBM Corp.*, 517 U.S. 843, 856 (1996).

[96] *Planned Parenthood of Southeastern Pennsylvania v. Casey*, 505 U.S. 833 (1992).

[97] Lawrence B. Solum, *The Supreme Court in Bondage: Constitutional Stare Decisis, Legal Formalism, and the Future of Unenumerated Rights*, 9 U. PA. J. CONST. L. 155, 184–201 (2006).

[98] Steven G. Calabresi, *Text, Precedent, and the Constitution: Some Originalist and Normative Arguments for Overruling Planned Parenthood of Southeastern Pennsylvania v. Casey*, 22 CONST. COMM. 311, 327 (2005) (stating that "the caselaw construing the [Constitution's] text is ... of critical importance").

3.4.4 *Originalist Precedent: Putting the Constitution into Effect*

3.4.4.1 Introduction

The most important way that originalism fits our current practice of utilizing constitutional doctrine created via precedent is through originalist precedent. Originalist precedent puts into effect the Constitution in the same manner as the Supreme Court's current constitutional doctrine.

I described in Subsection 2.4.2 how originalist precedent is identified using the Originalism in Good Faith standard. In this subsection, I describe how originalist precedent can and does account for the pervasive creation and employment of constitutional doctrine. Originalist precedent creates and employs constitutional doctrine that performs five functions: (1) specifying the Constitution's original meaning; (2) bringing to light implicit constitutional norms; (3) resolving perceived constitutional tensions; (4) embedding the Constitution's original meaning; and (5) creating – constructing – constitutional meaning.

It is through these five functions that originalist precedent puts into effect the Constitution. Putting into effect the Constitution is the label for making the Constitution effective. It is the process of taking the Constitution's original meaning and effectuating it such that, as I explain in Chapter 4, our society is able to overcome coordination problems, pursue the common good, and help Americans today pursue human flourishing.

Originalist precedent's role depends on the *mode* in which it is operating: whether it is operating in the field of constitutional interpretation or constitutional construction. The two modes are the interpretive mode and the constructive mode. I first discuss the functions of originalist precedent in the context of constitutional interpretation. Here, originalist precedent does not alter the Constitution's meaning. Originalist precedent provides determinate evidence of how the original meaning is connected to and governs the activity under its purview. It bridges the distance between the original meaning and the human activity subject to the Constitution's governance.

The next subsection then covers constitutional construction, where the originalist precedent operates in the constructive mode. Originalist precedent in this context ratifies the elected branches' constructions of the Constitution's meaning. In doing so, these originalist precedents *create* the governing constitutional doctrine. When operating in the constructive mode, originalist precedent does more than simply provide evidence of the Constitution's meaning: it constructs constitutional doctrine that fits the elected branches' created constitutional meaning.

These interpretive and constructive modes build on the distinction between epistemic and metaphysical legal determinacy I described in Subsections 2.3.3 and 2.4.3. The interpretive mode of originalist precedent preserves the epistemic "work" performed by originalist precedent. Originalist precedent is (presumptively binding) evidence of the Constitution's original meaning. The constructive mode of originalist precedent preserves the creative metaphysical "work" performed by the elected branches through their constitutional constructions. Originalist precedent is (defeasibly) binding evidence of that constructed constitutional meaning.

This precedent in both modes has greater capacity to guide Americans than the bare original meaning. This, coupled with the significant respect owed to originalist precedent, means that originalist precedent is a key means by which the Constitution coordinates Americans.

3.4.4.2 Originalist Precedent Operating in the Interpretive Mode

3.4.4.2.1 SPECIFYING THE CONSTITUTION'S ORIGINAL MEANING Specification is the process of answering a practical question – what course of action is appropriate? – in the context of a concrete situation. In the realm of law, specification means answering a legal question in the context of a legal case. Specification makes explicit how the Constitution's original meaning resolves a distinct legal question. It identifies the relevant constitutional norms and determines how those norms order human actions in a context. This is the primary practical role of originalist precedent. Most originalist precedent fulfills this function (though it may also, simultaneously, perform other functions).

Originalists argue that judges should enforce the original meaning of the Constitution's text, but it is an exceedingly rare case, especially today, that turns on the simple application of the original meaning to the facts presented in a case. Instead, federal courts have, from their inception, articulated legal norms that *specify*[99] the result in constitutional cases, thereby reducing or eliminating the need for direct appeals to constitutional text.

Specification is the main process by which courts create constitutional law. The creation of constitutional law and doctrine through the process of specification is entirely legitimate – indeed, it is a necessary component of constitutional adjudication. Without specification, the gap between the Constitution's original meaning and government officials' and private citizens' actions would be so great that the Constitution could not adequately guide their conduct. Reasonable Americans subject to the Constitution would disagree about what the Constitution required, undermining the Constitution's effectiveness as a mechanism of social coordination. The Supreme Court's constitutional law reduces that gap through specification.

A case before a court presents a set of factual circumstances that implicates one or more provisions of the Constitution. The litigants in the constitutional case each argue that the purportedly applicable constitutional provision has a certain meaning,

---

[99] I use the term "specify" to distinguish the activity of courts when they create constitutional law or doctrine from creative activity of courts.

and they argue that application of that meaning to the factual circumstances of the case leads to them prevailing. After entertaining these arguments, the court first determines the constitutional provision's original meaning. Second, the court applies that meaning to the case and determines which litigant's argument prevails. Through this two-step process, the court specifies that in factual situations analogous to that presented by the case, a particular result obtains. In doing so, the court announces a rule, standard, principle, test, or form of analysis, thereby creating constitutional law. That constitutional doctrine guides future courts' determinations of analogous constitutional cases.

By itself, the Constitution often lacks the specificity to govern a nation, especially a complex, dynamic nation such as our own. Terms like "Commerce" are not self-applying, and much less are phrases like "executive Power" or "necessary and proper." The process of specification takes the meaning of the Constitution's relatively spare terms and phrases and creates constitutional law capable of meeting society's need for coordination. These more-particularized norms of constitutional law created through adjudication and found in cases have the specificity to connect the meaning of constitutional terms to practical situations. And these norms have the determinacy to guide the conduct of society's members to a much greater degree than the constitutional text's original meaning standing alone.

The process of specification I have described is not unique to law. Philosophy, and ethics in particular, has grappled with an analogous situation since at least the time of Aristotle.[100] The fact that most philosophical traditions in the field of ethics have articulated means to specify how ethical norms decide concrete cases suggests that specification in law is likewise possible.

In the realm of practical ethics, philosophers have struggled to articulate how human conduct can be guided by norms – by reasons – that are, by definition, more general than the specific conduct they are supposed to guide. For example, one commonly accepted norm of human conduct is "do not steal."[101] The manner by which that norm guides specific human actions, however, is not always clear. In the property law context, to pick just one of many possible examples, there is a veritable cottage industry of philosophical arguments why – or why not – this norm applies to persons who use another's property in cases of necessity.[102] Strong arguments have been advanced on both sides,[103] indicating that application of the general norm (*i.e.*, do not steal) to some situations (*i.e.*, those of necessity) is not a mechanical process.

---

[100] *See* ALBERT R. JONSEN & STEPHEN TOULMIN, THE ABUSE OF CASUISTRY 19 (1988).

[101] EXODUS 20:15.

[102] The doctrine of necessity is where one is privileged to use another's property because of the need to protect one's or another's person or property. RESTATEMENT (SECOND) OF TORTS § 195 (1965).

[103] *See, e.g.*, ST, II-II, q. 66, a. 7 ("In cases of need, all things are common property, so that there would seem to be no sin in taking another's property for need has made it common.").

Philosophers have articulated a number of means to apply practical norms to particularized instances of human conduct.[104] These include, for instance, creating a practical syllogism with the general norm as the major premise, the specific conduct in question as the minor premise, and the conclusion giving the appropriate course of ethical conduct.[105] Another method is balancing competing reasons for and against action to determine which are of greatest import, and acting accordingly.[106] There are other methods,[107] and the existence, scope, and distinctiveness of each of these methods is contested by philosophers.[108] Regardless of the method used, however, the philosophical consensus is that practical norms can and do guide concrete human action.[109]

In law, judges face the same issue: how norms that are more abstract than the facts presented by a case specify the correct – legal – course of conduct of the parties in the case. The fact that specification occurs in ethics is a powerful reason to believe that it also occurs in law. We should not be surprised, therefore, by the numerous aspects of our legal practice that indicate that specification occurs in law in manners similar to ethics.

In fully developed systems of ethics, the appropriate methods of specification are identified, numerous intermediate norms are articulated,[110] and proper resolutions to frequent practical questions are recognized.[111] For instance, in the Aristotelian philosophical tradition, significant emphasis is placed on the faculty of the human mind, practical reason, which enables one to specify how one should act in a given context.[112] In law, similarly, scholars across the ideological spectrum have recognized the faculty that enables some judges to achieve excellence in adjudication. Examples include legal realist Karl Llewellyn's "situation sense,"[113] and natural lawyer Gerard Bradley's "legal reason[]."[114]

---

[104] John D. Arras, *Principles and Particularity: The Role of Cases in Bioethics*, 69 Ind. L.J. 983, 985–88 (1994).

[105] NE, 1144a; Aristotle, *De Anima*, in The Basic Works of Aristotle, at 434a16–22 (Richard McKeon ed., J. A. Smith trans., Random House 1941) (c. 384 B.C.).

[106] W. D. Ross, The Right and the Good (1930).

[107] Reasoning by analogy is a commonly identified third method of specifying the correct course of conduct.

[108] *See* Henry S. Richardson, *Specifying Norms as a Way to Resolve Concrete Ethical Problems*, 19 Phil. & Pub. Aff. 279, 284–90 (1990) (describing the disputes).

[109] *See* David DeGrazia, *Moving Forward in Bioethical Theory: Theories, Cases, and Specified Principlism*, 17 J. Med. & Phil. 511 (1992) (describing specification).

[110] *See* Paul R. Tremblay, *The New Casuistry*, 12 Geo. J. Legal Ethics 489, 503–07 (1998) (describing "principlism," which is the use of generally agreed-upon ethical principles as starting points of ethical judgment).

[111] Richard B. Miller, *Narrative and Casuistry: A Response to John Arras*, 69 Ind. L.J. 1015, 1015 (1993).

[112] ST, I-II, q. 57, a. 4.

[113] Karl N. Llewellyn, The Common Law Tradition: Deciding Appeals 60 (1960).

[114] Gerard V. Bradley, *Beguiled: Free Exercise Exemptions and the Siren Song of Liberalism*, 20 Hofstra L. Rev. 245, 251 (1991).

The same three phenomena of (1) identifying the appropriate methods of specification, (2) articulating numerous intermediate norms, and (3) recognizing resolutions to frequently-raised questions, has occurred in our legal practice. Precedent has been the primary mechanism of doing so. It is through originalist precedent that the Supreme Court applies the general norms of the Constitution's original meaning. Through precedent, the Court specifies how the Constitution's original meaning governs human conduct.

A commonly recognized facet of precedent is that the Court will frequently articulate an intermediate legal norm. Intermediate legal norms serve the same primary purpose as intermediate ethical norms. They bridge the space between the relatively abstract constitutional norms embodied in the Constitution's original meaning and the practical legal questions presented in cases. Legal officials, such as lower court judges and executive officials, and citizens have less of a burden on their judgment – and are more likely to make the correct and the same legal judgments – if they have intermediate legal norms to guide their conduct. The Court's criminal procedure case law, and more specifically the cases applying the Fourth Amendment's prohibition on unreasonable searches and seizures, provides an example of this.

Our legal practice has also resolved frequently-raised questions. These resolutions, because they are deeply embedded in precedent and practice, settle the resolutions to these questions. One such seminal resolution occurred during the Marshall Court. In two cases, the Court resolved the issue of whether, and to what extent, the Supreme Court could review state court judgments under Article III. In *Martin v. Hunter's Lessee*, the Court specified that its Article III "judicial Power" over "Cases" included appeals from state court civil suits.[115] Five years later, in *Cohens v. Virginia*, the Court specified that its "judicial Power" extended to state criminal appeals.[116] The Court's resolutions in *Martin* and *Cohens* are unchallengeable and have effectively specified the Constitution's meaning in this context.

To summarize my argument thus far, originalist precedent operating in the interpretive mode performs an epistemic role. Originalist precedent, as in ethics, specifies how concrete cases are governed by the original meaning. Originalist precedent is the "data" repository for later courts looking to decide analogous concrete cases.

Preserving the "work" done by originalist precedent is one of the reasons why Article III's requirement that federal judges give significant respect to constitutional precedent makes sense. Originalist precedent creates constitutional law that federal courts will use in future adjudications. If the constitutional law created through the process of specification is a faithful ascertainment and application of the

---

[115] *Martin v. Hunter's Lessee*, 14 U.S. (1 Wheat.) 304 (1816).
[116] *Cohens v. Virginia*, 19 U.S. (6 Wheat.) 264 (1821).

Constitution's original meaning – if it is an originalist precedent – then Article III requires later courts to work within that constitutional law to decide future cases.

With some constitutional texts, the need for constitutional doctrine is clearer than in others. For instance, the Fourth Amendment prohibits "unreasonable" searches and seizures. Assuming that the Search and Seizure Clause is a prohibition on unreasonable government action, the Court must create constitutional law to specify how the Clause's original meaning applies to different concrete circumstances. The constitutional doctrines the Court articulates will be applications of the Clause's principle of reasonableness to these concrete circumstances.

For instance, the Court announced, in the context of passenger automobile stops for traffic violations, that a police officer "may order passengers to get out of the car pending completion of the [traffic] stop."[117] In *Maryland v. Wilson*, the Court applied the principle of reasonableness to the facts of the case and created a per se rule that would govern future analogous cases. In so doing, the *Wilson* Court relied on the earlier case of *Pennsylvania v. Mimms*, which had ruled that police officers may order drivers of passenger cars to exit their vehicles on routine traffic stops.[118]

Thus, the *Mimms-Wilson* line of cases has, through application of the Search and Seizure Clause's reasonableness principle, created a rule of constitutional law. The *Mimms-Wilson* rule specifies how the principle of reasonableness applies in a given context, and the Court's specification is authoritative in future cases with analogous factual circumstances. Litigants in such future cases will not, absent exceptional circumstances, make appeals directly to the Search and Seizure Clause and instead will craft arguments based on the Court's precedent.

With other constitutional texts, the necessity of the creation of constitutional law is less clear, but it remains nonetheless. The Article II, § 1, cl. 4 requirement that the President "shall ... have attained to the age of thirty five years," possibly the most concrete phrase in the Constitution, provides an example. The age requirement is often used by scholars as the most prominent counter to claims by critical legal scholars that the law is indeterminate.[119] The rule-ness of the age requirement itself precludes many questions that would otherwise result in litigation and consequently precludes the significant need for constitutional law that exists with other, less rule-like constitutional provisions. However, situations may still arise that call for specification of the Presidential Age Clause and the creation of constitutional law.[120] For instance, a chronologically-underage plaintiff could advance the argument that the age requirement is more properly interpreted as a maturity

---

[117] *Maryland v. Wilson*, 519 U.S. 408, 415 (1997).

[118] *Pennsylvania v. Mimms*, 434 U.S. 106, 111 (1977).

[119] *E.g.*, Frederick Schauer, *Easy Cases*, 58 S. Cal. L. Rev. 399, 414, 420 (1985).

[120] *See* Richard A. Posner, The Problems of Jurisprudence 265–66 (1990) (listing potential variations in the meaning of the age requirement).

requirement, and that she is sufficiently mature.[121] An originalist judge faced with that argument would ascertain the original meaning of the age requirement and then apply that meaning to the facts presented by the case. In doing so, he could find that, while Article II, § 1, cl. 4 has, as one of its *goals*, the maturity of the President, its *meaning* is the rule of thirty-five years of age, instead of the standard of maturity, to define the requirement for the office. The court would then announce a rule that the age requirement requires that the President be thirty-five years old regardless of how mature a presidential candidate less than thirty-five years old might be. In doing so, the precedent would specify the Clause's meaning.

Today, of course, it is exceedingly rare for the Supreme Court to face an entirely new issue of constitutional law and hence the Court's decisions are frequently decided on the basis of the Court's constitutional doctrine. This results from the process of specification that began with the first constitutional law cases. For example, in *Marbury v. Madison*, Chief Justice Marshall relied on the nature of the judicial process to argue that, when faced with a statute that conflicts with the Constitution, a court must follow the Constitution.[122] Marshall characterized the judicial process as "apply[ing] the rule to particular cases" which requires a judge to "expound and interpret that rule."[123] The judicial process described by Marshall is one of specification. Judges determine the meaning of the Constitution, apply that meaning to the case at hand, and in doing so create constitutional law followed by later courts.

My theory of originalist precedent directs judges to give presumptive deference to originalist precedent that specifies constitutional meaning. This respects the originalist precedent's good faith articulation and application of the original meaning, thereby preserving the epistemic work performed by the precedent.

3.4.4.2.2 BRINGING TO LIGHT IMPLICIT CONSTITUTIONAL NORMS Much of the Constitution's original meaning is relatively patent; many of its norms are fairly obvious. To ascertain the original meaning in such cases does not require significant research or judgment. An example of such a patent originalist norm is the Coinage Clause, which authorizes Congress to "coin money." It is clear that this provision's original meaning grants Congress (at least) the authority to issue legal tender in the form of "metallic tokens."[124]

---

[121] Gary Peller, *The Metaphysics of American Law*, 73 CALIF. L. REV. 1151, 1174 (1985). Or, she could advance the claim that the age requirement in Article II was subsequently altered by the Fifth Amendment, which prohibits irrational age discrimination. Anthony D'Amato, *Aspects of Deconstruction: The "Easy Case" of the Under-Aged President*, 84 NW. U. L. REV. 250, 255–56 (1989).

[122] *Marbury v. Madison*, 5 U.S. (1 Cranch) 137, 177 (1803).

[123] *Id.*

[124] Robert G. Natelson, *Paper Money and the Original Understanding of the Coinage Clause*, 31 HARV. J. L. & PUB. POL'Y 1017, 1061 (2008).

However, even when the Constitution's original meaning is metaphysically and epistemically determinate, it often requires significant research and judgment to articulate that meaning. In these cases, the Constitution's original meaning is implicit and originalist precedent makes explicit – brings to light – that original meaning.

The Second Amendment's protection of an individual right to keep and bear arms is an instance of this. It is not manifest that the Second Amendment's original meaning protects an individual rather than collective right. Indeed, it was not until the early 1980s that significant support for the individual right interpretation of the Amendment – labeled the Standard Model – arose.[125] By the mid-1990s, however, the Standard Model had become, as the label suggests, the consensus interpretation.[126] Thereafter, the Supreme Court, in *District of Columbia* v. *Heller*, in an originalist opinion, made explicit the implicit original meaning of the Second Amendment by ruling that it protected an individual right.[127]

This same phenomenon occurs in ethics. Returning again to the Aristotelian tradition, some ethical propositions are patent,[128] while others are implicit. According to Aquinas, for instance, the first principle of natural law – do good and avoid evil[129] – is *per se nota*, or self-evident.[130] There are a handful of other natural law norms that are also manifest in a similar way.[131] However, there are many more implicit norms. These are norms the fuller explication of which took thought, argumentation, and time. For example, the Aristotelian tradition articulated the norm that it is "just to charge interest on a loan"[132] after centuries of discussion.[133] This norm was implicit in the tradition's broader philosophical commitments.[134] After significant thought, argumentation, and time, this ethical norm was made explicit in the tradition.[135]

The Constitution's original meaning will frequently not be apparent for a number of reasons. First, the data upon which to make a determination of what the original meaning is may be difficult to access or, if accessible, may present other obstacles such as an unmanageably large amount of data. Second, the factual situations that would provide an opportunity to make explicit the implicit norm may not previously have arisen or been presented. Third, the cultural, political, and economic

---

[125] The seminal scholarship articulating the Standard Model was Don B. Kates., Jr., *Handgun Prohibition and the Original Meaning of the Second Amendment*, 82 MICH. L. REV. 204 (1983).

[126] Randy E. Barnett & Don B. Kates, *Under Fire: The New Consensus on the Second Amendment*, 45 EMORY L.J. 1139, 1141 (1996).

[127] *Dist. of Columbia* v. *Heller*, 554 U.S. 570 (2008).

[128] ST, I-II, q. 94, a. 4.

[129] *Id.*, q. 94, art. 2.

[130] *Id.*; NLNR, at 29–32.

[131] ST, I-II, q. 94, a. 2.

[132] 2 GERMAIN GRISEZ, THE WAY OF THE LORD JESUS: LIVING A CHRISTIAN LIFE 833 (1993).

[133] JOHN T. NOONAN, JR., THE SCHOLASTIC ANALYSIS OF USURY (1957).

[134] AQUINAS, at 207.

[135] JONSEN & TOULMIN, *supra* note 101, at 193.

environment may make the search for or articulation of implicit constitutional norms imprudent or not well received.

My conception of originalist precedent directs judges to give presumptive respect to originalist precedent that brings to light implicit constitutional norms. This respects the originalist precedent's good faith articulation of the implicit original meaning norm, thereby preserving the precedent's epistemic work.

3.4.4.2.3 RESOLVING PERCEIVED TENSIONS IN THE ORIGINAL MEANING Originalist precedent resolves perceived tensions between constitutional norms by identifying, in a particular case, which of a stable of possibly-governing yet conflicting norms in fact governs the outcome of the case.

The norms embodied in the Constitution's original meaning have focal cases.[136] Given the care with which the Framers drafted the Constitution, it is unlikely that the focal cases of original meaning norms conflict. However, as one extends out from the focal case, it becomes more difficult to ascertain whether the norm governs a particular case. When aspects of two or more of the Constitution's norms (beyond their respective focal cases) plausibly apply to the same matter, a perceived tension between the norms exists. Originalist precedent resolves that perceived tension.

A notable instance of resolving perceived tensions was between the Bankruptcy Clause and the Contracts Clause, and the long-standing state practice of bankruptcy and insolvency laws. On the one hand, the Bankruptcy Clause authorized Congress to establish "uniform Laws on the subject of Bankruptcies," and the Contracts Clause prohibited states from passing laws "impairing the Obligation of Contracts." On the other hand, following adoption of the Constitution, states continued to pass bankruptcy and insolvency laws that applied to pre-existing debts.[137] Many Americans before, during, and following Ratification of the Constitution, plausibly argued that the Bankruptcy and Contracts Clauses prohibited states from passing such legislation.

The Supreme Court resolved the perceived tension in two cases: *Sturges* v. *Crowninshield*[138] and *Ogden* v. *Saunders*.[139] First, in an opinion by Chief Justice Marshall, the *Sturges* Court ruled that states could not pass bankruptcy and insolvency laws that discharged pre-existing debts.[140] Later, in *Ogden*, the Court ruled that state bankruptcy and insolvency laws that discharged debts incurred after passage of the laws were constitutional.[141] The Court in both cases reviewed the text and history

---

[136] NLNR, at 9–11; *see also* JED RUBENFELD, FREEDOM AND TIME: A THEORY OF CONSTITUTIONAL SELF-GOVERNMENT 178–95 (2001).

[137] PETER J. COLEMAN, DEBTORS AND CREDITORS IN AMERICA: INSOLVENCY, IMPRISONMENT FOR DEBT, AND BANKRUPTCY, 1607–1900, at 31–36 (1974).

[138] *Sturges* v. *Crowninshield*, 17 U.S. (4 Wheat.) 122 (1819).

[139] *Ogden* v. *Saunders*, 25 U.S. (12 Wheat.) 213 (1827).

[140] *Sturges*, 17 U.S. (4 Wheat.) at 197–208.

[141] *Ogden*, 25 U.S. (12 Wheat.) at 213.

of the Clauses in a good faith articulation and application of the original meaning.[142] *Sturges* and *Ogden* receive significant respect because they are evidence of how the Constitution's original meaning is not in tension, and this preserves the interpretive work performed by the Supreme Court.

This same phenomenon of perceived tension occurs in ethics.[143] In fact, one of the most powerful challenges to ethical theories is describing how to either avoid or resolve *prima facie* conflicts between ethical norms.[144] Different philosophical traditions have arrived at different mechanisms to resolve perceived tensions between ethical norms. In the Aristotelian tradition, for instance, many perceived tensions that arise between natural law norms are usually viewed as just that, *perceived* but not true conflicts. In other words, there is regularly a right answer to ethical questions.[145]

Over time, the tradition has addressed many perceived tensions. One of the most profound tensions, one that has received sustained attention in the Aristotelian tradition, is that between the obligation to tell the truth and the obligation to avoid harming others that arises, for example, when one is asked to disclose information that will lead to the unjust treatment of a person.[146] This occurs, for instance, when an unjust regime's agent asks a homeowner to disclose whether a fugitive is in the homeowner's house. The homeowner knows that the fugitive is in the house and that, if that fact is disclosed, the regime will treat the fugitive unjustly. Members of the Aristotelian tradition, over centuries, focused on this perceived tension. Today, the bulk of the tradition has concluded that the homeowner should not disclose the location of the fugitive.[147] It thereby resolved the perceived tension. Members of that tradition give this conclusion – this resolution of the perceived tension – significant respect.

My conception of originalist precedent directs judges to give presumptive respect to originalist precedent that resolves perceived tensions in the original meaning. This presumption respects the originalist precedent's good faith articulation and application of the original meaning, and thereby preserves the precedent's epistemic work.

3.4.4.2.4 EMBEDDING THE CONSTITUTION'S ORIGINAL MEANING Originalist precedent embeds the Constitution's original meaning in the Supreme Court's constitutional law. The process of entrenching the original meaning in case law protects and defends that meaning – and therefore protects and defends the originalist precedents' epistemic work. It does so in a number of ways.

---

[142] *Sturges*, 17 U.S. (4 Wheat.) at 197–207; *Ogden*, 25 U.S. (12 Wheat.) at 215.
[143] Miller, *supra* note 112, at 1015–16.
[144] Arras, *supra* note 105, at 995–96; Richardson, *supra* note 109, at 284–90.
[145] 1 GRISEZ, *supra* note 133, at 98.
[146] JONSEN & TOULMIN, *supra* note 101, at 195–215.
[147] *Id.* at 213.

First, case law puts the Court's institutional prestige behind the original meaning. The Court's originalist precedent carries with it both the respect for the Constitution's original meaning and the Court's own, independent weight. Second, the original meaning is protected by the Court's explanation of the reasons behind it in the Court's opinions. Frequently, the Court provides reasons why the result reached by the Court – in accordance with the original meaning – is substantively good.[148] Articulating why the original meaning is good ensures wider support for it. The Court has also argued why, even though the original meaning is not ideal (in general or in a particular case), it is better to follow that meaning rather than create a different meaning.[149]

Embedding the Constitution's original meaning in originalist precedent also protects that meaning from alteration. First, this is valuable because the original meaning itself is valuable: it resolves coordination problems in a manner superior to judicial coordination, the most commonly proposed alternative.[150] Second, embedding the original meaning advances Rule of Law values, such as stability of the law. Third, the embedded original meaning permits it to better perform its function of preserving the epistemic work accomplished by the precedent.

3.4.4.3 Originalist Precedent Operating in the Constructive Mode

The roles played by originalist precedent in the context of constitutional interpretation – specifying constitutional meaning, bringing to light implicit constitutional norms, resolving perceived tensions in the original meaning, and embedding the Constitution's original meaning – are also played by originalist precedent in the construction zone. There are three significant differences, however. First, originalist precedent in the construction zone facilitates the resolution of original underdeterminacy. Second, the constructed constitutional meaning is defeasible by the elected branches. Third, originalist precedent that constructs constitutional law has a gravitational effect on other areas of (constructed) constitutional law. I will address each of these differences in turn.

As a reminder, I argued earlier that constitutional construction occurs when the Constitution's original meaning is metaphysically determinate and epistemically underdeterminate.[151] In this category, the constructive mode applies. I first explain why this is the case, and then I describe in more detail the unique aspects of the constructive mode.

---

[148] E.g., *Crawford* v. *Washington*, 541 U.S. 36, 63–69 (2004); *United States* v. *Lopez*, 514 U.S. 549, 564–68 (1995).

[149] *Buckley* v. *Valeo*, 424 U.S. 1, 118–37 (1976); *INS* v. *Chada*, 462 U.S. 919, 944 (1983); *DeShaney* v. *Winnebago County Dep't of Soc. Servs.*, 489 U.S. 189, 202–03 (1989).

[150] *Infra* Subsection 4.5.6; McGinnis & Rappaport, *supra* note 4, at 81–99.

[151] *Supra* Subsection 2.3.3.

Originalist precedent operating in the constructive mode, *in addition to* providing evidence of the Constitution's (epistemically underdetermined) original meaning, also identifies determinate constitutional law as constructed by the elected branches. In the construction zone, when an elected branch construction is subject to litigation, the Supreme Court will affirm that construction and, in doing so, construct constitutional doctrine that will govern in subsequent analogous cases. These precedents are entitled to significant respect because they create the legal doctrine that coordinates social activity. Until a later Court determines that the originalist precedent should be overruled,[152] or the relevant elected branch changes its construction of the Constitution, the Supreme Court's constructed constitutional doctrine is the governing constitutional law.

Second, the originalist precedent's construction of constitutional law is defeasible. Originalist precedent that constructs constitutional law is subject to defeasance by the elected branches. Therefore, if the Court at Time 1 constructed Meaning X, and Congress then passes a statute that is constitutional only under Meaning not-X, then Congress has (re)constructed the Constitution's meaning. So, in a case at Time 2 involving the constitutionality of the statute, the Court should adopt Meaning not-X (so long as it is consistent with what is known about the original meaning).

The third difference when originalist precedent operates in the constructive mode is the gravitational force of precedent. Gravitational force is the power of cases and the legal principles they instantiate to influence the law around them, including later cases.[153] Originalist precedent that constructs constitutional doctrine is analogous to common law adjudication because, in both, the courts are creatively articulating legal doctrine. The legal principles in both influence the law – exert gravitational force. Originalist precedents that do not construct constitutional law do not have gravitational force because they do not create the governing legal principles. Instead, the Constitution's determinate original meaning provides those legal principles, and originalist precedent instantiates them.

3.4.4.4 Conclusion

In summary, originalism's extensive use of originalist precedent provides originalism with the capacity to create extensive constitutional doctrine, an essential facet of the Supreme Court's practice. This originalist precedent performs all of precedent's many functions, including preserving its epistemic and constructive work.

---

[152] Because, for example, the constructed constitutional doctrine did not adequately account for the elected branch's construction.

[153] RONALD DWORKIN, TAKING RIGHTS SERIOUSLY 111–17 (1977).

3.4.5 *Constitutional Construction: Fitting and Justifying Elected Branch Constructions*

3.4.5.1 Introduction

Constitutional construction occurs when the Constitution's original meaning is epistemically underdetermined, and within the construction zone, elected branches possess the authority to construct constitutional meaning. In this subsection, I describe how constitutional construction helps originalism fit our constitutional practice. Construction facilitates originalism's congruence with our practice because it allows for the creation of constitutional doctrine that fits and justifies elected branch constructions.

3.4.5.2 There Is More-Than-De Minimis Constitutional Construction

The relative quantity of construction is an empirical question that must be answered on a case-by-case, doctrine-by-doctrine basis, and there is little discussion among scholars on this point.[154] My tentative view is that many of the most important constitutional questions currently debated between originalists and nonoriginalists are issues of interpretation and not construction. Here, I have in mind debates such as those over whether Congress' Commerce Clause power authorizes it to require Americans to purchase government-approved health insurance,[155] whether Congress' power to spend authorizes it to attach conditions to its grants to states (to effect regulation not authorized by an enumerated power),[156] whether the Due Process Clauses require the states and federal government to permit abortion,[157] or whether the Establishment Clause prohibits public religious holiday displays.[158] These are just a few of the many important constitutional issues settled by the original meaning, and in each of these, the Constitution's original meaning provides a determinate answer to the questions posed.

At the same time, there are constitutional issues that the original meaning does not determinatively answer. Given the existence of closure rules and the original meaning's metaphysical determinacy,[159] the scope of underdeterminacy is limited to cases of epistemic underdeterminacy. In this book, I do not identify the quantity of constitutional issues within this category.

---

[154] *But see* Lawrence B. Solum, *Communicative Content and Legal Content*, 89 NOTRE DAME L. REV. 479, 483 (2013) (describing the category of construction, though differently articulated by Solum, as relatively very large).

[155] *NFIB v. Sebelius*, 567 U.S. 519 (2012).

[156] *South Dakota v. Dole*, 483 U.S. 203 (1987).

[157] *Roe v. Wade*, 410 U.S. 113 (1973).

[158] *McCreary County v. ACLU*, 545 U.S. 844 (2005).

[159] *Supra* Subsection 2.3.3.

There are, however, sound reasons to believe that the category of epistemically underdetermined cases is not de minimis. For instance, there are many provisions in the Constitution that utilize a legal norm – such as a principle or standard – the application of which may be underdetermined. The Fourth Amendment's reasonableness requirement for searches and seizures is a possible example. It will at least occasionally be the case that it is epistemically underdetermined whether a particular search or seizure is reasonable, and the originalist closure rules do not provide sufficient weight to provide a determinate answer. In this and similar contexts,[160] construction exists, and originalism would not *prima facie* reject existing constitutional constructions.

3.4.5.3 Constitutional Construction Helps Originalism Fit Our Widespread Constitutional Practice of Deference to Elected Branch Constructions

In the construction zone, federal judges should defer to elected branch constructions.[161] Therefore, to the extent current Supreme Court doctrine approves of elected branch constructions, originalism fits both the employment and content of current constitutional doctrine. When Congress is working within the underdeterminate constitutional meaning, it may not violate the determinate original meaning that exists but, within those strictures, Congress can be creative. In these situations, because the original meaning is not completely constraining, Congress can use its prudential judgment to address policy issues in the manner it sees fit.

For example, assume that the Commerce Clause does not determinately authorize – or not authorize – Congress to regulate the Internet. Congress has repeatedly passed statutes constructing its authority under the Commerce Clause.[162] It has exercised authority to regulate the Internet. Consequently, the (by hypothesis) underdetermined nature of the Commerce Clause's original meaning has permitted Congress to construct a response to changed technology.

Existing constitutional law contains many deference doctrines. Taking just one prominent example, the Supreme Court defers to Congress' judgments about the necessity of means to achieve enumerated ends.[163] In many other areas of law, though the law does not contain an explicit requirement of deference, the Supreme Court's practice is to defer to elected branch interpretations in close cases.[164] Originalism has the capacity to retain elected branch constructions.

---

[160] Other likely examples include the Necessary and Proper Clause (necessary) and the Cruel and Unusual Punishment Clause (cruel).

[161] *Supra* Subsection 2.3.3.

[162] *See, e.g.,* 47 U.S.C. §223 (2006) (regulating online decency); *id.* §231 (regulating online pornography).

[163] *See McCulloch* v. *Maryland*, 17 U.S. (4 Wheat.) 316, 421 (1819) ("plainly adapted").

[164] This occurs not only today, but also when the Supreme Court more fulsomely followed the original meaning. *See, e.g., Swift & Co.* v. *United States*, 196 U.S. 375, 397 (1905) (upholding Congress' exercise of its Commerce Clause authority and stating that "[t]he two cases are near

3.4.6 *Originalism's Embrace of Some Nonoriginalist Precedent Helps It Fit Our Constitutional Practice*

3.4.6.1 Introduction

"But what about nonoriginalist precedent?," a critic is likely to ask. How is the constitutional doctrine contained in the Supreme Court's nonoriginalist precedent consistent with originalism? Does the adoption of originalism require the overruling of cases that are both just and widely accepted by society? The paradigm example of such a case (from the critic's perspective) is *Brown v. Board of Education*,[165] which, nonoriginalists claim, originalism rejects. In this vein, Professor Michael Gerhardt has argued that "[u]nitary theories," like originalism, "face an inescapable dilemma." Originalists "have to choose between rejecting most of [the Supreme Court's] precedents, thereby precipitating constitutional turmoil, or rejecting or seriously modifying the proposed unitary theory to ensure stability or continuity in constitutional decision-making."[166] This dilemma, according to critics, comes from originalism's commitment to following the original meaning coming into conflict with cases decided based upon reasons other than the original meaning.

Many critics of originalism perceive originalism's "problem" with nonoriginalist precedent as its major defect. Furthermore, nonoriginalist precedent is potentially the most powerful obstacle to my claim that originalism is the best description of our legal practice. In this subsection, I show that originalism's retention of some nonoriginalist precedent helps it fit our constitutional practice.

3.4.6.2 The "Problem" of Nonoriginalist Precedent

The list of likely and potential[167] nonoriginalist precedents, and constitutional law doctrines built on these precedents, is long and presents a strong challenge to originalism. Precedents that have been identified as nonoriginalist – though not

---

to each other, as sooner or later always must happen where lines are to be drawn, but the line between them is distinct").

[165] *Brown v. Board of Education*, 347 U.S. 483 (1954).

[166] Gerhardt, *supra* note 11, at 132.

[167] I included "potential" because one cannot know, a priori and without performing sufficient research, what the original meaning is and whether a particular precedent is an incorrect articulation or application of that meaning. Further, one would also have to know if the original meaning is epistemically underdetermined because, if it is, then a particular case may fall into the "construction zone," which would allow creative construction of constitutional doctrine. That being said, the conventional view is that much Supreme Court precedent, including important cases, is nonoriginalist.

necessarily by originalists![168] – include *Brown* v. *Board of Education*,[169] which held that racially segregated public schools violated the Equal Protection Clause; *Roe* v. *Wade*[170] (and its progeny), which held that laws prohibiting abortion violated the Due Process Clause; *Everson* v. *Board of Education*,[171] which held that the Establishment Clause incorporated a principle of strong separation between church and state; various free speech cases[172]; *Wickard* v. *Filburn*,[173] which held that Congress' Commerce Clause power extended to purely intrastate activity; nondelegation doctrine cases[174]; the incorporation doctrine[175]; and recently *Obergefell* v. *Hodges*,[176] which appeared to hold that the Due Process and Equal Protection Clauses required states to marry people of the same sex. This list of nonoriginalist precedents and doctrines, though not close to exhaustive, shows that, if the originalist account of our constitutional practice is to be plausible, originalists must explain the status of these precedents and doctrines. But, originalism's answer cannot be the complete elimination of nonoriginalist precedent, because that would be too harmful to the common good; and originalism's answer cannot be to retain all nonoriginalist precedent because that would destroy originalism's own capacity to secure the common good.

While there is much nonoriginalist precedent, I do not want to overstate the problem of nonoriginalist precedent for originalism. First, most cases decided by federal courts are not constitutional cases and hence would not be impacted by the overruling of nonoriginalist constitutional precedent. Second, there are instances when the original meaning of the text of the Constitution will be underdetermined. In these situations, the Supreme Court has no authority to strike down a statute in the first instance, so a shift by the Court away from nonoriginalist precedent would not impact these constitutional constructions. Third, as I describe in the next subsection, instead of outright overruling a nonoriginalist case, the Supreme Court may initially limit the case, employ an originalist methodology that will further limit the nonoriginalist case in future cases, and eventually, after the jurisprudential landscape has changed, overrule the case. This process protects reliance interests,

---

[168] Frequently, nonoriginalists will point to cases as nonoriginalist as a means to discredit and undermine originalism. This is especially true of *Brown*. *E.g.*, FRANK B. CROSS, THE FAILED PROMISE OF ORIGINALISM 92 (2013); Michael J. Klarman, *Brown, Originalism, and Constitutional Theory: A Response to Professor McConnell*, 81 VA. L. REV. 1881 (1995); Earl M. Maltz, *Originalism and the Desegregation Decisions – A Response to Professor McConnell*, 13 CONST. COMMENT. 223 (1996).

[169] *Brown v. Board of Education*, 374 U.S. 483 (1954).

[170] *Roe v. Wade*, 410 U.S. 113 (1973).

[171] *Everson v. Board of Education*, 330 U.S. 1 (1947).

[172] *E.g.*, *Texas v. Johnson*, 491 U.S. 397 (1989); *Bates v. State Bar of Ariz.*, 433 U.S. 350 (1977); *Cohen v. California*, 403 U.S. 15 (1971); *Stanley v. Georgia*, 394 U.S. 557 (1969).

[173] *Wickard v. Filburn*, 317 U.S. 111 (1942).

[174] *Mistretta v. United States*, 488 U.S. 361 (1989).

[175] *McDonald v. Chicago*, 561 U.S. 742, 791 (2010) (Scalia, J., concurring).

[176] *Obergefell v. Hodges*, 135 S. Ct. 2584 (2015).

allows society to slowly move with the Court, and prepares individuals and social institutions for the eventual overruling of the nonoriginalist case.

Before moving on, let me note that, while nonoriginalists often use the existence of nonoriginalist precedent as a club against originalists, nonoriginalists as well are faced with their own problem of mistaken precedent. Nonoriginalist theories of constitutional interpretation must account for precedents and doctrines that are justified by the original meaning of the Constitution but not by the nonoriginalist's methodology. Important precedents criticized by nonoriginalists include *United States v. Lopez*,[177] and more recently *NFIB v. Sebelius*.[178] Moreover, there exists the pervasive aspect of our legal practice of making arguments based on the original meaning of the Constitution even in bodies of law considered nonoriginalist.[179] Consequently, the "problem of precedent" is one shared by both originalists and nonoriginalists.

3.4.6.3 A "Three-Step Program" for Originalism

When the Supreme Court determines that a nonoriginalist precedent should be overruled, it may, but does not have to, immediately overrule the precedent. Instead, the Court may, if the balance of three factors identified in Subsection 2.4.4 warrants, slowly move the law back toward the original meaning. As Keith Whittington pithily summarized the Court's capacity to manage the transition to an originalist jurisprudence, "[a]n originalist Court need not seek to overturn the existing corpus of constitutional law overnight, or even over a decade."[180] Doing so helps originalism better fit our constitutional practice in the medium and long term while also protecting and working toward a fully originalist legal practice. This is a three-step process.[181]

The first step is that the Court refuses to extend a nonoriginalist precedent. In this step, the Court is presented with the natural extension of an existing nonoriginalist precedent to an analogous situation. The Court refuses to do so. Ideally, the Court would justify its refusal to extend the nonoriginalist precedent because of the original meaning pulling the doctrine back home. This refusal to issue a natural extension is itself a minor ripple in the law. It also signals to the nation, in the case's substantive holding and in the Court's reasoning, that the nonoriginalist precedent's authority has weakened. It is not yet clear how much. At minimum,

---

[177] *United States v. Lopez*, 514 U.S. 549 (1995).

[178] *NFIB v. Sebelius*, 567 U.S. 519 (2012).

[179] *See, e.g., Everson v. Board of Education*, 330 U.S. 1, 14–15 (1947) ("The meaning and scope of the First Amendment, preventing establishment of religion [is construed] in light of its history and the evils it was designed forever to suppress.").

[180] WHITTINGTON, INTERPRETATION, *supra* note 5, at 169.

[181] This analysis is similar to Lawrence B. Solum, *The Constraint Principle: Original Meaning and Constitutional Practice* 85 (April 11, 2018), https://papers.ssrn.com/sol3/papers.cfm?abstract_id=2940215 (visited Sept. 30, 2018).

the precedent's weakened authority reduces or eliminates the precedent's gravitational effect on the law. Furthermore, the Court's signal will induce parties to further challenge the nonoriginalist precedent. This sets up the second step.

As parties begin to contest constitutional doctrine built on the nonoriginalist precedent, they will challenge cases and doctrines analytically closer to the precedent's core, and they will succeed. The Court will utilize these challenges to further undermine the nonoriginalist precedent and further signal that it is moving constitutional doctrine in this area back to the original meaning. At this point, the signal is unmistakable and the law is clearly shifting its center of gravity away from the nonoriginalist precedent and toward the original meaning. Once the center of gravity shifts, astute lawyers will recognize that the underlying nonoriginalist precedent's authority is severely limited and its lifespan short. Still, the process is multi-year, giving reliance interests time to adjust.

Third, the Court overrules the nonoriginalist precedent. At this point, the overruling is not surprising and there are few if any remaining reliance interests harmed by it. Instead, the continued existence of the nonoriginalist precedent itself caused a wrinkle in the law's surrounding fabric. It was an anachronism in that area because of the surrounding law's movement back toward the original meaning and away from the precedent. The precedent itself was causing harm to the Rule of Law and the common good through, for instance, the legal instability and unfairness it caused. Its extinguishment is a cause for rejoicing.

The Supreme Court has numerous tools at its disposal to lengthen (or shorten) this process of moving constitutional doctrine toward the original meaning.[182] For instance, docket control permits the Supreme Court to selectively take cases that push or pull doctrine toward the original meaning and in the timeframe the Supreme Court believes is prudent.

This movement away from one point of doctrinal stasis to another is fairly common. A good example is the Supreme Court's mid-twentieth century state action doctrine case law. The state action doctrine is the rule that the Constitution applies only to government and governmental actors.[183] In the early twentieth century, the Court moved toward limiting and possibly eliminating the doctrine. One step in the direction was a series of cases dealing with privately owned shopping centers. In these cases, private mall owners were sued for violating the Constitution. For instance, in the first in this series of three major cases, *Amalgamated Food Employees Union v. Logan Valley Plaza*, a private mall was alleged to have violated the Free Speech Clause because it prohibited its tenant-store's employees from engaging in labor picketing on the shopping center's grounds.[184] The Court held that the mall was a state actor. Four years later, however, the Court halted its course

---

[182] Whittington, Interpretation, *supra* note 5, at 169.
[183] With limited exceptions, most prominently the Thirteenth Amendment.
[184] *Amalgamated Food Emps. Union v. Logan Valley Plaza, Inc, et al.*, 391 U.S. 308 (1968).

in a factually indistinguishable case, and rejected the claim that a private mall owner was a state actor.[185] The Court's reasoning signaled its discomfort with *Logan Valley* because it weakly distinguished it and its reasoning was inconsistent with *Logan Valley*. Then, four years after that, the Supreme Court overruled *Logan Valley*.[186] Over a four-year period, the legal system was on notice that the Court's erosion of the state action doctrine was unlikely to survive and planned accordingly.

Another way to think about originalism's capacity to move constitutional doctrine back to the original meaning is in terms of the original meaning's own gravitational pull.[187] Or, one can think of the Constitution's original meaning like a religious tradition's sacred text that anchors the tradition and that has the power to pull the tradition back to its own best self.[188] The Constitution's original meaning is so powerful and attractive that is authorizes overturning nonoriginalist precedent and reorganizing the constitutional doctrine built on that precedent. It pulls the doctrine back to itself, not overnight, but slowly.

3.4.6.4 Preserving (Some) Nonoriginalist Precedent Fits Our Practice of Preserving (Some) Legal Mistakes and Is Normatively Attractive

Originalism better fits our legal practice because it preserves some nonoriginalist precedent, and it does so in two main ways. First, originalism's retention of some nonoriginalist precedent provides originalism with an error-correction mechanism, which is necessary because our legal system contains error-correction mechanisms.

Our legal system is operated by humans, and humans make mistakes. Typically, mistakes are the result of inadvertence, such as when a judge mis-states the law or applies the law incorrectly, though it is likely that at least some legal errors are the result of intentional mis-statements or mis-applications. Our legal system has many mechanisms that acknowledge mistakes and deal with them. For example, property law has a number of these doctrines, including most prominently adverse possession, that anticipate mistakes and that manage those mistakes for the sake of the common good. Some error-correction mechanisms reject the mistake, while others treat the error either as not a mistake, or as only a partial mistake.

The practice of constitutional law likewise has error-correction mechanisms, and precedent is the most important such mechanism. Stare decisis pushes courts to follow prior erroneous articulations of the law or erroneous applications of the law. A theory of interpretation that lacked an error-correction mechanism, or lacked one with precedent's capacity to follow mistakes, would be discontinuous with existing legal practice.

---

[185] *Lloyd Corp. v. Tanner*, 407 U.S. 501 (1972).
[186] *Hudgens v. NLRB*, 424 U.S. 507 (1976).
[187] Randy E. Barnett, *The Gravitational Force of Originalism*, 82 FORDHAM L. REV. 411, 420–30 (2013).
[188] SANFORD LEVINSON, CONSTITUTIONAL FAITH (1988).

Originalism's constitutionally mandated retention of some nonoriginalist precedent is originalism's primary mechanism to acknowledge mistakes and account for them. Originalism therefore possess an error-correction mechanism, one with the capacity to follow mistakes, and fits this important facet of constitutional practice.

Second, the continued viability of some nonoriginalist precedent helps originalism fit our existing constitutional practice by maintaining the substantive continuity of constitutional law. The extent to which preserving some nonoriginalist precedent helps originalism fit constitutional law depends on two factors: (1) how much nonoriginalist precedent exists; and (2) how much of that precedent would be overruled. Neither of these factors is readily amenable to quantification, though I will suggest that there are good reasons to believe that originalism would continue to fit the bulk of constitutional practice in the short term.

Looking initially to the first factor, there is a relatively broad consensus among nonoriginalists and among most originalists that there is widespread nonoriginalist precedent.[189] I will not belabor the point.

It is clear that, under the three-factor analysis of nonoriginalist precedent that I laid out previously,[190] some nonoriginalist precedents would be immediately overruled. I gave *Roe* as an example because of its unjustness. I also gave *Crawford* as an example where Rule of Law values pushed toward immediate overruling of *Roberts*. *Home Building & Loan Ass'n* v. *Blaisdell* may be a possible example of a case subject to immediate overruling because of its dramatic deviation from the Constitution's original meaning.[191]

However, these cases are relatively extreme. Instead, the three factors will often point to gradual rather than immediate overruling of nonoriginalist precedent. This is because of two main reasons. First, much precedent creates reliance interests. Constitutional questions in the United States are nearly always, in some form, questions of government power to regulate. This is especially clear in the context of interpreting the federal government's limited and enumerated powers. The government and regulated parties both rely on a precedent's identification of the proper scope of governmental regulation to plan and act. On the government side, the government may create statutes and regulations and institutions premised on the precedent. For example, the Supreme Court's expansive interpretation of the taxing power in *NFIB* v. *Sebelius* authorized the federal government to entrust the Department of Health and Human Services with implementing the Affordable Care Act. On the regulated party side, *NFIB* v. *Sebelius* required insurance companies to

---

[189] The major holdout from this consensus is Professor Balkin, but his conclusion that there is a relatively small amount of nonoriginalist precedent arose from his relatively thin conception of the original meaning and correspondingly robust conception of construction.

[190] *Supra* Subsection 2.4.4.

[191] *Home Bldg. & Loan Ass'n* v. *Blaisdell*, 290 U.S. 398 (1933); RUBENFELD, *supra* note 94, at 67–68.

dramatically restructure to comply with the Act, employers to modify their employee health insurance plans, and individuals to renegotiate their plans.

Reliance interests also occur in the context of limitations on government, though here the situation is more complicated and more difficult to generalize. These interpretations draw a line beyond which individuals may act, and in doing so, build reliance. This reliance is less robust if the parties that relied are able to modify their positions relatively quickly with relatively little cost. However, the reliance interests will tend to be higher when they are in the form of major life-choices and institutions. For example, the Supreme Court's interpretation of the Free Speech Clause to protect "adult entertainment" as speech, enabled the creation of businesses which purvey that "speech."[192] Or, when the Court interpreted the Due Process Clause to protect same-sex sexual intimacy, individuals could construct their lifestyles in reliance on that ruling.[193]

Second, most nonoriginalist precedent was created because it was perceived to reach a just result. The point of nonoriginalism is that it authorizes judges to interpret the Constitution in a way (that is perceived to be) more normatively attractive than the original meaning. One can see this analytically by comparing originalism's "modalities" – permissible arguments – with those of nonoriginalism. Both contain modalities like text, structure, and history. However, nonoriginalism additionally includes normative considerations either directly or indirectly. Ronald Dworkin's law-as-integrity conception of law is an example of the former. According to Dworkin, judges must choose the morally best constitutional interpretation.[194] Popular Constitutionalism is an example of the latter. Popular constitutionalists argue that constitutional interpretation should reflect popular movements' interpretation which, in turn, embody those movements' normative perspectives.[195] The Warren Court's rhetoric is littered with references to the normative attractiveness of its nonoriginalist interpretations.[196] In sum, nonoriginalist precedents will frequently have a claim to justness because, by definition, they deviated from the original meaning *because of* their perceived normative attractiveness.

To the extent that a nonoriginalist precedent reflects what their authors believed were normatively attractive qualities, and to the extent those authors perceptions were accurate, then the third factor in the analysis I prescribed for nonoriginalist precedent will push the Supreme Court to overrule the precedent over time, and not immediately.

If the "problem" of nonoriginalist precedent is the biggest obstacle to originalism's ability to fit our practice, as many nonoriginalists argue, then the argument

---

[192] *E.g., Erie v. Pap's A.M.*, 529 U.S. 277 (2000).

[193] *Lawrence v. Texas*, 539 U.S. 558 (2003).

[194] Dworkin, *supra* note 3, at 228.

[195] Larry D. Kramer, The People Themselves: Popular Constitutionalism and Judicial Review 8 (2004).

[196] *Reynolds v. Sims*, 377 U.S. 533, 555 (1964).

developed here surmounts that problem. Originalism requires the immediate over-ruling of some nonoriginalist precedents. However, this is not all nonoriginalist precedents; it is only those that are significant deviations from the original meaning, that severely undermine Rule of Law values (or whose overruling does not under-mine the Rule of Law), and that are strongly unjust, or some combination of those three factors. This means that a precedent will not be overruled when doing so would harm the common good. Upon what basis could a critic argue otherwise? The critic cannot claim, for example, that originalism will destabilize the entire legal system, because the analysis prevents that. Nor may the critic assert that overruling a particular precedent is destabilizing because, by hypothesis, neither the Rule of Law nor justice is unreasonably harmed by overruling.

Furthermore, for the other nonoriginalist precedents that are not immediately overruled, their gradual overruling cannot be a basis for complaint from the perspective of feared systemic destabilization and harm to the Rule of Law. As I have argued, the deliberate and slow alteration to nonoriginalist doctrine will minimize harm to reliance interests and, at the point at which the doctrine's center of gravity tips toward the original meaning, the Court should eliminate the non-originalist doctrinal vestiges *for the sake of* the Rule of Law. Upon what basis may a critic argue to the contrary? The critic cannot claim that reliance interests are destabilized because, by definition, the second factor (in these cases) has required the slow alteration of constitutional doctrine until the tipping point is reached.

3.4.6.5 This Solution to the Challenge of Nonoriginalist Precedent Avoids the Problems of Other Responses

My resolution of the challenge posed by nonoriginalist precedent to originalism's ability to claim a satisfactory description of our constitutional practice is more attractive than responses suggested by other originalists. This occurs for two reasons. First, the rejection by some originalists of all nonoriginalist precedent does not fit the Constitution's original meaning. Second, rejection of all nonoriginalist prece-dent is normatively unattractive.

For originalists, the Constitution's original meaning should be the first place to look for an answer to a constitutional question. Of course, as I have described, the Constitution's original meaning does not always provide a determinate answer to questions, but originalists must first look to see if it does, and only then proceed to other types of analyses to resolve outstanding issues. I argued in Subsection 2.4.4 that the original meaning of "judicial Power" in Article III requires federal judges to give constitutional precedent significant respect.

To my knowledge, originalists supporting a get-rid-of-it all position have not rebutted this historical case, nor have they provided an alternative historical account. Instead, their position on nonoriginalist precedent is unmoored from the Constitution's original meaning. For example, Professor Gary Lawson argued that the Supremacy Clause requires federal courts to not follow nonoriginalist prece-dent.[197] Professor Lawson argued that the Supremacy Clause makes the Constitution superior to all other sources of law, including Supreme Court precedent that incorrectly interpreted the Constitution. Professor Lawson's only comments on the claim that "judicial Power" includes stare decisis is that "there is not much to support the claim"[198] and that the evidence does not show courts following precedent contrary to the Constitution.[199]

Bolstering my historical claim is the likely majority of originalist scholars who have investigated the evidence agree that "judicial Power" includes stare decisis, though these scholars disagree about the weightiness of this consideration. Professors McGinnis and Rappaport have most thoroughly canvassed the historical evidence, and their basic conclusion coincided with mine.[200]

Second, the practice of precedent is a good thing.[201] It is an extraordinarily widespread phenomenon in human life and in our legal practice. Precedent also advances crucial Rule of Law Values and preserve the epistemic and metaphysical "work" performed by courts in their precedents. Some nonoriginalist precedents created just relationships. A total or near-total immediate rejection of nonoriginalist precedent would cause originalism to not fit our legal practice, dramatically hurt the Rule of Law, and eliminate just relationships.

My conception of originalism avoids those difficulties because of its three-factor analysis coupled with its capacity to slowly move constitutional doctrine back to the original meaning. My conception is targeted to preserve and recover the original meaning while, at the same time, preserving the value in nonoriginalist precedent and reducing, to the extent possible, harm to the Rule of Law.

3.5 ORIGINALISM ACCOMMODATES SOCIETAL AND CONSTITUTIONAL CHANGE

3.5.1 *Introduction*

The United States has changed significantly since the Founding, and the Supreme Court's constitutional doctrine itself changes in response to, among other reasons, societal change. In this chapter, I show that originalism has six interpretative tools that accommodate societal and constitutional change. These six tools are: (1) an originalism of principles (2) abduced-principle originalism; (3) constitutional

---

[197] Gary Lawson, *The Constitutional Case Against Precedent*, 17 HARV. J. L. & PUB. POL'Y 23 (1994); Gary Lawson, *Mostly Unconstitutional: The Case Against Precedent Revisited*, 5 AVE MARIA L. REV. 1 (2007).

[198] Lawson, *Mostly Unconstitutional*, *supra* note 198, at 13.

[199] *Id.* at 12 n.39.

[200] McGINNIS & RAPPAPORT, *supra* note 4, at 154–74.

[201] RANDY J. KOZEL, SETTLED VERSUS RIGHT: A THEORY OF PRECEDENT 6 (2017).

construction; (4) Article I and state police power; (5) Article V; and (6) nonoriginalist precedent. These mechanisms are capable of sufficiently accommodating societal and constitutional change – to a greater or lesser degree when used individually, and effectively when taken as a whole. This capacity to flex with changes in society often occurs through the mechanism of constitutional doctrine, so these tools also help originalism fit our practice of constitutional doctrine.

3.5.2 Ongoing, Transformational Change

Our Constitution is over 225 years old. It is the oldest functioning national written constitution in the world.[202] A lot has changed over the past two centuries. The United States has grown tremendously and in many ways. Our population has grown from approximately 4 million in 1793[203] to over 325 million today.[204] Our nation's geographic extent grew from that of a small nation hugging the Atlantic coast to that of a giant spanning the North American continent.[205]

Even more importantly, the American People and how they live are dramatically different from 1789. The American People's religious and cultural life has been altered by the passage of time. The United States of 1791, when the First Amendment was ratified, was more Christian than today's United States. The percentage of Americans identified as Christians was, as one would expect given immigration by religious dissenters, high.[206] Many states retained state established churches and, even those that did not, officially recognized Christianity, or at the very least theism.[207] Today, by contrast, though Americans likely remain the most religious of any Western country, the rate of Christian identification has changed,[208] and Christianity no longer has a legally sanctioned position.

Culturally, the society of 1789, or 1868 for that matter, was more "conservative," as that term would be employed today in political discourse, regarding many important

---

[202] Massachusetts' constitution was submitted to and adopted by the Commonwealth's citizens in a specially called convention in 1780, and remains in force today (with modification, of course). LEONARD LEVY, SEASONED JUDGMENTS: THE AMERICAN CONSTITUTION, RIGHTS, AND HISTORY 307 (1995).

[203] U.S. Census Bureau, *Return of the Whole Number of Persons within the Several Districts of the United States* (1793), www.census.gov/library/publications/1793/dec/number-of-persons.html.

[204] U.S. Census Bureau, *U.S. Population Projected to Cross 325 Million Threshold*, www.census.gov/newsroom/press-releases/2017/cb17-tps43.html (May 5, 2017).

[205] Akhil Reed Amar, *The David C. Baum Lecture: Abraham Lincoln and the American Union*, 2001 U. ILL. L. REV. 1109, 1126–30.

[206] PAUL JOHNSON, A HISTORY OF THE AMERICAN PEOPLE 204 (1997).

[207] Lee J. Strang, *The Original Meaning of "Religion" in the First Amendment*, 40 DUQ. L. REV. 181, 220–24 (2002).

[208] U.S. Census Bureau, U.S. Dep't of Commerce, *Statistical Abstract of the United States: 2004–2005*, at 55 tbl.67 (2005), www.census.gov/prod/2004pubs/04statab/pop.pdf; Gary Langer, *Poll: Most Americans Say They're Christian*, ABC NEWS, July 18, 2001, http://abcnews.go.com/US/Story?id=90356&page=1.

issues. Possibly the most dramatic change is in the area of sexual mores. While perhaps honored in the breach, norms governing human sexuality privileged married, heterosexual sexual intimacy.[209] Today, by contrast, marriage as the sole forum for sexual intimacy sounds quaint.

The rise of urbanization and industrialization presented changes that dramatically altered the daily life of average Americans. Until 1910, the United States was primarily a rural nation with its people living either on farms or in small communities.[210] Thereafter, and increasingly, Americans lived in larger, urban areas. Relatedly, Americans of previous generations worked in agriculture or smaller businesses, but since the late nineteenth century, Americans have increasingly come to work in larger businesses focusing on industrial or other commercial endeavors.[211] And today, the American economy is post-industrial.

Since it is unlikely that many will contest the claim that there has been great change over the past two centuries, I will not further belabor the point other than to sound a note of caution. The transformation in American society over the past two centuries can be exaggerated. A standard criticism of originalism in the scholarly literature and Supreme Court opinions is that the factual presuppositions that initially supported the original meaning have changed so dramatically that it no longer makes sense to follow the original meaning. Of course, if the factual presuppositions that undergirded the original meaning have not been altered, or at least not materially so, this regularly proffered criticism loses much of its strength.

For example, in the Religion Clause context, proponents of nonoriginalist interpretations of the Clauses often claim that a nonoriginalist interpretation is necessary because the Framers and Ratifiers in 1791 could not have foreseen the rise of religious pluralism and hence did not take that fact into account when crafting the Clauses.[212] This claim underestimates the scope of religious pluralism at the time of the Framing and Ratification. It also underestimates the Framers' and Ratifiers' knowledge of their world's religious pluralism and the history of religious pluralism. They were concerned with religious pluralism; in fact, religious pluralism on the state and local level was the primary motivation for the inclusion of the Religious Tests and Establishment Clauses.[213]

---

[209] Charles J. Reid, Jr., *The Augustinian Goods of Marriage: The Disappearing Cornerstone of the American Law of Marriage*, 18 B. Y. U. J. Pub. L. 449, 462–70 (2004); Charles J. Reid, Jr., *The Unavoidable Influence of Religion upon the Law of Marriage*, 23 Quinnipiac L. Rev. 493, 500–13 (2004).

[210] U.S. Census Bureau, U.S. Dep't of Commerce, 1990 *Census of Population and Housing: Population and Housing Unit Counts: United States* 5 tbl.4 (1993), www.census.gov/prod/cen1990/cph2/cph-2-1-1.pdf.

[211] Arthur S. Link et al., The American People: A History 507 (Arthur S. Link et al. eds., 1981).

[212] *Van Orden v. Perry*, 545 U.S. 677, 734 (2005) (Stevens, J., dissenting); Erwin Chemerinsky, Constitutional Law 1455 (2d ed. 2002).

[213] Akhil Reed Amar, The Bill of Rights: Creation and Reconstruction 32, 34, 301 (1998).

The religious pluralism in 1791 America, it is true, consisted mostly of Protestant Christianity. However, within Protestant Christianity, there was a wide variety of doctrines and practices.[214] Further, the existence of a relatively large Catholic population centered in Maryland,[215] along with vibrant Jewish communities, expanded the scope of religious pluralism yet further.[216] The Framers and Ratifiers were also aware of religious pluralism – including atheism – throughout history and its continuing existence in many parts of the world, especially in the Far East and among the tribes that peopled the American frontier.[217] Given their concern with and knowledge of religious pluralism, the standard criticism of the Religion Clauses' original meaning is, at a minimum, overstated.

3.5.3 *The Purported Problem Posed to Originalism*

Regardless of exactly how much change has occurred within the United States, it has been substantial. This leads to a powerful criticism of originalism, one that nonoriginalists have not been shy about making. The criticism is that originalism's faithfulness to the Constitution's original meaning prevents it from adequately responding to and accommodating societal change.

Justice Stevens, no fan of originalism, chastised originalists on the Supreme Court for failing to recognize that "our understanding of the Constitution does change from time to time."[218] In the academy, Mark Tushnet was representative when he claimed that "the general problem of originalism ... is that social change makes it a theory of constitutional interpretation that regularly fails to provide guidance on matters of contemporary constitutional controversy because it disregards the complexities of ... the current situation."[219] Nor is this a new critique. Justice Douglas anticipated this argument in 1949, writing that today's judge cannot let "men long dead and unaware of the problems of the age in which he lives do his thinking for him."[220] Indeed, even scholars sympathetic to originalism find the challenge of change compelling.[221]

The challenge of change is especially pronounced in our society because we have both a written Constitution and a society that has undergone tremendous change in the period during which the Constitution has been in force. Originalism, by arguing

---

[214] JOHNSON, *supra* note 207, at 108–17, 204–11; SAMUEL ELIOT MORISON, THE OXFORD HISTORY OF THE AMERICAN PEOPLE 292–94 (1965).

[215] JOHNSON, *supra* note 207, at 55–61.

[216] *Id.* at 305–07.

[217] *See* FOREST MCDONALD, NOVUS ORDO SECLORUM: THE INTELLECTUAL ORIGINS OF THE CONSTITUTION 5 (1985) (describing the deep historical learning of the Framers).

[218] *Roper v. Simmons*, 543 U.S. 551, 587 (2005) (Stevens, J., concurring).

[219] Mark Tushnet, *Religion and Theories of Constitutional Interpretation*, 33 LOY. L. REV. 221, 229 (1987).

[220] William O. Douglas, *Stare Decisis*, 49 COLUM. L. REV. 735, 736 (1949).

[221] *E.g.*, Larry Kramer, *Fidelity to History – and through It*, 65 FORDHAM L. REV. 1627, 1636 (1997).

that the Constitution's authoritative meaning is its historically-fixed meaning, ties itself to the "writtenness" of the Constitution and thereby opens itself to the challenge of change.

On a deeper level, this critique is powerful because, for a law to serve its purpose, it must adequately fit the society that it governs. For instance, legal norms governing road use in a pre-automobile society needed adjustment to fit the advent of widespread automobile usage. Legislators had sound reasons to modify rules governing, for example, speed limits on roadways in light of the automobile's different capabilities. Similarly, the argument goes, our Constitution's original meaning, which came of age in a society so different from our own, needs to be adjusted to fit modern American realities. Judges, on this account, have sound reasons to modify the Constitution's meaning to fit the new realities.

In the following subsection, I show that originalism has the resources to meet the challenge of change. There are at least six interpretive tools by which originalism can accommodate social change. These mechanisms are capable of sufficiently accommodating societal and constitutional change – to a greater or lesser degree when used individually, but effectively when taken as a whole. This capacity to flex with changes in society permits originalism to adequately fit existing constitutional doctrine.

3.5.4 *Originalism Sufficiently Accommodates Societal and Constitutional Change*

3.5.4.1 Introduction

Originalism has the interpretive tools to be sufficiently flexible in the face of changed societal conditions. These six tools are: (1) an originalism of principles, standards, and rules; (2) abduced-principle originalism; (3) constitutional construction; (4) Article I and state police power; (5) Article V; and (6) nonoriginalist precedent. Next, I explain how each tool contributes to originalism.

3.5.4.2 An Originalism of Principles

The first of originalism's facets that enables it to accommodate changed societal conditions are the varying levels of generality of the Constitution's original meaning. Legal norms, including those embodied in the Constitution's original meaning, can exist at an infinite number of levels of abstraction, from a very particularized rule to a broadly encompassing principle. Legal philosophers, however, have commonly divided the possible levels of abstraction of legal and other norms using a tripartite division: rules, standards, and principles.[222] Using this framework, I will show how

---

[222] There is substantial disagreement on what the differing types of legal norms are and the respective characteristics of those types. STEVEN J. BURTON, JUDGING IN GOOD FAITH 168 (1992). The

originalism is well equipped to tackle societal change. My claim is that the Constitution's original meaning – especially regarding its more important clauses[223] – is frequently sufficiently abstract so that originalism can fulsomely accommodate change. This occurs when a judge applies this relatively abstract constitutional norm to new situations.

The most concrete type of legal norm is the rule. One of the characteristics of rules is that they cover a limited number of social circumstances. They take the form of: if fact(s) A (B, C, etc.) exist(s), then result(s) X (Y, Z, etc.).[224] Rules are narrow because of the limited number of facts they cover. Rules have an on-off quality. Only if the limited number of pertinent facts exists does the result follow. Rules are generally considered to provide little space for normative evaluation.

Standards are more abstract and less constraining than rules. They lack the on-off quality that characterizes rules. Instead of a particular result following from the existence of a specified (list of) fact(s), a standard directs the decision maker to take into consideration a set of factors that will guide the decision maker's decision. No one factor is determinative, and the factors that guide the decision maker may themselves have varying weights and hence influence on the decision maker's decision.

The standard provides the universe of factors that the decision maker must utilize, but how the factors interact to produce a result is not predetermined. The factors could each have a specific weight, and the decision maker must determine on which side the different factors fall and then balance the two sets of factors. Or, the standard could direct that the factors will have different weights depending on their interrelationship.[225]

Principles, like standards, provide reasons that decision-makers must utilize. Unlike standards, however, principles do not preclude the decision maker from employing additional considerations in making a decision. Instead of providing the tools to resolve a particular issue, as do rules and standards, principles have, in the words of Ronald Dworkin, "gravitational force."[226] That is, principles push or pull a decision maker in one direction or another – they put their thumb on the scale, so to speak.[227]

---

tripartite division of legal norms reflects a common convention. Lawrence B. Solum, Legal Theory Blog, *Legal Theory Lexicon: Rules, Standards, Principles, Catalogs, and Discretion* (Dec. 24, 2017).

[223] By "more important clauses," I am referring to those portions of the Constitution that have the highest product of frequency of use, broadness of coverage of social life, and the centrality of those facts of social life covered. As an example, the Commerce Clause is more important than the Third Amendment's prohibition on quartering soldiers.

[224] Richard A. Wasserstrom, The Judicial Decision 36–38 (1961).

[225] Burton, *supra* note 223, at 51–62.

[226] Dworkin, *supra* note 154, at 111.

[227] Burton, *supra* note 223, at 170. The relatively clean trichotomy described in the text does not account for the frequency with which legal norms possess aspects of multiple types of legal norms. "Most legal norms are hybrids, in that they have both rule-like and standard-like

Here, the aspect of these three basic legal norms with which I am most concerned is their ability to apply to new situations. I will focus on the relative abstraction of the norms, or their component parts, because this characteristic most readily permits a norm to apply to new circumstances. Principles generally have, to a greater extent than rules or standards, the ability to apply to new circumstances because of their relatively greater abstraction. Principles are not limited, in the manner of rules or standards, to a fact or discrete set of facts. Lastly, principles often employ component parts that require judgments of value or practical reason. None of this is to say, however, that rules do not have the capacity to apply to new situations – only that they do not have as great a capacity as do principles and standards.

Principles (along with other legal norms, but to a greater degree than those other norms) can apply in ways unforeseen by their author(s). In the Fourth Amendment context, for example, the Supreme Court has repeatedly faced cases that presented circumstances unforeseen (and unforeseeable) by the Amendment's framers and ratifiers. A good illustration of this is *Kyllo* v. *United States*.[228] There, the Court faced the question of whether a thermal image scan of a house, which revealed information about the house's interior, was a "search[]" within the Fourth Amendment's meaning. The Court ruled that the image scan was a search. The Court relied, in part, on the reasoning that the Constitution guaranteed a minimum level of protection for homes and that the Court must ensure that new technology does not erode that protection. "To withdraw protection of this minimum expectation would be to permit police technology to erode the privacy guaranteed by the Fourth Amendment."[229] The Court applied the Fourth Amendment's principle of special protection to the home to a situation unforeseen by its framers and ratifiers. In fact, later judges applying a legal principle may apply it to situations known to exist by the principle's author(s), but in a manner *contrary* to how the principle's author(s) did or would have applied it.

It is widely agreed that the Constitution embodies all three types of legal norms.[230] A commonly given example of a constitutional rule is the requirement that the President be thirty-five years of age.[231] The relative "ruleness" of the Clause does create difficulty in responding to change. Arguably, as presently constituted, the Clause does not take into account the relatively longer maturation period for modern Americans in contrast to the founding generation. Members of the founding generation, at a relatively young age, performed at the highest levels of

elements." Larry Alexander & Ken Kress, *Against Legal Principles*, 82 Iowa L. Rev. 739, 740 (1997).
[228] *Kyllo* v. *United States*, 533 U.S. 27 (2001).
[229] *Id.* at 34, 40.
[230] Barnett, *supra* note 5, at 123; Ronald Dworkin, Freedom's Law: The Moral Reading of the American Constitution 7–9 (1996); Whittington, Interpretation, *supra* note 5, at 202, 216.
[231] U.S. Const. art. II, §1, cl. 5.

state and society, and with exemplary skill. For example, some of the most influential and important members of the Philadelphia Convention – including Alexander Hamilton and Edmund Randolph – were younger than thirty-five, and James Madison was only thirty-six.[232]

A possible example of a standard is the Necessary and Proper Clause.[233] Scholars have argued that judges, when faced with the question of whether a statute is constitutional under the Necessary and Proper Clause, must utilize a number of elements to make the determination.[234] Judges must, of course, determine whether the statute is both necessary and proper, but both elements can be further particularized. A statute is *necessary* if it is more than simply convenient, but it need not be indispensable or absolutely necessary.[235] Also, a statute is *proper* only if: (1) it does not violate individual rights, (2) it does not violate the separation of powers, and (3) it does not violate federalism.[236] A judge, therefore, must utilize all of these elements to arrive at a conclusion of whether a given statute is constitutionally necessary and proper.

The Necessary and Proper Clause's component parts are relatively capacious in their sweep in that they can bring within their sway statutes addressing any subject within Congress' enumerated powers. Justice Scalia's concurrence in *Gonzales v. Raich* is an example of how the Clause may apply to unforeseen activities – the interstate market for illicit drugs – that Congress seeks to regulate under its Article I powers.[237]

Scholars have argued that Article IV's Privileges and Immunities Clause[238] embodies the principle that states must give citizens of other states the rights a state gives its own citizens. Akhil Amar has called this the "interstate-equality principle."[239] This principle applies to new forms of state differential treatment of noncitizens. For instance, in *Saenz v. Roe*, the Court struck down a California statute that gave reduced welfare benefits to new residents during their first year of residency.[240]

Given that the Constitution does contain, not only rules, but also more capacious standards and principles, which of these types of legal norms predominates in frequency and regarding the most important constitutional provisions, is an

---

[232] *The Age of the Framers in 1787*, www.teachingamericanhistory.org/convention/delegates/age .html (last visited May 17, 2009).
[233] U.S. Const. art. 1, §8, cl. 18.
[234] Barnett, *supra* note 5, at 153–90; Gary Lawson & Patricia B. Granger, *The "Proper" Scope of Federal Power: A Jurisdictional Interpretation of the Sweeping Clause*, 43 Duke L.J. 267, 285–326 (1993).
[235] Barnett, *supra* note 5, at 178.
[236] Lawson & Granger, *The "Proper" Scope*, *supra* note 235, at 326–34.
[237] *Gonzales v. Raich*, 545 U.S. 1, 33–42 (2005) (Scalia, J., concurring).
[238] U.S. Const. art. IV, §1, cl. 1.
[239] Akhil Reed Amar, America's Constitution: A Biography 254 (2005).
[240] *Saenz v. Roe*, 526 U.S. 489, 492, 498–507 (1999).

empirical question. Critics of originalism have not provided significant evidence on this point. Instead, originalist scholarship has identified many and important constitutional provisions the original meaning of which is a standard or principle. This finding fits both the historical data from the period of the Framing and Ratification, and what reasonable Framers and Ratifiers would do when creating the Constitution.

First, the Framers and Ratifiers were cognizant of the challenge of change.[241] They had witnessed the Articles of Confederation's inability to adapt to the changes that took place following the Revolution and its consequent failure.[242] Professor Philip Hamburger summarized this history finding that the Framers and Ratifiers "strove for a constitution that would survive changes in American society and therefore attempted to exclude from the Constitution all that might become obsolete."[243] For instance, one of the mechanisms the Framers and Ratifiers utilized to achieve their goal of permanence was to give the national legislature discretion to meet unforeseen situations (within its limited and enumerated powers). Another mechanism was to embody principles in the Constitution's text – principles that would apply to changed future circumstances.

This makes sense if one is creating a governmental structure intended to be a "novus ordo seclorum: a new order of the ages."[244] A reasonable person in the position of the Framers and Ratifiers would "draw their Constitution loosely enough so that it might live and breathe and change with time."[245]

The question of which type of legal norm a constitutional text embodies is primarily an empirical and not a normative question.[246] To determine what form the legal norm in question takes, one must conduct an inquiry into the original meaning of the constitutional text. That inquiry will reveal – if the data is sufficiently determinate – whether the original meaning is a legal rule, standard, or principle.[247]

It may be the case that some (perhaps many) of the Constitution's norms embody not only an abstract principle, but a principle of critical morality. The difference between these two types of principles – conventional moral principles and critical moral principles – is that the first is drawn from conventional morality while the second is drawn from critical morality.[248] A principle drawn from critical morality has, as its object, an accurate statement of the requirements of morality, regardless of what society believes on the subject. A judge faced with the task of interpreting a

---

[241] Philip A. Hamburger, *The Constitution's Accommodation of Social Change*, 88 MICH. L. REV. 239, 240–42 (1989).

[242] *Id.* at 276.

[243] *Id.* at 325.

[244] McDONALD, *supra* note 218, at 262.

[245] *Id.* at 293.

[246] GREGORY BASSHAM, ORIGINAL INTENT AND THE CONSTITUTION: A PHILOSOPHICAL STUDY 79–83 (1992).

[247] WHITTINGTON, INTERPRETATION, *supra* note 5, at 213–14.

[248] H. L. A. HART, LAW, LIBERTY AND MORALITY 20 (1963).

critical moral norm embodied in the Constitution will use both his speculative[249] and his practical reason[250] to determine, respectively, how best to define and apply the moral norm in the case. The judge's analysis will include determining the best conception of the critical moral norm in question.

Lastly, the well-accepted distinction in the philosophy of language, between sense and reference, bolsters my argument for an originalism of principles.[251] Sense is the meaning of a text that identifies and encompasses the text's referents. A text's sense provides the analytic mechanism connecting the text to its referents. This mechanism is the "set of identifying properties or descriptions associated with [the text]."[252] For instance, if the text in question is "human," its sense is rational animals. Referents, by contrast, are objects in the world identified by the sense of the text in question. Recurring to our previous example of "human," Aristotle would be a referent.

The distinction between sense and reference, and related philosophy of language concepts,[253] helps originalism meet changing circumstances because the Constitution's sense can apply to referents not in existence when the Constitution was ratified. If, for example, the publicly understood referents of the Cruel Punishments Clause of the Eighth Amendment included ten specific examples of wicked government punishment, that does not exhaust the possible referents to which the Clause may apply. If, as is likely the case, the Clause's sense was approximately those punishments that are, in fact, cruel,[254] then the Clause's sense can apply to new referents not in existence when the Clause was ratified (it could apply, for instance, to the electric chair).

The Clause's sense could also apply to known practices in ways *contrary* to the framers' and ratifiers' understandings. This could be the case regarding the death penalty, for instance. Despite the framers' and ratifiers' beliefs that the death penalty was consistent with the Eighth Amendment, later interpreters could legitimately conclude that the death penalty is unconstitutionally cruel if it is, in fact, cruel. The distinction between sense and reference is analogous to the distinction between legal norms and the original applications of those norms.

---

[249] ST, I-II, q. 79, a. 2.

[250] NLNR, at 100–27.

[251] Gottlob Frege, *Uber Sinn und Bedeutung* [*Sense and Reference*], translated in 57 PHIL. REV. 209 (1948); *see* Christopher R. Green, *Originalism and the Sense-Reference Distinction*, 50 ST. LOUIS U. L.J. 555, 563–74 (2006).

[252] BASSHAM, *supra* note 247, at 75.

[253] For example, John Stuart Mill used the terms "connotation" and "denotation." JOHN STUART MILL, A SYSTEM OF LOGIC 34–41 (8th ed. 1872). Rudolf Carnap also used the terms "intension" and "extension." RUDOLF CARNAP, MEANING AND NECESSITY 177–79 (1947).

[254] John F. Stinneford, *The Original Meaning of 'Cruel'*, 105 GEO. L.J. 441 (2017).

3.5.4.3 Abduced-Principle Originalism

Second, and relatedly, originalism has at its disposal abduced-principle original-ism.[255] I use the label abduced-principle originalism to refer to the phenomena where there was no original public meaning of a constitutional text and, instead, there was a societal consensus only on a discrete set of practices – what I label archetypal practices – that the text permitted, proscribed, or required. Abduced-principle originalism abduces a norm – a rule, standard, or principle – that fits this existing data of constitutional meaning. Abduced-principle originalism focuses on the practices that the Framers and Ratifiers believed the term or phrase required, proscribed, or permitted. Abduced-principle originalism provides a mechanism to increase the area of usable original meaning. Interpreters can, in turn, apply these abduced norms to new circumstances.

Abduced-principle originalism relies on the form of reasoning variously described as "abductive inference,"[256] "inductive inference,"[257] and "analogical reasoning in law."[258] Abduction is the process of "discovering the rules to be applied, of making sense of patterns of characteristics, and of putting characteristics into rule-like patterns."[259] The process of abduction has four steps: (1) identify the data in need of explanation; (2) articulate hypotheses to explain the data; (3) test the hypotheses to determine which best explains the data; and (4) the best hypothesis is applied to new data in need of explanation.[260]

Abduced-principle originalism follows this same process. Abduced-principle originalism applies to constitutional texts for which there was no or limited original meaning, but regarding which there was a public consensus on what archetypal practices the text acted upon. First, an interpreter must identify the data – the archetypal practices regarding which there was a consensus that the text permitted, proscribed, or required. Second, the interpreter must put forward possible norms that explain the data. Third, the interpreter will test the possible norms utilizing fit

---

[255] What follows is a brief summary of what I argued in prior work. Lee J. Strang, *Originalism and the "Challenge of Change": Abduced-Principle Originalism and Other Mechanisms by Which Originalism Sufficiently Accommodates Changed Social Conditions*, 60 HASTINGS L.J. 927 (2009).

[256] Scott Brewer, *Exemplary Reasoning: Semantics, Pragmatics, and the Rational Force of Legal Arguments by Analogy*, 109 HARV. L. REV. 923, 947 (1996).

[257] Dan Hunter, *No Wilderness of Single Instances: Inductive Inference in Law*, 48 J. LEGAL EDUC. 365, 365 (1998).

[258] Larry Alexander, *The Banality of Legal Reasoning*, 73 NOTRE DAME L. REV. 517, 525 (1998). There is vigorous debate on the existence of and scope of abduction. *Id.* at 531–33; Emily Sherwin, *A Defense of Analogical Reasoning in Law*, 66 U. CHI. L. REV. 1179, 1186–94 (1999); Cass R. Sunstein, *On Analogical Reasoning*, 106 HARV. L. REV. 741 (1993).

[259] Brewer, *supra* note 257, at 978.

[260] *Id.* at 947–48, 962–63, 980–81, 983.

and, if necessary, the Framers' and Ratifiers' perspective,[261] to ascertain which norm is the best explanation of the archetypal practices. Fourth, the interpreter will apply that norm in the case before her, the case that had required her to articulate the constitutional text's original meaning through the process of abduction. Abduced-principle originalism can increase the relative coverage of the original meaning and thereby decrease the relative constitutional underdeterminacy by filling in the gaps between and beyond archetypal practices.

Regarding those provisions for which there was not a coherent original meaning, other than a social consensus on the discrete practices affected (or not affected) by the provisions, the originalist interpreter has three possible responses: (1) restrict the provision's authoritative meaning to that discrete set of practices regarding which there was a consensus; (2) abduce the rule, standard, or principle that best fits and justifies the discrete set of practices; or (3) determine which rule, standard, or principle best fits the provision's text. The originalist's correct response is option two.

Abduced-principle originalism permits originalism to avoid the problematic first option: limiting the Constitution's original meaning to the archetypal practices. If it were otherwise, then the problem of change would be acute. The Constitution's original meaning would be limited to the circumstances at the time of ratification. Since the discrete set of practices would not change – and, most importantly, would not expand to include new practices – the Constitution's original meaning would quickly become outdated. It would be limited to the archetypal cases existing at the time of ratification.

Assume, for instance, that the original meaning of "cruel" in the Cruel and Unusual Punishment Clause did not create a rule, standard, or principle. Instead, assume that the historical evidence showed that the public understanding of the Clause was that only five discrete practices were prohibited by the Clause. Given government's ability to devise new punishments, the efficacy of the Clause would be greatly undermined if the Clause's original meaning could not reach new punishments because it was limited to the then-existing five practices.

Abduced-principle originalism prevents this from occurring. The interpreter would abduce a rule, standard, or principle that fits the practices regarding which there was an original meaning. Abduced-principle originalism would, like the principled originalism I described previously, be able to apply the abduced norm to new and unforeseen circumstances. This would include new punishments that were proscribed by the abduced norm of "cruel."

Option two is the correct originalist response for the following three reasons: First, the resultant meaning of the provision – in the form of a rule, standard, or principle – is the Constitution's original meaning. By ensuring that the original meaning that does exist is retained, abduced-principle originalism respects the authority of the Framers and

---

[261] By the Framers' and Ratifiers' perspective, I mean approaching a given issue with their knowledge and purposes.

Ratifiers to make the prudential, coordinating decisions that are embodied in the Constitution. The norms articulated using abduced-principle originalism likewise respect the Framers' and Ratifiers' authority. Second, while option one does respect the Framers and Ratifiers' authority, option two ensures that originalism can surmount the challenge of change, unlike option one. Third, while option three can meet the challenge of change, it does not – unlike option two – respect the Framers' and Ratifiers' authority because it does not fit the Framers' and Ratifiers' decisions.

3.5.4.4 Constitutional Construction

Originalism's third tool to accommodate societal change is constitutional construction. When the Constitution's original meaning is underindeterminate, Congress has the authority to make constitutional constructions, and when Congress is working within the underdeterminate constitutional text, it can be creative. In these situations, because the original meaning is not completely constraining, its rootedness in the past is not an issue and, hence, the problem of change is not an issue. Instead, Congress can use its prudential judgment to address current issues in the manner it sees fit.

3.5.4.5 Legislative Power

Originalism's fourth tool is legislative power. Federal and state legislative power facilitate originalism's capacity to fit constitutional and societal change. Article I of the Constitution grants to Congress all of the federal government's legislative power. Correspondingly, state governments have plenary legislative power except where specifically restricted by the federal or state constitutions. This power is known as the police power.[262]

In those many areas where the federal or state legislatures have legislative authority, they can react to changed circumstances as their judgments dictate. The Framers and Ratifiers, in response to the recognized problem of changing social conditions, deliberately chose to enable Congress to address change.[263]

Given the continuing legislative ability to respond to changed conditions, we should not be surprised to find that there are numerous instances where Congress or the states have legislated in reaction to what was perceived as an inadequate original meaning. In the Fourth Amendment context, for instance, the Supreme Court overruled *Olmstead* v. *United States*[264] in *Katz* v. *United States*.[265] The *Katz* Court replaced the *Olmstead* Court's originalist reading of the Fourth Amendment with

---

[262] D. Benjamin Barros, *The Police Power and the Takings Clause*, 58 U. MIAMI L. REV. 471, 471–72 (2004).
[263] Kay, *American Constitutionalism*, *supra* note 43, at 38.
[264] *Olmstead* v. *United States*, 277 U.S. 438 (1928).
[265] *Katz* v. *United States*, 389 U.S 347 (1967).

the "reasonable expectation of privacy" concept.[266] Congress, however, perceived *Katz's* level of protection against wiretapping as inadequate, so it enacted Title III in 1968.[267] Congress expanded protection beyond the Fourth Amendment's original meaning, and it did so using its legislative power.

Originalism accords state legislatures broad legislative authority (compatible with the Constitution's limits). This book is not the place to make detailed claims regarding the scope of this legislative power other than to note that states have relatively broad authority to meet new challenges.

3.5.4.6 Nonoriginalist Precedent

Fifth, originalism's ability to meet the challenge of change is augmented by its openness to nonoriginalist precedent. The third factor judges should utilize to evaluate nonoriginalist precedent requires judges to determine how effectively the legal norm embodied in the nonoriginalist precedent rightly orders social relations. This inquiry encompasses the question of how well the norm fits today's society. If the norm fits changed conditions better than the original meaning, it is more likely to rightly order social relations and hence be retained.

The second factor will also, in many instances, counsel against overruling a precedent because doing so would harm Rule of Law values. In many areas of the law, nonoriginalist precedents have become embedded in the law, and social practices that fit the nonoriginalist precedents, but fit less well the Constitution's original meaning, have encrusted themselves on the precedents. Overruling those precedents would, therefore, undermine Rule of Law values. This potential for harm to Rule of Law values counsels against overruling the precedents and therefore for preserving precedents that fit current social practices.

Many nonoriginalist precedents and doctrines arose in response to (at least perceived) societal changes, and some (or many) of these originalism can incorporate. The New Deal "transformation," for instance, was in large measure motivated, both on and off the Court, by changes in society.[268] The justices who participated in modifying constitutional doctrine repeatedly and explicitly invoked changed conditions as a justification.[269] If in fact the nonoriginalist New Deal precedents are normatively attractive responses to societal change, then an originalism that can retain some of them is better able to meet the challenge of change.

---

[266] *Id.* at 361 (Harlan, J., concurring).
[267] Omnibus Crime Control and Safe Streets Act of 1968, Pub. L. No. 90–351, 82 Stat. 197, 211–225 (1968).
[268] ACKERMAN, TRANSFORMATIONS, *supra* note 60, at 308–09.
[269] E.g., *NLRB* v. *Jones & Laughlin Steel Corp.*, 301 U.S. 1, 41 (1937); *West Coast Hotel, Co.* v. *Parrish*, 300 U.S. 379, 390 (1937).

3.5.4.7 Amendment

Sixth, and obviously, the Constitution contains within itself the means to modify its meaning. Article V permits amendment of the Constitution if approved by two-thirds vote of Congress and three-fourths of the states.[270] The Framers and Ratifiers understood Article V to be a way for future generations to meet "new challenges and opportunities in the unforeseeable future [that] might require new approaches."[271]

There is a scholarly debate over whether Article V is an attractive vehicle of amendment. The extent to which one is persuaded that Article V is sufficiently viable to permit amendment when necessary, while at the same time sufficiently resistant to change to preserve the Constitution's enduring character, will influence one's view on whether and to what extent Article V helps originalism meet the challenge of change. It is clear that Article V has not been used frequently and that part of the "blame" for that failure lies at the feet of the relatively high hurdles Article V places before proposed amendments. However, the lack of a larger number of amendments does not by itself indicate that the Constitution is unduly difficult to amend.

It is likely that the Constitution would have been amended more frequently than it has been if the Supreme Court had hewed more closely to the Constitution's original meaning.[272] Perhaps the best example of this occurred during the New Deal. President Roosevelt considered a written constitutional amendment to place the New Deal on solid constitutional footing.[273] In the end, though, the Court's famous "switch in time" relieved the pro-New Deal pressure for formal constitutional change, and the New Deal "amendments" came in the form of nonoriginalist precedents.[274] This is simply another way of saying that there exists a prodigious number of nonoriginalist precedents that may have eliminated the popular support necessary for amendments. Nonetheless, *absent* recourse to "amendments" via judicial precedent, Article V likely remains a viable option.

3.5.4.8 Conclusion

The six originalist tools I summarized provide significant flexibility to originalism to accommodate societal change. Originalism primarily does so, however, through the mechanism of constitutional doctrine. The first five tools all employ constitutional doctrine to meet new societal circumstances. For example and obviously, nonoriginalist precedent is precedent that forms constitutional doctrines. However, even the tools that, at least at first blush, do not appear to employ constitutional doctrine,

---

[270] U.S. Const. art. V.
[271] Amar, America's Constitution, *supra* note 239, at 285.
[272] McGinnis & Rappaport, *supra* note 4, at 88–94.
[273] Ackerman, Transformations, *supra* note 60, at 298–301.
[274] *Id.* at 314–15, 326–27.

do so. Article I and state police power both become the subject of cases in which the scope of those powers is elucidated and defined. As a result, originalism's built-in capacity to meeting societal change is simultaneously an opportunity for it to fit our constitutional practice of employing constitutional doctrine.

3.6 CONCLUSION

This chapter argued that originalism provides an accurate description of our current constitutional practice. Originalism fits the key facets of our practice, including our written Constitution and Supreme Court practice, and widespread aspects of our practice such as the pervasive use of precedent and constitutional doctrine. However, like every theory of interpretation, originalism does not fit all facets of our practice. For example, not all nonoriginalist precedents would continue in an originalist world. The argument in this chapter has been that these outlier practices – the nonoriginalist precedents that would be overruled under originalism but not under current practice – should be marginalized because of the practice's deeper commitments to originalism. In other words, American constitutional practice's commitment itself has the force to move the practice toward originalism.

Let us say, however, that this chapter has *not* persuaded you. Perhaps you believe that our constitutional practice's most important commitments are not originalist, or that its nonoriginalist aspects are simply too numerous in kind and quantity for the practice to be accurately labeled originalist. In Chapter 4, I argue that originalism is the most normatively attractive theory of interpretation because, systematically followed, it secures the common good and thereby provides the background conditions under which Americans today may most effectively pursue their human flourishing. This is the law-as-coordination account of originalism.

The law-as-coordination account in Chapter 4 can be coupled with Chapter 3's descriptive claim. Tied to Chapter 3, the law-as-coordination account provides a reason to embrace originalism even if (and to the extent) it is a reform movement. Law-as-coordination shows that it is reasonable for interpreters and for Americans to move our constitutional practice away from eclecticism and towards a coherent originalist practice because of the goods secured by doing so: the national common good and individual human flourishing.

On the other hand, if this chapter has persuaded you, then the law-as-coordination account of originalism can also stand on its own as a justification for our (current) originalist constitutional practice. It explains why our practice is valuable, and it gives sound reasons to participants in that practice to continue it.

4

Originalism Best Advances Americans' Human Flourishing: The Law-as-Coordination Account of Originalism

The end of the state is the good life and these are the means towards it.

Aristotle, *The Politics*[1]

4.1 INTRODUCTION

In this chapter, I show that originalism is the most normatively attractive interpretive methodology because it best secures the background conditions under which Americans can pursue their own individual human flourishing. Originalism does so by enabling the Constitution to overcome coordination problems and thereby secure the common good. I call this the law-as-coordination account of originalism. It is a natural law justification for the American Constitution. This argument proceeds in four parts.

First, I explain that the end of human beings is flourishing – what the Greeks called *eudaimonia*, often translated as happiness. Human flourishing occurs when we pursue the basic human goods, such as life, friendship, and knowledge, and do so excellently – virtuously.

Second, I show that individual human beings can achieve human flourishing only in community with others – in a society that effectively pursues the common good through (among other types of authority) legal authority. Only a society can provide the organization necessary to produce the goods (broadly conceived to include material, emotional, and spiritual goods) and provide the conditions (peace, structures for the expression of individual personality, and structures for social cooperation) for individual human flourishing.

Third, I describe how every society of more-than-modest complexity must utilize legal authority and positive law to coordinate its members to secure the common

---

[1] ARISTOTLE, THE POLITICS 1280b (B. Jowett trans., 1885).

good and human flourishing because the natural law is underdetermined. These legal authorities characteristically coordinate members of their societies through judgments that are (1) authoritative, (2) prudential, (3) coordinating, and (4) embodied in positive law. A legal authority's laws coordinate members of a society by providing exclusionary reasons in the members' practical deliberations. The positive law's meaning is the mechanism by which the law conveys its exclusionary reasons to citizens.

Fourth, I apply this conception of legal authority to the United States Constitution and show how the Constitution contains America's fundamental authoritative, prudential, coordinating decisions. Americans at the time of the Founding – as well as today – point to the state ratification conventions as having the authority to adopt the Constitution. The Constitution's decisions on how to order American society are prudential; they are all-things-considered judgments. The Constitution's authoritative, prudential decisions coordinated – and continue to coordinate – Americans' lives toward the common good and individual human flourishing. Americans in 1789, and Americans today, employ the Constitution's authoritative, prudential, coordinating decisions in their practical deliberations – and thereby effectively coordinate their actions and effectively pursue their individual goods – by utilizing originalism.

This law-as-coordination account of originalism provides not only an attractive normative justification for originalism, it also dovetails with many other facets of my conception of originalism. For instance, I argued in Subsection 2.4.4 that originalism must preserve some nonoriginalist precedent for the sake of the common good. My law-as-coordination account also connects well with my employment of the judicial virtues in Section 2.6 to describe the kinds of judges needed for originalism to succeed.

Before describing my law-as-coordination account of originalism, let me first briefly provide three reasons why originalism needs a normative justification.

4.2 ORIGINALISTS MUST PROVIDE A NORMATIVE ACCOUNT FOR ORIGINALISM

4.2.1 *Introduction*

To be clear, originalists have and continue to provide a wide variety of attractive normative justifications, and I described them in Subsection 1.4.3. However, some originalists have claimed that a normative justification is not necessary for originalism,[2] and others have claimed that a normative justification is not necessary because

---

2   E.g., Gary Lawson, *Originalism Without Obligation*, 93 B. U. L. Rev. 1309, 1312–15 (2013).

our current legal practice requires originalism,[3] so this subsection details three responses to those claims.

4.2.2 *A Normative Account Is Needed to the Extent That Originalism Is a "Reform Project"*

I argued in Chapter 3 that the important and widespread facets of our current constitutional practice are committed to originalism. To the extent you were not persuaded by that argument and you believe that our legal practice is instead eclectic – that it has a relatively even mix of both originalism and nonoriginalism such that legal officials have discretion on whether to follow its originalist or nonoriginalist components – then both you and official interpreters will need additional reasons to choose originalism. This state of affairs would mean that originalism is partly a reform project and that it is trying to move legal practice toward a point that is all or mostly originalist. Since the practice itself (by hypothesis) is internally conflicted and does not commit officials to originalism or to nonoriginalism, current American law does not provide a reason for officials to choose one over the other.

The law-as-coordination account of originalism provides reasons for legal officials to choose originalism. This chapter argues that originalism best secures the United States' common good and thereby preserves and protects the conditions for Americans today to flourish. A practically reasonable interpreter will include those reasons in his practical-legal deliberations. It also argues that legal officials themselves are made better persons when they are faithful to the Constitution's original meaning, which is also a reason for them to follow originalism.

4.2.3 *Originalists Must Respond to Critics' Frequent Claim That Originalism Is Substantively Unjust*

Professor David Strauss' first chapter in *The Living Constitution* is titled "Originalism and Its Sins."[4] This is only one instance of the broader phenomenon of critics' common claim that originalism fails as a theory of constitutional interpretation because it leads to unacceptably unjust or imprudent results.[5] Perhaps most famously, Justice Thurgood Marshall argued in his bicentennial speech that the Constitution's origins were mired in slavery and the exclusion and oppression of many Americans so that, as a result, modern Americans should interpret the

---

3 William Baude, Essay, *Is Originalism Our Law?*, 115 COLUM. L. REV. 2349, 2392 (2015); Stephen E. Sachs, *Originalism as a Theory of Legal Change*, 38 HARV. J. L. & PUB. POL'Y 817, 819 (2015).

4 DAVID A. STRAUSS, THE LIVING CONSTITUTION 7 (2010).

5 Paul Brest, *The Misconceived Quest for the Original Understanding*, 60 B. U. L. REV. 204, 222, 229 n.96, 230 (1980); RICHARD H. FALLON, JR., IMPLEMENTING THE CONSTITUTION 22 (2001).

Constitution using non-original meanings.[6] Originalism, Professors Barber and Fleming claimed, "demands that courts uphold admittedly unjust conceptions of constitutional provisions ... [The originalist] contends, in brief, that justice at the wholesale level can demand injustice at the retail level."[7] Professor William Marshall made a nuanced version of this move by evaluating constitutional theories based on whether they support nonoriginalist "landmark decisions."[8] This nonoriginalist criticism is ubiquitous.[9]

My view of this argument is threefold. First, this criticism of originalism is a category mistake. The meaning of a text is distinct from whether that meaning is normatively attractive.[10] A person who receives a letter from an acquaintance that states "You are an a**hole," will not "interpret" the letter to mean something positive. Instead, the recipient will understand the letter's meaning as a negative comment on him. The recipient will not adopt a different theory of "interpretation" to achieve a more positive meaning. Similarly in the legal context, a court will not adopt an unconventional theory of contractual interpretation in the face of contractual language that leads to negative results (from one contracting party's perspective).

The Constitution's meaning and the real-world impact of that meaning are likewise distinct, though – obviously – causally connected. I argued in Section 2.2 that the Constitutional Communication Model described the Framers, Ratifiers, and Americans generally as utilizing the Constitution's original meaning to achieve substantive and normatively attractive goals, such as reducing interstate trade barriers. I also described in Sections 2.3 and 2.4 how substantive justice impacts the Constitution's meaning in the contexts of constitutional construction and nonoriginalist precedent. However, because many scholars and Americans evaluate *theories* of constitutional interpretation on the basis of substantive normative attractiveness, in this chapter I argue that originalism, as a theory of constitutional interpretation, leads to normatively attractive results.

Second, taking the nonoriginalist criticism at face value: all plausible theories of interpretation – not only originalism – are subject to it, and therefore it cannot winnow the nonoriginalist wheat from the originalist chaff. Every plausible theory of interpretation purports to interpret the U.S. Constitution: an artifact created and adopted by limited and imperfect Americans. A purported theory of interpretation that failed, at least occasionally, to reach suboptimal substantive results would not be

---

[6] Thurgood Marshall, *The Bicentennial Speech* (May 6, 1987), http://thurgoodmarshall.com/the-bicentennial-speech/ (visited Sept. 20, 2017).

[7] Sotirios A. Barber & James E. Fleming, Constitutional Interpretation: The Basic Questions 85 (2007).

[8] William P. Marshall, *Progressive Constitutionalism, Originalism, and the Significance of Landmark Decisions in Evaluating Constitutional Theory*, 72 Ohio St. L.J. 1251 (2011).

[9] *See* Joel K. Goldstein, *Constitutional Change, Originalism, and the Vice Presidency*, 16 U. Pa. J. Const. L. 369, 376 n.22 (2013) (listing sources making this claim).

[10] Randy E. Barnett, Restoring the Lost Constitution 109–10 (2004).

a plausible theory of interpretation of that artifact. Therefore, even if one were to evaluate theories of constitutional interpretation based on their normative attractiveness, *every* theory would lead to substantively unattractive results, and the question would be one of *relative* normative attractiveness. This would be a daunting inquiry in a pluralistic society. In this chapter, I argue that originalism leads to normatively more attractive results than other theories.

Third, again taking the criticism at face value: it overstates the unjust results to which originalism leads. A common move by critics of originalism is that the Constitution's meaning, fixed in 1789, or 1867, or 1919, or some other time historical period, did not achieve sufficiently just results and that, therefore, originalism *today* is counted out as a theory of interpretation. For instance, the fact that the Constitution's original meaning did not outlaw slavery in the slave states, or that it did not mandate that states open the franchise to women, shows that originalism is tainted, root and branch.[11] More nuanced critics charged that the Constitution's original meaning, even after amendments to correct more egregious injustices, remained unacceptably normatively flawed. Professor David Strauss, for example, catalogued six current "sins" by originalism.[12]

These and other objections overstate originalism's imperfections. The Constitution's original meaning today is reasonably and adequately – not perfectly – just. Constitutional amendments including, most importantly, the Reconstruction and Nineteenth Amendments, have eliminated unjust constitutional meaning and replaced it with just meaning. Furthermore, within the scope of federal and state power, statutes have achieved just results that the Constitution itself could not. For instance, even if the federal government were not bound by a principle of equal protection,[13] it has produced significant civil rights legislation. Originalism's incorporation of some nonoriginalist precedent further ameliorates possible injustice by requiring the retention of precedent that (from the critics' perspective) provides more-just legal norms. Lastly, of course, the amendment process is a vehicle for changing (by hypothesis) unjust constitutional meaning (once the tremendous disincentive of nonoriginalism is removed).

This chapter details my law-as-coordination account of originalism as a response to this criticism. I argue that originalism is normatively attractive because it provides and protects the background conditions necessary for Americans today to effectively pursue their corporate common good and individual human flourishing. This argument does not entail the claim that the Constitution's original meaning is perfect; it's not, and the law-as-coordination account provides an explanation for why it's not.

---

[11] Thurgood Marshall, *supra* note 6.
[12] STRAUSS, *supra* note 4, at 12–17.
[13] Which is contested.

4.2.4 *The Constitution Makes Normative Claims upon Its Subjects*

Originalism needs a normative account because of the type of document originalism interprets. The Constitution is law, and law makes normative claims on those subject to its sway. Law tells people what to do and what not to do; it provides reasons for humans to take into account in their practical deliberation whether to act or to not act. However, reasonable human beings need – and are entitled to – reasons to act upon the law's reasons; they must know that the larger normative system of which the law's reasons are a part is itself valuable. Humans must know that their law-directed actions and inactions – especially those different from the actions they would otherwise have taken – serve human flourishing. In particular, the law must give its subjects reason to believe that its reasons advance human flourishing.

Ohio's legal system is basically just, while the Soviet Union's was not. Both were legal systems; however, only one gave the humans subject to its sway *reasons* – as opposed to compulsion – for action. Only Ohio's legal system provided sound reasons for Ohioans to cooperate with its laws. It promised – for the most part and generally – to secure the background conditions for Ohioans to flourish, including for instance distributive and commutative justice. The Soviet legal system dictated actions to its subjects; it did not provide distributive or commutative justice and therefore did not – for the most part and generally – provide sound reasons for its subjects to cooperate.

The Constitution makes normative claims on Americans. It tells Americans who are officers how to act. In turn, it authorizes those officers to direct other Americans with the force of law through statutes, executive actions, and judicial orders. Americans therefore need reasons for action: reasons why the Constitution's reasons are valuable and worthy of following are important to justify Americans' following the Constitution. Otherwise, the Constitution would be no better than a dictator ordering Americans without regard for their well-being. The law-as-coordination account provides reasons for Americans to follow the Constitution's and its legal system's reasons.

4.2.5 *Conclusion*

Originalists need to provide a normative account for originalism to provide reasons for American officers and American citizens to employ the Constitution's reasons in their practical deliberations. Though this chapter provides such a normative justification for originalism, it is not a full-throated argument grounded in contested conceptions of justice and good. Instead, as I explain in the following section, the law-as-coordination account is intentionally "thin."

4.3 LAW-AS-COORDINATION IS A "THIN" ACCOUNT

The law-as-coordination account of originalism is "thin," and in three basic ways. First, it is a thin account because it avoids directly relying on the substantive outcomes of constitutional interpretation to support its normative attractiveness. For instance, I do not argue that the Religion Clauses' original meaning is normatively attractive and that, therefore, originalism is a normatively attractive theory of constitutional interpretation because it will lead to that interpretation. Law-as-coordination is not and does not rely on deeply contested claims about substantive constitutional meaning, such as claims about the proper scope of religious liberty. Instead, it relies on premises, claims, and arguments shared with most Americans. It employs arguments and claims, like the existence of coordination problems and the Rule of Law, that enjoy widespread acceptance. From a more descriptive perspective, my argument is thin because it relies on the widely-accepted facets of the origin and operation of our Constitution including, for instance, its unique Framing and Ratification process.

It is common for originalists to make this move. Originalists will typically present their normative arguments for originalism as advancing some good or set of goods that Americans widely share. For instance, Professors McGinnis and Rappaport argued that the Constitution's original meaning secured the most good consequences because it went through supermajoritarian processes.[14] Their claim was agnostic about what particularly counted as good consequences and instead hinged on their less-controversial account of supermajoritarian political processes. Likewise, my law-as-coordination account is agnostic about many important though controversial issues.

Law-as-coordination is thin in a second way. Its argumentative structure currently is tied to the concepts of the common good and human flourishing. The conceptions of these concepts I employ are themselves relatively thin. The conception of the common good used here is the common good as social coordination, and it cashes out into three primary components – the Rule of Law, justice, and offices – that themselves have widespread acceptance. The conception of human flourishing – the excellent pursuit of the basic human goods – employed here is also thin because it does not require one to accept more controversial claims about human nature and metaphysical propositions.

Third, the law-as-coordination account is thin because one may detach it from its grounding in human flourishing. This means that, if one believes that law generally, and the Constitution in particular, serve a function other than securing

[14] John O. McGinnis & Michael B. Rappaport, Originalism and the Good Constitution (2013).

human flourishing, the law-as-coordination account may serve that alternative function too.[15] One would substitute *that* goal for human flourishing in the account and the form of the argument would remain fundamentally the same.

The law-as-coordination account's thinness is a virtue because it allows a wide variety of Americans, with reasonably different conceptions of the good life, to accept its premises. This is valuable, and let me note a second way it is valuable. The law-as-coordination account's thinness also distinguishes it and makes it preferable to many *non*originalist theories. I recounted at the beginning of this chapter how nonoriginalists criticized originalism for leading to (what the critic argued was) substantively unjust interpretations. That criticism frequently assumed a particular – contested – conception of justice, one with which many reasonable Americans of good faith do not agree. For instance, this criticism relies on contested views about the size and role of government, the nature of human sexuality, and contested public policy issues like affirmative action. By contrast, the law-as-coordination account argues that originalism is normatively attractive because it facilitates Americans' coordination. This argument does not rest on such controversial claims and instead rests on the widely accepted function and operations of positive law.

4.4 THE LAW-AS-COORDINATION ACCOUNT OF POSITIVE LAW

4.4.1 *Introduction*

This chapter argues that originalism is the most normatively attractive theory of constitutional interpretation because it best secures the corporate common good, which provides the background conditions that permit Americans to effectively pursue their individual human flourishing. Originalism does so by protecting and following the authoritative, prudential, coordinating decisions made by the Framers and Ratifiers and embodied in the Constitution's original meaning. This is the law-as-coordination account of originalism.

This account utilizes tenets from the Aristotelian philosophical tradition. This subsection summarizes for readers the Aristotelian tradition's conception of positive law as a system of authoritative, prudential, coordinating decisions the purpose of which is to overcome coordination problems, secure societal common good, and promote individual human flourishing. Then, in Section 4.5, I apply this conception of law to the U.S. Constitution.

My description of and arguments for the law-as-coordination account are grounded in the Aristotelian philosophical tradition's conception of human beings,

---

[15] This flexibility makes my law-as-coordination account structurally similar to Professor Barnett's normative justification for originalism. He argued that originalism was normatively justified because it provided adequate assurances that the Constitution and law would respect natural rights. BARNETT, *supra* note 10, at 45. However, as Barnett noted, one could make the same move with good consequences or popular sovereignty or even other conceptions of rights.

law, and legal authority.[16] This is not mechanical application of the tradition's claims; instead, the tradition provides my point of departure for evaluating the U.S. Constitution, its purpose, its authority, and how Americans – especially judges – should interpret it.

I next describe the concepts that are important for my claim that originalism is the best way to interpret the Constitution. These concepts are: human flourishing, natural law, virtue, the common good, authority, and positive law. These concepts will function as the key "tools" I utilize to justify originalism.

4.4.2 *Human Flourishing, Natural Law, and Virtue Ethics*

4.4.2.1 Introduction to the Aristotelian Philosophical Tradition

The Aristotelian philosophical tradition is the central Western philosophical tradition.[17] It has its origin in Greek thought, particularly Aristotle, Plato, and Socrates.[18] In the High Middle Ages,[19] after the fall of the Western Roman Empire, St. Thomas Aquinas began the synthesis of Aristotle's thought with the Christian philosophical inheritance, especially from St. Augustine.[20] The Aristotelian tradition flourished throughout the West until the onset of the Reformation when, due to many factors,[21] other philosophical traditions eclipsed it.[22] The alacrity and comprehensiveness of this move away from the Aristotelian tradition varied. By the late nineteenth century, however – outside of subcultures, such as Catholic institutions – the Aristotelian tradition was eclipsed in the West.[23]

A revival of the tradition occurred in the late nineteenth and early twentieth centuries.[24] Focus on Aquinas' thought characterized what is commonly labeled the

---

[16] I intend my description and use of the tradition to be as ecumenical as possible among different schools of thought, though my arguments are influenced by the sources upon whom I most relied.

[17] ROBERT P. GEORGE, IN DEFENSE OF NATURAL LAW 5 (1999).

[18] ALASDAIR MACINTYRE, WHOSE JUSTICE? WHICH RATIONALITY? 89–90 (1988).

[19] CHRISTOPHER DAWSON, RELIGION AND THE RISE OF WESTERN CULTURE 140–217 (1991).

[20] ALASDAIR MACINTYRE, THREE RIVAL VERSIONS OF MORAL ENQUIRY: ENCYCLOPAEDIA, GENEALOGY, AND TRADITION 120, 123–24 (1990). For a history of Thomism, see ROMANUS CESSARIO, O. P., A SHORT HISTORY OF THOMISM (2005). For a history of late-nineteenth to mid-twentieth century Neo-Thomism, see GERALD A. MCCOOL, S. J., THE NEO-THOMISTS (1994), and GERALD A. MCCOOL, S. J., FROM UNITY TO PLURALISM: THE INTERNAL EVOLUTION OF THOMISM (1989).

[21] ALASDAIR MACINTYRE, AFTER VIRTUE 165 (2d ed. 1984); JAMES GORDLEY, THE PHILOSOPHICAL ORIGINS OF MODERN CONTRACT DOCTRINE 112–21 (1991).

[22] MACINTYRE, *supra* note 18, at 209–13; John Finnis, *Natural Law Theory: Its Past and Its Present*, 57 AM. J. JURIS. 81, 92 (2012).

[23] GORDLEY, *supra* note 21, at 161.

[24] MACINTYRE, *supra* note 20, at 72–77; MCCOOL, THE NEO-THOMISTS, *supra* note 20, at 25–40.

Neo-Scholastic or Neo-Thomistic revival.[25] This revival was, to a large but not complete degree,[26] limited to the Catholic intellectual world. However, this movement fragmented in the late 1950s and early 1960s.[27]

Over the past forty years, nearly contemporaneous revivals of interest in natural law and virtue ethics occurred, especially in the Anglo-American world. The commonly cited initiation of this natural law revival was the publication of John Finnis' *Natural Law and Natural Rights* in 1980. The modern revival of interest in virtue ethics is identified at different dates,[28] but it certainly occurred by the publication of Alasdair MacIntyre's *After Virtue* in 1981. I discuss natural law and virtue ethics as key components of the Aristotelian tradition's account of law in Subsections 4.4.2.3 and 4.4.2.4.

My goal here is to introduce readers to the key facets of the Aristotelian philosophical tradition, not to defend or justify it; that is the role of philosophers and theologians. The Aristotelian tradition has many facets. The key concepts I employ for constitutional interpretation fall into the category of practical philosophy. Practical philosophy's goal is human action, such as ethics, the subject matter of which includes the licitness of human actions.[29]

In the following subsections, I first describe the architectonic concept of human flourishing. Then, I explain the tradition's two primary mechanisms to guide humans to human flourishing: natural law and virtue ethics. Third, I illustrate legal authority's and its positive law's essential role securing the common good – the background conditions – needed for individuals to secure human flourishing.

Then, in Section 4.5, I employ these concepts to argue that the Constitution is the product of legal authority's exercise of creative practical reason to implement the natural law and secure the common good for the United States. This common good, I argue, provides the conditions for Americans to flourish.

4.4.2.2 Key Facets of Human Flourishing: The Basic Human Goods, Practical Reason, and Free Will

The Aristotelian philosophical tradition identifies human flourishing as humans' end, both the goal of a well-lived human life and the goal of discrete practical

---

[25] McCool, From Unity to Pluralism, *supra* note 20, at 29–32; McCool, The Neo-Thomists, *supra* note 20, at 9–11, 31–45, 151–57.

[26] An example of the penetration of the Neo-Scholastic revival was Jacques Maritain's involvement in drafting the U.N. Declaration on Human Rights. Julie Kernan, Our Friend, Jacques Maritain (1975).

[27] McCool, From Unity to Pluralism, *supra* note 20, at 34–35, 224–30.

[28] The revival of interest in virtue ethics is frequently tied to Elizabeth Anscombe's 1958 piece *Modern Moral Philosophy*. In Catholic circles, the Second Vatican Council's call for a renewal of moral theology is frequently cited as the cause for renewed interest in virtue ethics. Cessario, *supra* note 20, at 129–30, 241–42.

[29] Aquinas, at 21, 23–25.

activities. As Aquinas, following Aristotle, pithily put it, "All men agree in desiring the last end, which is happiness."[30] The tradition also shows how humans have the capacity to identify their end and to freely and reasonably pursue it.

Happiness is doing that which a human does as a human, because this shows how specifically human creatures are fully actualized.[31] Humans are distinguished from other creatures by their capacity to reason.[32] A human's unique end, then, consists of acting rationally.

Humans act rationally by reasonably participating in the "basic human goods."[33] The basic human goods are activities in which humans engage and which form the basis, foundation, and goal for all practical activity. These goods are analytically distinct components of overall human flourishing. The basic human goods include at least: life, knowledge, leisure, friendship, beauty, practical reasonableness, justice, and religion.[34]

The goods that are the basic human goods are those that together constitute the good life for beings like us: beings with human characteristics. Human life operates on at least three fundamental (and inter-related) levels including: (1) the basic life functions that maintain our bodily integrity, (2) the activities that pertain to us as social animals, and (3) our rational pursuits.[35] The various basic human goods correspond to those different facets of human life. Humans, for example, need the basic good of life to exist. Or – and unlike Tasmanian Devils – humans need interaction with other humans, including the basic human good of friendship, to flourish. Additionally, because humans speculate about their own life's ultimate meaning in a way that chickens do not, religion is a basic human good for us and not chickens.

The basic human goods are both identified and pursued by a faculty of our minds called practical reason. Practical reason has two key facets. First, it provides humans with the capacity to identify what is truly good for us.[36] Practical reason identifies what is constitutive of happiness. Our practical reason identifies the basic human goods as activities that are valuable and worth pursuing, and their opposites as bad and in need of shunning. Practical reason does so through an unmediated recognition of the basic human goods and not as an inference from some other data source. For example, if you come across a law student studying a case book in the law school library, you perceive the student as engaged in a valuable activity: acquiring knowledge. You know this without drawing an inference from some other

---

[30] ST, I-II, q. 1, a. 7.
[31] *Id.* at I-II, q. 1, a. 7. Aristotle used the term *eudaimonia* to describe the end goal of human action. NE,1095a. Aquinas used the term *beatitudo.* ST, I-II, q. 1, a. 7.
[32] *Id.* at I-II, q. 1, a. 1.
[33] NLNR, at 97.
[34] *Id.* at 85–92.
[35] ST, I-II, q. 94, a. 2.
[36] NLNR, at 64–73.

source of data or metaphysical principle. You do not have to, for instance, read sociological studies on the impact of studying law on human well-being.

Second, practical reason is the capacity to identify the best means to pursue a basic human good, or to coordinate one's overall pursuit of the congeries of basic human goods.[37] The basic human goods do not come prepackaged and easy to assemble. Instead, humans must identify the means to pursue a good, through creation, exchange, or other form of cooperation. For example, to participate in leisure, one might play solitaire, or rent a movie, or play a game of basketball with friends. Each of these pursuits requires planning and execution. Much more challenging is coordinating one's life's pursuit of all of the basic human goods. There are inevitably trade-offs between goods, questions of efficiency, and coordination of goods toward long-term goals, among many, many judgments that one must make. For instance, the pursuit of a profession requires prioritizing the goods associated with that profession over other goods, and most professions necessitate minimizing some goods, such as leisure.

At the same time as the tradition identifies reason as central to human beings' practical life and the pursuit of human flourishing, the tradition also identifies a central role for human will.[38] The will is the capacity that allows humans to choose,[39] both between different goods and between good and bad actions. Human will is necessary for human flourishing for two primary reasons. First, it enables humans to exercise the human trait of freedom. Relatedly, it enables humans to pursue the goods that constitute a full life via the characteristically human manner of rational choice.

Freedom is one of humanity's distinguishing characteristics,[40] and will is the faculty that makes freedom possible.[41] If a human is forced to perform an act against his will, or if the action is performed without human volition (as in the case of sleepwalking), that act is nonhuman.[42] Those nonhuman actions are akin to instinctive actions by nonhuman animals. They are not wrong; they simply are not characteristically human.

Human will, in the Aristotelian tradition, is a "rational appetite" because human will directs humans (only) to goods that, as discussed earlier, are identified as good by practical reason.[43] Human will is rational because it is ordered by practical reason toward participation in the basic human goods. Actions of this rational intellect precede and direct one's will. One's reason, first, identifies some good worthy of

---

[37] *Id.* at 100–25.
[38] ST, I-II, q. 1, a. 1.
[39] *Id.*
[40] *But see* ALASDAIR MACINTRYE, DEPENDENT RATIONAL ANIMALS: WHY HUMAN BEINGS NEED THE VIRTUES (1999).
[41] ST, I-II, q. 1, a. 3.
[42] *Id.* at I-II, q. 1, a. 2.
[43] *Id.* at I-II, q. 1, a. 2 (emphasis deleted).

pursuit, and then one's intellect places that good before one's will's consideration, and lastly one's will pursues that good in conjunction with and through the means devised by one's practical reason.

In sum, human flourishing is the voluntary and rational participation in the basic human goods. Our practical reason identifies those goods and reasonably structures our free pursuit of them. This account of human flourishing will serve as the foundation for my account of positive law generally, and originalism in particular. I argue in Subsection 4.4.4 and Section 4.5 that both positive law and originalism provide the common good – the means – by which Americans today freely and rationally secure their human flourishing.

The Aristotelian tradition identifies two primary mechanisms that facilitate pursuit of human flourishing.[44] The first is natural law and the second is virtue. These two instruments complement each other because natural law provides an "external" guide that facilitates human pursuit of happiness, while virtue provides "internal" guidance.[45] Next, I describe each in turn.

4.4.2.3 Natural Law

Natural law is the body of non-humanly-posited norms that identifies which actions are, and which are not, conducive to human flourishing.[46] One may think of the natural law as containing the "external" guides to human flourishing. They are external because the natural law norms are not chosen by individual humans or a community of humans.[47]

Natural law norms are natural because they are tied to human nature: they identify which actions are conducive to or destructive of human flourishing by reference to a being with human characteristics.[48] Natural law precepts are tied to human nature via the goods that natural law norms direct humans to instantiate.[49] Primary among the characteristics of humans is both a rational and animal nature. For instance, the first principles of practical reason (discussed next in the text) include the directions to act practically reasonably (a manifestation of our rational nature), and to preserve oneself (a manifestation of our animal nature).[50]

---

[44] CESSARIO, *supra* note 20, at 94–95.

[45] *See* ST, I-II, q. 49, introduction (describing virtue as the "intrinsic principle" of human action while natural law is the "extrinsic principle[]").

[46] *Id.* at I-II, q. 90, a. 2.

[47] In the Aristotelian tradition, most historical members of the tradition, and many of the tradition's members today, identify God as the being who promulgated the natural law in and through human nature, and it is this promulgation by someone other than a particular human or humanity in general, that makes natural law "external."

[48] ST, I-II, q. 91, a. 2; *id.* at I-II, q. 94, a. 4; NLNR, at 34.

[49] 1 GERMAIN GRISEZ, THE WAY OF THE LORD JESUS: CHRISTIAN MORAL PRINCIPLES, ch. 5, q. D, a. 11(1983); NLNR, at 59–126.

[50] ST, I-II, q. 94, a. 2.

The first principles of practical reason provide the structure for our practical reasoning. The fundamental first principle of practical reason is to pursue good and avoid evil.[51] The other first principles of practical reason are high-level specifications of that principle.[52] They identify what is good in a general way and, by implication, distinguish what is bad. There are three overarching first principles of natural law: (1) one should preserve oneself and grow and flourish biologically; (2) one should pursue society with fellow humans; and (3) one should engage in rational activity.[53]

These principles of practical reason are the architecture of all practical decision making. They describe *how* humans decide to act in the multitude of situations they face. These first principles of natural law, are *per se nota*, frequently translated, self-evident.[54] This means, at a minimum, that all humans who reflect on their own practical decision making process would identify these as part of the structure of their decision making. For example, when a person decides to act a certain way, they always pursue something they perceive as good (the fundamental first principle of natural law). This is especially in evidence when one later reflects on one's actions and concludes that, though formally pursuing some good, in fact, one was mistaken and should have made a different choice.

Immediately one notices that these first principles of natural law are abstract; too abstract, in fact, to guide most concrete decision making, including legal decision making. The Aristotelian philosophical tradition has identified a number of mediating structures to bridge the analytical gap between these more-abstract natural law norms and the concrete practical situations typically faced by humans. A key such bridge is virtue ethics, described in the following subsection. Other important structures include specification and *determinatio*, which I now describe.

Specification is where relatively abstract natural law principles are applied to specific situations through a practical syllogism with relative confidence, and thereby create more-concrete, intermediate norms.[55] Over the years, the Aristotelian philosophical tradition has recognized a wide array of intermediate – "specified" – norms. These intermediate norms are one mechanism used to bridge the decisional space between general natural law norms and particular practical situations.[56] Intermediate norms can themselves be relatively abstract, such as the prohibition on taking innocent human life,[57] which is derived from the more abstract natural law norms of doing good and avoiding evil and preserving biological human life.

---

[51] *Id.*
[52] AQUINAS, at 79–90.
[53] *Id.*
[54] NLNR, at 64–69.
[55] GEORGE, *supra* note 17, at 52.
[56] Henry S. Richardson, *Specifying Norms as a Way to Resolve Concrete Ethical Problems*, 19 PHIL. & PUB. AFF. 279, 298 (1990).
[57] EXODUS 23:7; ST, q. 100, a. 1.

They may also be relatively concrete, such as the norm permitting the killing of uniformed enemy soldiers in a just war, which is itself a further specification of the more abstract norms just discussed.[58] This process became institutionalized, for a period of time, through the practice of casuistry.[59]

Through this articulation of intermediate norms, the natural law is better able to guide practical conduct. For instance, soldiers have the far easier task of judging whether the war in which they are fighting is just using the criteria set forth in the Just War Tradition, and whether their opponents are uniformed enemy soldiers, than whether they are "doing good and avoiding evil."

Both ethical life and legal practice utilize specification. In ethical life, parents specify the norm "treat others with respect" to prohibit one child from yelling angrily at another child. In our legal system, specification is likewise common. For example, using the same norm, treat others with respect, our legal system prohibits one person from battering another person.

The second primary method of bridging the gap between relatively abstract natural law principles and the concrete realities of life is called *determinatio*. *Determinatio* is a reasoned process of applying the natural law to concrete situations that also involves significant freedom and creativity because of the wide analytical gap between natural law norms and most practical situations. *Determinatio* involves those situations where the distance between the natural law norm and the fact-situation is too great for a practical syllogism to provide confidence in a purported answer. An analogy used by Aquinas to describe this phenomenon is architecture.[60] The rules of physics and requirements of functionality require that a house have more than two sides, that it possess a roof, at least one door, some windows, etc. These are the "natural laws" of architecture within which the architect must work, but they leave wide scope to the architect's freedom and creativity.

Determinatio is ubiquitous in ethical life and in legal practice. To take a homey example, parents wish their children to grow up to be full, happy, well-rounded adults. At least in the United States, one facet of that is some – reasonable – usage of electronic media such as television. At the same time, children must participate in many, many activities other than using electronic media to become full human beings. Parents must make determinations on how much electronic media they will guide their children to utilize. The answer cannot be all of the time, nor can it be none of the time. Parents have creative, though constrained, freedom to determine the appropriate level.

The law is likewise filled with *determinatio*. Indeed, this is the manner by which most positive law implements the natural law.[61] The number of examples is nearly

---

[58] CATECHISM OF THE CATHOLIC CHURCH § 2309 (1993).
[59] The outstanding modern example of casuistry is Germain Grisez's four-volume opus, I-IV GERMAIN GRISEZ, THE WAY OF THE LORD JESUS: CHRISTIAN MORAL PRINCIPLES (1983–1997).
[60] ST, I-II, q. 95, art. 2.
[61] GEORGE, *supra* note 17, at 108–11.

limitless. Driving regulations provide a ubiquitous illustration. Driving regulations are subject to constraints. A regulator must respect the laws of physics: two cars cannot be in the same place at the same time. A regulator wishes to maximize a number of goods, such as speed, efficiency, safety, and environmental protection, which are in some tension with one another and in complex ways. However, within these broad bounds, regulators retain significant freedom and creativity to craft regulations that fit the community and its needs.

Human creativity – the coupling of practical reason and will – plays a key role in implementing the natural law in legal systems because of the roles this creativity plays in specification and, more so, in *determinatio*. Human creativity crafts the positive law's determination within broad bounds. The natural law's "openness" to human agency is also the point at which, in the legal system, positive law is most important. This is because, by hypothesis, without the positive law's determinations, humans could come to many, many reasonable, and many mutually-inconsistent, alternative conclusions, so members of a community would not naturally coalesce around a consensus point. For instance, without highly specific driving regulations, drivers would reasonably utilize the highways in inconsistent manners. Instead, the positive law's determination is crucial to resolving the natural law's indeterminacy and creating the conditions under which humans may live well together.

Natural law is the Aristotelian philosophical tradition's "external" guide to human flourishing. It consists of a set of norms of various levels of abstraction that identify actions conducive to human flourishing and actions harmful to it. The natural law has built into it a need for human practical reason and will to provide posited and more-concrete guides to human life. This sets the stage for my argument that the Constitution and originalism provide this posited, more-concrete guidance to Americans.

4.4.2.4 Virtue Ethics

Virtue is the second key mechanism to guide us to human flourishing.[62] Unlike natural law, virtue is an "internal" guide because it is an aspect of an individual's own habits and character. This character was built up over time through an individual's repeated choosing of virtuous (or vicious) actions. I first summarize virtue ethics, and then I show the relationship between virtue ethics and natural law.

Virtue ethics is primarily characterized by its focus on the concept of virtue, and the related concept of character, in the ethical life.[63] In answer to what is usually taken as the fundamental ethical question of "what sorts of action should I do?,"[64]

---

[62] I introduced virtue ethics earlier in Subsection 2.6.2, so my explanation here will focus on virtue ethics' relationship to human flourishing.

[63] ROSILAND HURSTHOUSE, ON VIRTUE ETHICS 1 (1997).

[64] *Id.* at 26.

a virtue theorist answers, "what a virtuous agent would characteristically ... do in the circumstances."[65]

Virtue is a habit[66] – an entrenched disposition of character[67] – to perform a type of human activity well. For example, the virtue of fortitude enables one to ascertain what courage requires in concrete situations and to willingly act accordingly.[68] Virtues enable persons to perform activities excellently. A person who possesses fortitude will know what courage requires in particular situations, have the intellectual disposition to act courageously when called to do so, be emotionally disposed to act courageously, and will reliably act courageously.[69]

The acquisition of virtue is like the acquisition of any habit. One must, first, perform acts consistent with virtue and, after the habit has formed (or during the process), one comes to realize that these virtuous acts are valuable in themselves, and then one pursues the acts because one enjoys acting virtuously. But the converse is also true. One can acquire a vice by continuously performing vicious acts. One then becomes more and more corrupt, less able to resist the vice and less able to pursue virtue.

Virtue is both constitutive of human flourishing and instrumental to securing it. Human flourishing is the state of being most fully human, which means acting rationally excellently.[70] A person's excellent utilization of his faculties is acting virtuously.[71] Therefore, human flourishing is partially constituted by virtue.

Virtue also equips humans to achieve human flourishing.[72] The virtues are those habits of character that perfect the portion of their possessor to which they apply.[73] For example, a human does not flourish if he is not temperate. A person who characteristically eats excessively has the vice of intemperance.[74] That person has difficulty controlling his pursuit of physical goods, like food and drink. The desire for food controls the person[75] so that the person acts, not in accord with his practical reason, but instead by dictate of his passion. This person, because of his lack of virtue, is prevented from flourishing. To flourish, the intemperate person must acquire the means to do so – a temperate disposition.

Let me say a few more words about the relationship between natural law and virtue ethics. The virtues work hand in hand with natural law directives to facilitate

---

[65] *Id.* at 28.
[66] ST, I-II, q. 56, a. 3.
[67] HURSTHOUSE, *supra* note 63, at 10–12.
[68] JOSEF PIEPER, THE FOUR CARDINAL VIRTUES: PRUDENCE, JUSTICE, FORTITUDE, TEMPERANCE 115–41 (1965).
[69] *See* HURSTHOUSE, *supra* note 63, at 10–12 (making a similar claim regarding honesty).
[70] ST, I-II, q. 1, a. 1; *id.* at I-II, q. 3, a. 5.
[71] *Id.* at I-II, q. 3, a. 2.
[72] *Id.* at I-II, q. 49, introduction; *id.* at I-II, q. 55, a. 1.
[73] *Id.* at I-II, q. 55, a. 1.
[74] *Id.* at II-II, q. 148, a. 1.
[75] The intemperate person is, to his degree of intemperance, unfree.

pursuit of human flourishing. Most important, the virtue of practical wisdom perfects one's capacity to correctly *identify* the principles of natural law via identification of the goods toward which natural law directs human actions.[76] Practical wisdom also facilitates the choice of the best *means* to secure the basic human goods.[77]

The moral virtues ensure that one's appetites for goods are properly ordered by one's reason.[78] This ensures that one's vision of what the natural law requires is not blurred, and that one's passions do not overawe one's (otherwise correct) judgment about what the natural law requires one to do. In sum, virtue and natural law are complementary tools that work hand in hand to facilitate one's pursuit of happiness.

The virtues assist, not only with improving particular facets of human beings themselves, such as temperance and one's appetites, but also the roles and tasks humans perform. Parenting, for instance, requires the virtue of (sometimes tremendous!) patience on the part of parents. Flourishing family life also requires the virtue of obedience by children to their parents. Particular vocations also require corresponding virtues. Judges, for example, must possess the virtue of justice-as-lawfulness, the disposition to follow the law.

As I will explain, the Aristotelian philosophical tradition has developed a line of thought as part of virtue ethics that describes the habits of character necessary to make relationships of authority function as well as possible. The person or persons occupying authority roles need the virtues particular to the specific types of authority they exercise. A parent, for instance, needs the particular form of practical wisdom geared toward rearing children. A legislator, whose purview encompasses the entire society, needs the virtue of political wisdom.[79] A child and a citizen also both need virtues corresponding to their respective and different positions. A child's virtue includes obedience to parents. This obedience is initially nearly-unquestioning and slowly, as the child grows into an adult, moves toward that of a free and equal friend. A citizen's proper virtue is rational engagement in the society's political and legal systems as an independent, patriotic member of the society.

In sum, virtue ethics is the internal guide humans possess to identify and secure human flourishing. This account will form the foundation for my arguments that the virtues help explain why interpreters should follow the original meaning and provide tools to best do so.

---

[76] ST, I-II, q. 94, a. 1; NLNR, at 34.

[77] NLNR, at 88.

[78] ST, I-II, Q. 94, art. 4; NLNR, at 88.

[79] For an aretaic theory of legislation see Lawrence B. Solum, *Virtue as the End of Law: An Aretaic Theory of Legislation*, 9 JURIS. 6 (2018).

4.4.3 *Social Beings Pursuing the Common Good and Human Flourishing through Legal Authority and Law*

In the prior subsection, I described the goal of human beings to secure human flourishing, and how natural law and virtue were complimentary aids in that quest. In this subsection, I show that humans pursue human flourishing in a society that secures the common good through positive law created by legal authority. To do so, I make three moves. First, I describe humans' social nature. Second, I describe the common good. Third, I show that society can secure the common good only via legal authority and the positive law it promulgates. I then use these arguments in Section 4.5 to explain the Constitution as the product of the Framing and Ratification's promulgation of positive law to secure America's common good.

4.4.3.1 Humans Flourish as Part of a Community with Others

Aristotle famously said that "man is by nature a political animal."[80] This central commitment of the tradition is built on a number of bases. First, living in society directly facilitates human flourishing by providing the means to exercise many of the basic human goods, such as friendship. Second, society indirectly facilitates human flourishing by providing the background conditions – a just order, material, spiritual, and cultural goods – that make the pursuit of happiness possible. This latter basis is most relevant to my argument.

Social life is necessary for human flourishing because it provides the social, material, spiritual, and cultural background that makes the pursuit of excellence possible, and in two key ways. First, the fact of human dependency makes solo human flourishing practically impossible, and, second, individual *in*ability to secure the basic human goods by oneself makes solo human flourishing practically impossible.

First, humans are dependent throughout our lives.[81] We are born entirely helpless. Without parents (or, lacking that, other people to care for him), an infant quickly dies. Indeed, the level of care needed for an infant to robustly grow and develop is high, and infants therefore require significant "investment" by parents (or others). Similarly, at the end of life – and often enough at some point during an individual's life – an individual becomes significantly dependent on others for both his basic and higher needs. Frequently, an individual's dependency requires considerable assistance by family and others. Indeed, it is this phenomenon that made

---

[80] ARISTOTLE, *supra* note 1, at 1253a.
[81] This discussion is drawn from ALASDAIR MACINTYRE, DEPENDENT RATIONAL ANIMALS: WHY HUMANS NEED THE VIRTUES (1999).

Justice Ginsburg's claims in *NFIB* v. *Sebelius* about health insurance need and usage powerful.[82]

Beyond the expected occasions of dramatic of human dependency, however, throughout our lives, we are periodically dependent on others because of impairment. Perhaps we are overcome with grief at the passing of a spouse, and we need family and friends to provide emotional support. Or, perhaps we have developed an addiction, and family and friends intervene to break the addiction. In these and countless other unexpected ways, we are dependent on our fellow humans.

Furthermore, humans are all born with the capacity for virtue.[83] However, we need education and training to enable us to actualize virtue. For some, the guidance of parents is enough to lead them to virtue. For others, something more is needed. That something may include effective societal intervention to prevent the individual from harming himself and/or others, and to help the individual continue his advancement toward his virtue. For example, the legal proscription against theft not only prevents theft, it also acts as a pedagogue to (especially, young) people and habituates (especially, young) people to not take others' goods.

Second, society is necessary to provide support for individuals to access the basic human goods. Though it is theoretically possible to participate in some of the basic human goods without other people, such as leisure, it is practically impossible to flourish on one's own.[84] For instance, one can hardly acquire knowledge except from another who has knowledge of the subject, either immediately from a teacher or mediately from an author. Or, though one could conceivably participate in the basic human good of religion solely on one's own, few, if any, people do so. Instead, religious inquiry and expression nearly invariably contain communal elements. This includes receiving, passing along, expressing, and discussing religious beliefs or the concepts within which religious beliefs are conceptualized and expressed.

Through the division of labor and cooperation, both private and public, societies provide the ensemble of goods and conditions needed for individual flourishing. The division of labor, coupled with cooperation, does two important things. First, it allows greater productivity, both in quantity and diversity of goods, than was otherwise possible.[85] The division of labor applies to material goods, of course, but it also applies to other goods – including, for instance, the good of religion, where theologians focus their energies on particular facets of that good.

---

[82] *NFIB* v. *Sebelius*, 567 U.S. 519, 590–92 (2012) (Ginsburg, J., dissenting).

[83] NE, 1103a.

[84] The cases of feral children suggest that humans who do not live in community with other humans fail to develop many of the basic faculties of humans, including even language. *See, e. g.*, Laura Smith, *Literally raised by wolves, this Indian boy was found wandering in the wilderness as a six-year-old*, TIMELINE (Nov. 20, 2017) (describing the story of Dina Sanichar), https://timeline.com/dina-sanichar-feral-children-ea9f5f3a80b2 (visited Sept. 19, 2018).

[85] ST. THOMAS AQUINAS, ON THE GOVERNANCE OF RULERS (DE REGIMINE PRINCIPUM) 34–35 (Gerald B. Phelan trans., Sheed & Ward 1938).

The historical evolution of human communities from the family unit shows the value of the division of labor. From clans and tribes consisting of related families, the larger society expanded into the city-state, and later the modern nation-state was born. The twentieth century has seen the establishment of the United Nations and calls for a global state.[86] At each step along the way toward the nation-state (and arguments for a global state), the needs of humans – spiritual, intellectual, and material – compelled the further expansion of society. Each larger unit of society was better able to provide for its members' wants and needs and better enabled its members to reach their end.

Second, the various goods produced through the division of labor are exchanged and the participants in the exchanges mutually enriched. Much of this exchange occurs, at least in the United States, in the market system. It occurs, however, against a nonmarket background of social and legal norms that ground and structure the market. Additionally, exchange also occurs through nonmarket governmental means, to effectuate distributive justice among members of the society.

This subsection argued that human beings must live in a community in order to flourish. The brute fact of living in a community is, however, by itself not sufficient to create the conditions for flourishing. Instead, the following subsection identifies three key mechanisms by which community members work together for their own and each other's benefit.

4.4.3.2 The Common Good as Social Coordination: Justice, the Rule of Law, and Offices

This subsection describes the common good. The conception of the common good I employ here is intentionally thin.[87] The common good is central to my argument because it is going to be one of the primary reasons interpreters employ in their practical deliberations to justify following the Constitution's original meaning.

---

[86] JACQUES MARITAIN, MAN AND THE STATE 188–94 (1951).

[87] There is robust debate over different conceptions of the common good. *See, e.g.*, Mark C. Murphy, *The Common Good*, 59 REV. OF METAPHYSICS 133, 133–64 (2005) (describing three conceptions of the common good, including instrumental, aggregative, and distinctive conceptions). My tentative view is that my argument does not depend on a particular conception of the common good because, under any of the conceptions, the common good is at least a means to secure individual human flourishing. This is labeled the instrumental conception, and it is the one I employ. *See* George Duke, *The Common Good*, in NATURAL LAW JURISPRUDENCE 382–83 (George Duke & Robert P. George eds., 2017) (proposing a synthesis of the three conceptions). Special thanks to Dr. V. Bradley Lewis for his advice on the relevant scholarship in this area including his own valuable work. V. Bradley Lewis, *Is the Common Good an Ensemble of Conditions?*, 84 ARCHIVIA DI FILOSOFIA 121 (2016); V. Bradley Lewis, *Personalism and Common Good, Thomistic Political Philosophy and the Turn to Subjectivity* 175, in SUBJECTIVITY ANCIENT AND MODERN (R.J. Snell & Steven McGuire, eds., 2016); V. Bradley Lewis, *Aristotle, The Common Good, and Us*, 87 PROCS. OF THE AM. CATHOLIC PHIL. ASS'N 60 (2013).

The common good is the common ordering – the common working together – of a society's members to achieve their communal and individual goods. In the Aristotelian tradition, there is a connection between human flourishing and the common good because the common good is the ensemble of conditions in a society that enables the society's members to flourish as individuals.[88] The common good includes "a set of conditions which enables the members of a community to obtain for themselves reasonable objectives, or to realize reasonably for themselves the value(s), for the sake of which they have reason to collaborate with each other."[89] With the common good, individual flourishing can occur more fruitfully, and humans therefore have reason to support the common good.

The common good is the metric by which one measures whether a society is successful or failing *as a society*. Without the common good, a society is wicked and/ or inept; with the common good, a society is properly performing its supportive role for human life.[90]

For the purpose of my focus on constitutional interpretation, I describe two important facets of the common good's social coordination: justice, and the Rule of Law. Then, I describe the offices that are the necessary instruments for social coordination via justice and the Rule of Law.

First, justice is giving each his due.[91] It has two components: commutative and distributive justice. Both govern the allocation of goods in a society, broadly conceived to include material and nonmaterial goods.

Distributive justice concerns the overall distribution of goods in a society. Distributive justice requires that societies distribute goods in such a manner that each member has the capacity to live a distinctively human life.[92] As Aristotle noted, without sufficient material, cultural, religious, and intellectual resources, a human cannot live a virtuous life.[93] Each society – and the same society at different points in time – will have different amounts and distributions of these goods; hence, what distributive justice requires is relative to the society's circumstances.[94]

Commutative justice governs the relationship between a small number of identifiable individuals. Commutative justice ensures that participants in exchanges[95]

---

[88] The common good is "nothing else than the unification of men for the purpose of performing some one thing in common." St. Thomas Aquinas, Contra Impugnantes Dei Cultum Et Religionem, at iii, *quoted in* The Political Ideas of St. Thomas Aquinas: Representative Selections, at x–xi (Dino Bigongiari ed., 1953).

[89] NLNR, at 155.

[90] The common good is therefore analogous to human flourishing in an individual. Both are the goals or ends towards which and the purposes to which they—societies and individuals—aim.

[91] For discussions of justice in the tradition, see ST, II-II, at qq. 57–61; NE 1129a–1138b; NLNR, at 161–97.

[92] NLNR, at 166–67.

[93] NE, 1130b, 1020a-b, 1144b.

[94] Gordley, *supra* note 21, at 13.

[95] Both voluntary and nonvoluntary.

receive approximately the same or greater goods than the goods they conveyed.[96] It requires that individuals treat others in such a way during transactions that the transactions do not deprive others of their just share of society's goods. Much of private law is most directly associated with commutative justice.[97] For example, property law governs how individuals interact with the world's resources and with other individuals' property. One such rule of property law governs the relationship between the owner of a driveway easement, the dominant tenant, and the owner of the land upon which the easement travels, the servient tenant. American property law provides a detailed inventory of the respective rights and duties of both tenants. These aspects of easement law coordinate how individual Americans coordinate their property relations, and these laws are an aspect of commutative justice.

Commutative justice is related to distributive justice[98] because appropriate norms of commutative justice are needed to preserve or facilitate a distributively-just distribution of goods in society. For instance, insufficiently robust laws of trespass and ejection could upset the distribution of real property by permitting nonconsensual acquisition by people with relatively greater power.

Justice is a central facet of the common good. Justice prescribes guidelines for the quantity and mix of goods for each member of society, so that they can effectively pursue their own flourishing. Without distributive justice, at least some members of society would not have the resources needed for flourishing, and other may have such a superabundance that they become vicious. For example, if education were reserved only for a segment of society, then the children of other members would not have the tools to fully actualize their potential. Without commutative justice, a reasonably just distribution of resources would be upset after a series of unjust transactions, depriving some members of the capacity to flourish. For instance, the more powerful members of a society could utilize their power to take goods from less-powerful members.

The second key aspect of the common good is the Rule of Law. The Rule of Law is the governance of law over human affairs, rather than discretionary, ad hoc decisions made by humans regarding other humans.[99] The Rule of Law's contribution to the common good is both intrinsic and instrumental. In both modes of contribution, the Rule of Law facilitates individual human flourishing.

The Rule of Law is intrinsically valuable because, "[w]here it is observe[d], people are confronted by a state which treats them as rational agents due some

---

[96] GORDLEY, *supra* note 21, at 8.
[97] AQUINAS, at 200.
[98] GORDLEY, *supra* note 21, at 8.
[99] NLNR, at 270–71; LON L. FULLER, THE MORALITY OF LAW 39 (rev. ed. 1969); Joseph Raz, *The Rule of Law and Its Virtue*, 93 LAW Q. REV. 195 (1977). For an earlier and influential formulation of the components of the Rule of Law, *see* A.V. DICEY, INTRODUCTION TO THE STUDY OF THE LAW OF THE CONSTITUTION 202–03 (10th ed. 1960).

respect as such."[100] Human beings grasp and act based on practical reasons.[101] "Laws," in turn, "provide beings capable of grasping and acting on reasons with (additional) reasons for action"[102] because laws facilitate social cooperation, without which the members of a society could not achieve many goods or achieve goods as effectively.[103] Therefore, the Rule of Law, which provides members of a society with reasons for action,[104] treats the members respectfully – as rational beings – and is valuable as a result. With the Rule of Law, the members of a society are treated as they are: as reasoning beings.

Instrumentally, the Rule of Law is a necessary facet of the background environment so that members of a society can pursue goods constitutive of human flourishing. The primary manner in which the Rule of Law facilitates the common good is that it is the means by which legal authority overcomes coordination problems. I describe this function in the following subsection.

For our immediate purposes, the Rule of Law is also instrumentally valuable because it provides a relatively stable and relatively secure environment, one free from arbitrary manipulation.[105] Building an individual life is a long-term endeavor, and it requires frequent interaction with other people. Building communal life for communities is even more challenging. Life-building of either sort cannot occur, or cannot occur effectively, if the "rules of the game" change unexpectedly or if other people[106] can arbitrarily undermine one's or one's community's pursuit of a life plan. For instance, if private property law relationships are subject to sudden or arbitrary change, then individuals will not invest in long-term property relationships such as family housing or land for businesses.

Distributive justice is fundamentally related to the Rule of Law because it includes, as one facet within its purview, the good of the Rule of Law. Distributive justice requires that the legal system's benefits and burdens be apportioned fairly among the law's subjects. The fundamental equality of all people as reasonable beings requires the law to burden and benefit people equally. For example, it would be unjust for a citizen to not follow the law in situations where the legal system burdens her and follow it (and expect others to follow it) when it benefits her. A driver should not follow only those traffic laws that benefit her while expecting other drivers to follow all the traffic laws. That driver would receive the legal system's benefits, but not its restrictions, and thereby off-load those restrictions on her fellow citizens.

---

[100] Neil MacCormick, *Natural Law and the Separation of Law and Morals, in* Natural Law Theory: Contemporary Essays 105, 123 (Robert P. George ed., 1992).

[101] George, *supra* note 17, at 116.

[102] *Id.* at 120.

[103] NLNR, at 155.

[104] George, *supra* note 17, at 120.

[105] NLNR, at 272–73.

[106] Both private and public individuals.

In sum, without justice and the Rule of Law, a society's coordination of its members will not exist or exist in limited form. In either case, the members of such a society would not be able to effectively pursue their human flourishing. For example, absent the Rule of Law, private property would not be safe from government or private theft. At the same time, such depredations would violate commutative justice and ultimately distributive justice. By securing a just order, the society ensures that its members can carry on their daily work of securing the basic human goods unmolested. To achieve a just order, the society will impose standards of conduct on its members and enforce those standards through social institutions.

Third, societies create offices with political authority to curate the common good. The purpose of these offices is to oversee the common good either for portions of society (in the case of a federal administrative agency, a state court judge, or a town mayor) or the entire society (in the case of a king, a president, a parliament, or a Congress). Such offices are necessary because individuals and subsidiary entities, in the reasonable pursuit of their own goods, may pursue goods or pursue them in such a manner that society's overall pursuit of the common good is harmed.

This can occur for a number of reasons. Here, I will briefly identify two.[107] First, an individual's or subsidiary entity's good may conflict with the overall common good. For example, a father may want his son to attend college and engage in the profession of the son's choice, whereas, because of a dire war, the society needs the son for military service, which may entail the son's death, and the responsible officer conscripts the son for that purpose. The father in this scenario rightly wills his son's happiness. However, the officer, who has the care of the entire society's common good, has the authority to – and rightly does so – conscript the son for service of the common good.

Second, different individuals and subsidiary entities, in the reasonable pursuit of their respective goods, may clash. The common good requires that an officer have authority to coordinate these respective pursuits, so that all the pursuits are as effective as possible and consistent with the overall common good. For example, the Fish and Wildlife Service reasonably working to protect an endangered species of animals under the Endangered Species Act may come into dispute with the Tennessee Valley Authority reasonably constructing a dam that would limit flooding and provide electricity.[108] Since both the Service and the Authority are reasonably pursuing their objectives, the common good needs an officer who has care of the overall societal common good to decide what the common good in fact requires in that dispute.

Like the Rule of Law, though even more so, these offices – including their existence, duration, jurisdiction, structure, and powers – are a positive creation and

---

[107] A more fulsome explanation of the need for political and legal authority is provided in the next subsection.
[108] *Tennessee Valley Auth. v. Hill*, 437 U.S. 153 (1978).

are not in their particulars a requirement of the natural law. There is no natural law norm that requires the lodging of official authority in a particular person or institution. As a result, the officers of a particular society receive their political and legal authority from that society's prudential, coordinating decisions. For instance, one's neighbor could not regally proclaim herself the neighborhood watch-leader because, whether that position exists and its characteristics, are not determined by natural law and are instead created by one's community's members and conventions.

The particular coordinations each society makes to achieve the common good are heavily context dependent. More specifically, justice, the Rule of Law, and offices are open to a wide variety of reasonably different instantiations. A society may choose from different manners of ordering economic life as well as private life. It may choose the Anglo-American common law or continental civil law system. A society can also order itself under various forms of government, various governmental structures, and various legal regimes. One cannot, as Robert P. George has argued,

> [I]dentify a uniquely correct scheme of ... regulation which can be translated from the natural law to the positive law ... A number of different schemes—bearing different and often incommensurable costs and benefits, risks and advantages—are consistent with natural law. So the legislator must exercise a kind of creativity in choosing a scheme. He must move, not by deduction, but rather by an activity of the practical intellect that Aquinas called *determinatio.*[109]

This description of the common good as social coordination sets up my argument in Section 4.5 that the Constitution is American society's key mechanism to secure the common good. It does so through securing justice and the Rule of Law through the machinery of offices.

Not explicitly discussed thus far in my description of the common good – though latent throughout the discussion – is the subject of authority. In the next subsection, I describe the Aristotelian philosophical tradition's conception of authority generally, and then focus on legal authority. My description will show that authority is necessary for effective pursuit of the common good because of authority's essential role coordinating society's members which, in turn, is necessary for members of society to pursue their own flourishing. Thereafter, I describe the crucial role played by a legal authority's positive law in the natural law tradition.

4.4.3.3 The Need for Authority, Particularly Legal Authority, to Secure the Common Good

4.4.3.3.1 INTRODUCTION In the preceding subsection, I described the common good as social coordination of society's members, and I particularly focused on the coordination provided by justice and the Rule of Law through the mechanism of

---

[109] GEORGE, *supra* note 17, at 108.

offices. Here, I argue that the social coordination that constitutes the common good is *necessarily* the result of authority and, in particular, legal authority.[110] This account of authority will support my argument in Section 4.5 that the Constitution's original meaning is authoritative and operates as an exclusionary reason in judges' interpretive calculus because of its capacity to secure the common good.

4.4.3.3.2 AUTHORITY INSTEAD OF UNANIMOUS CONSENT TO SECURE THE COMMON GOOD Before describing authority in greater detail, let me first briefly dispose of a possible alternative account of social coordination and law: consent. Perhaps, one might think, members of a society can coordinate their activities and render laws doing so authoritative through their consent. This account is attractive because we normally think of people as possessing the capacity to consent to ethical and legal obligations. I argue that there are two primary reasons why consent cannot be the basis for the social coordination needed for the common good. First, unanimous consent is unlikely under the conditions of large societies. Second, unanimous consent is unsecurable when there are reasonably different means of pursuing the common good.

First, consent is not practical in large, complex societies like the United States. Human beings are rational and free agents. Consequently, they may bind themselves to commitments, including commitments that limit their freedom. Odysseus' binding himself to his ship's mast to control himself is a classic example.[111] In a small, simple community, the community could *perhaps* operate on a principle of unanimous consent. These communities are characterized by trust, face-to-face transactions, and long-term relationships. Married couples may be an example of this. The family does nothing that both husband and wife do not agree to.[112] Small religious communities, such as monasteries, may be another example. However, these conditions do not obtain in the United States.[113] As Finnis pithily put it: "Now there is no need to labor the point that unanimity about the desirable solution to a specific co-ordination problem cannot in practice be achieved in any community with a complex common good."[114]

Second, and more fundamentally, consent is unsecurable because there are reasonably different ways to pursue the common good in a society of more-than-modest

---

[110] My account of authority is primarily derived from YVES SIMON, A GENERAL THEORY OF AUTHORITY *passim* (1962); NLNR, at 231–90; 4 John Finnis, *Law as Coordination, in* THE COLLECTED ESSAYS OF JOHN FINNIS 66 (1989) (2011); 4 John Finnis, *Law's Authority and Social Theory's Predicament, in* THE COLLECTED ESSAYS OF JOHN FINNIS 46 (1984) (2011); *see also* JEAN PORTER, MINISTERS OF THE LAW: A NATURAL LAW THEORY OF LEGAL AUTHORITY (2010).

[111] THE ODYSSEY OF HOMER 173 (S. H. Butcher & A. Lang trans., 1909)

[112] This spousal consent could take the form of agreement to a particular familial action, or it could take the form of agreement to a division of authority by which different spouses possess different spheres of primary decision-making authority.

[113] BARNETT, *supra* note 10, at 9.

[114] NLNR, at 232–33.

complexity. To take a classic example, every reasonable person would agree that safe highway usage is a facet of the common good in the United States under current societal conditions. In the United States, automobile use of the highways is necessary for individual flourishing. Most Americans need to travel on roads to purchase food, educate their children, engage in gainful employment, receive healthcare, meet with friends, and for leisure. There are, however, numerous reasonable and mutually-exclusive means to pursue that facet of the common good. Highway usage is a complex coordinated activity, and most of the particular manners of cooperation are arbitrary. For instance, the speed for a particular stretch of road, or for a certain category of roads, could reasonably be set at a number of different points.

Furthermore, the range of reasonableness increases as the complexity of the subject good increases. Complexity is compounded by the nearly infinite variety of *combinations* of means to pursue highway safety. For instance, add to the simple speed limit hypothetical, the additional variables of car design safety, road design, and driver habits, and there emerge a wide array of reasonable combinations to secure reasonable highway safety.

But the complexity of coordinating all of these individual conventions is exponentially compounded by the multifarious *interactions* among them. This is challenging because of the sheer scope of the coordination and because of the trade-offs between the various particular possible coordinations. The speed limit bumps into safety and environmental impact. Vehicle safety bumps into environmental impact and efficiency and so on. In principle, there is not a uniquely correct *system* of coordination for highway usage. Effective use of the highways thus presents a deep coordination problem.

This complexity is further compounded by the interaction of the good of highway safety with other components of the common good. Highway safety, along with some of the variables that constitute a reasonable approach to highway safety, interacts with other facets of the common good. For example, highway safety has a complex relationship with productivity. To pick just two facets of that relationship: on the one hand, the safer highways are, the fewer man-hours that are lost from work, while, on the other hand, if highway safety is increased by reduced speeds, than more man-hours are used driving. As summarized by Yves Simon, "[t]he existence of a plurality of genuine means in the pursuit of the common good excludes unanimity as a sufficient method of steadily procuring unity of action."[115]

This phenomenon – where reasonable members of a community cannot rationally arrive at a mutually-agreed-upon path to pursue a good like highway travel – is called a coordination problem. Coordination problems are obstacles to achieving the social cooperation necessary for individuals to effectively pursue the common good and their own human flourishing. Coordination problems occur in situations

---

[115] SIMON, *supra* note 110, at 47.

where everyone in a society has reason to cooperate with others in a particular, unified manner but, because a specific mode of cooperation is underdetermined – because there are multiple reasonable, yet mutually exclusive, means to cooperate – a consensus will not spontaneously arise, making coordination impossible. I rely on this concept of coordination problems when I show how positive law is the key mechanism to overcome them, and I argue that the Constitution is our society's solution to fundamental coordination problems.

For these reasons, consent is not a possible route to secure the coordination necessary for the common good. This leaves only an authority crafting coordinating decisions toward the common good.

4.4.3.3.3 THE NATURE AND ORIGINS OF LEGAL AUTHORITY Authority is pervasive in human life; it is natural. In family life, children are under their parents' authority. In the workplace, employees are subject to their bosses' authority. In religious life, leaders authoritatively articulate and apply religious doctrines. And, of course, in political and legal spheres, authorities decide political and legal issues. And yet, scholars have struggled to articulate the contours and justification – and limits – of authority.

In the Aristotelian philosophical tradition, authority is the characteristic of a person or institution that warrants the authority directing the actions of those subject to the authority's directives because that characteristic provides sound reasons for those subject to the authority to follow the authority's directives. For example, parents possess the natural capacity to direct their children's practical activities and are hence their children's authority because the parents' authority helps the children flourish. Authority plays an essential role securing the common good and human flourishing. Without authority, a community would not be able to overcome coordination problems and effectively pursue the common good, and the community's members would not be able to effectively pursue human flourishing. This rationale both justifies authority's existence and identifies its limitations.

Authority's authority is justified by its "perfective" rationale[116] – its capacity to help its subjects secure the basic human goods. An authority enables its society's members to achieve human flourishing in a way the members would not be able to absent the authority. Parents possess natural authority over their children because the parents direct their children toward flourishing adulthood. Similarly, as I discuss in Subsection 4.4.4, legal authority rightfully directs those subject to its authority via positive law because of the legal authority's crucial role creating and preserving the common good.

At the same time, this rationale limits authority to those instances when the structure of authoritative directives employed by the authority facilitates its subjects' flourishing. For instance, parents who systematically fail to direct their children

---

[116] SIMON, *supra* note 110, at 22.

toward flourishing adulthood should lose control of their children. Similarly, as I describe in Subsection 4.4.3.3.6, legal authority loses its justification when it systemically fails to achieve the common good. Legal authority's authority is therefore presumptive and defeasible.

Authority arises both naturally and conventionally.[117] The mix of nature and convention varies, but all human relationships of authority contain facets of both, and these different facets complement each other. Authority is natural, for instance, in family relationships, between parents and children, though, even here, there is a large measure of convention. For example, in American families today, authority typically resides with the nuclear family's parents over their children, while in ancient Rome, by contrast, the *paterfamilias* possessed authority over all his descendants.[118]

Authority is also conventional; for example, the coach of a youth basketball team exercises a socially-constructed scope and depth of authority over the team members. Even here, however, there is an aspect of the coach's authority that is natural. The coach's authority is natural because the purposes served by the basketball team are natural. The team is constituted for leisure, one of the basic human goods, and also character formation for the team members, an aspect of rearing one's children, among other natural purposes. The coach's authority is necessary to achieve these natural purposes, and is therefore natural.

Political authority – the authority in a political community such as the United States – is likewise both conventional and natural. The natural law does not identify one person or institution in a particular society as the uniquely correct political authority.[119] One neighbor has no authority to say to another neighbor: "You must mow your yard at least once a week." That bossy neighbor has no "neighborhood authority" to issue such a command. Instead, political authority is constituted through convention.[120] Conventions identifying political authorities may arise in

---

[117] This argument is drawn from PORTER, *supra* note 110.

[118] H.F. JOLOWICZ & BARRY NICHOLAS, HISTORICAL INTRODUCTION TO THE STUDY OF ROMAN LAW 119 (3d ed., 1972).

[119] To the extent that the Catholic Church is a temporal political society, its leadership is uniquely correct because the institutions of leadership and the membership of at least the Bishopric of Rome are divinely identified. Vatican II, *Christus Dominus* § 2 (1965); John Paul II, *Fundamental Law of Vatican City State*, Art. 1, § 1 (Nov. 26, 2000); CODE OF CANON LAW § 331 (1983).

[120] Here, I put to one side the unusual situations where political authority is not based on human convention – at least not solely – and is instead identified by divine proclamation, such as the case of the Jewish People, 1 KINGS 16: 12–13, and Roman Catholic Church. MATTHEW 16:18–19.

any number of ways: through slow accretion,[121] rational social designation,[122] or sheer brute force.[123]

Political authority also has natural facets to it. Political authority is natural primarily because it serves natural purposes. Political authority has the over-arching supervision of a society, and it therefore has care of the society's common good. Securing the common good is *the* key natural purpose of political authority, and a political authority's pursuit of that goal is subject to natural constraints, such as justice.

Political authority serves its natural purpose in many ways. One is to provide a forum for the citizens of the society to exercise their own practical-political rationality by participating in the political process (at all levels). Citizens deliberate with each other and with their political leaders about the common good and how best to secure it. For example, in the United States, one of the perennial subjects of debate and discussion is the relative relationship of the federal and state governments both generally[124] and regarding specific issues.

For purposes of my argument, the fundamental way political authority serves its natural purposes is by establishing legal authority. Legal authority is the aspect of a society's legal system that creates and authorizes the society's positive law. Legal authority is a necessary mechanism to enable a society to pursue the common good and to help its members pursue their own human flourishing. Legal authority is tasked with providing legal directions to implement the indeterminate natural law and provide sufficient guidance to a society's members so that they can cooperate in the way(s) necessary for the common good and full human flourishing.

Though legal authority is a necessary and natural component of political authority because of the natural purposes it serves, the form that legal authority takes is itself, within broad contours, underdetermined. Therefore, legal authority is also conventional. Focusing just on the office of judge, for a moment: judicial offices may have different jurisdictions, powers, and terms and protections of office, depending on the circumstances. In the United States itself, many different manifestations of judicial office exist, and these testify to the deep conventionality of the office. Federal judges have limited jurisdiction, robust tenure protections, and significant power (within their jurisdiction). State court judges typically have broad jurisdiction, there is a wide variety of tenure protections, and they possess significant power (within their broad jurisdiction). Administrative agencies utilize judge-like

---

[121] For example, the House of Commons' slow gathering of authority, culminating in the Parliament Acts of 1911 and 1949, which reduced the House of Lords' authority to block and delay the Commons' legislation.

[122] For example, the American states' identification of the state ratification conventions as having the authority to authorize the Constitution.

[123] For example, William the Conqueror's authority in England at some point after his conquest in 1066.

[124] One of the "stock" moves in American political argumentation is to claim that a particular federal policy is good or bad by how it facilitates or harms federalism.

officials for intra-agency adjudication, and these offices possess a variety of characteristics that vary widely from those of federal and state court judges.

4.4.3.3.4 LEGAL AUTHORITY OPERATES AS AN EXCLUSIONARY REASON IN PRAC-
TICAL DELIBERATIONS Authority operates within individuals' practical deliberations about what actions they should and should not take. Normally, when a
person is deciding on a course of action to take, that person will have before him
a number of reasons, some of which point in one direction, and some of which
point in other directions. To take a moderately complex example, parents deciding
how to educate their children have to take into account a plethora of reasons. For
instance, Saint Francis High School may be more expensive than other schools, but
it has a robust academic track record. Its students are very intelligent, but they also
lack character development in key areas. Classical Christian School is less expensive
than St. Francis, but it does not have St. Francis's academic track record because it
is newer, though the curriculum it uses itself has a very long and successful track
record. Its students are intelligent and have received well-rounded character development, and so on. Parents must choose one of the two schools. Their course of
action will be reason-guided, though not reason-determined.

However, when a practical authority enters the picture, the authority may provide
an additional reason to take (or not take) a particular course of action, and a subject
of the authority will include *that* reason in his practical deliberations. For instance, a
child, Alex, would like to go to the little neighboring general store to buy a soda with
money he earned mowing lawns. Alex has considered different routes to get to the
store, and he has settled on taking the most direct route because it is quicker and less
complicated. Alex's Mom asks Alex which way he plans to go and, after he tells her,
she says "No, even though that route is quicker and easier, it is too dangerous
because it has more cars on it. I want you to take the Brint Road." In Alex's practical
reasoning – assuming Alex is a good son – his Mom's directive operated as an
additional reason for him to consider.

However, an authority's reason is not simply *another* practical reason for a person
to consider; it displaces or *excludes* the subject's other reasons: it is an exclusionary
reason.[125] Continuing my hypothetical, Mom's directive was not just one reason
among many for Alex to consider; it excluded Alex's other reasonable reasons. In
Alex's practical reasoning process, the only reason that remains open to Alex to act
upon is the reason identified by his mother because she directed it. Alex could not –
at least not in a manner consistent with respect for his mother – say, "Mom has a fair
point, but I think that she's over-emphasizing the danger from the extra cars, and,
besides, I'm a careful rider, so I'll take my original route."

Legal authority likewise operates by providing citizens subject to its authority with
additional, exclusionary reasons to act or not act in the manner directed by the legal

---

[125] JOSEPH RAZ, THE AUTHORITY OF LAW 17, 22–23, 26–27, 32–33 (2d ed., 2009).

authority's legal norms. For example, traveler X is traveling from point A to point B early in the morning in a city and would normally consider a number of factors in her practical reasoning – which route is shortest, which route is safer, which route is more scenic, and so on – to decide between routes 1 and 2. If, however, the city council has designated a street along route 2 as a one-way street with traffic going in the direction opposite that being taken by traveler X, the city has contributed another reason to traveler X's practical reasoning. But not just another reason, an exclusionary reason, one that will exclude traveler X's other reasons and push traveler X to take route 1 instead of route 2.

As I describe in more detail in Subsection 4.4.3.3.6, the ability of an authority's reason to exclude other reasons from a person's practical reasoning process has limits; it is defeasible. These limits vary depending on the authority's claim to authority, the countervailing reason(s), and the action(s) at issue, among other circumstances. For instance, let's assume that traveler X is racing to point 2 because she is driving her father, who is suffering from a heart attack, to the hospital. In that situation, traveler X's countervailing reason may be powerful enough to cause her to reject the city council's decision to make the street one-way.[126]

4.4.3.3.5 SOUND REASONS TO FOLLOW LEGAL AUTHORITY'S DIRECTIVES The basic human goods and the requirements of morality are reasons for action that operate within our practical deliberation. We see a book in which we are interested, and the basic good of knowledge provides a reason for us to pick up the book and start reading it. By contrast, the statement of a person or group of people containing a directive "read this book" does not, by itself, provide a reason for action. Assuming that morality does not itself already require the action prescribed or proscribed by such a directive, then it is simply a proposition that, without some additional reason, its audience has no need to take into account in its practical deliberations. Stated differently, you don't have to listen to your neighbor's orders.

So, what reason(s) do we have to listen to the directives – the laws – of legal authority? What follows is the natural law tradition's explanation for how the fact of authority itself provides reasons for its subjects to take account of the authority's directives in their practical deliberations.

A legal authority's authority is justified by its unique role securing the common good and individual human flourishing. Without legal authority, the great goods provided by social life, including (but not limited to) justice and the Rule of Law, would be either not available or available in a more limited manner. One need only

---

[126] In this situation, if a police officer failed to exercise appropriate executive discretion by arresting traveler X, and the prosecutor failed to exercise appropriate prosecutorial discretion by prosecuting traveler X, a judge would be justified utilizing an equitable interpretation of the city ordinance to not find traveler X guilty of violating the ordinance. For a more in-depth discussion of Aristotle's theory of equity, see Roger A. Shiner, *Aristotle's Theory of Equity*, 27 LOY. L. A. L. REV. 1245 (1994).

look at current societies such as Venezuela[127] and past societies, such as the Holy Roman Empire during the Thirty Years War,[128] where legal authority broke down, to observe the frequently terrible impact this had on members of those societies. Therefore, absent reasons to defeat a legal authority's authority, which I will discuss shortly, a practically reasonable person will entertain a legal authority's directives in his practical deliberations because of the good that legal authority accomplishes for that individual and his fellow citizens.

The key to my argument is my adoption of the perspective of a practically reasonable citizen in a society with a reasonably just legal system. What reasons does this citizen have to incorporate the law's reasons in his practical deliberations? Practical reasonableness is the reasonable pursuit of the basic human goods, all things considered. Practical reason includes within its calculations the societal common good. A practically reasonable person facing a concrete choice situation, or a person constructing and pursuing a life plan, knows the necessary role that the common good plays in both situations. Without the common good – without a reasonably just and legally directed social ordering – one will have a difficult and, in many cases, impossible time pursuing some or all of the basic human goods in a long-term, coherent manner. For example, the good of leisure provided by golf depends on a robust network of social ordering, both public and private, that enables golf courses to exist and function. Or, a person constructing a life plan, which must include the good of knowledge in order to be a reasonable life plan, knows that her ability to participate in the good of knowledge requires, among other things, the coordination of a complex educational system. Practically reasonable citizens will therefore include in their *own* practical deliberations their commitment to support the legal authority that makes the common good and their own (and their fellow citizens') flourishing possible.

This commitment to support the legal authority and its legal system through inclusion of its law's reasons in one's practical deliberations and by following its legal norms is supported by at least nine interrelated reasons.[129] These reasons each identify why a practically reasonable person has reason to follow his society's legal authority (though, as I explain, defeasibly), and to not, on a case-by-case basis, decide whether to follow the legal authority's law. A practically reasonable member of a society with a basically-just legal system therefore has sound reasons to take the law into account as he determines what courses of action to take, including those where the law provides a reason for the person to act differently than his practical deliberations would otherwise have led him to act.

---

[127] *See* Amanda Taub & Max Fisher, *In Venezuela's Chaos, Elites Play a High-Stakes Game for Survival*, N.Y. Times A12 (May 6, 2017) ("Even as Venezuela sinks into chaos ...").

[128] J. V. Polisensky, The Thirty Years War 225 (Robert Evans trans., 1971).

[129] These reasons are derived from NLNR, at 314–20; Finnis, *Law as Coordination, supra* note 110; Finnis, *Law's Authority, supra* note 110.

To exemplify these nine reasons, I employ a hypothetical situation that fits my personal experience and, based on conversations, the experience of many Americans. Put yourself in the situation of a traffic jam on a divided four-lane road. Traffic is moving, though slowly, and it is not clear when the blockage will clear. An aggressive driver begins to illegally drive on the shoulder and to pass her fellow drivers, and then she passes you. If you are like me and, I suspect, most Americans, you think that it was wrong of this aggressive driver to do so, and you remain on the highway despite its relative costs to you.

But why is that? It cannot be because of the mere fact of driving on a highway shoulder because there is nothing unethical about that, *simpliciter*. Indeed, there are times when most Americans would agree that it is ethical for one to do so – for instance, if one were an ambulance driver taking a severely injured person to the hospital. Instead, it is the fact of the aggressive driver acting *illegally* that makes her actions unethical. In the following text, I provide nine reasons why a practically reasonable person in your (hypothetical) situation should follow the law and should not act like the aggressive driver. My claim is that these reasons capture and illuminate your intuition why the aggressive driver acted unethically and you acted ethically.

First, legal authority and the legal system through which it operates functions as a whole – as a seamless web – and practically reasonable subjects of the legal system will take *that* fact into account in their practical deliberations and give its laws support. The legal system secures many goods, including justice and the Rule of Law, that create the conditions for society's members to secure their own flourishing. In doing so, the legal authority distributes the benefits and burdens of the legal system among society's members. This means that, at any given point in time, a particular member of society may receive relatively greater benefits from the system and a different member may receive relatively greater costs from the system. However, because each member's capacity to flourish is secured by the legal system as a whole, and that whole is a seamless web, they each have reason to follow the system as a whole. Members do not have a reason to support the system only when it advances their parochial interests, and they know that if all members selectively followed the legal authority, it would fatally undermine the legal system's effectiveness.

For instance, the legal system allocated a burden to our aggressive driver. The law directed her to continue on the highway even though it was relatively slower than driving on the shoulder. However, a practically reasonable driver would recognize that the legal system as a seamless web is fundamentally just, that her jurisdiction's highway regulations also are basically sound, and that they remain so even though the particular law in question burdens her on that particular occasion. The practically reasonable driver knows that the legal system has also allocated significant benefits to her, such as its protection of his person and property interests – including the goods required by distributive justice and the benefit of the Rule of Law – and is likely to do so again (just as it is likely to also allocate burdens to her in the future). The authority and its seamless legal system are the unique system for securing the common good, and practically reasonable members of society will take that fact into account when they deliberate. A practically reasonable driver cannot reasonably exclude the onerous law from his practical deliberations and not follow it, because the legal system as a seamless web has provided him with the capacity to flourish. Furthermore, the practically reasonable driver knows he cannot do so consistent with other citizens also doing so, which would undermine the legal authority's and its system's capacity to secure the common good.

Second, a member of a society will include that society's legal authority's reasons in his practical deliberations because doing so supports distributive justice. Distributive justice identifies the appropriate distribution of goods in a society. One of society's goods is its legal authority itself: who decides when, as well as how, to instantiate justice and the Rule of Law. A person who follows the legal authority acts justly, by giving the authority and her fellow citizens their due, while a person who acts contrary to it acts unjustly, because that person arrogates to herself authority that was distributed to the legal authority – in particular, to the system's system of distributing authority. Distribute justice has allocated to the legal authority the authority to make allocating decisions. A practically reasonable person will take distributive justice into account in her deliberations and act consistently with the legal system's distribution of authority to distribute.

A practically reasonable driver from our hypothetical will abide by the law's limits on his driving because he knows that to do otherwise would be to act unjustly. This would be arrogating to himself a decision reasonably allocated to the legal authority. He would be taking responsibility for the decision on how to allocate benefits and burdens of highway use, which his state's legal system had allocated to the state legislature and department of transportation.

Third, a just legal system treats those subject to the law as equals, and this equal treatment is a reason for a practically reasonable person to take the legal authority's laws into account in her practical deliberations. The law treats its subjects equally in many ways; let me identify two key ways. First, the law acts nonpreferentially by providing that its subjects are subject to the law in the same manner and to the same extent: high- or low-born, rich or poor, the law treats everyone as a rational subject, as a human being capable of acting based on reason. Second, the law avoids preferential treatment by nonpreferentially distributing the benefits and burdens of social life among the law's subjects. The law is an important mechanism of achieving distributive and commutative justice, and the law's pursuit of those goals avoids unreasonably preferential treatment. An individual's practical deliberations will acknowledge the law's equal treatment by including the legal authority's legal directives in his practical deliberations. He knows that if he does not follow the legal authority's directives, then he undermines the law's otherwise equal treatment of its subjects. One manner of doing so is by treating himself as not subject to the law's reasons, or as subject to the law in a way different from his fellow citizens.

Our practically reasonable driver's legal system's equal treatment of its citizens is a reason for him to take its laws into account in his practical deliberations. He knows that, by following the burdensome highway law, he facilitates the legal system's equal treatment and maintains the principle that everyone is subject to the law because of their fundamental rationality. Staying in his lane also maintains the legal system's equal distribution of benefits and burdens. To do otherwise – to join the aggressive driver – would be to exempt himself from the legal authority's authority and cause inequality in the legal system's treatment of its subjects and distort its (by hypothesis) reasonably just distribution of benefits and burdens.

Fourth, and a corollary to the third reason, a practically reasonable person does not have a reason to exclude the law's reasons in her practical reason as a means to prefer his own well-being over that of her fellow citizens. If a person decides, on a case-by-case basis, whether following a legal authority or not is more advantageous (to that person) in that case, then that person will periodically decide to not follow the law. In doing so, the person will occasionally advantage herself at the expense of her fellow citizens by giving to herself more of the legal system's benefits than it had allocated to her. Yet, a person does not possess a sound reason to do so because of the fundamentally equal rationality of humans.

For example, the aggressive driver decided that it is more advantageous to *her* to (illegally) drive on the shoulder and to go past her fellow drivers. The driver's self-dealing is at the expense of the legal system's distribution of goods to her fellow drivers. Under the legal system's coordination of highway usage, non-emergency driving should occur only on the designated lanes and not on the shoulders, and the hypothetical aggressive driver is taking more highway usage than her allotted share. The aggressive driver is also taking use of the shoulder, which is designated for emergency usage, from fellow citizens who may need to utilize the shoulder for those purposes. Yet, she had no reason to prioritize her own interests over those of other equally rational drivers. A practically reasonable driver would choose to follow the law and not privilege herself over her fellow drivers.

Fifth, the practically reasonable person manifests and builds the virtue of civic friendship when he follows the law (and refuses to privilege himself), and this constitutes a reason to follow the legal authority and to entertain its laws in his practical deliberations. Civic friendship, like friendship more generally, is willing the good of another; in this case, the good of one's fellow citizens. A citizen's support for his society's legal system, the legal system that creates the conditions for the flourishing of his fellow citizens, is a manifestation of civic friendship. A citizen's refusal, selective or otherwise, to follow the law undermines the legal system and displays antipathy to or disinterest in his fellow citizens.

The aggressive driver expressed antipathy for her fellow citizens when she violated the law and used the shoulder instead of staying in the lane with her fellow citizens.

A practically reasonable driver will take her fellow citizens' interests into account in her deliberations to follow the legal system. She will recognize that the system of highway regulations facilitates her fellow citizens' flourishing, even if – in that instance – it imposed a modest burden, and that illegally driving on the shoulder will harm that system. Doing so will build the virtue of civic friendship in her character, and this provides a reason for the driver to uphold the system by not driving on the shoulder.

Sixth, maintenance of the Rule of Law's systemic character provides practically reasonable individuals with reasons to support a legal authority and its legal system. Legal authority creates and maintains the Rule of Law through its legal system. The Rule of Law is valuable because it is necessary for effective coordination which, in turn, is a necessary element for the common good and individual human flourishing. Furthermore, the Rule of Law prevents harm, both public and private, to individuals.

The Rule of Law's value derives partly from its systemic character. The system's laws apply to *all* actions *prior* to application. This facilitates coordination and it prevents harm by making all actions law-governed. Therefore, the Rule of Law's value depends on individuals following the system and not evaluating laws one-by-one. The Rule of Law is not consistent with law's subjects picking-and-choosing which laws to follow post-hoc. A practically reasonable person has good reason to follow the legal system as a system, and therefore good reason to include the legal authority's laws in his practical deliberations.

Our aggressive driver is doing the opposite. She is taking the laws, one-by-one, and deciding whether to follow them based on whether, prior to application, she directly benefits from doing so. Her actions harm the Rule of Law as a system of laws and are therefore practically unreasonable. The driver is treating the law as not applicable to her actions prior to her actions; instead, she is deciding case-by-case, what to do based on her own practical judgment.

Seventh and relatedly, a practically reasonable citizen will take into account in his deliberations the fact that the consistent commitment of citizens to follow the law is necessary to avoid a vicious cycle of greater and greater disobedience to the law resulting, ultimately, in undermining or destroying the common good. This will occur when the coordination benefit from law-following becomes relatively less and the personal gain from lawbreaking becomes relatively greater.

For the large majority of positive law, the most important value it provides is the coordination it effectuates. The positive law itself is typically not intrinsically right or wrong. Laws governing traffic intersections are an example. The legal rule that the vehicle on the right may proceed first through the intersection at a four-way stop is arbitrary, but the coordination such a rule provides is valuable. In many situations where positive law's value is its social coordination, an individual regularly has incentives to not follow the law's guidance in particular instances. For example, an individual could save a little time by going through an intersection even as and slightly after the traffic light turned red. However, as other citizens witness this self-regarding behavior, the positive law's coordination value diminishes, and this incentivizes other citizens to engage in similar self-regarding behavior. "Since everyone else is running red lights, I might as well too to save myself a little time," a person might say. This vicious cycle will increase as more and more people privilege themselves over the law's social coordination. This will reduce or destroy the individual positive law's value and, if unchecked, the cycle will culminate in the development of vicious habits of disobedience of the law and a broader culture of lawlessness.

Of course, this cycle would not reach its nadir overnight, and it might never reach the level of lawlessness of a society in utter chaos. Legality is not an all-or-nothing proposition. The duty to support one's legal system prevents not only anarchy but – more frequently and more likely – it prevents impediments to the common good that, though negative and harmful to human flourishing, are not devastating. To take a colorful example, in New York City in the late 1970s and early 1980s, the subway system nearly collapsed because of the disorder caused by crime, vandalism, and subway train breakdowns.[130] The disorder grew over a lengthy period of time and became a cycle of ever greater disorder until the subway system was left relatively empty because so few New Yorkers braved the disorder to utilize it. The disorder had not reached total chaos, but it made the subway unusable for most people.

A practically reasonable person treats the legal authority's legal directives as reasons for action because he has sound reason to believe that his own adherence to the positive law helps secure the law's coordination benefits for himself and others, and avoids the cycle of self-regarding disobedience that harms social coordination for himself and others. This is unlike our aggressive driver. Her ostentatious privileging of herself suggests to the lawful drivers that they do the same, and as more and more drivers follow her lead, the benefits of coordination evaporate, and the cycle becomes even more aggressive.

Eighth, a legal authority's social coordination via legal directives treats its subjects as rational beings, and for this reason its laws should be taken account of in practical deliberations. Positive law directives enter into a subject's practical deliberations as reasons for acting or not acting. Law's mode of operation treats its subjects as beings who act based upon reasons, and this is valuable. A practically reasonable person would take law's reasons into account in his own practical deliberations because of this value.

The law is like a friend you know. This friend treats everyone equally well, even in situations when you yourself may not have, like speaking with an annoying person. The friend always explains why he did something, he patiently explains things to

---

[130] William Bratton with Peter Knobler, Turnaround: How America's Top Cop Reversed the Crime Epidemic 152–64 (1998).

others who may be a little "thick," and he disagrees with others in a reasonable manner. You have good reason to treat this friend well. You have good reason to engage with him in a reason-giving manner, as he does with you. Like this reasonable friend, you have good reason to treat the law in the same manner it treats you, and this means that you have a reason to treat the law well because of its essential characteristic of reason-giving. Our aggressive driver treated the law poorly.

The aggressive driver is like an acquaintance who always does what *she* wants. Even when everyone is supposed to be working together to achieve a common goal, the aggressive driver ostentatiously refuses to contribute to the goal, and her only "reason" is because it does not benefit *her* sufficiently.

Ninth, the formation and preservation of the virtue of justice-as-lawfulness provides a reason for a practically reasonable person to include the law's reasons in his deliberations. Acknowledging that one's society's legal authority's legal directives possess authority is a manifestation of the virtue of justice-as-lawfulness. Justice-as-lawfulness is one's habitual disposition to follow one's society's laws. A person with this virtue has formed his character so that his practical reasoning automatically takes into account the law's valuable function of securing the common good as a reason to follow the legal system's directives. Building one's character is a reason to act, and it leads the practically reasonable person to employ the law in his practical deliberations.

The aggressive driver failed to exercise the virtue of justice-as-lawfulness, and her lawlessness harmed her character; it made it more difficult for her to see the law's value. The other, practically reasonable, drivers saw the point of the highway laws, including of the law that burdened them. Their following the law built-up their character, and this gave them a reason to follow the law.

In sum, members of a society with a properly functioning legal authority act practically reasonably when they take into account the legal authority's laws in their practical deliberations. As John Finnis summarized this line of argument, "Generally speaking, an individual most appropriately acts for the common good not by trying to estimate the needs of the community at large, nor by second guessing the judgments of those who are directly responsible for the common good, but by performing his particular undertakings and fulfilling his other responsibilities."[131]

It is unlikely that many will challenge a legal authority's authority when following an authority's law leads a person to a better state of affairs than if the person had followed the person's own practical reasoning (and not taken into account the law).[132] It remains the case, however, that a single person, or some minority of people, could irregularly (or perhaps systematically) deviate from an authority's determination without catastrophic harm to the authority's ability to coordinate for its community, in order to achieve a (perceived) short-term personal advantage.

---

[131] Finnis, *Law as Coordination*, *supra* note 110, at 73.
[132] This situation involves Raz's powerful and influential service conception of authority.

Perhaps, for example, a person briefly drives on the right-hand shoulder of a highway to pass a traffic jam. Or, a child sneaks a small cookie before mealtime and when no one is watching. The reasons I identified, grouped into two categories, continue to provide sound reasons to follow the legal authority's determination.

One class of reasons focuses on the person himself. A child who sneaks a cookie hurts himself. He has treated his family unjustly by taking more than his share, and acted viciously by sneaking and not following his parents' directive, all of which deforms his character. Similarly, a person who illegally uses the road's shoulder to avoid a traffic jam hurts himself. He has treated his fellow citizens unjustly by taking a route that was not his to take, and acted viciously by ostentatiously flaunting the traffic laws, all of which deform his character. Indeed, a person whose character is typified by rejection of social and legal conventions is a sociopath or psychopath.

The second class of reasons looks at the resulting negative effects on the authority's capacity to coordinate for the common good. In a family where one child sneaks a cookie and her siblings learn about it, the others are tempted to and may do likewise. This undermines the parents' authority and their ability to guide all of their children to adulthood. In society, other citizens may similarly break the traffic laws with ever-greater regularity, which would undermine the legal authority's ability to effectively coordinate highway travel.[133] The greater the disorder in a community, the more disorder that will occur in the community. At its most egregious, snowballing breaches of highway regulation would undermine other great goods of society like the Rule of Law.

4.4.3.3.6 THE DEFEASIBILITY OF LEGAL AUTHORITY Members of a reasonably just society with a properly functioning legal authority that, through its laws, coordinates society, have many and sound reasons to include those laws as exclusionary reasons in their practical deliberations. However, there are limits to law's reasons' authority.

A legal authority's legal norms, though authoritative for individuals in that society through their role as an exclusionary reason in the individuals' practical deliberations, are *defeasible*.[134] Legal authority, within the Aristotelian philosophical tradition, is nested within political authority and within the still broader concept of authority. Legal authority, like other forms of authority, is both necessary because of and *limited* by its rationale: service to the common good and the facilitation of human flourishing. In each type of community, from the family up to the nation-state, authority is necessary for members of each such community to achieve flourishing, and it is also limited by that rationale. For this reason, for instance,

---

[133] In a nutshell, this is the claim of the "broken windows theory." George L. Kelling & James Q. Wilson, *Broken Windows: The Police and Neighborhood Safety*, THE ATLANTIC, Mar. 1982, www.theatlantic.com/magazine/archive/1982/03/broken-windows/304465/.

[134] ST, I-II, q. 96, a. 4.

gross parental abuse of authority justifies the modification or elimination of that authority. A parent who grievously and regularly mistreats his child is acting contrary to that child's flourishing and beyond his authority. Similarly, wicked legal systems, like the Nazi legal system, did not possess authority. It did not serve the common good – it served the "good" of some at the expense of others – and it harmed the human flourishing of nearly everyone under the regime's sway.[135] Defeasibility is legal authority's limit.

Defeasibility is a concept common to law. To say that a legal relationship is defeasible is to say that it is not unlimited; that triggering facts may limit or change or eliminate the relationship. Perhaps the classic example in American law are the defeasible fees, such as the fee simple determinable and the fee simple condition subsequent.[136] These are interests in property that, absent the occurrence of an event, are equivalent to the highest form of property ownership in our legal system, the fee simple absolute. However, when a triggering event occurs, the property relationship ends. For instance, if Landulf granted Blackacre "to Thomas, so long Thomas does not enter a religious order, then to James," Thomas has a defeasible fee. When Thomas enters the Order of Preachers, then Thomas automatically ceases to own Blackacre, and James does; Thomas' interest defeased.

In fact, the situation of a person subject to legal authority having a sufficiently strong reason to not follow the legal system's authoritative legally-prescribed reason, is so common that our legal system has developed a series of mechanisms that limit the use of legal authorities' otherwise-exclusionary reasons. These mechanisms build into the legal system itself opportunities for subjects to defease the legal system's reasons. In property law, for example, the standard rule in the United States is that a property owner has the authority to exclude others.[137] The law provides an exclusionary reason for a person who wishes to trespass on another's property for a run-of-the-mill reason. But, the law also removes that reason in cases of necessity.[138] In these situations, a person experiencing necessity will reason about his course of action without the law's exclusionary trespass-prohibition reason. If, all things considered (except trespass law, which is *not* considered because of the law's own exclusion of that reason), the person would use another's property for emergency shelter, for example, the law will not change that practical calculus.

Let me summarize when and how the authority of a legal authority's directives' is defeasible. The primary way legal authority's law is defeasible is if it lacks one or

---

[135] Even those who, at surface-level, may seem to have appeared to flourish under and because of the Nazi legal system in fact did not because their characters were warped by their participation in the regime's wickedness or by turning a blind eye toward its wickedness. *See generally* Daniel Jonah Goldhagen, Hitler's Willing Executioners: Ordinary Germans and the Holocaust (1996).

[136] Rest. (Third) of Property: Wills & Donative Trans. §24.3, comms. (2011).

[137] Restatement (Second) of Torts § 158 (1965).

[138] *Id.* § 263.

more of the four necessary facets of a law.[139] My argument here depends on the concept of a focal case.[140] The focal case of something is its best, most robust, fullest version of that thing. The concept of the focal case applies to human beings as well.

A legal authority's directives that possess all four facets of law are law's focal case. They are not defective. A statute passed by Congress (and signed by the President) that regulates the commercial transportation of goods on railroads across state lines to preserve competition and avoid price gouging is American federal law in the focal sense.[141] It was issued by the proper authority for such laws; it was promulgated in the Statutes at Large; it was for the common good of the United States; and it was reasonable. This law may not be the wisest law, and it may not even be very effective achieving its goals; the key is the legal authority utilized its practical wisdom to solve a coordination problem with the common good.

By contrast, positive law that lacks one or more of law's four essential characteristics is a marginal instance of law. At some point, a positive law becomes so marginal that it loses its authority: its authority is defeased. For example, the purported law may not have been promulgated by a legal authority or, more commonly, it may have been promulgated by a (recognized) legal authority beyond that authority's jurisdiction.[142] If Congress passed a "law" not authorized by its limited and enumerated powers, or if a state passed a "law" that infringed the Privileges or Immunities Clause, these laws are beyond the respective governments' jurisdictions. Or, a "law" that served one person's or one class' interests at the expense of the common good would fail one of the criteria.[143] These "laws" retain some but lack other necessary facets of law. They are marginal laws. For these positive laws, a citizen no longer has a *prima facie* duty to follow them because they are not fully laws. The "laws'" authority is defeased.

However, the fact that a "law" is only marginally a law because of its lacking one or more of the characteristics of law does not mean that it is not law intra-systemically. It is possible – indeed, highly likely in a basically just and mature legal system – that a citizen may still have sound reasons to follow such an imperfect law for the overall sake of the common good that the legal authority, through the legal system, still instantiates (despite this – and likely other – marginal law(s)).[144] In a basically-just legal system, the citizen should follow the marginal law to preserve the Rule of Law and justice, which continues to exist in the jurisdiction despite the existence of the imperfect law. A concrete manifestation of this widespread

---

[139] The facets are: proper authority, promulgated, for the common good, and reasonable. ST, I-II, q. 90, a. 4.

[140] NLNR, at 9–18.

[141] An Act to regulate commerce, 24 Stat. 379 (1887).

[142] This is more common because, in a mature legal system, the legal authorities are identified and their existence is static, so it is uncommon to have non-authorities purporting to promulgate "law."

[143] *Yick Wo v. Hopkins*, 118 U.S. 356 (1886).

[144] ST, I-II, q. 96, a. 4.

phenomenon is the practice of Americans generally, and government officials in particular, adhering to Supreme Court precedents even when the precedents are not consistent with the Constitution.[145] This includes the Supreme Court itself! They do so for the sake of the Rule of Law and justice, and the common good they secure.

My argument here, therefore, identifies two steps in an individual's analysis of whether that individual should follow a legal authority's legal directives. First, a situation must exist in which a positive law lacks one or more of law's four necessary characteristics: it must be marginal. Second, even if that occurs and law's *prima facie* authority is defeased, a citizen must still ascertain whether the law is part of a basically just legal system, one that is continuing to secure the common good.

There are two caveats to my claim. First, when a marginal law (in an otherwise basically just legal system) affirmatively commands that a person perform a gravely wicked act, that person does not have reason to do so. A powerful example is the 1850 Fugitive Slave Act's requirement that state officials in northern states enforce the Act, even upon flimsy evidence provided by a purported slave owner.[146] Second, when a marginal law occurs in a basically unjust legal system, a person does not have a reason to take the marginal law's reason into account in his practical deliberations.[147] In this situation, even though the imperfect law may be intra-systemically recognized as law – perhaps *because of* its imperfection! – the broader legal system does not give the person a reason to follow the law because it is failing to secure the common good.

Defeasibility may apply on a law-by-law basis, or systemically. My discussion up to now has focused on discrete legal enactments, though systemic defeasance can also occur. For example, a purported legal authority could not possess legal authority if, for instance, it had unjustly usurped the previously identified legal authority's place.[148] Unjust revolutions, like the communist overthrow and murder of the Czar, are examples of this phenomenon. Or, a legal authority could lose its authority because its legal pronouncements have generally become extremely imprudent or unjust, or important facets of it have become imprudent or unjust. This occurred in Germany in 1918 shortly before Kaiser Wilhelm II formally abdicated.

Absent defeasibility, however, a legal authority and its legal pronouncements retain their *prima facie* claim to authority over those subject to it because of the

---

[145] *See, e.g.,* Abraham Lincoln, *Speech on the Dred Scott Decision* (June 26, 1857) ("But we think the *Dred Scott* decision is erroneous. We know the court that made it, has often over-ruled its own decisions, and we shall do what we can to have it to over-rule this. We offer no *resistance* to it . . .").

[146] The Fugitive Slave Act, 9 Stat. 462 (1850).

[147] ST, I-II, q. 95, a. 4.

[148] This claim applies in the short- and medium-term, but not in the long-term. Following Finnis, I think that an initially-unlawful authority could become a polity's legitimate legal authority over the long term, if it reasonably pursues the common good. NLNR, at 246–52. This likely occurred in William the Conqueror's England, but did not occur in the Soviet Union.

good reasons for legal authority. This authority manifests itself as an exclusionary reason in the practical deliberations of its subjects.

4.4.3.3.7 CONCLUSION In this subsection, I described legal authority. Authority is both natural and conventional. It is necessary to secure the common good and human flourishing. This rationale both justifies authority's existence and its authority, and it also identifies authority's limitations. The focal case of authority is that its commands direct the conduct of persons subject to the authority by providing exclusionary reasons in their practical deliberations. Authority's indispensable function in a community's organization which, in turn, is indispensable to an individual's flourishing, is what justifies authority. Political and legal authority are the fullest manifestation of this need for coordination and authority, on a societal level. As summarized by Yves Simon, "authority is neither a necessary evil nor a lesser good nor a lesser evil nor the consequence of any evil or deficiency – it is, like nature and society, unqualifiedly good."[149]

In the Aristotelian philosophical tradition, authority is not justified by reference to consent or the voluntary taking-on of obedience or reciprocity of accepted benefits. Instead, authority's claim to compliance is because, without authority and its directives, communities and the individuals who comprise those communities would not be able to flourish.

4.4.3.4 Conclusion

This subsection explained why legal authority is so important to every complex community of human beings. This sets up my argument for originalism, where I argue that Americans during the Framing and Ratification period, and Americans today, recognize that the state ratification conventions possessed the authority to designate the Constitution as our society's legal resolution of fundamental coordination problems. The Constitution, because of its role securing the common good, provides sound reasons for legal officials, and Americans of all stripes, to employ its reasons in their legal and practical deliberations.

4.4.4 *The Law-as-Coordination Account of Positive Law: Positive Law's Essential Role Pursuing the Common Good and Human Flourishing*

4.4.4.1 Introduction

In Subsection 4.4.3, I explained the Aristotelian philosophical tradition's description of human beings, including our end of human flourishing and the crucial roles for the common good and legal authority securing that end. This subsection describes

---

[149] YVES R. SIMON, PHILOSOPHY OF DEMOCRATIC GOVERNMENT 59 (1951).

how human-created law – positive law – performs a critical function in the Aristo-telian tradition's conception of law. Positive law is essential for any society of more than the merest degree of complexity to effectively pursue the common good of the community and provide the appropriate conditions for its members' human flourishing. Positive law's essential roles are to resolve coordination problems and specify the natural law in a society. It does so though authoritative, prudential, coordinating decisions, which it – the positive law – embodies. This is the law-as-coordination account of positive law. In Section 4.5 I apply the law-as-coordination account to the U.S. Constitution and explain why it requires an originalist interpretation.

4.4.4.2 The Conventional View of Natural Lawyers' Conception of Positive Law

The centrality of positive law to the law-as-coordination account of law may seem counterintuitive to many readers. One common claim about the natural law tradition's conception of law is that it possessed insufficient analytical space for positive law to play the role it obviously plays in mature legal systems. This happened because the natural law either excluded all ethically non-ideal positive laws from the category of law,[150] or because the natural law norms themselves provided the needed law in a society.[151] Critics argued that natural lawyers' conception failed to fit the common situation of an unjust positive law that continued to be a recognized legal norm within the legal system,[152] and failed to fit the ubiquitous situation of positive law originating from the choices of identified human sovereigns.[153] These conclusions followed from natural law theories' supposed injunction that "an unjust law is not a law."[154] H. L. A. Hart famously described the Aristotelian philosophical tradition as holding something like this position.[155] This strong injunction, it was believed, crowded out positive law that was not ethically ideal and, for natural law to have the ability to identify positive law as unjust, there had to be a tremendous number of natural law norms which *themselves* could supplant positive law and its coordination and specification functions.

This perspective is incorrect, at least as applied to the Aristotelian philosophical tradition. The Aristotelian philosophical tradition has expounded an elaborate description of the relationship between natural and positive law. In particular, the Aristotelian philosophical tradition recognizes the necessary and important function

---

[150] *E.g.,* Jules L. Coleman & Brian Leiter, *Legal Positivism, in* A COMPANION TO PHILOSOPHY OF LAW AND LEGAL THEORY 241, 244 (Dennis Patterson ed., 1996).

[151] *E.g.,* HANS KELSEN, GENERAL THEORY OF LAW AND STATE 416–17 (Anders Wedberg trans., Harvard University Press, 1945).

[152] Jules L. Coleman, *The Architecture of Jurisprudence,* 121 YALE L.J. 2, 11 (2011).

[153] JOHN AUSTIN, THE PROVINCE OF JURISPRUDENCE DETERMINED (1832).

[154] ST. AUGUSTINE, ON FREE CHOICE OF THE WILL 8 (Thomas Williams trans., 1993).

[155] H. L. A. Hart, *The Separation of Law and Morals,* 71 HARV. L. REV. 593, 617, 620, 626 (1958).

of positive law. As John Finnis summarized Aquinas' conception of positive law: "Aquinas asserts and illustrates positive law's variability and relatively to time, place, and polity, its admixture of human error and immorality, [and] its radical dependence on human creativity."[156]

The purported natural law injunction that "an unjust law is not a law" does not mean that non-ideal positive laws are not law intra-systemically, nor does it imply that there is a thick panoply of natural law norms waiting in the wings and capable of substituting for positive legal enactments. Instead, the injunction distinguishes between the focal case of law and marginal cases.[157] In its focal case, positive law reasonably guides its society's members toward the common good, while marginal cases do so poorly or not at all. However, with most marginal laws, though it is defective in some way, it remains intra-systemically authoritative in a basically just legal system because of the *legal system's* important role securing the common good.[158]

This is why Aquinas still called an unjust law a "law," and did not use some other label with a different connotation, such as decree or edict, labels that were available to him because Aristotle (among others) utilized them.[159] Furthermore, Aquinas qualified his description of unjust laws with characterizations of "more outrages than law,"[160] and "not law but a corruption of law,"[161] indicating that unjust positive law was still law, though defective in some way and so only marginally law. His locution is similar to that used when Americans today call someone a "fair-weather friend," to indicate that a person is a defective friend. Aquinas summarized his position: "A tyrannical law, though not being according to reason, is not a law, absolutely speaking, but rather a perversion of law; and yet, in so far as it is something in the nature of a law, it aims at the citizens being good."[162]

Lastly, Aquinas distinguished situations where an unjust positive law is so unlike law's focal case that a subject is obligated to *not* follow it. These are instances where the purported positive law requires a citizen to perform an intrinsically evil action.[163] An intrinsically evil action is one where the act is wicked, regardless of the circumstances. For instance, the Roman authorities periodically ordered Christians to worship the emperor's or pagan gods' images.[164] This shows that a run-of-the-mill

---

[156] JOHN FINNIS, *The Truth in Legal Positivism*, in THE AUTONOMY OF LAW: ESSAYS ON LEGAL POSITIVISM 195 (Robert P. George ed., 1996).

[157] NLNR, at 9–11.

[158] ST, I-II, q. 95, a. 4; NLNR, at 363–66 (describing this).

[159] NE, 1134b.

[160] ST, I-II, q. 96, a. 4.

[161] *Id.* at I-II, q. 95, a. 2.

[162] *Id.* at I-II, q. 92, a. 1.

[163] *Id.* at I-II, q. 96, a. 4.

[164] *Compare id.* ("[L]aws may be unjust through being opposed to the Divine good: such are the laws of tyrants inducing to idolatry.").

marginal positive law retains sufficient characteristics of law to be deserve the appellation "law."

In the following subsection, I describe how positive law has a central place in a properly functioning legal system both because the natural law itself is unable to perform positive law's functions, and because the natural law itself calls for positive law to have its own legitimate and autonomous functioning in legal systems.

4.4.4.3 Positive Law's Central Place within the Tradition: Instantiation and Coordination

4.4.4.3.1 INTRODUCTION Positive law's importance stems from its two main functions in a properly functioning legal system: (1) the positive law's necessary role *instantiating* or implementing the natural law's norms; and (2) the positive law's necessary role *coordinating* society's members toward the common good. The first source is that positive law bridges the gap between the natural law's general prescriptions for individuals and societies and the goals it identifies for them, and concrete human life. The natural law underdetermines a great deal of the guidance needed in human societies, and positive law provides (much of) that guidance. The positive law bridges the gap between the natural law's prescriptions and concrete human societies through two modes: the first mode is specification and the second mode is *determinatio*.

The second source of positive law's necessary place is that positive law provides the means by which citizens coordinate their activities and secure the common good, which in turn enables them to pursue their own individual goods. Positive law overcomes coordination problems that undermine the social cooperation necessary to achieve the common good.

4.4.4.3.2 INSTANTIATION VIA SPECIFICATION AND DETERMINATIO The natural law sets out the thin contours of *how* individuals achieve the identified goal of human flourishing. Relatedly, the natural law provides only spare outlines of *how* a society pursues the identified goal of the common good. The Aristotelian philosophical tradition provides relatively little guidance on how to achieve the abstract goals of human flourishing and the common good. In addition to identifying the goods themselves, it identifies some principles of natural law to guide pursuit of those goods. The Aristotelian philosophical tradition also includes virtue ethics that provides guidance on character formation and which generates "v-rules" that prescribe and prohibit virtuous and vicious conduct, respectively.[165] These resources are insufficient, however, to answer many important questions facing societies. To take just one narrow but important example: should the United States have one

---

[165] HURSTHOUSE, *supra* note 63, at 37.

federal civil cause of action for sexual torts,[166] or should its states adopt separate positions? Natural law and virtue ethics do not have the resources to provide a determinate answer, but the Aristotelian philosophical tradition clearly requires the prohibition, punishment of, and rectification for sexual torts.

This gap between human flourishing and the common good, on the one hand, and the natural law's thin guides on how to achieve them, on the other, is one of the primary reasons for the positive law's crucial place in the Aristotelian philosophical tradition and the dominant role positive law plays in developed legal systems. This gap-bridging or implementing function of positive law occurs through the modes of specification and *determinatio*, discussed in the following text.[167]

First, the positive law makes the natural law determinate through specification. This process is one of drawing "detailed proximate conclusions,"[168] or "demonstrated conclusions"[169] from the natural law. In these situations, the positive law makes express and applicable to that jurisdiction the natural law's primary, secondary, and intermediate principles, and in doing so provides practical guidance to humans. For instance, the natural law requires respecting other people, including their physical integrity, so each person can pursue his own flourishing unimpeded by others.[170] The positive law applies that norm to society by, among other things, prohibiting rape. Or, the natural law requires respect for others' private property.[171] One specification of that norm is to return the property one has borrowed to its owner.

Specification's impact is relatively limited (compared to *determinatio*) because, as the analytical distance between the natural law norm and the concrete circumstances increases, or more than one natural law norm applies and they push in different directions, humans quickly begin to disagree about the proper specification and, at some point, humans lack the capacity to reliably specify. For example, though one must return the private property one has borrowed, it is less clear whether one must return a borrowed knife to an owner if one has a suspicion the owner may utilize it to harm others.

The second, and more commonly employed, mode by which the positive law instantiates the natural law is through the process called *determinatio*. *Determinatio* is the relatively unrestricted, creative field where human lawmakers create positive law that comports with the natural law's general guidelines and advance their society's common good. *Determinatio* occurs when, in principle, there is more than one reasonable manner by which to instantiate the natural law. In these situations,

---

[166] Putting aside questions of the federal government's constitutional authority to do so.
[167] John Finnis, *Natural Law Theory: Its Past and Its Present*, 57 Am. J. Juris. 81, 93–94 (2012).
[168] ST, I-II, q. 94, a. 5.
[169] *Id.* at I-II, q. 95, a. 2.
[170] *Id.* at I-II, at q. 94, a. 2; Catechism of the Catholic Church, §§ 2297–98.
[171] ST, II-II, q. 66, a. 1, 2; Catechism of the Catholic Church, § 2402.

the choice of reasonable manner is arbitrary, and the key is that a flesh-and-blood human makes a choice and embodies that choice in law.

Take, for example, the question of the appropriate regulation of easements.[172] Easements involve one party's consensual use of another's property. A driveway across a neighbor's property is a common example. The natural law provides broad bounds to such relationships, including commutative and distributive justice, and respect for private property. Within these bounds, however, human lawmakers possess significant discretion to construct reasonable and reasonably different bodies of law governing easements. For instance, one jurisdiction may reasonably prohibit any expansion of the dominant tenement served by the easement,[173] while another jurisdiction may reasonably permit such expansion so long as it did not increase the use-burden on the servient estate.[174]

Aquinas analogized a legislator operating in the mode of *determinatio* to the architect of a house.[175] An architect works within broad outlines – *e.g.*, a door, walls, and a roof are mandatory, gravity applies to the house, the bearing capacity of the structure's supports is a given – that are analogous to the natural law's general goals and norms. However, within these broad bounds, the architect has tremendous creativity to design a unique house. Similarly, within the natural law's broad bounds, humans exercise significant legislative creativity to choose and craft a reasonable manner of implementing the natural law.

4.4.4.3.3 COORDINATION   The second source of the positive law's necessary role in the natural law tradition is its coordination of society's members. I described coordination problems earlier when I showed that authority, and not consent, was the only means to achieve the social cooperation necessary for the common good.[176] Here, I show that positive law is the essential mechanism that legal authority employs to resolve coordination problems and secure that cooperation.

As a reminder, coordination problems are obstacles to achieving the social cooperation necessary for individuals to effectively pursue their own human flourishing. Coordination problems occur in situations where everyone in a society has sound reasons to cooperate with others in a particular, unified manner but, because a specific mode of cooperation is rationally underdetermined, a consensus will not spontaneously arise making coordination impossible without authority. Coordination problems regularly occur in the context of *determinatio*, though they also

---

[172] RESTATEMENT (FIRST) OF PROPERTY § 450 (1944).
[173] This is the traditional American rule. *Id.* § 484.
[174] This is the minority position. RESTATEMENT (THIRD) OF PROPERTY (SERVITUDES) § 4.8 (2000).
[175] ST, I-II, q. 95, a. 2.
[176] *Supra* Subsection 4.4.3.

occur in the specification context as well.[177] The classic example of a coordination problem is highway usage.

Coordination problems are ubiquitous, and the reason for this is the natural law's underdetermination of the specific modes of social life. The natural law has no prescription for highway speed limits, nor does it prescribe the overall mix of coordinations for the highway system. It does, however, prescribe the common good and human flourishing, and moderately more detailed norms – such as distributive and commutative justice – within which human legislators must work. These and other natural law prescriptions, however, leave a wide berth for human creativity in providing solutions to coordination problems. Like the architect designing a house, human legislators overcoming coordination problems work within broad bounds through use of positive law. This natural law underdeterminacy accounts for the robust role of positive law *determinatios* in modern legal systems, and it also accounts for the reasonable and reasonably diverse different *determinatios* utilized by different societies.[178]

The positive law overcomes coordination problems by providing publicly identified and identifiable means that members of a society then utilize to cooperate with others. Americans that drive on highways initiate yellow blinking lights on their cars when they wish to turn right or left, and others on the highways cooperate by slowing down to accommodate the turn. This usage by citizens of the positive law's solutions to coordination problems is crucial. Without it, the problems would go unremedied, cooperation would be impeded or cease, and the common good and human flourishing would be hindered. If highway users did not utilize signals – for example, turned without signaling – or if they used the wrong signals – for instance, used the horn in place of the turn signal – then the positive law's resolutions would be ineffective.

The positive law's solution to a coordination problem is *salient*. The law makes what might otherwise be – and what might otherwise be perceived to be – mere uniformity of action among members of a group more than simple happenstance: a properly functioning legal system makes such uniformity of action salient because the participants in the activity and observers know that the coordination is the product of the legal system's coordination through law. Positive law's salience sets it apart from informal solutions to coordination problems.

Imagine that you are from a foreign country that is un-urbanized and un-industrialized and has remote, mountainous terrain, so that it has very few cars. You have not driven a car before you come to the United States and attempt to drive on its roads. You notice that whenever anyone wishes to stop, red lights in the back of the car light up. You also see yellow lights blink on and off on cars, and the cars

---

[177] For instance, though the natural law requires that the positive law proscribe sexual torts, it leaves underdetermined what the punishments should be.

[178] MARITAIN, *supra* note 86, at 99.

then turn left and right. Even though you do not know how Americans drive, you *do* know that Americans do drive and that we have a functioning legal system that regulates driving. The existence of a properly functioning legal system makes what might otherwise be mere uniformity of action salient – it is law-coordinated activity.

4.4.4.3.4 CONCLUSION The twofold function of positive law is to instantiate the natural law and to coordinate society's members toward the common good. Both of these functions are fulfilled when law orders its subjects' actions. Law's instantiation of the natural law norm identifying human life as good and worth protecting via prohibitions against murder succeeds when it protects human life in its jurisdiction. Law secures the common good, and the basic human good of knowledge, when it structures and supports education of children in its jurisdiction. In both instances, law provides reasons taken into account in its subjects' practical deliberations, reasons that guide citizens to not take innocent human life and to pay taxes to support the provision of education.

4.4.4.4 The Law-as-Coordination Account of Positive Law: Authoritative, Prudential, Coordinating Decisions for the Common Good

Here, I synthesize my prior arguments regarding legal authority and positive law and provide the law-as-coordination account of positive law.[179] On this account, positive law remedies natural law's underdeterminacy, overcomes coordination problems, and secures the common good through judgments that are: (1) authoritative, (2) prudential, (3) coordinating, and (4) embodied in (positive) law. I will use the example of highway regulations in Ohio to show that this account captures the focal case of American positive law. Speed limit laws enable Ohioans to use highways reasonably effectively, and use of highways is necessary to human flourishing in Ohio;[180] absent coordinated usage of highways, this would not be possible, or at least not as effectively so.

The Ohio legislature's (and its positive law's) determinations are recognized as *authoritative* by legal officials and people in that jurisdiction. For example, Ohio's state legislature is recognized by Ohio public officials, Ohioans generally, and others present within Ohio as having the authority to make legal determinations for the state.[181] If a state highway patrolman cited a person on Ohio's highways for

---

[179] My account is primarily drawn from NLNR, at 125, 154–56, 231–33, 335; AQUINAS, at 35–36; 255–58; Finnis, *Law's Authority, supra* note 110; Finnis, *Law as Coordination, supra* note 110; *see also* Larry Alexander, *All or Nothing at All? The Intentions of Authorities and the Authority of Intentions, in* LAW AND INTERPRETATION: ESSAYS IN LEGAL PHILOSOPHY 357, 359 (Andrei Marmor ed., 1995).

[180] This is true at least as our society is presently structured.

[181] OHIO REV. CODE ANN. § 4511.21(B) (Baldwin's 2018).

exceeding the applicable speed limit, the speeder would not be able to claim an exception from the speed limit on the basis that it was not passed by the body with authority to do so. Ohioans, both officials and private citizens, appreciate that speed limit laws passed by the state's legislature are authoritative because they were enacted by the state legislature.

The Ohio legislature's judgments (embodied in the positive law) are *prudential* because, in this area of *determinatio*, there is not a uniquely correct answer either to most individual highway regulation questions or to the question of which body of regulations is best. The question of the proper speed limit on Ohio's highways has no uniquely correct answer. Some answers are clearly better than others, but there are a wide variety of reasonable but not reason-determined possibilities.[182] The Ohio legislature, when it made speed limit determinations, employed its prudential judgment, weighed the numerous factors that go into the determination – safety, environmental concerns, efficiency, and citizens' need for quick travel, to name a few – and made a judgment.

The Ohio legislature's legislation governing highways is the product of both the legislature's reason and its will. The Ohio legislature responded to reasons. For instance, a speed limit that was too slow would harm efficiency, or a speed limit that was too fast would cause too many or too severe accidents. It deliberated on the reasons before it and debated various legislative proposals to address those reasons.

The Ohio legislature also exercised its will and selected a proposal and enacted it into law. It could have selected a different speed limit law or a different body of regulations, so its actual exercise of reasoned choice is crucial to the positive law's existence.

The Ohio legislature's judgments, embodied in the positive law, are *coordinating* because they organize and structure the activities of citizens and thereby overcome coordination problems. Ohio's speed limit laws coordinate the actions of citizens of Ohio. People traveling on Ohio's highways – both Ohioans themselves and people from surrounding states – refer to the speed limit signs along the roadside to learn how fast they should travel. The law – its direction – then acts as an exclusionary reason in their practical deliberations as they travel on the roadways. Drivers drive at cautious speeds in school zones and high speeds on interstate highways as a result of the speed limits.

Lastly, the Ohio legislature's judgments are *embodied in positive law* because that is the mechanism by which the judgments are communicated – promulgated – to citizens, so they can coordinate their activities. The Ohio legislature's authoritative, prudential, coordinating decisions, embodied in law, achieve the legislature's goal of overcoming coordination problems and securing the common good through the

---

[182] The wide variety of interstate variation of speed limits suggests the range of reasonableness. *Compare* MONT. CODE ANN. § 61-8-303 (2017); CAL. VEH CODE § 22349 (Deering 2018); OHIO REV. CODE ANN. § 4511.21 (Baldwin 2018); R. I. GEN. LAWS § 31-14-2 (2018).

direction the law provides to its subjects. To achieve this end, Ohio embodies its speed limit regulations in statutes and regulations for Ohioans to know and follow. Ohioans, to properly understand the substance of the legislature's speed limit decision, will look to the statute in which the legislature placed Ohio's speed limit. Ohioans will use the statute's text, structure, historical context, and other information relevant to ascertaining the meaning the legislature intended to convey to them.[183] Ohioans' interpretive goal is to accurately understand the legislature's authoritative, prudential, coordinating decision on speed limits, and then employ that limit in their practical deliberations.

Ohioans follow the legislature's authoritative, prudential, coordinating decisions, embodied in law, for the sound reasons I have already outlined.[184] The first category of reasons is that Ohioans are better people when they follow the law. For instance, Ohioans treat their fellow citizens well when they follow the law because Ohioans know that Ohio's legal system helps those fellow citizens pursue human flourishing. Making oneself a better person is a reason to include the law's reasons within one's practical deliberations. The second class of reasons is that Ohioans know that following the law maintains the legal system's capacity to perform its essential function securing the common good. For example, if everyone began to run red lights, others would too, and a vicious cycle of ever-greater law breaking would occur until the coordination value of the traffic signals was diminished or lost. Maintaining the common good of one's community is a reason to include the law's reasons within one's practical deliberations.

In Section 4.5, I apply the law-as-coordination account to the U.S. Constitution, and I show that it provides an accurate and normatively attractive description of the Constitution, its origins and operations. The Constitution embodies the authoritative, prudential, coordinating decisions of the Framers and Ratifiers, and Americans today should follow those judgments, both for their own sake and for the sake of the common good. Next, I draw out three implications of the law-as-coordination account of positive law that I will also apply to the Constitution.

4.4.4.4.1 POSITIVE LAW EMPLOYS LINGUISTIC MEANING TO ACHIEVE SOCIAL COORDINATION Positive law employs the linguistic meaning of its laws to achieve social cooperation among its subjects.[185] (At this point in my argument, I make no claim about what type of meaning this is – whether it is textual, or purposive, or

---

[183] Or, Ohioans may employ attorneys trained in the language of the law, as a form of linguistic division of labor, to translate these legal materials for the layperson.

[184] *Supra* Subsection 4.4.3.3.5.

[185] In my law-as-coordination account of originalism, *infra* Section 4.5, I argue that the original public meaning of the text is its meaning *Compare* RICHARD EKINS, THE NATURE OF LEGISLATIVE INTENT 180–217 (2014) (defending the view that statutory meaning is the legislature's intended meaning, which is the conventional semantic meaning in its context, which includes the reasons for which the legislature legislated).

intended, or some other type of meaning – only that it is the positive law's text's meaning.) Positive law employs linguistic meaning to create and guide citizens' cooperation and, to do this, the law's subjects must know what the positive law's prescriptions are. They must have notice of the positive law's solutions to the coordination problems and be capable of incorporating those solutions into their practical deliberations.

Citizens derive from the positive law's meaning its reasons, which they then incorporate into their practical deliberations. Citizens come to know and understand the law's reasons through its linguistic meaning. For example, they see a road sign and learn that the speed limit is 55 miles per hour on the rural two-lane road, and then incorporate that legal prescription into their decision about how fast to drive on the road. Without a sign indicating what the speed limit is on a stretch of highway, highway users will be unable to coordinate their usage, resulting in less efficient and more dangerous use of the highways.

Citizens need not just a general knowledge of the positive law's meaning in a general way; their knowledge must be effective: citizens must also be able to understand the positive law's reasons and employ them in their reasoning. If the positive law were in a language different from the society's primary language(s), or if the positive law were hidden from citizens, or if the positive law utilized language in a nonstandard manner, the citizens subject to the law would not receive its guidance and would be unable to cooperate with it and each other. For example, if an American state suddenly replaced its highway mileage and speed limit signs with kilometers, most Americans would be confused about what the speed limit actually was, and how far it was until the desired stop or exit.[186] This would undermine the efficacy of highway usage.

In our legal system, the mechanism by which the participants in our legal system create, enforce, apply, and follow the law is the positive law's linguistic meaning. This reliance on meaning is a manifestation of many things, including our legal system's commitment to inanimate justice.[187] Whatever the reason, the key tool for positive law's coordination is its meaning.[188]

---

[186] *See, e.g.*, Mark Sableman, *Metric plan for road signs killed*, WASHINGTON POST, (June. 30, 1977), www.washingtonpost.com/archive/local/1977/06/30/metric-plan-for-road-signs-killed/edd5e38c-8b0a-4519-b991-c599b347b5a8/?noredirect=on&utm_term=.7b89af4e7c7d ("The highway agency's proposal called for converting all speed limit signs to metric measure by the end of 1979, and all other regulatory and advisory signs by late 1982. It was killed because of objections based on both cost and safety.").

[187] ST, I-II, q. 95, a.1.

[188] My claim does not exclude the possibility (and occurrence) of the positive law's meaning misfiring in some way. The law's meaning may not achieve what the legislator hoped it would achieve because he employed a meaning obtuse to that end; the law's meaning may be insufficient in some way (*e.g.*, the meaning could be vague or ambiguous), so that it cannot guide citizens; or the law's meaning may be susceptible to executive or judicial manipulation.

An important implication of positive law's linguistic meaning's centrality to law's capacity to coordinate is that a change in its meaning will result in a change in the positive law's coordination. Using an old chestnut as an example: "No vehicles in the park."[189] Assume that the positive law's meaning was its conventional meaning, which would prohibit an ambulance on an emergency run from entering the park. Assume further that a judge ruled that the ordinance did not prohibit the ambulance from going on an emergency run into the park in response to a park patron's call, and that the judge did so utilizing another meaning, perhaps an equitable interpretation of the ordinance taking into account the ordinance's purpose. This change in meaning changed the ordinance's coordination. The different meanings differently affected the ambulance driver, the park victim, and other vehicles and park patrons into the future.[190] Thereafter, the now-modified meaning of the ordinance will enter into community members' practical deliberations differently than it had done before. No longer, for instance, does the law provide a reason for ambulance drivers on emergency runs to not enter the park. The consequences of the changed coordination may be positive (or negative), but the fact of altered coordination caused by changed linguistic meaning is clear.

Both legislators and citizens have incentives to ensure effective communication via positive law's meaning. Legislators who are in good faith seeking to overcome a coordination problem and secure the common good[191] have strong incentives to craft the positive law's text so that citizens can understand their directive and therefore follow it. They will choose words and organize them in such a way that the meaning of the law, as understood by citizens and employed in their practical deliberations, will lead to the citizens acting in a coordinated manner as the legislators' intended. Even legislators operating from less laudable motives still have an incentive to make their enactment comprehensible to achieve whatever their goals are. For instance, a farm state senator's goal to enrich his dairy farmer constituents would need to clearly identify the mechanisms by which the constituents could extract economic rents from consumers.[192] Citizens are also incentivized to understand a positive law's resolution to a coordination problem so that they can effectively go about their lives.

In Section 4.5, I apply this implication to the U.S. Constitution and argue that its original meaning is the means by which it coordinates Americans.

---

[189] H. L. A. HART, THE CONCEPT OF LAW 126 (2d ed., Oxford U. Press, 1994).

[190] Most obviously, the ambulance driver went from violating the ordinance to not violating it. The park victim went from causing a legal violation to not. Other vehicle users, such as drivers of nonmotorized vehicles, like bicycles, will now think they may drive in the park. Park patrons may be more likely to utilize the park because of more-ready access to emergency help; or, they may be less likely to utilize the park if and because of greater driving in the park (of all sorts).

[191] See GRÉGOIRE WEBBER ET AL., LEGISLATED RIGHTS: SECURING HUMAN RIGHTS THROUGH LEGISLATION 86–115 (2018) (describing the focal case of a legislature as an institution making reasoned choices for the good of the community).

[192] Compare Block v. Community Nutrition Institute, 467 U.S. 340 (1984).

4.4.4.4.2 HUMAN CREATIVITY AS A FUNDAMENTAL ASPECT OF POSITIVE LAW Up to now in this subsection, I have described a necessary and robust role for positive law in society. I showed that this role was to make the natural law effective in the society through instantiation (specification and *determinatio*) and coordination. There is a second important implication to draw from the importance of positive law, and it is that positive law is a manifestation of deep and increasing human creativity.

Human legislators use both their reason and their will to implement the natural law, pursue the common good, and provide for human flourishing. They *choose* one of the many reasonable manners to implement the natural law and embody that choice in positive law. For this reason, different societies' responses to the same basic issue will be different, and legitimately so.

Human legislators' creativity also explains why the positive law of a particular society is authoritative for members of that society, even if other reasonable paths were not embodied in positive law. There is so much contingency in so much of positive law that one may nearly always be able to identify other reasonable alternative bodies of positive law. Therefore, the mere fact that positive law is subject to reasonable substantive criticism is not a reason to reject it. Furthermore, this deep contingency highlights the need to respect a legal authority's choice of positive law because it is not the substantive goodness of the positive law that is its efficient cause; it is the mere fact that it was chosen by the authority.

The profound creativity exercised by human legislators is a manifestation of high regard for human reason. Humans are unique and valuable because of our capacity for reason, and we are also valuable because of our capacity for creativity and choice, which manifests itself in many areas of endeavor, of which law is an important instance.

The Constitution, I argue in Section 4.5, was the product of creative choice by the Framers and Ratifiers.

4.4.4.4.3 POSITIVE LAW'S INCREASING ROLE IN LEGAL SYSTEMS A third implication of the importance of positive law is that, over time, and as a legal system develops, positive law fills-in the jurisprudential vacuum left by natural law and builds-out a legal edifice to govern community life.[193] Over time, a legal system's positive law will tend to hide from view the role and place of natural law norms. Positive law is crucial because it implements the natural law through instantiation and coordination. These reasons push a legal system to create more and more

---

[193] *See* HEINRICH A. ROMMEN, NATURAL LAW 230 (Thomas R. Hanley, trans., 1936) ("The natural law calls, then, for the positive law. This explains why the natural law, though it is the enduring basis and the norm of the positive law, progressively withdraws, as it were, behind the curtain of the positive law as the latter achieves a continually greater perfection.").

positive law. For example, the law governing the basic fact pattern of one human being killing another has developed into a more detailed set of criminal prohibitions[194] than the original common law crimes.[195] Likewise, the evolution of property law from simple easements and profits to the modern doctrines of easement, real covenants, and equitable servitudes, shows legal determination of how agreements regarding property uses should be conducted.[196]

Similarly, the U.S. Constitution called forth positive law, especially through elected branch constructions and judicial precedent.

4.4.5 *Conclusion*

This section summarized the key facets of the Aristotelian philosophical tradition's law-as-coordination account of positive law. My description showed that human flourishing is the goal of human life, and that natural law and virtue help guide humans toward flourishing. Legal authority and positive law are necessary means to instantiate the natural law and coordinate human activity, and thereby secure the common good, which is necessary for individual humans to effectively pursue their flourishing. The positive law coordinates its subjects by employing exclusionary reasons, conveyed through linguistic meaning, in their practical deliberations. I employ this account of positive law in the following section to explain why originalism is the most normatively attractive theory of constitutional interpretation.

4.5 THE LAW-AS-COORDINATION ACCOUNT OF ORIGINALISM

4.5.1 *Introduction*

Turning now to the Constitution: originalism is essential to ascertaining and preserving our society's solution to fundamental coordination problems, securing the common good, and promoting human flourishing. The Constitution embodies numerous authoritative, prudential, coordinating judgments. Originalism is the means for Americans today to accurately access those judgments and employ them in their practical deliberations. Use of originalism, therefore, is necessary to overcome coordination problems, secure the common good, and create the background conditions for Americans today to flourish.

---

[194] Model Penal Code § 201 (2017).

[195] Oliver Wendell Holmes, Jr., The Common Law 51–62 (1881).

[196] Uriel Reichman, *Toward and Unified Concept of Servitudes*, 55 S. Cal. L. Rev. 1177, 1183–1230 (1982).

4.5.2 *The Constitution's Original Meaning Resolves Fundamental Coordination Problems to Secure the Common Good and Human Flourishing*

4.5.2.1 Introduction

There were dozens of fundamental coordination problems, and likely hundreds of other coordination problems, that needed resolution to enable the fledgling United States to effectively pursue the common good. Just a sampling of the fundamental issues facing the nation included: should the constitution be written?; what propositions should be included and not included in the written constitution, just statements of law or statements of political principle as well?; how should the constitution be interpreted?; in what manner shall the constitution take effect or receive authorization?; what theory of political sovereignty shall undergird the constitution?; how many branches of government should there be?; how shall the legislative branch be constructed?; what manner of selection shall be employed for members of the legislature?; what powers shall the legislature have?; how should the legislature's powers be identified?; how shall the federal government be prevented from becoming too powerful?; shall the executive be plural or unitary?; how long shall the executive's term be?; what powers shall the executive possess and how shall they be identified?; shall the executive play a role in the legislative process?; how shall the executive be selected?; how shall the judiciary be structured?; what powers shall the judiciary possess?; how should judges' independence be protected?; what terms of office shall judges have?; what limits and checks should restrain judges?; what role shall the states (continue to) play in the constitutional system?; shall the constitution enumerate rights protections and, if so, what rights should be so protected and to what extent?; and how shall the constitution be modified?

Each of these fundamental issues – and many other important questions – needed resolution if American society was going to be able to order itself sufficiently to secure the common good. For instance, without a power to tax, a national government would be ineffective.[197] Yet, because "the power to tax involves the power to destroy,"[198] this federal power had to be limited to protect individuals and states, and to ensure the Constitution's ratification. The Framers and Ratifiers answered this essential question in the Constitution.[199] That the Constitution decides numerous fundamental issues is clear, so I will not belabor the point.

The basic coordination obstacles resolved by the Constitution in 1787 and via subsequent amendments have not evaporated with the passage of time. All or most of the same fundamental obstacles to coordination remain. For instance, the President's term's length remains in need of resolution. Indeed, if anything,

---

[197] Like the Articles government, which was hamstrung by lack of resources.
[198] *McCulloch v. Maryland*, 17 U.S. (4 Wheat.) 316, 431 (1819).
[199] U.S. CONST. art. I, § 2 cl. 3, § 8 cl. 1, § 9 cl. 4.

the passage of time has *compounded* the gravity of obstacles to coordination. For example, the importance of settlement of the office held by George Washington was important; the office held by Donald Trump is vastly more consequential because it wields vastly more power with fewer formal and informal checks, and so, therefore, fundamental agreement on its contours is likewise more consequential.

And it is not only so-called structural issues that remain in need of resolution. Coordination of individual liberties also remains in need of resolution. Religious exercise, for instance, is subject to reasonably different conceptions, yet one must be employed. And today, Americans deeply disagree over the protection, if any, to provide to religious exercise, and that assumes Americans agree on a conception of religious exercise, which is unlikely.

The Constitution's coordinating judgments, which resolve fundamental and important coordination problems, represent a principal facet of the Aristotelian philosophical tradition's description of lawmaking. The natural law identifies the goal of human life – flourishing – but it does not provide detailed guidance on how to achieve that goal. Flourishing is accomplished in a society of fellow human beings, and societies advance their members' flourishing by securing the common good. Yet, the common good too, is underdetermined by the natural law. Hence, one of positive law's key roles is to resolve coordination problems that impede the common good. The Constitution performed, and continues to perform, this role in our society.

4.5.2.2 The Constitution's Resolutions to Fundamental Coordination Problems Are Authoritative

The Constitution, and the coordination-problem-resolving judgments it embodies, was adopted by American society through means recognized as authoritative both then and today.[200] I call this the Constitution's provenance, and I explained this concept in Subsection 3.3.3.

Constitutional provenance is the origin of a constitution. Constitutional provenance is crucial because it is the characteristic that explains why a particular document, and not another, is a polity's governing constitution. A constitution's provenance comes from authorization by the constituent authority that possessed the authority to designate a document as the constituent authority's polity's constitution. This authority is identified and recognized by the legal system's officials as well as, typically, the system's subjects. For instance, the Articles of Confederation was adopted by the Second Continental Congress and was authoritative because of

---

[200] Akhil Reed Amar, America's Constitution: A Biography 6–21 (2005); Paul Johnson, A History of the American People 190–95 (1997); Jonathan Gienapp, The Second Creation: Fixing the American Constitution in the Founding Era 6 (2018); Jack N. Rakove, Original Meanings: Politics and Ideas in the Making of the Constitution 110–12 (1996).

its provenance. Americans at the time recognized that the Continental Congress had the authority to adopt the Articles. The Articles' text still today claims that *it* is the United States of America's constitution; however, it is not, because it lacks the U.S. Constitution's provenance; it was not adopted by the relevant constituent authority – *i.e.*, the thirteen state ratification conventions.

The United States Constitution is identified by its provenance. Only the United States Constitution originated from the Philadelphia Convention on September 17, 1787, and was ratified by nine state ratifications conventions by 1788. Americans in 1789 recognized that the Constitution became the Constitution upon its ratification,[201] at least by the time New York had ratified it in 1788, making it the eleventh state to do so and the last of the major states. (Only North Carolina and Rhode Island had not ratified at this point.) Key evidence for this is that opposition to the new Constitution, though fierce during the Ratification debates up to this point, died away.[202] Further, the pre-existing legal system's legislature, the Articles of Confederation's Continental Congress, recognized that Ratification was the defining moment and mechanism for the new Constitution's identification as the governing Constitution by, among other things, acknowledging New Hampshire's ratification, calling for elections under the newly-ratified Constitution, and the holding of the new Congress' first session.[203]

Our constitutional practice today continues to identify the Constitution by its provenance. Americans today recognize that the Framing and Ratification process identified the Constitution, and that the Ratifiers possessed the authority to designate the document now located in the National Archives as the U.S. Constitution.[204]

This authoritative U.S. Constitution contains coordinating judgments that revolve fundamental coordination problems facing American society. These judgements possess the Constitution's authority.

---

[201] At least for those states that ratified it.

[202] JOHN HART ELY, DEMOCRACY AND DISTRUST: A THEORY OF JUDICIAL REVIEW 6 (1980); KEITH E. WHITTINGTON, CONSTITUTIONAL INTERPRETATION: TEXTUAL MEANING, ORIGINAL INTENT & JUDICIAL REVIEW 146 (1999); *see also* 3 RECORDS OF THE FEDERAL CONVENTION OF 1787, at 372, 374 (James Madison) (Max Farrand ed., 1911) ("As the[Constitution] came from [the Framers] it was nothing more than the draft of a plan, nothing but a dead letter, until life and validity were breathed into it by the voice of the people, speaking through the several State Conventions.").

[203] 1 THE DOCUMENTARY HISTORY OF THE FIRST FEDERAL ELECTIONS 1788–1790, at 131 (Merrill Jensen & Robert A. Becker eds., 1976) (September 13, 1788 Resolution).

[204] This is evidenced by, for instance, the Supreme Court's constant refrain that, even in its most controversial decisions, it is interpreting the Constitution. *Dickerson* v. *United States*, 530 U.S. 428, 442 (2000). The document in the National Archives is identified by federal officers as the document signed by the Framers and approved by the Ratifiers. *See Charters of Freedom–The Declaration of Independence, The Constitution, The Bill of Rights*, www.arch ives.gov/exhibits/charters/charters_of_freedom_6.html (visited May 17, 2009). (stating that the document contained in the glass case in the Archives' rotunda was the "signed [and] engrossed parchment" from the framing Convention); STRAUSS, *supra* note 4, at 101.

Americans in 1787–1789, and Americans today, had and have good reason to treat the Constitution and its coordinating judgments as authoritative. The Framing and Ratification was an act of intentional – reasoned and chosen – lawmaking. The purpose and effect of the lawmaking was to overcome coordination problems and secure the common good. Treating the Framing and Ratification as authoritative is necessary for the Constitution's coordinating judgments – for the intentional law-making – to achieve their goal.

The fact that the Constitution's coordinating decisions are authoritative is a manifestation of the broader phenomenon of legal authority I described. Legal authority makes a decision on how to overcome a coordination problem. A legal authority's decision, embodied in positive law, operates as an exclusionary reason in the practical reasoning of citizens through the mechanism of law's meaning. In doing so, it coordinates citizens' activities, thereby overcoming coordination problems. This creates the background conditions within which citizens may effectively pursue their flourishing.

4.5.2.3 The Constitution's Resolutions to Fundamental Coordination Problems Are Prudential

The Constitution's resolutions of fundamental coordination problems are the result of prudential determinations about how American society could best pursue human flourishing, under the circumstances. For all or nearly all of the fundamental coordination problems faced by the Framers, there was not a uniquely correct resolution to the problem (though, in many instances, circumstances narrowed the range of reasonable resolutions). As a result, the Framers utilized their pruden-tial judgment, honed by debate and deliberation, to determine solutions to the coordination problems. The Ratifiers similarly utilized their prudential judgment, likewise honed by debate and deliberation, to evaluate and, ultimately, adopt the proposed constitution.

There was not one uniquely correct answer to the fundamental questions deter-mined by the Constitution. For instance, even on the matter of whether our Constitution should be written, which at first blush presented a relatively easy binary choice,[205] the Framers and Ratifiers still employed their prudential judgment to choose among reasonable options because of the strong reasons that argued for an unwritten or partially unwritten constitution. There was a long-standing and rela-tively well-functioning tradition of an unwritten constitution in the United King-dom, which provided a plausible route. Furthermore, Americans were familiar with and generally proud of their common law inheritance from Great Britain, a system of unwritten law.

---

[205] Or, maybe a ternary choice: written, unwritten, or some written and some unwritten.

There were, however, more and less reasonable answers to most of these fundamental issues, given the context in which the Framers found themselves in 1787. On the question of a written or unwritten constitution, for example, by 1787 the American People had developed a tradition of written charters as colonies and, upon independence, most states adopted written constitutions.[206] Further, Americans had negative experiences with the unwritten English constitution in the period leading up to the Revolution, both in the form of ambiguity about what that constitution authorized Parliament to do, and plausible – though debatable – claims by Parliament that it had the authority to enact laws to which the colonists objected.[207] The Framers and Ratifiers exercised their prudential judgment, informed by their experiences, and chose a written Constitution. This choice was not a uniquely correct one; instead, it was an all-things-considered and on-balance judgment.

The subject of the President's term of office, however, is a different sort of issue – one that was more typical than the written-unwritten constitution issue – where the Framers were not presented with a binary choice. Instead, there was a wide range of options. The range of options available to the Framers included everything from one-year to a lifetime in office (with all sorts of potential mechanisms to end a term of office before its expiration[208]). Furthermore, the length of the President's term of office did not possess the background circumstances to guide practical deliberation. Americans, of course, were familiar with the United Kingdom monarch's lifetime reign, but this had few American followers.[209] They also faced a brief post-Revolution practice of state executives with very short terms of office,[210] which was generally perceived as a failure. Other than these two extremes – lifetime or very-short – the Framers and Ratifiers had little first-hand experience upon which to draw. The exclusion of these extremes, however, left significant room for reasonably different positions, and the debate in the Philadelphia Convention was correspondingly robust.[211] Resolution of the issue and debate over it were made more complex by the numerous relationships between the President's term of office and other issues, such as congressional removal of the President, the method of presidential

---

[206] Steven G. Calabresi, *The Historical Origins of the Rule of Law in the American Constitutional Order*, 28 HARV. J. L. & PUB. POL'Y 273, 277–78 (2004).

[207] WHITTINGTON, INTERPRETATION, *supra* note 202, at 50–53.

[208] Here, I have in mind mechanisms like votes of no confidence, recalls, and impeachment, among others.

[209] There are (disputed) historical claims that Alexander Hamilton supported an elected monarch. RICHARD BEEMAN, PLAIN, HONEST MEN: THE MAKING OF THE AMERICAN CONSTITUTION 169 (2009).

[210] Thomas E. Cronin, *Presidential Term, Tenure and Reeligibility*, *in* INVENTING THE AMERICAN PRESIDENCY 61–63 (Thomas E. Cronin ed., 1989).

[211] *Id.* at 65.

election to office, and the President's role in the legislative process.[212] The Framers and Ratifiers settled on a particular term, after a robust debate. For this, as with most other fundamental issues, the Framers and Ratifiers possessed a relatively open field of deliberation.

For many of these fundamental matters addressed by the Constitution, we are so used to the answer that the Constitution provides us that we gloss over the fact that a choice was made – that a choice *had* to be made – to coordinate our society. For example, few Americans would think to raise the question of a unitary or plural executive,[213] but it was a live issue at the Philadelphia Convention, with precedent in the states and colonies, and more remotely.[214] This shows how powerful the Constitution's resolution of coordination problems are to Americans.

The aspect of the Constitution's decisions as prudential represents an important facet of the Aristotelian philosophical tradition's description of human acts and lawmaking. Human acts are characteristically human when they are reason-based, when they proceed from a practical judgment about reasonably pursuing basic human goods. Similarly, legislative actions are fully legislative when they proceed from the lawmakers' practical wisdom.

4.5.2.4 The Constitution's Resolutions to Fundamental Coordination Problems Are Coordinating

These authoritative and prudential decisions, embodied in the Constitution, co-ordinated and continue to coordinate members of our society toward the common good. The Constitution's resolutions of fundamental coordination problems re-ordered American life and the legal system, and continue to do so today.

The Constitution embodied many fundamental determinations that coordinated the United States. Clear evidence of this is that the Articles of Confederation no longer operated. Following the Constitution's going into effect, no one in the legal system acted upon or appealed to the Articles. Instead, government officials acted under the Constitution's directions and appealed to it to justify their actions.

For instance, one of the major re-orderings effectuated by the Constitution was the creation of federal control over most commerce. The Interstate Commerce Clause embodied the Framers' and Ratifiers' authoritative, prudential judgment that the Articles of Confederation's approach to interstate commerce had failed,[215] and

---

[212] James Randolph Peck, Note, *Restoring the Balance of Power: Impeachment and the Twenty-Second Amendment*, 8 Wm. & Mary Bill Rts. J. 759 (2000) (making these and other connections).

[213] For a prominent exception, see David Orentlicher, Two Presidents Are Better than One: The Case for a Bipartisan Executive Branch (2013).

[214] Steven G. Calabresi & Nicholas Terrell, *The Fatally Flawed Theory of the Unbundled Executive*, 93 Minn. L. Rev. 1696, 1696–97 (2009).

[215] The Federalist No. 22 (Alexander Hamilton).

that federal control was needed. The First Congress, in its first session, in its very first acts, employed the Foreign Commerce Clause,[216] the Interstate Commerce Clause,[217] and the Indian Commerce Clause[218] to re-order Americans' commercial life for the common good. The Statutes at Large are filled with Congress creating positive law to build-out the apparatus of national government and order Americans' common economic life.

The Constitution's coordinating judgments continue to order Americans today. Legal officials of all stripes, and Americans generally, act pursuant to the Constitution and justify their actions by its standards. As I described in Subsection 3.4.2, the Supreme Court claims that the Constitution governs its actions within its purview. For instance, the Constitution's allocation of authority between the federal and state governments over interstate commerce governs the United States.[219]

The fact that the Constitution is not always – or, in some contexts, regularly – cited as controlling legal questions or that other legal authorities are directly relied upon to decide legal issue *supports* my claim. I described originalist precedent in Subsection 2.4.3. I showed that originalist precedent is the primary mechanism by which the Constitution is implemented. I also described how this fundamental role is the Constitution's own creation. Consequently, as precedent has built up over the centuries, the Constitution's authoritative role has naturally receded into the background.

Similarly, federal statute law created by Congress since the Republic's beginning has proliferated, creating a thick web of positive law that decides most (federal) legal issues in the United States. I described this phenomenon in Section 4.4. The Constitution's grant of powers to Congress in Article I, Section 8, authorized it to resolve coordination problems. *That* constitutional judgment by the Constitution continues to coordinate Americans' lives today, and the Constitution itself has naturally receded into the background.

The Constitution's solutions to the United States' fundamental coordination problems generally and for the most part secure the common good. I described a thin conception of the common good in Subsection 4.4.3 that included justice, the Rule of Law, and offices. The Constitution (at least) secures this conception of the common good. It does not command Americans to commit serious injustice. It does secure justice through its protection of individual rights and, more importantly, through the creation of structures of federal lawmaking and its preservation of state lawmaking. It also secures the Rule of Law through the process of creation and preservation of law-making, law-executing, and law-applying institutions. The

---

[216] An Act for laying a Duty on Goods, 1 Stat. 24 (July 4, 1789).
[217] An Act for Registering and Clearing Vessels, 1 Stat. 55 (Sept. 1, 1789).
[218] An Act to regulate trade and intercourse with the Indian Tribes (July 22, 1790).
[219] For a recent and thoughtful evaluation of the history of the Supreme Court's Dormant Commerce Clause jurisprudence see Daniel Francis, *The Decline of the Dormant Commerce Clause*, 94 Denv. L. Rev. 255 (2017).

federal offices created by the Constitution, and the state offices preserved by it, guide and superintend justice and the Rule of Law. Consequently, even if one believes that the Framers and Ratifiers were motivated by their own (elite) self-interest,[220] that does not preclude the law-as-coordination account's applicability.

4.5.2.5 Originalism Is Necessary to Access the Constitution's Authoritative, Prudential, Coordinating Resolutions to Fundamental Coordination Problems

Originalism is necessary to understand the Constitution's authoritative, prudential, coordinating decisions. Without originalism, Americans at the time of Ratification, and today, could not access and therefore could not be guided and coordinated by the Constitution's authoritative, prudential, coordinating decisions. The original meaning was the mechanism of communication employed by the Framers and Ratifiers to present the Constitution's reasons to Americans for inclusion in their practical deliberations.

I described the Constitutional Communication Model of Originalism in Section 2.2, where I argued that the Constitution's original meaning is identical to its originally intended meaning and its meaning derived via the original methods. The Framers and Ratifiers debated, drafted, and adopted the Constitution with the common goal of communicating with each other, with government officers, and with other Americans, both contemporary and subsequent.[221] The Constitution's original public meaning made that communication possible and effective. That Model has additional payoff here.

The Constitution's original meaning is the Constitution's authoritative meaning because only it accesses the intentional law-making acts performed by the Framers and Ratifiers. Americans have sound reasons to employ that meaning because the Framers' and Ratifiers' intentional law-making actions used the original meaning to communicate their coordinating decisions toward the end of securing the common good.

From the Framers' perspective, they were working to create a functioning national government by resolving the problems that had plagued the Articles of Confederation, and to provide the mechanisms for Americans to cooperate into the future. For the Framers to achieve those goals, they needed to communicate with the Ratifiers, who would authorize the Constitution; with governmental officials, both federal and state, who would implement the Constitution's directions; and with Americans, both contemporary and in the future, who would live under the

---

[220] CHARLES A. BEARD, AN ECONOMIC INTERPRETATION OF THE CONSTITUTION OF THE UNITED STATES (1913).

[221] See BARNETT, *supra* note 10, at 89–117 (arguing that the Framers and Ratifiers understood that the Constitution's original meaning was authoritative); WHITTINGTON, INTERPRETATION, *supra* note 202, at 180 (same).

Constitution's suzerainty. From the Framers' own perspective, the meaning the Framers employed had to be accessible to all of these different groups of Americans. Therefore, the Framers intended their meaning to be the Constitution's public meaning. This was the meaning that Americans beyond the confines of Independence Hall would be able to retrieve and follow. The Constitution's original meaning is, therefore, authoritative, because it is the form within which the Constitution's authoritative decisions were and are communicated to members of our society, enabling Americans to pursue the common good reasonably effectively.

From the Ratifiers' perspective, the meaning they used when authorizing the Constitution was also its public meaning. They did not have access to the private intentions of the Framers (if they had even wished to learn them). The Ratifiers' own debates, by necessity, employed the Constitution's public meaning because that was the meaning to which they all had access. Like the Framers, the Ratifiers wished other Americans to know and follow the Constitution, including especially government officers – how else would the Constitution function? – and the only way for these other Americans to access the Constitution's meaning was through its public meaning. James Madison affirmed this conception of the Constitution's authoritative meaning: "I entirely concur in the propriety of resorting to the sense in which the Constitution was accepted and ratified by the nation. In that sense alone it is the legitimate Constitution."[222]

From the perspective of Americans more generally, they did not know what the Framers' or the Ratifiers' private intentions were (if they even wished to know them). Americans' ability to know and conform their actions to the Constitution's instructions meant they had to utilize the Constitution's public meaning. In particular, governmental officers, who swore an oath to the Constitution, could know the Constitution's meaning, discuss it with each other, and coordinate their activities pursuant to the Constitution's directions, only via accessing its public meaning.

Take, for example, Art. IV, § 4's Domestic Violence Clause. The Clause authorizes federal intervention in a state in cases of "domestic violence."[223] The Clause was the Framers' attempt to strike a prudent balance between, on the one hand, preserving state autonomy from excessive federal intrusion and, on the other hand, providing the states with federal assistance when they could not maintain their institutional integrity.[224] The paradigm example of what the Framers feared was another Shay's Rebellion. During that Rebellion, the state government ceased functioning in western Massachusetts, and for a time, the state appeared unable to cope with the Rebellion. A strong central government, authorized to assist states in situations such as these, was the Framers' goal. At the same time, the Framers

---

[222] *Letter from James Madison to Henry Lee* (June 25, 1824), *in* 9 THE WRITINGS OF JAMES MADISON 190, 191 (Gaillard Hunt ed., 1910).

[223] U.S. CONST. art. IV, § 4.

[224] Jay S. Bybee, *Insuring Domestic Tranquility: Lopez, Federalization of Crime, and the Forgotten Role of the Domestic Violence Clause*, 66 GEO. WASH. L. REV. 1, 32–40 (1997).

created a federal system with the states retaining an indispensable role, and they did not wish the federal government to possess the authority to interfere with state institutions absent good reason.

The Domestic Violence Clause was the result of the Framers' intentional law-making that employed their complex practical reasoning. The Framers knew that to convey the results of their prudential judgment – to convey the Constitution's coordinating decision – to the Ratifiers and the American People, they had to employ a meaning these audiences could understand. The Ratifiers, debating and adopting the Domestic Violence Clause, likewise had to utilize a meaning access-ible to them and to other Americans, to both access the Framers' and their (the Ratifiers') own prudential judgment. Lastly, the American People needed then, and still need today, to utilize the original public meaning to learn the Framers' and Ratifiers' authoritative and prudential decision to follow the Constitution's instruc-tions and thereby coordinate their actions.

The Constitution's original meaning was the Constitution's key mechanism for coordinating American society. It provided the vehicle by which the Constitution's directives to its subjects could operate as reasons in their practical deliberations. For instance, during the First Bank Controversy, the congressmen in good faith grappled with the Necessary and Proper Clause's instructions to them.[225] Their goal was to ascertain the Clause's public meaning and to follow it, and they worked hard to do so. Each side in the debate, once they ascertained the Clause's public meaning, employed it in their practical deliberations to determine whether Congress did or did not possess the power to charter a national bank. No one appealed to a different constitutional meaning; no one argued for a non-original meaning because of its normative attractiveness.

Use of a meaning other than the original meaning would change the Constitution's coordination. This is uncontroversial. For instance, and obviously, constitutional amendments change the Constitution's original meaning and there-fore Americans' coordination. The Eleventh Amendment prohibited federal courts from taking jurisdiction over states, thereby stopping a practice the Supreme Court had previously employed.[226] Nonoriginalist Supreme Court precedent, by defin-ition, does as well.

Use of a meaning other than the original meaning would short-circuit the Consti-tution's capacity to coordinate in three key ways. First, any unauthorized change to the Constitution's original meaning would disconnect resultant coordination from the Framers' prudential judgment. This new meaning would substitute a different practical judgment for the Framers' all-things-considered judgments embodied in

---

[225] Lee J. Strang, *An Evaluation of the Historical Evidence for Constitutional Construction From the First Congress' Debate Over the Constitutionality of the First Bank of the United States*, 14 U. St. L.J. 193 (2018).
[226] *Chisholm v. Georgia*, 2 U.S. (2 Dall.) 419 (1793).

the original meaning. For example, the Supreme Court's nonoriginalist interpretation of the Contracts Clause in *Home Bldg. & Loan Ass'n v. Blaisdell*, which authorized impairment of contracts by states, embodied a different practical judgment than the Framers' employed in the Clause's original meaning.[227]

If American governmental officials today – in particular, federal judges – used a different meaning for the Domestic Violence Clause, one based on contemporary meaning of the Clause, they would cut themselves off from the Framers' and Ratifiers' authoritative, prudential, coordinating decision. The Framers and Ratifiers made an all-things-considered judgment – one that, by definition, was not, in principle, susceptible to a uniquely correct answer. Different reasonable people may have struck different prudential balances. But that is the point: the written Constitution in the National Archives embodies one prudential judgment and does not employ the potentially infinite variety of alternative prudential judgments. Only the original meaning can access the Framers' and Ratifiers' unique prudential decision.

Second, any unauthorized change to the Constitution's original meaning would disconnect coordination from the Ratifiers' authority. This new meaning would be the product of a person or institution other than the Ratifiers. For instance, the Supreme Court's interpretation of the Fifth Amendment's Due Process Clause to strike down the Missouri Compromise in *Dred Scott v. Sandford*, replaced the Fifth Amendment's ratifiers' meaning with the Supreme Court's nonoriginalist meaning.[228] The Supreme Court was not authorized by the American legal system to substitute its determination for that of the Fifth Amendment's ratifiers because our legal system's constitutional provenance does not include the Supreme Court.

Similarly, if current officials rejected the Domestic Violence Clause's original meaning, doing so would also reject the Ratifiers' authoritative judgment. In our legal system, only the Ratifiers possessed the authority to adopt the Constitution as our governing document. No federal or state officers claim for themselves the authority to adopt the written Constitution in the National Archives. Utilizing the original meaning is the only meaning that respects the Ratifiers' authority to adopt the Clause.

Third, multiple points of coordination caused by government officials following a variety of constitutional meanings would hinder the Constitution's coordination from operating. For instance, if some government officials followed the original meaning, while others followed the conventional contemporary meaning, while still others followed (what they each perceived to be) the most normatively attractive meaning(s), these government officials would not be able to coordinate their actions. For instance, current officials that rejected the original meaning would unsettle the coordination provided by the Domestic Violence Clause with

---

[227] *Home Bldg. & Loan Ass'n v. Blaisdell*, 290 U.S. 398 (1934).
[228] *Dred Scott v. Sandford*, 60 U.S. (19 How.) 393, 449–52 (1857) (Taney, C.J.).

its fine-tuned federalism balance. The Clause's original meaning identifies one reasonable mechanism (among many) to navigate the tension between state autonomy and state anarchy, and between federalism and national power. Once that reasonable approach is rejected, in principle, innumerable alternative approaches to that tension become available. For instance, a reasonable Supreme Court today might interpret the Clause to authorize federal intervention when incidence of home-related crime reaches a certain level. Furthermore, not only is the particular judgment unsettled; different current officials may arrive at different, incompatible – yet reasonable – prudential judgments. Congress may identify a different permissible response to home-related crimes than might the Supreme Court. Utilizing the original meaning is the only meaning that maintains the level of stable coordination provided by the Framers and Ratifiers.

In sum, the Constitution's original meaning is the only means to access the written Constitution's authoritative, prudential, coordinating decisions. Utilizing other meanings undermines the Framers' and Ratifiers' prudential judgments, rejects their authority, and destabilizes the social coordination established by the Constitution. In place of the Constitution's reasons operating in Americans' practical deliberations, alternative nonoriginalist meanings would cause different reasons to operate and result in different coordinations and a lack of coordination.

4.5.3 *The Law-as-Coordination Account of Originalism Applies to the Whole Constitution*

At this point, one may think that the law-as-coordination account of originalism is most persuasive (to the extent it is persuasive) as applied to the Constitution's structural provisions and issues of institutional settlement. These are the provisions that create, structure, and empower the federal government. For instance, most of Article I governs Congress' structure. These provisions serve as clear coordination points.

However, one might question whether this same rationale applies to the Constitution's rights-protecting provisions. One could do so on a number of bases. For instance, one could hold the view that rights are more determinate than governmental structures and that, therefore, there is less need for coordination. The freedom of speech's scope and contours, for instance, leave less room for debate than a legislature's structure because of the right's categorical nature.[229] Or, one might believe that it is improper to deliberate about the scope of rights because of their fundamental nature. This view was on display in the Supreme Court's

---

[229] Ronald Dworkin, Taking Rights Seriously xi (1977).

famous pronouncement that "[o]ne's right to … free speech … may not be submitted to vote."[230]

On the contrary, the law-as-coordination account applies to all of the Constitution's provisions, including those that protect individual rights. Reasonable people and reasonable legal systems protect different individual rights and protect them in different manners. Americans of good faith reasonably disagree over, for example, the extent of free speech protection for hate speech.[231] Similarly, Western nations that protect the freedom of speech take different approaches to hate speech.[232] This means that, just like the Constitution's structural provisions, its rights-protecting provisions were subjects of specification and *determinatio*, which requires reasoned creativity by drafters. This is born out in the legislative records of drafters reasonably debating whether and how to protect rights.[233] Therefore, just like structural provisions, rights provisions coordinate Americans' lives.

Furthermore, fundamentalness is not correlated with the need for coordination. The fact that rights protect fundamental aspects of human flourishing does not make them *more* fundamental than mechanisms that, for instance, provide structures for the provision of education to children. And yet, the subject of the provision of education is one of the most challenging subjects of *determinatio* in need of coordination. The relationship between fundamental subjects and coordination is evidenced by the widespread phenomenon of parliamentary systems historically not having bills of rights and yet protecting individual rights to a degree similar to other systems, because their parliamentary systems were well ordered. Indeed, because reasoned participation in political debate by citizens and legislators is itself a facet of human flourishing, debates over protection of individual rights and the form that protection will take contributes to the flourishing of Americans.

4.5.4 *The Law-as-Coordination Account of Originalism Precludes Resort to the Reasons Employed by the Framers and Ratifiers to Reject the Constitution's Original Meaning*

Through the law-as-coordination account of originalism, I painted a picture of the Constitution's original meaning as a reasonable solution to the United States' fundamental coordination problems. This account is an application of the standard account of why societies create legal systems: to secure the benefits of the relative

---

[230] *West Va. St. Bd. of Educ. v. Barnette*, 319 U.S. 624, 639 (1943).
[231] *Compare RAV v. St. Paul*, 505 U.S. 377, 391–96 (1992) (Scalia, J.), *with id.* at 401–02 (White, J., concurring).
[232] Robert A. Kahn, *Why do Europeans Ban Hate Speech? A Debate Between Karl Loewenstein and Robert Post*, 41 Hofstra L. Rev. 545 (2013).
[233] For instance, the congressional debates over the Fourteenth Amendment were long, deep, and contested. 36 Congressional Globe: Debate and Proceedings, 1833–73, https://memory.loc.gov/cgi-bin/ampage?collId=llcg&fileName=070/llcg070.db&recNum=106 (visited Oct. 28, 2018).

clarity and determinacy of positive law solutions to coordination problems. I also argued that the Constitution's solutions are not the only reasonable solutions, nor are all of its solutions the most reasonable. This means that Americans can reasonably contend that they would have written the Constitution differently. For example, one could reasonably argue that the robust structural protections for states prevent the United States from achieving other valuable ends, like the election of presidents who are selected by a majority of the voting electorate. Or, one could reasonably claim that the Constitution's focus on "negative" rights and limited powers prevents its protection for "positive" rights, like a right to welfare. In principle, these, and a nearly-infinite variety of similar reasonable arguments, remain open to Americans of good faith because of the rationally-guided but not rationally-determined nature of implementing the natural law and securing the common good.[234]

However, a practically reasonable American has sound reasons to not use these arguments to reject the original meaning because doing so is inconsistent with the point and maintenance of the constitutional system. The point of the Framing and Ratification of the Constitution as an intentional law-making act was to provide a constitutional system that overcomes fundamental coordination problems and secures the common good. The Constitution's original meaning did so, and created and governs a reasonably just legal system. That law-making process included consideration of all facets of the common good including federalism, selection of the President, and rights protection. Indeed, because one could *always* (reasonably) criticize *any* legal system for its resolutions to coordination problems, such criticisms are inconsistent with the point of legal authority, which is to settle indeterminacy, and a practically reasonable person will therefore not use them to reject all or part of a legal system.

A practically reasonable person will not reject the Constitution's original meaning, or parts of it, for reasons considered in the law-making process because doing so would be inconsistent with the maintenance of the constitutional system and in tension with the great goods secured by it. This is because, in principle, if one American may (re)raise such reasons as reasons to not follow the Constitution's original meaning, then all Americans may (re)raise them. If more than *de minimis* numbers of Americans do so, then the system weakens and may break down. Moreover, since the constitutional system presents itself as a seamless web – where one may not pick and choose which facets to follow – a practically reasonable person will take that fact into account and not reject all or part of the Constitution's original meaning because of already-considered reasons.

4.5.5 *The Law-as-Coordination Account of Originalism Makes Sense of the Framing and Ratification in a Manner Nonoriginalism Cannot*

The Framing and Ratification process was unique in our legal system, one that harnessed the Framers' prudential judgment to the Ratifiers' authority to create and

---

[234] Thank you to Professor Francisco Urbina for raising this criticism.

adopt the Constitution with the goal to secure the United States' common good. Originalism makes sense of that process; nonoriginalism does not.[235] There are three ways that originalism better accounts for the Framing and Ratification: first, it respects the Ratification process' authority; second, it values the Framing process' exercises of prudential judgment; and third, it explains why the Constitution is imperfect.

All three of these manifestations of originalism's more accurate account of the Framing and Ratification derive from a fundamental insight of originalism: the Framing and Ratification of the Constitution was an intentional act of lawmaking by humans and understood to be such by the lawmakers themselves. Originalism's account of how to interpret the Constitution fits this fact. The Framers and Ratifiers had reasons to write and authorize the Constitution; those same reasons explain and justify the Constitution's legal instructions to Americans; and those legal instructions are communicated via the Constitution's original meaning. Originalism treats the Constitution as an act of reasoned lawmaking and tries to understand its product as rational communication.

The Framing and Ratification process is unique in our legal system for two primary reasons: it was the starting point of our current legal system,[236] and (in part, because of that) it was the source of our legal system's most authoritative legal norms.[237] The Framing and Ratification is architectonic to originalism because the original meaning was the Constitution's public meaning at the time it came into existence, and it was the meaning utilized by the Ratifiers who authoritatively adopted it.

Nonoriginalism, by definition, uses some other meaning chosen by someone other than the Ratifiers: it is not the original meaning the Framers and Ratifiers employed to draft and authorize the Constitution. The fact of the unique Framing and Ratification of our Constitution is superfluous in nonoriginalist methodologies – it does not do any analytical work in interpretation. Instead, the Constitution's text is an historical accident – a given – a vessel that must be filled with meaning of the interpreter's choice. For example, the Due Process Clauses were primarily about the process the government owes before it takes away a person's life, liberty, and property.[238] However, that meaning does not achieve many or the correct substantive goals (from nonoriginalists' perspective(s)), such as a constitutional right to

---

[235] This argument is partly based on Steven D. Smith, Correspondence, *Law Without Mind*, 88 MICH. L. REV. 104 (1989).

[236] Stephen E. Sachs, *Originalism as a Theory of Legal Change*, 38 HARV. J. L. & PUB. POL'Y 817, 844–45 (2015).

[237] I described this as our Constitution's provenance in Subsection 3.3.3.

[238] Ryan C. Williams, *The One and Only Substantive Due Process Clause*, 120 YALE L.J. 408 (2010).

abortion, and so justices must make implausible claims about, for instance, the meaning of "liberty."[239]

By contrast, originalism embraces the unique process that identified and authorized our written Constitution, even when its meaning leads to imprudent or unjust results.[240] Originalism treats the Constitution as authoritative, as having originated from flesh-and-blood humans with the authority to designate a document as our Constitution.

Second, the Framing and Ratification process also identified and adopted prudential solutions to our society's basic coordination problems through the Framers' prudential judgment. Originalism privileges these judgments by maintaining faithfulness to the Constitution's original meaning, which expresses those judgments.

Nonoriginalism, by contrast, is an inherently poor way to overcome coordination problems. Nonoriginalist methodologies are "stuck with" the Constitution's text, with the particular words and their arrangement on the parchment. This text is a given that most nonoriginalists will not – at least not explicitly – reject. So, nonoriginalists have to try to wedge their preferred meaning into the text. This leads to very creative "interpretations" of the Constitution's text. For example, the Contracts Clause means that states may impair the obligation of contracts,[241] and that Congress can regulate *non*economic, *intra*state activity "among the several States."[242] This is an ineffective manner to overcome coordination problems because no human ever deliberately and rationally directly addresses the substantive prudential issue. Instead of a human being (or group of human beings) directly applying their practical reason to a coordination problem and finding a solution, the nonoriginalist interpreter has to find a solution that plausibly fits the Constitution's text *and* that, from the nonoriginalists' perspective, is still a more-reasonable substantive solution to the coordination problem. For instance, the New Deal Court wished to rule that Congress possessed plenary power under the Commerce Clause over economic issues,[243] but it felt constrained to articulate the substantial effects test as *an interpretation of* the Commerce Clause's text.[244]

A rational community designing a legal system would not choose nonoriginalism as the way for the legal system to respond to coordination problems. A reasonable legal system would not identify one legal authority and task it with creating positive

---

[239] *See, e.g., Planned Parenthood of S.E. Pa. v. Casey*, 505 U.S. 833, 852 (1992) ("At the heart of liberty is the right to define one's own concept of existence, of meaning, of the universe, and of the mystery of human life. Beliefs about these matters could not define the attributes of personhood were they formed under compulsion of the State.").

[240] One of the most dramatic such instances of injustice in the Due Process Clause context is *DeShaney v. Winnebago County Department of Social Services.* 489 U.S. 189 (1989).

[241] *Home Building & Loan Ass'n v. Blaisdell*, 290 U.S. 398 (1934).

[242] *The Healthcare Cases*, 567 U.S. 519, 589 (2012) (Ginsburg, J., dissenting).

[243] *See* Barry Cushman, *Formalism and Realism in Commerce Clause Jurisprudence*, 67 U. CHI. L. REV. 1089, 1143–46 (2000) (describing the history behind the *Wickard* decision).

[244] *Wickard v. Filburn*, 317 U.S. 111 (1942).

law that resolves coordination problems, and then task *another* legal authority with the job of attributing different meaning to the law's text to resolve the same coordination problems. Yet, that is how nonoriginalist methodologies approach the Constitution.

Third, the law-as-coordination account helps explain why the Constitution's meaning is imperfect. I began this chapter by recounting the ubiquitous nonoriginalist criticism that originalism failed as a theory of constitutional interpretation because of its substantively unjust interpretive results. This criticism is powerful because it has some truth to it. Regardless of one's perspective, the Constitution's original meaning is imprudent or unjust in at least some ways. This criticism also assumes that nonoriginalist methodologies would lead to (at least relatively) perfect results.

However, originalism's *im*perfections show how the law-as-coordination account provides a more accurate picture of the Constitution's provenance than nonoriginalism. The Framers and Ratifiers were limited and imperfect humans, and any artifact they produced – especially one so complex as a national constitution – would be imperfect too. Originalism's imperfections testify and tie originalism to the Framers' imperfect prudential judgment and the Ratifiers' authority. Nonoriginalism, by contrast, with its "perfect Constitution,"[245] unmoors itself from the very process that created and authorized the Constitution.

4.5.6 *Judges (and Other Government Officials) Have Sound Reasons to Follow the Constitution's Original Meaning*

4.5.6.1 Introduction

Up to this point, my argument has been a straightforward application of the more-general law-as-coordination account of positive law to the U.S. Constitution. I argued that the Constitution is normatively attractive because its authoritative, prudential, coordinating decisions resolved fundamental coordination problems and thereby created the conditions for societal common good and individual American human flourishing. I coupled this with the claim that the Constitution's original meaning was the mechanism by which Americans could access the Constitution's decisions and utilize them in their practical deliberations.

A critic may argue, however, that my argument does not sufficiently justify Americans today following the Constitution's coordination solutions.[246] A critic may contend that, even if the Constitution's solutions to coordination problems

---

[245] Henry P. Monaghan, *Our Perfect Constitution*, 56 NYU L. REV. 353 (1981).
[246] I am grateful to Professor Richard Primus for articulating this type of criticism.

gave Americans in the early Republic, and for some period of time thereafter, good reason to follow it, it is *prima facie* implausible that the Constitution's solutions are better than the coordination solutions provided by common law constitutionalism today.[247] This criticism could come in at least two forms.

First, a critic could argue that the goal of coordination could be served *as well* by common law constitutionalism coupled to a robust practice of stare decisis. Like the private law, where the common law is generally considered to provide a stable system of coordination, courts could – indeed, have – created a stable system of coordination in constitutional law.

Second, and relatedly, a critic could point to (relatively more) recent nonoriginalist Supreme Court precedents as offering a suite of *better* coordination points. These alternative coordination points provide better coordination than the Constitution's original meaning because they were decided more recently by justices more familiar with current views on how to respond to coordination problems and, therefore, nonoriginalist meaning is more normatively attractive. For example, a critic could point to the New Deal Supreme Court's nonoriginalist Commerce Clause interpretation, which the Court explicitly justified based on its better fit with modern economic conditions,[248] as a better coordination point than the Clause's original meaning. (This argument is a subspecies of the more general claim that originalism is not a normatively attractive theory of interpretation because it leads to unjust results.)

In this subsection, I argue that federal judges (and other government officials) should follow the Constitution's original meaning, both for the sake of the judge's own flourishing and for the sake of the common good. But first, I identify the relevant point of comparison.

4.5.6.2 Common Law Constitutionalism Does Not Serve Coordination Better Than Originalism

The relevant comparison point between common law constitutionalism and originalism is originalism with a robust conception of precedent. I argued in Section 2.4 that originalism employs precedent to implement the Constitution and secure the common good. Originalism is not, at least not in a mature legal system like ours, *de novo* recovery and application of the original meaning in each new case. Instead, originalist precedent is a judge's bread and butter. So, whatever value common law constitutionalism possesses, originalism also has it.

Next, I argue that originalism also has additional reasons why it provides better coordination points than common law constitutionalism.

---

[247] STRAUSS, *supra* note 4, at 106.
[248] *Wickard v. Filburn*, 317 U.S. 111, 118–29 (1942).

4.5.6.3 Indistinguishable from Run-of-the-Mill Lawbreaking

Many scholars hold to the position that recent nonoriginalist Supreme Court precedents offer a suite of better coordination points. What makes this criticism *prima facie* attractive is the time-gap and the purported changes that have occurred between when the Constitution's coordination solutions were articulated and authorized (Framing and Ratification) and when they are applied (today). However, this situation is, in principle, indistinguishable from many instances of ordinary lawbreaking because of our legal system's commitment to inanimate justice, and for that reason, should be rejected.

Ordinary lawbreaking involves one of the law's subjects not following the law. In the context of positive law, this lawbreaking *always* occurs some time after the law's authorization because of our legal system's deep commitment to inanimate justice.[249] Inanimate justice is when a legal system separates the legal system's law-making and law-applying mechanisms.[250] Our system does not rely on King Solomon dispensing solomonic wisdom on a case-by-case basis.[251] Instead, our legal system creates legal norms, primarily through the mechanism of legislatures, and then applies these posited norms later, primarily through the mechanisms of the executive and judicial branches of government. Even the run-of-the-mill speeder violates a traffic law that has likely been on the books for decades. In our legal system, with its commitment to inanimate justice, speeders and other lawbreakers cannot justify their lawbreaking because of the passage of time or the changes that have occurred during that time. A speeder could not, for instance, successfully argue that he had the capacity to disregard the positive law. Nor could the speeder argue that he did not break the law because the speed limit was established before the advent of numerous vehicle safety improvements that make faster driving safer.

This same phenomenon occurs as well even in those domains governed primarily by the common law. Outside of the rare occasion when a court articulates a new common law rule and applies that new rule in the same case,[252] common law is articulated at one point in time and applied by courts thereafter with references to the establishing precedent.

A federal judge's failure to follow the Constitution's original meaning today is analogous to run-of-the-mill lawlessness. Our legal system has divided up and

---

[249] Our legal system did not have to adopt a strong commitment to inanimate justice – other legal systems throughout history have employed different balances between animate and inanimate justice – and our legal system retains facets of animate justice. For example, our system continues to employ a collection of doctrines that go under the heading of equity that, among other things, introduce facets of animate justice into the legal system. Samuel L. Bray, *The System of Equitable Remedies*, 63 UCLA L. Rev. 530 (2016).

[250] ST, I-II, q. 95, a.1.

[251] 1 Kings 3:12.

[252] This description assumes a non-Dworkinian conception of the common law, and I make this description only for the sake of argument.

distinguished the points of constitutional creation and authorization from constitutional application, and judicial misinterpretation fails to respect that fundamental commitment like ordinary lawbreaking. It does so by substituting one (nonoriginalist) meaning that contains one set of reasons and that produces one form of coordination, for the original meaning that produced a different type of social coordination. The nonoriginalist judge, like the speeder, cannot argue that he has the authority to modify the Constitution, nor could he argue that the passage of time and the change of circumstances authorized his modification of the Constitution.

A critic might respond that the situations are different because the stakes are so much higher in the constitutional context. Unlike the speeding context, where the speeder may save himself a couple of minutes or a couple of dollars in fines, in the constitutional context, important interests of the national society are at stake. For instance, a nonoriginalist may argue, the Court's nonoriginalist interpretation of the Commerce Clause was necessary because the vastly expanded national economy in the early twentieth century needed effective regulation by the national government in order to function well.[253] This distinction does not work, and for two related reasons.

First, the distinction cannot be cabined to constitutional interpretation. Many issues of statutory interpretation, for instance, are as or more important than at least some constitutional issues. The Supreme Court's interpretations of the Sherman Anti-Trust Act are nearly as consequential as its interpretations of the Commerce Clause. Second, and conversely, the distinction cannot be cabined because it would license run-of-the-mill lawbreaking – *i.e.*, low-stakes lawbreaking – that has few or no negative consequences. If avoiding major negative consequences (or securing important good consequences) justifies departure from constitutional meaning, then – under this line of thinking – lawbreaking with few or no negative consequences, and modest positive consequences, should be permitted. For example, a speeder's speeding causes little harm, and provides the speeder with a modest benefit, and he should be able to secure those benefits.

Another piece of evidence for my argument – that nonoriginalist precedent is like ordinary lawbreaking because of our system's commitment to inanimate justice – is that few, if any, scholars argue that federal judges (and other government officials) should be able to update federal statutes to provide better coordination points. Here is how that argument would go. Statutes, when they are passed, serve as effective mechanisms of coordination for Americans. However, statutes that were passed long ago, or whose regulatory subjects have experienced substantial changes, provide less effective points of coordination than judicial interpretations that vary from the statutes' initial meanings. For example, one would argue that the 1964 Civil Rights Act's protection of "sex" – which, at the time, did not include discrimination on the basis of "gender identity" – should nevertheless cover gender identity because our

---

[253] *E.g., Wickard* v. *Filburn*, 317 U.S. 111 (1942) (regulation of national market for grain).

understanding of this phenomenon has changed substantially. This argument parallels the argument that nonoriginalist precedents provide better coordination points than the Constitution's original meaning.

The most prominent expression of this argument in the statutory context is Guido Calabresi's *A Common Law for the Age of Statutes*.[254] Regardless of the power of Judge Calabresi's arguments, they were not adopted by American legal practice and continue to be exotic in legal scholarship.[255] The failure of this analogous argument in the statutory context is evidence that it lacks power as well in the constitutional context.

Consequently, the argument that Supreme Court nonoriginalist precedent provides better points of coordination for our legal system because they are newer than the Constitution's original meaning, and therefore take into account changes that have occurred since the original meaning was authorized, is merely identifying a consequence of our legal system's commitment to inanimate justice. This argument is in principle indistinguishable from ordinary lawbreaking and should be rejected.

Next, I employ the perspective of the practically reasonable judge and argue that federal judges have sound reasons to follow the Constitution's original meaning. I categorize these reasons into two classes, the first focused on judges themselves and the second focused on the effects of following the original meaning. These reasons are particular applications of the arguments given in Subsection 4.4.3.3 for following legal authority and positive law; *this application assumes prior knowledge of that earlier and more-detailed explanation of those reasons*.

To help me describe the sound reasons judges have to follow the Constitution's original meaning, I employ a hypothetical federal judge who does not follow the Constitution's original meaning. The Judge believes he has sound reasons for this refusal. For example, the Judge does not "believe that any document drafted in the 18th century can guide our behavior today. Because the people in the 18th century could not foresee any of the problems of the 21st century."[256] He thinks that "[t]here are things that are in the text of the Constitution that are absurd."[257] In place of the original meaning, the Judge "think[s] we can forget about the 18th century, much of the [Constitution's] text. We ask with respect to contemporary constitutional issues, ask what is a sensible response."[258] I explain next that the Judge harms both himself and the common good by rejecting the sound reasons for following the original meaning.

---

[254] Guido Calabresi, A Common Law for the Age of Statutes (1982).

[255] *See, e.g.*, T. Leigh Anenson, *Equitable Defenses in the Age of Statutes*, 36 Rev. Litig. 659, 706 (2018) (stating that Calabresi's argument "remains controversial"); Nicholas S. Zeppos, *Judicial Candor and Statutory Interpretation*, 78 Geo. L.J. 353, 357, 361–62 (1989) (stating that Calabresi's argument is "radical").

[256] *Compare* Josh Blackman, *Judge Posner on Judging, Birthright Citizenship, and Precedent*, Josh Blackman's Blog, http://joshblackman.com/blog/2015/11/06/judge-posner-on-judging-birthright-citizenship-and-precedent/ (visited Oct. 28, 2018) (quoting Judge Richard Posner).

[257] *Id.*

[258] *Id.*

4.5.6.4 Judges Have Good Reason to Follow the Constitution's Original Meaning for the Sake of Their Own Flourishing

Judges (and other government officials) should follow the Constitution's original meaning for the sake of their own flourishing, and for two types of reasons. First, the Constitution's original meaning provides a sound practical reason for judges to follow it, and judges who incorporate the Constitution's reasons in their practical-legal deliberations act fully reasonably. Second, following the Constitution's original meaning accords with and builds sound judicial character. Both of these reasons are reasons for judges to follow the Constitution's original meaning even when the judge may believe that an alternative meaning would provide a more effective coordination point in a case or area of doctrine.

Stepping back for a moment, recall from Subsection 4.4.2 that a key facet of one's own human flourishing to act practically reasonably. This means that one should freely choose to act for reasons that conduce to one's fulfillment. I argued in Subsections 4.4.3 and 4.4.4 that a basically just legal system provides at least nine sound reasons for those subject to the positive law to follow it. These reasons flow from positive law's necessary role securing societal common good which, in turn, makes individual human flourishing more likely. Positive law is needed to resolve coordination problems, and the law's solutions to coordination problems work only if the law's subjects take the law into account in their practical deliberation. As a result, a practically reasonable person will employ the law's reasons in her practical deliberations. Failure to incorporate the law into one's practical reasoning would make one less than fully reasonable. One would make impaired – and not fully reasoned – practical judgments.

Likewise, a judge (or other government official) who follows the Constitution's original meaning acts fully reasonably. The Constitution's original meaning is our legal system's mechanism that secures the common good, and this provides a reason for a practically reasonable judge to follow it. Such a judge includes the Constitution's reasons within her practical-legal reasoning. The Constitution's reasons are important for a judge to include because they are the legal system's unique and authoritative mechanism to overcome coordination problems and secure the common good.

Our ostentatiously nonoriginalist Judge harmed himself by acting with limited practical reason. The Judge "missed the point" of the Constitution. The Constitution is the United States' authoritative solution to fundamental coordination problems, and its original meaning is the means to effectuate those solutions. The Judge's nonoriginalism harms the Constitution's capacity to achieve its purpose.

Second, judges (and other government officials) that follow the Constitution's original meaning preserve and build their characters. Building one's character is a reason to act in a particular way. I described in Subsection 4.4.2.4 how the virtues